THE BEIJING CONVENTION ON THE JUDICIAL SALES OF SHIPS

AF867513

MARITIME AND TRANSPORT LAW LIBRARY

Ship Building, Sale and Finance
Edited by Bariş Soyer and Andrew Tettenborn

The Modern Law of Marine Insurance
Volume 4
Edited by D. Rhidian Thomas

Air Cargo Insurance
Malcom A. Clarke and George Leloudas

Offshore Oil and Gas Installations Security
An International Perspective
Mikhail Kashubsky

International Trade and Carriage of Goods
Edited by Bariş Soyer and Andrew Tettenborn

Maritime Law and Practice in China
Liang Zhao and Lianjun Li

Maritime Cross-Border Insolvency
Lia Athanassiou

The Law of Yachts and Yachting
Second Edition
Edited by Filippo Lorenzon and Richard Coles

Maritime Liabilities in a Global and Regional Context
Edited by Bariş Soyer and Andrew Tettenborn

New Technologies, Artificial Intelligence and Shipping Law in the 21st Century
Edited by Bariş Soyer and Andrew Tettenborn

The Law of Wreck
Nicholas Gaskell and Craig Forrest

Codification of Maritime Law
Challenges, Possibilities and Experience
Edited by Zuzanna Pepłowska-Dąbrowska and Justyna Nawrot

Transport Documents in Carriage of Goods by Sea International Law and Practice
By Caslav Pejovic

Maritime Law
Fifth Edition
Edited by Yvonne Baatz

Ship Operations: New Risks, Liabilities and Technologies in the Maritime Sector
Edited by Bariş Soyer and Andrew Tettenborn

Maritime Safety in Europe
Edited by Justyna Nawrot and Zuzanna Pepłowska-Dąbrowska

Fresh Produce Shipping
Damages and Compensation
Rex C. Tester

Freeports and Free Zones
Operations and Regulation in the Global Economy
Mark Rowbotham

Disruptive Technologies, Climate Change and Shipping
Edited by Bariş Soyer and Andrew Tettenborn

Responsibility and Accountability in Maritime Law
The Criminalisation of the Ship's Master
Simon Daniels

Cartner on the International Law of the Shipmaster
On the New Command at Sea
Second Edition
John A C Cartner

Illegal Charters and Aviation Law
Alena Soloveva

Commercial and Maritime Law in China and Europe
Shengnan Jia and Lijun Zhao

Offshore Floating Production
Legal and Commercial Risk Management
Stuart Beadnall, Simon Moore and Max Lemanski

The Modern Law of Marine Insurance
Volume Five
Edited by D. Rhidian Thomas

Merchant Ship's Seaworthiness: Law and Practice
Xiankai Zhan & Pengfei Zhang

Inland Waterway Transport
The European Legal Framework
Massimiliano Grimaldi

Unmanned Ships and the Law
Bulent Sozer

Damages, Recoveries and Remedies in Shipping Law
Edited by Bariş Soyer

Commercial Disputes
Resolution and Jurisdiction
Edited by Bariş Soyer

International Maritime Law and Practice
Comparative Law in Context
Časlav Pejović

LNG Offshore Production and Regasification
Legal and Commercial Risk Management
Stuart Beadnall, John Simpson & Max Lemanski

The Beijing Convention on the Judicial Sales of Ships
Edited by D. Rhidian Thomas

THE BEIJING CONVENTION ON THE JUDICIAL SALES OF SHIPS

EDITED BY

PROFESSOR D. RHIDIAN THOMAS

informa law
from Routledge

First published 2025
by Informa Law from Routledge
4 Park Square, Milton Park, Abingdon, Oxon OX14 4RN

and by Informa Law from Routledge
605 Third Avenue, New York, NY 10158

Informa Law from Routledge is an imprint of the Taylor & Francis Group, an informa business

© 2025 selection and editorial matter, D. Rhidian Thomas; individual chapters, the contributors

The right of D. Rhidian Thomas to be identified as the author of the editorial material, and of the authors for their individual chapters, has been asserted in accordance with sections 77 and 78 of the Copyright, Designs and Patents Act 1988.

All rights reserved. No part of this book may be reprinted or reproduced or utilised in any form or by any electronic, mechanical, or other means, now known or hereafter invented, including photocopying and recording, or in any information storage or retrieval system, without permission in writing from the publishers.

Trademark notice: Product or corporate names may be trademarks or registered trademarks, and are used only for identification and explanation without intent to infringe.

British Library Cataloguing-in-Publication Data
A catalogue record for this book is available from the British Library

Library of Congress Cataloging-in-Publication Data
Names: Thomas, D. R. (D. Rhidian), editor.
Title: The Beijing Convention on the Judicial Sales of Ships / edited by Professor D. Rhidian Thomas.
Description: Abingdon, Oxon [UK] ; New York, NY : Routledge, 2025. | Series: Maritime and transport law library | Includes bibliographical references and index.
Identifiers: LCCN 2024056390 (print) | LCCN 2024056391 (ebook) | ISBN 9781032814544 (hardback) | ISBN 9781032814575 (paperback) | ISBN 9781003499930 (ebook)
Subjects: LCSH: United Nations Convention on the International Effects of Judicial Sales of Ships (2023) | Arrest of ships. | Judicial sales. | Maritime law. | Maritime law—United States. | Merchant marine.
Classification: LCC K1188.A7 B45 2025 (print) | LCC K1188.A7 (ebook) | DDC 343.09/65—dc23/eng/20241125
LC record available at https://lccn.loc.gov/2024056390
LC ebook record available at https://lccn.loc.gov/2024056391

ISBN: 978-1-032-81454-4 (hbk)
ISBN: 978-1-032-81457-5 (pbk)
ISBN: 978-1-003-49993-0 (ebk)

DOI: 10.4324/9781003499930

Typeset in Times New Roman
by Apex CoVantage, LLC

For Product Safety Concerns and Information please contact our EU representative:
GPSR@taylorandfrancis.com
Taylor & Francis Verlag GmbH, Kaufingerstraße 24, 80331 München, Germany.

CONTENTS

DETAILED CONTENTS

TABLE OF CASES

E

F

G

H

I

J

O

P

Q

R

TABLE OF LEGISLATION

Note: Page numbers in **bold** indicate original text

National legislation

International Treaties and Conventions

CONTRIBUTOR BIOGRAPHIES

EDITOR AND CONTRIBUTOR

D. Rhidian Thomas is Professor Emeritus of Maritime Law and Founder Director of the Institute of International Shipping and Trade Law at Swansea University, Wales, UK. He previously held academic positions at the University of Wales, Cardiff, and the University of East Anglia; and visiting positions at universities in Europe, Scandinavia, Far East and North America. He held the Francqui Chair at the University of Leuven in 2010/2011 and is the recipient of an honorary doctorate of law from the University of Gothenburg.

He is Editor-in-Chief of the Journal of International Maritime Law and member of the editorial boards of Shipping and Trade Law and Comparative Maritime Law. He is a member of the Comite Maritime International (and the International Standing Committee on Marine Insurance Law), the British Maritime Law Association, Chartered Institute of Arbitrators and an honorary member of the Croatian Maritime Law Association.

His principal teaching and research interests are in the fields of admiralty jurisdiction and practice, maritime and shipping law, marine insurance law, international trade law and commercial dispute resolution. He has written, edited and contributed to many books on a range of maritime and admiralty topics and commercial arbitration, and published widely in academic and professional journals.

He is a frequent speaker at conferences and seminars and also acts as an expert witness and consultant.

CONTRIBUTORS

Abhinayan Basu Bal is a Reader at the School of Business, Economics and Law at University of Gothenburg. He lectures and researches in commercial and maritime laws with emphasis on digitalisation and sustainability. He holds a Ph.D in law and MSc in informatics.

Since 2013, he has been the accredited Swedish observer to UNCITRAL Working Group-IV on E-Commerce. Earlier, he worked at Lund University where he managed the delivery of the LLM in maritime law programme. Currently, he is engaged in designing the governance of a transport ecosystem that aims to foster visibility in international trade.

Martin Davies is the Admiralty Law Institute Professor of Maritime Law at Tulane University Law School in New Orleans and the Director of the Tulane Maritime Law Center.

He is an Overseas Fellow of the Australian Academy of Law and a Titulary Member of the Comité Maritime International (CMI). Before joining Tulane, he was Harrison Moore Professor of Law at The University of Melbourne in Australia and before that, he taught at Monash University, The University of Western Australia, and Nottingham University. He has also been a visiting professor at universities in China, Italy, Azerbaijan and Singapore.

He is an author (or co-author) of books on maritime law, international trade law, conflict of laws and the law of torts. He has also published many journal articles on these topics. He has extensive practical experience as a consultant for over 35 years on maritime matters and general international litigation and arbitration, in Australia, Hong Kong, Singapore and the USA. He is presently a senior consultant with the firm of Clyde & Co.

Ann Fenech was elected president of the CMI in Antwerp in 2022 after serving as vice president in 2018. She is head of the marine litigation department at Fenech & Fenech Advocates and past Managing Partner from 2008 to 2020. She qualified in 1986 and joined HFW in London from where she moved to Chaffe McCall Phillips Toler and Sarpy in New Orleans. On joining Fenech & Fenech in 1992, she created the marine litigation department and has dealt exclusively with maritime issues for the past 37 years.

She lectures worldwide on maritime law, particularly at the University of Malta and International Maritime Law Institute. She is the immediate past president of the Malta Maritime Law Association, founding member of the Malta Maritime Forum and board member of the European Maritime Law Organisation since 2008. She is co-chair of the CMI international working group on the ratification of the Convention on the International Effects of Judicial Sales of Ships and was the CMI co-ordinator of the project at UNCITRAL, which led to the approval by the Commission of the Draft Convention in June 2022 and its adoption by the General Assembly in December 2022. She was heavily involved in the organisation of the second signing ceremony of the Convention held in Malta in June 2024.

She has been involved in drafting a number of shipping laws in Malta, including amendments to the Merchant Shipping Act, the Pilotage Regulations and the articles on actions in rem in the Code of Organisation and Civil Procedure.

She has been listed in the Lloyds List Top 100 People – The Shipping Industry's most influential people in 2022 and 2023.

Paul Myburgh is currently a professor of law at the Auckland University of Technology (AUT) Law School and an adjunct research professor in the Centre for Maritime Law (CML) at the National University of Singapore (NUS).

Paul is the Chief Editor of the CML CMI Database on Judicial Decisions on International Conventions, the New Zealand correspondent for Lloyd's Maritime and Commercial Law Quarterly and sits on the editorial boards of the Journal for International Maritime Law and the Maritime Business Review.

His research interests include admiralty and shipping law, international trade and transport law, international commercial law and the protection of underwater cultural heritage.

George Theocharidis is a professor of maritime law and policy at the World Maritime University. A member of the Piraeus Law Bar and qualified advocate before Areios Pagos (Supreme Court) with extensive shipping litigation practice.

He is a member of the IMO Roaster of Experts and of the Working Group of the Legal Committee on "Measures to Prevent Unlawful Practices Associated with Fraudulent Registration and Fraudulent Registries of Ships". He served as an ordinary member of the Law Commission that recently revised the Code of Private Maritime Law of Greece and Joint Rapporteur of the International Working Group of the Comité Maritime International (CMI) on "Liability for the Wrongful Arrest of Ships".

He is author of many books and articles on various fields of law. And holder of a LL.M. degree from the University of Cambridge (UK) and Ph.D. from Aristotle University of Thessaloniki (Greece).

FOREWORD

In April 1992 a vessel named *Cerro Colorado* was arrested in England by mortgagees who later obtained judgment against the vessel. The Admiralty Marshal was authorised to sell the vessel. But before he did so the Spanish Embassy advised the Marshal that any purchaser would be liable for the claims of the master and crew and an advertisement was placed in Lloyd's List in June 1992, stating that:

> Any eventual offeror or purchaser must be aware that the ship *Cerro Colorado* . . . [is] encumbered with several seizures, especially by virtue of a judgment of the Spanish Courts awarding its crew an amount of 700 million pesetas which is a privilege-rank debt, the enforcement of which shall remain prevailing notwithstanding any sale under the Orders of Admiralty.

I was instructed by the Admiralty Marshal to seek clarification from the Admiralty Court of the legal effect of a sale by the Admiralty Court. Thus, was raised for determination the issue which later gave rise to the Convention on the International Effects of Judicial Sales of Ships (known as the Beijing Convention).

That issue had rarely troubled the Admiralty Court but when it did so a clear answer was given. In 1841 Dr Lushington addressed the issue in *The Tremont*[1] and in 1961 Hewson J again did so in *The Acrux*.[2] Sheen J, the Admiralty Judge in the case of *The Cerro Colorado*,[3] was therefore able to state with clarity the effect in English law of a sale of a ship by the Admiralty Court.

The principles of English law may be stated as follows:

First, the title conferred by the Admiralty Court when it sells a vessel in the exercise of its admiralty jurisdiction in rem is a valid title against the whole world. Thus, a sale by the Admiralty Marshal confers a clean title, free of any encumbrance. The practical justification for the clean title is that it ensures that the sale price achieved is the market value of the vessel, which is in the interests of creditors with rights *in rem*, and thereby facilitates and encourages the financing, construction and purchase of vessels and the carriage of goods by sea.

Second, the Admiralty Court also recognises that sales by admiralty courts of other jurisdictions will also confer a clean title. This flows not only from the principles of the maritime law but also from the respect accorded to the comity of nations.

---

1 (1841) 1 Wm Rob 163.
2 (1962) 1 LR 405.
3 (1993) 1 LR 58.

The Admiralty Court expects (it can do more) that these general principles of the maritime law will also be respected by other maritime nations.

It may be that the paucity of cases where those principles have not been respected suggests that that expectation is well founded. But the study of this subject which has resulted in the Beijing Convention suggests that the Admiralty Court may be to some extent optimistic. My own view is that admiralty courts of the world are very conscious of the fact that they each seek to apply the same principles of admiralty law and are very respectful of the decisions of their sister courts. Although, from time to time, the detailed application of those principles may differ, the principle that an admiralty sale confers a clean title is of such importance, not only internationally, but also with regard to the efficacy of each admiralty's courts' own judicial sales, that the occasions on which it may not be respected are likely to be few.

The consequence of those general principles is that the Admiralty Court will not permit a creditor with a claim in rem to arrest the vessel in its new ownership, whether the sale was ordered by the English Admiralty Court or by the Admiralty Court of another maritime nation.

The corollary or supporting rule of these general principles is that a creditor with a claim in rem may, where the vessel has been sold by an order of the Admiralty Court, exercise their claim in rem against the proceeds of sale; see *The Union Gold*[4] and *The Sanko Mineral*.[5] This supporting rule seeks to ensure that a creditor with a claim in rem will not be prejudiced by a judicial sale of the vessel. In the latter case, this principle was applied in the context of an arrest in England by a mortgagee bank, a cargo claim in rem arising in the United States (US) and a shipowner subject to a reorganisation in Japan recognised in England under the Cross-Border Insolvency Regulations. Thus, the principle is of clear relevance and importance in the modern commercial world.

The essays in this book by the most distinguished of commentors on admiralty matters examine critically and with much learning not only the existing understanding in the common law world of the legal effect of an admiralty sale[6] but also the specific provisions of the Convention which seek to give effect to its important and necessary aim of ensuring that there is no doubt or misunderstanding as to the effect of a judicial sale of a ship.[7] The case of *The Cerro Colorado* and the more recent case of *The Bright Star*[8] discussed by Ann Fenech in Chapter 1 indicate that those with claims against a ship may indeed misunderstand or fail to recognise the effect of a judicial sale of a ship.

From the viewpoint of an English Admiralty lawyer the Beijing Convention seeks to give effect to the general principles of maritime law recognised by the English Admiralty Court. Although the Convention has been described as being marked by its "simplicity"[9] it is to be noted that, by contrast with an approach based upon general principles, the Convention creates a formal and prescriptive scheme which seeks to

---

[4] (2014) 1 LR 53.

[5] (2015) 1 LR 247.

[6] See, in particular, Chpt 4 by Professor Myburgh of Auckland University at ss. 2 and 3. The position in the USA is described in Chpt 5 by Professor Davies of the Tulane University Law School.

[7] See, in particular, Chpt 2 by Professor Rhidian Thomas of Swansea University.

[8] (2023) App. Civ. 846/18/2 92023.

[9] See Chpt 1 by Ann Fenech.

define when a sale of a ship will confer a clean title and, by inference when it will not. In this regard, it is to be noted that Professor Rhidian Thomas has said in Chapter 2 of this book that the Convention:

> sets out explicitly in precise terms, procedural and technical, the circumstances when the judicial sale of a ship confers a clean title on the purchaser. Thus exposed a potential challenger is presented with a precise target by which to seek to undermine the purchaser's title, with challenges mustered or manufactured on procedural and technical issues.

An example, he suggests, is the concept of a "clean title" which, as used in the Beijing Convention, does not extend to unregistered charges such as statutory rights of action in rem (that is, maritime claims which do not give rise to a maritime lien but may be enforced in rem pursuant to statute).

Whether the Convention succeeds in its aim to a greater extent than the principles of the maritime law reflected in English Admiralty law will depend upon the number of such nations who ratify and enforce the Convention. I have no doubt that the essays in this book will be carefully studied by those nations who have not yet ratified the Convention. The essays not only explain the beneficial aim of the Convention and the methods by which that aim is sought to be realised but also point out its limitations.[10] In addition, there is a glimpse into the future of "on-line" admiralty sales and how they may fit into the structure of the Beijing Convention.[11]

In that context, it may be helpful to bear in mind that the detailed scheme in the Convention does not seek to displace the general principles of the maritime law to which the English Admiralty Court and many other courts give effect but sits alongside those principles. For those principles are preserved by Article 14 of the Convention which provides that nothing in the Convention shall preclude a state from giving effect to a judicial sale in another State under any applicable law. Thus, the Beijing Convention and the long-established principles of the maritime law can work together to secure the necessary aim of ensuring that the courts of maritime nations, or perhaps more relevantly, those with claims against ships, respect the clean title conferred by an admiralty judicial sale.

Sir Nigel Teare
Admiralty Judge 2011–2020 of the
High Court of England and Wales

10 See Chpt 3 by Professor George Theocharidis of the World Maritime University in Malmo.

11 See Chpt 6 by Abhinayan Basu Bal.

PREFACE

The Beijing Convention (The UN Convention on the International Effects of Judicial Sales of Ships) is a recent arrival on the international maritime scene and is currently in the process of seeking international acceptance. It addresses a relatively inconspicuous yet critically important aspect of international litigation relating to shipping. Its object is to unify and entrench recognition of the principle that when a ship is sold by judicial sale, as an integral incident of litigation relating to ships, the purchaser acquires clean title free of all encumbrances. This principle is long established and ostensibly free from contention, but recent cases have been identified which reveal the principle being ignored or even rejected, with diverse adverse consequences. These include disruption to shipping and international maritime trade and threat to the viability of judicial sales as a vital aspect of litigation and as a branch of the ship sale and purchase market.

The Convention has been in preparation for some 20 years. The subject was initially taken up by the CMI which over a period of years, following its well-established procedures, prepared a draft convention. Thereafter responsibility for the initiative was transferred consensually to UNCITRAL which continued to develop the draft in collaboration with the CMI. Their joint endeavours were successful and resulted in an agreed Draft Convention. This was duly submitted to the UN General Assembly which agreed to adopt the proposal and decreed that it should be known as the Beijing Convention. At the time of writing the Convention is open to signature and ratification but has yet to come into effect in international law.

The Convention provides an illustration of one of the ways international maritime law is made in the contemporary world. It also attracts questions about the approach to be taken to the interpretation of such an international maritime convention. The way a convention functions will ultimately depend on the interpretation of its terms. Although the core concept addressed by the Convention is familiar, its precise application and wider recognition may vary with the jurisprudential context. Differences may exist between the common law and civilian traditions and also between different branches of these traditions. These differences may have implications for the way the Convention is responded to and on the potential impact incorporation may exert. Some of the chapters examine the diverse possibilities.

The text also takes matters beyond the Beijing Convention and looks to the future. It is doubtful if the current practice of judicial sales predominantly based on public auctions and posted paper bids can survive for much longer. The prospect of judicial sales being conducted online is considered and also the extent to which this development may be facilitated by the Beijing Convention and the prospect of the IMO providing a third-party digital platform.

Over the course of six chapters written by specialists in the field the Beijing Convention is subjected to close scrutiny and analysis. The contributions are not to be viewed as the compilations of a traditional book with individual chapters building up a systematic understanding of the chosen subject. Each chapter represents the particular perspective of the individual writer and in developing their theses a degree of overlap, particularly of introductory matters, is to be anticipated. Also, different responses are expressed to the potential benefits and deficiencies of the Convention.

The editor

CHAPTER 1

The evolution of the UN convention on the international effects of judicial sales of ships (the Beijing convention)

*Ann Fenech**

1.1 The process leading up to the adoption of the Convention

1.1. It was a significant day for the Comité Maritime International (CMI) when on the 8th December 2022 the United Nations Information Service, Vienna, announced in a press release that –

> The United Nations General Assembly adopted the United Nations Convention on the International Effects of Judicial Sales of Ships on the 7th December 2022. The General Assembly authorized a signing ceremony for the Convention to be held as soon as practicable in 2023 in Beijing and recommended the Convention be known as the "Beijing Convention on the Judicial Sale of Ships.[1]

1.2. This announcement represented the culmination of many years of dedicated work. In 2004, Prof Henry Li from China brought to the attention of the executive committee of the CMI the need for a convention to introduce order to an important matter adversely effecting international trade, namely the recognition of the legal effect of judicial sales of ships.

1.3. An International Working Group was formed and the product of its industry, a Draft Convention on the Judicial Sale of Ships and their Recognition was approved by the General Assembly of the CMI in Hamburg in 2014.

1.4. The CMI subsequently approached the IMO Legal Committee in 2015 and 2016 with the object of progressing the draft into international law, but the Legal Committee decided not to accept the proposal. The matter was deferred to be considered again at a later date. The CMI then approached the Hague Conference on Private International Law (HCCH), which at the time (July 2019) was working on what became known as the Convention on the Recognition and Enforcement of Foreign Judgments in Civil or Commercial Matters. At the same time, opinions were expressed by some delegations in the CMI that the topic might be better suited for consideration by UNCITRAL.

1.5. In 2017 the CMI submitted a proposal titled, "Proposal of the Comité Maritime International (CMI) for possible future work on cross-border issues related to the judicial sale of ships", to the 50th Session of United Nations Commission on International Trade Law (UNCITRAL) held in Vienna.[2] The proposal was considered

---

* Ann Fenech President of the CMI and CMI co-ordinator in Working Group VI at UNCITRAL 2018–2022, Partner and head of the marine litigation department Fenech & Fenech, Advocates, Malta.

1 UN Press release UNIS/L/335.

2 A/CN.9/923.

DOI: 10.4324/9781003499930-1

and the suggestion made that it would be useful to hold a Colloquium to provide further information about the proposal made to the Commission.[3]

1.6. In response a Colloquium was organised in Malta in February 2019 by the CMI, together with the Maltese Ministry for Transport, Infrastructure and Capital Projects and the Malta Maritime Law Association. It was attended by some 150 delegates from over 60 countries, representing a cross-section of the international maritime industry. Apart from maritime lawyers, members of the judiciary, representatives of ship repairers, financial institutions, port authorities and flag administrations attended. There was also the active presence and participation of international bodies such as BIMCO, ITF and ICS.

1.7. The Colloquium was moderated by Dr Suzanne Shaw, Vice President of the Malta Maritime Law Association, and held over an entire day. It was addressed by myself, then President of the Malta Maritime Law Association, Stuart Hetherington, then President of the CMI, the Maltese Minister for Transport, Infrastructure and Capital Projects and Ryan Harington, Senior Legal Officer at UNCITRAL.[4] The introductory speeches focused on current challenges and the necessity of a universal solution. They were followed by two panel discussions. The first dealt with "*Available Enforcement Proceedings*"[5] and the second with "*Current Challenges faced by Financiers, Creditors and Owners*".[6]

1.8. Numerous international stakeholders contributed and there was unanimous support for the necessity of a convention.[7] It was noted that there were far too many instances when, notwithstanding the fact that a vessel had been sold in a valid judicial

---

[3] The Report of the 50th session (ibid (n 2)) stated at note 465,

> The Commission thanked CMI for its proposal and noted the importance of the issues raised. It decided not to refer the proposal to a working group at the present time but agreed that UNCITRAL, through its Secretariat, and States would support and participate in a colloquium to be initiated by CMI to discuss and advance the proposal.

[4] CMI Yearbook 2017–2018 pp. 329–364.

[5] This panel consisted of the Moderator, Ann Fenech, CMI Executive Councillor and Managing Partner, Fenech & Fenech Advocates, Malta; Camila Mendes Vianna Cardoso, Managing Partner, Kincaid, Mendes Vianna, Advogados, Rio de Janeiro, Brazil; Jan-Erik Pötschke, Partner Ahlers & Vogel, Hamburg, Germany; Lawrence Teh, Administrator CMI, Senior Partner, Dentons Rodyk & Davidson LLP, Singapore; Charles Buss, Partner Watson Farley & Williams, London, UK and Brooke Shapiro, Associate, Winston & Strawn LLP, New York, USA.

[6] This panel consisted of the Moderator, Alexander von Ziegler, CMI Executive Councillor, Partner Schellenberg Wittmer AG, Switzerland; Tilman Stein, Director and Senior Counsel, Deutsche Bank, Hamburg, Germany; Peter Laurijssen, Manager Legal Department, CMB Group, Antwerp, Belgium; Cornelia Zammit German, CEO Falzon Group of Companies, Malta; Simon Ward, Fellow Chartered Shipbroker, Institute of Chartered Shipbrokers, London, UK; Ivan Sammut, Maltese Registrar General of Shipping and Seamen, Malta; Norman Martinez, Associate Professor, International Maritime Law Institute, Malta.

[7] Tilman Stein, Senior Counsel, Head Group Legal Deutsche Bank AG, was of the view that "Legal certainty; maximisation of the asset value; the availability of ship finance; and ease of registration are the key ingredients of an efficient and effective system of judicial sales"; Peter Laurijssen, Manager, Legal Department CMB Group Antwerp, was of the view that: "Any failure by one state to recognise sales in other jurisdictions impacts severely on each of those ingredients"; Charles Buss, Partner at Watson Farley & Williams and co-author of the "The Law of Ship Mortgages", expressed the view that "bidding interest needs to be stimulated"; Ivan Sammut, Registrar General of Maltese Ships, underlined that "there is need for more certainty to avoid unnecessary delays in the registration of ownership and deletion of previous mortgages following judicial sales" Alexandra Willcox, Eggar Forrester Shipbrokers, said "Potential buyers need to be confident with the process in order to attract them to bid and buyers need to be satisfied with the title they are going to attain".

sale free and unencumbered, nonetheless shipowners, financiers and crew members were compelled to deal with claims resulting from the failure of institutions within states to give effect to the clean title obtained by the purchaser;[8] or were unable to obtain the deletion of registered mortgages;[9] or obtain the deletion of the ship from the ship registry;[10] or the vessel was arrested by old creditors of the ship.[11]

1.9. These recent factual experiences underlined how important it is that when a judicial sale results in the free and unencumbered transfer of title in the vessel, that in the hands of the new purchaser, the clean title is given full effect. This leads to certainty and peace of mind, not only for the purchaser but also the creditors of the vessel. It is in their interest that the maximum price is obtained for a ship sold by judicial sale, which also ensures their best chance of being adequately reimbursed.

1.10. There was also consensus that any uncertainty about the title of the purchaser would seriously impact the availability of finance for ships sold in judicial sales and influence the price obtained to the detriment of the vessel's existing creditors. The colloquium ended with overwhelming support for the reforms proposed by the CMI in the Beijing Draft.

1.11. The outcome of the Colloquium, together with the CMI Beijing Draft, was presented by Switzerland under the title "Proposal of the Government of Switzerland for possible future work on cross-border issues related to the judicial sale of ships" at the 51st session of UNCITRAL in June of 2018.[12] In response, the Commission supported the proposal and noted that the issue had the potential to affect many areas of international trade and commerce, not only the shipping industry, with several examples of that impact provided.[13]

1.12. The subject was referred to Working Group VI and Prof Beata Czerwenka was elected Chair. The WG considered the draft convention over six sessions, from the thirty-fifth session in New York in May 2019 to the fortieth session in New York in February 2022. In the fortieth session, the WG completed its article-by-article review of the substantive provisions of the fifth revision of the draft convention. And on the 30th June 2022 in New York, the 55th session of UNCITRAL adopted the draft convention and recommended that it be referred to the United Nations General Assembly for consideration at its forty-seventh session in New York in December 2022.

1.13. The Convention was duly adopted by the General Assembly of the UN at the forty-seventh session. At the same time, it authorised a ceremony for the opening for signature of the Convention to be held as soon as practical in 2023 in Beijing. It also recommended that the Convention be known as the Beijing Convention on the Judicial Sale of Ships.[14]

---

[8] *The Galaxias (Canada)* 1988 LMLN No 240 p. 2, relates to the difficulties encountered in Greece in obtaining recognition of a judicial sale in Canada.

[9] *The Sam Dragon (Ireland)* 2012 IEHC 240, was concerned with a judicial sale in Belgium and the difficulties encountered by the buyer to delete the mortgagees interests in the vessel, registered in Korea.

[10] *Pelamis No 68 Federal Court of Australia No NSD379/2017*, related to the difficulties encountered by the Australian buyer of a vessel in connection with a judicial sale in Singapore. The Taiwanese authorities where the ship was registered refused to recognise him as the new buyer.

[11] *Ann Fenech nominee v Jebmed Srl – The Bright Star (Malta)* [2023] App. Civ. 846/18/2. Considered infra par. 1.5.

[12] UN A/CN.9/944/Rev.1.

[13] Report of UNCITRAL, 51st session A/73/17.

[14] Report of UNCITRAL, 55th session A/77/17.

1.2 Signing ceremony in Beijing

1.14. The signing ceremony took place in Beijing on the 5th of September 2023, in accordance with the authorisation of the General Assembly of the UN in December 2022.[15] It was held at the Beijing National Convention Centre and organised by the Chinese Government and UNCITRAL.

1.15. The Convention was attended by senior officials and representatives from more than 30 countries.[16] It was signed by 15 countries: China, Burkina Faso, Comoros, El Salvador, Grenada, Honduras, Kiribati, Liberia Sao Tome and Principe, Saudi Arabia, Senegal, Sierra Leone, Singapore, Syria and Switzerland, in the presence of numerous state representatives.

1.16. The signing ceremony was preceded by introductory speeches by members of the Chinese Government and Chinese Judiciary and was followed by an international symposium organised by the Supreme People's Court of the People's Republic of China, UNCITRAL, China Maritime Law Association and Dalian Maritime University, with persons from a cross section of the industry taking the floor.[17] It was followed by an international symposium which addressed the main features and potential impact of the Convention.[18]

1.17. Regrettably, in September 2023, the European Union had not yet finalised its internal processes so as to be able it to sign the Convention and therefore no EU Member State was in a position to sign.

1.18. On the 21st of December 2021, the European Council published its decision on the signing of the Convention on behalf of the European Union. The President of the Council was authorised to designate the persons empowered to sign the Convention on behalf of the Union.[19] On the 15th of March 2024, the European Union signed the

---

[15] <comitemaritime.org/the-convention-on-the-international-effects-of-judicial-sales-of-ships-open-for-signature/>.

[16] At the time of writing 28 states have signed the Convention but only one state, El Salvador, has ratified it. The European Union has signed under its status as a Regional Economic Integration Organisation (REIO); see Article 19, Beijing Convention.

[17] Speakers included Wang Shumei – Justice of the People's Republic of China, Anna Joubin-Bret, Secretary of UNCITRAL, Zang Mingqi – Vice President and Secretary-General of China Law Society, Yu Jianlong – Vice Chairman of the China Council for the Promotion of International Trade, Gao Xiaoli – Chief Judge of the Fourth Civil Division of the SPC of China, Hu Fang – Deputy Chief Judge of the Fourth Civil Division of the SPC of China, Xu Chun – Deputy Director General of the Maritime Safety Administration of China, Zhang Yuejiao – Expert member of the International Commercial Expert Committee of the SPC of China, Peter Wong Hing Hong – Deputy Law Officer of the Department of Justice of the Hong Kong Special Administrative region of China, Zhai Juan – General Manager of the Legal Department of China Merchants Energy Shipping Co Ltd, Wang Bo – Principal of the Legal Department of ICBC Financial Leasing Co Ltd, Chu Beiping – Vice President of Dalian Maritime University, Ann Fenech – President of the CMI, co-chair of CMI IWG on Judicial Sales and CMI co-ordinator for CMI during Working Group VI at UNCITRAL, Prof Henry Li – co-chair of CMI Working Group on Judicial Sales, Jose Angelo Estrella Faria – Principal Legal Officer UNCITRAL, Jan De Boer – Senior Legal Officer IMO, Soren Larsen – Deputy Secretary General BIMCO, Peter Laurijssen – ICS representative and CMI IWG rapporteur, Lawrence Teh – Administrator CMI.

[18] Publication of the International Symposium on the Beijing Convention on the Judicial Sale of Ships; 5 September 2023 Beijing, China.

[19] EU 2024/414 "on the signing, on behalf of the European Union, of the United Nations Convention on the International Effects of Judicial Sales of Ships, adopted by the United Nations General Assembly in New York on 7 December 2022".

Convention in New York, as also did Belgium which held the Presidency of the EU Council; it was the first EU Member State to sign the Convention.

Subsequently, Tanzania, Equador, Luxembourg, Dominican Republic and Libya have signed the Convention.

1.3 Second signing ceremony

1.19. From March 2024 EU Member States were able to sign the Convention. This led to the idea that it might give the Convention further impetus if a celebratory event were to be organised in an EU Member State and at which EU and non-EU Member States were given the opportunity of signing the Convention. Malta showed an interest and the CMI assisted in the facilitation of a celebratory event organised by the Maltese Ministry of Foreign and European Affairs and Trade, CMI and UNCITRAL.

1.20. The Secretariat of UNCITRAL persuaded the Treaty Section of the United Nations that it would be of great benefit if the Treaty Book could be brought to Malta for what would effectively be a second signing ceremony of the Convention. This was an exceptional request since historically the Treaty Book only leaves on a single occasion to the country designated by the General Assembly as the country where the signing ceremony is to take place, in this case, Beijing. Nonetheless, the Treaty Section appreciated the advantages of the proposal and agreed.

1.21. The celebratory event was held in Malta on the 19th of June 2024.[20] The Treaty Book was brought to Malta by Mr. David Nanopoulos, Chief, Treaty Section, Office of Legal Affairs at the UN. The event was of high status at which the significance of the Convention was explained to states and their representatives. It also gave states the opportunity to sign.[21] Seven states took this opportunity and signed the Convention, namely Malta, Spain, Cyprus, Italy, Croatia, Cote d'Ivoire and Antigua and Barbuda.[22] And subsequently Gabon and Ghana have signed.

1.22. This brings the present number of signatories to 31, including the EU, and one ratification. It is also significant that the signatory states include four of the ten largest flag states in the world, namely, Liberia, China, Singapore and Malta.

1.4 The principal provisions of the Convention

1.23. The Convention has 23 Articles,[23] but only 11 are substantive. It is its simplicity which will probably be the key to its success.

[20] <comitemaritime.org/convention-on-the-international-effects-of-judicial-sales-of-ships/>.

[21] The event was held under the auspices of the President of the Republic of Malta Her Excellency Miriam Spiteri Debono and addressed by three Maltese Ministers – Ian Borg, Minister of Foreign Affairs, Jonathan Attard, Minister of Justice and Chris Bonett, Minister of Transport; and Jose Angelo Estrella Faria Principal Legal Officer and Head Legislative Branch, Law Division, Office of Legal Affairs at UNCITRAL; Ann Fenech President of the CMI; Dorota Lost Sieminska, Director, Legal Affairs and External Relations Division at the IMO and Richard Sonnenshein, Director General DG Justice. In my address I invited the EU to now proceed to the next step of finalising the necessary processes to enable EU Member States to ratify the convention. In response Mr Sonnenshein confirmed that the EU was totally committed to ensuring that EU Member States would be able to ratify the convention as soon as possible.

[22] <comitemaritime.org/beijing-convention-signing-ceremony-2/>.

[23] UN A/RES/77/100.

1.4.1 The primary provision

1.24. The central provision of the Convention is contained in Article 6, which states:

> A Judicial sale for which a certificate of judicial sale referred to in Article 5 has been issued shall have the effect in every other State Party of conferring clean title to the ship on the purchaser.

1.4.2 Ship arrest

1.25. The Convention, as stated in Article 3, applies only to a judicial sale of a ship if (i) it is conducted in a State Party and (ii) the ship is physically within the territory of the State of judicial sale at the time of the sale.

1.4.3 Notice of sale and IMO as repository

1.26. Various criteria need to be satisfied for the Convention to apply and for a judicial sale to have international effect, notably compliance with the notice of sale criteria in Article 4.

1.27. Article 4 provides that a number of persons need to be notified. During the deliberations relating to the Convention, this was one of the articles which generated significant debate. A number of delegations, accompanied by maritime lawyers, understood that in today's age, with the technology available on our smartphones, it is very easy to track vessels and establish whether they have been arrested and about to be sold in a judicial sale. However, there was still significant concern whether all parties having an interest in the process would be adequately notified. The end result was the list of parties to be notified contained in Article 4.

1.28. However, given the extent of the concern and to ensure consensus, the idea of giving notice through the agency of a third-party public site started to gather momentum. This led to the conclusion that it would be highly desirable if notices of judicial sale could be transmitted to an entity such as the IMO, which already had the GISIS platform which could host such an additional module and which would be readily accessible.

1.29. Discussions followed between the CMI, UNCITRAL and IMO and the idea was presented to LEG 107 at the request of UNCITRAL. During the session, the Secretariat explained how UNCITRAL had contacted the IMO Secretariat to explore options for IMO to host a possible online repository under the draft instrument, as a new GISIS module.[24] At that same meeting the CMI presented its case in support of the idea that the Repository should be the IMO, explaining all the advantages and how using the GISIS platform provided would offer a range of benefits and, importantly, transparency. The CMI concluded its statement by stating that it wholly supported the idea and was of the firm view that this would be a perfect opportunity for two UN organisations, the IMO and UNCITRAL, to provide a solution to a matter which had important ramifications and effects on international shipping and trade.[25] LEG107 agreed to invite the Secretariat to make the necessary arrangements to host a possible

---

[24] LEG 107/18/2 para 17.4.

[25] LEG 107/18/2 Annex 3 p. 21.

online repository under the UNCITRAL draft instrument on the foreign judicial sale of ships and their recognition, as an additional GISIS module.[26]

1.30. This led to the introduction of Article 11 which identifies the IMO as the Repository of the Notices of Judicial Sales and the Certificate of Judicial sale. In practice, the notices of judicial sales and certificates of judicial sales will be sent to the IMO which is creating a special module on the Global Integrated Shipping Information System – the GISIS platform, enabling the uploading of these documents. Thus anyone, anywhere in the world will be able to see and check at the press of a button whether a particular vessel is about to be sold in a judicial sale.

1.31. This idea satisfied those delegations who were concerned about the adequacy of the notice provisions. Article 4 consequently provides that, apart from the list of recipients, notice of judicial Sale must also be sent to the IMO.

1.4.4 Certificate of Judicial Sale

1.32. Article 5 contains the provisions relating to the Certificate of Judicial Sale. This article, in practice, provides state parties with the tools to ensure that they can effectively implement the Convention if called upon.

1.33. On completion of a judicial sale that confers clean title to the ship under the law of the state of the judicial sale, conducted in accordance with the requirements of that law and the Convention, the court or other public authority that conducts the judicial sale shall issue a Certificate of Judicial Sale.

1.34. The Convention provides a model of the certificate in Annex 11. The certificate confirms that "the Judicial sale has conferred clean title to the ship on the purchaser".

1.4.5 Flag state registration and ship arrest

1.35. The certificate of judicial sale in effect enables flag administrations and courts to act effectively in line with Articles 7 and 8.

1.36. Article 7 provides that at the request of a purchaser who produces a Certificate of Judicial Sale, a registrar of ships is "obliged" to delete the vessel, or effect a transfer of ownership, and is "obliged" to delete any pre-existing mortgages, hypothecs or registered charges.

1.37. Article 8 provides that an application for an arrest of a ship for a claim pre-existing the sale free and unencumbered "shall be refused" on the production of the certificate of judicial sale by the new owner of the vessel. And if the vessel has been arrested in *ex parte* proceedings the court "shall" upon the production of a Certificate of Judicial Sale, order the release of the vessel.

1.38. Articles 7 and 8 constitute *the raison d'etre* of the Convention. Great instability may be caused after a ship is sold free and unencumbered in a judicial sale if the previous owner brings pressure to bear on the registrar of ships to refrain from deleting the vessel or registering the vessel in the name of the new owner; or to refrain from deleting a mortgage or registering a new mortgage in favour of a new mortgagee: and

---

[26] LEG 107/18/2 para 17.6.

because of the great uncertainty and chaos which ensues when vessels are arrested post judicial sales by unscrupulous existing creditors.

1.39. These possibilities make Articles 7 and 8 very significant. They underpin the entire Convention. They provide an effective mechanism which enables registrars of flag administrations and courts to act immediately and decisively. Registrars and courts are *obliged* to act in the way indicated on the presentation of a Certificate of Judicial Sale.

1.40. The feedback from flag administrations and members of the judiciary in countries which witness numerous ship arrests has been positive. The general view is that the certainty which is produced by the significance given to the certificate of judicial sale will eliminate much wasted time, meaningless exchanges and applications before both flag administrations and courts.

1.4.6 Jurisdiction of court of judicial sale

1.41. The Convention provides in Article 9 that it is the court of the State of judicial sale which has exclusive jurisdiction to hear a claim or application to avoid a judicial sale and not the court of any other state.

1.42. This was considered important to avoid forum shopping under the Convention. It is only the court of the State of judicial sale that can reasonably be expected to enquire into the facts of a judicial sale and determine whether the sale complies with its own laws and the provisions of the Convention, or should be avoided.

1.43. Of course, the decision to avoid a sale after a judicial sale; or after the vessel is registered in the name of the new owners; or after mortgages are entered by new financiers; or after creditors have actually been paid out of the purchase price, would have serious repercussions and lead to many complications. Therefore, the decision to avoid a judicial sale is one to be made with caution. The UNCITRAL Secretariat's Explanatory Notes on the Convention, paragraph 207 states[27]

> In practice, avoidance of a judicial sale is exceedingly rare. It is a remedy of limited availability given the difficulty of unwinding the effects of a judicial sale and restoring the parties to their previous positions once action has been taken on registration under article 7 and the proceeds of sale have been distributed. . . . The inclusion of article 9 in the Convention is not intended to suggest that challenges to a judicial sale should be encouraged as a matter of course; rather it is designed to ensure that the validity of a certificate of judicial sale and the conditions for issuance are scrutinized exclusively by the State of judicial sale.

1.4.7 Public policy

1.44. The clear provisions of Articles 7 and 8 are subject to only one exception which relates to public policy.

1.45. If an application thereunder would result in the court making an order that would be "manifestly contrary to the public policy" of the State in which the court

[27] UN Convention on the International Effects of Judicial Sales of Ships: Text and Explanatory Note <uncitral.un.org/sites/uncitral.un.org/files/media-documents/uncitral/en/united_nations_convention_on_the_international_effects_of_judicial_sales_of_ships.pdf>. See Appendix 2.

is located, the court may dismiss the application. The exception is clearly set out in Articles 7(5) and 8(4).

1.46. Article 10 sets out the core application of the "public policy" defence in the following terms –

> A judicial sale of a ship shall not have the effect provided in article 6 in a State Party other than the State of Judicial sale if a court in the other State Party determines that the effect would be manifestly contrary to the public policy of that other State Party.

1.47. This exception may attract criticism as possibly interfering with the certainty which is otherwise provided by the Convention. Whilst such observations cannot be dismissed, it is equally important that there should be an understanding of what led to the exception and, importantly, how the exception is to be applied.

1.48. During the deliberations, there were a number of delegations who were of the view that there was not any need for a public policy exception. However, a significant number of delegations were of the contrary view and also insisted on exceptions that were so varied and far-reaching that their adoption would have effectively removed the clarity and certainty which the Convention was seeking to achieve. The debate was lively and the lack of consensus clearly exposed. Nonetheless, consensus was finally reached.

1.49. The range of exceptions suggested was eliminated and the sole exception based on "manifestly contrary to public policy" was retained. This is in keeping with the position commonly occupied in private international law. However, it was made abundantly clear during the deliberations that this exception was to be strictly interpreted and a very high threshold adopted.

1.50. The Explanatory Notes on the Convention, paragraph 212,[28] clearly stipulates –

> This sets a high threshold, which reflects recent treaty practice. The threshold is designed to avoid an abusive or overly expansive application of the public policy exception and requires a compelling reason as to why giving effect to a foreign judicial sale is contrary to an identified matter of public policy. It emphasizes that the public policy is expected to apply only in exceptional cases.

1.4.8 Limitation

1.51. Article 15 of the Convention makes it clear that the Convention is not dealing with the procedure or priority in the distribution of proceeds of a judicial sale. Nor with any claims *in personam* against the owner of the vessel.

1.4.9 Coming into force

1.52. Article 21 of the Convention provides that the Convention shall enter into force 180 days after the date of the deposit of the third instrument of ratification, acceptance, approval or accession.

---

[28] Ibid. See also Appendix 2.

1.53. The Explanatory Notes on the Convention, paragraph 258,[29] indicate that multilateral treaties prepared by UNCITRAL have required as few as three and as many as ten State ratifications to enter into force.

1.54. Naturally, the real benefit of the Convention to international trade depends on it giving effect to judicial sales in as many countries as possible and this is dependent on its ratification by as many states as possible. Discussions focused on what would be the best route to follow. A significant number of delegations agreed that a low number would encourage states to ratify in the knowledge that once they had ratified the Convention would be close to coming into force. It was considered that this approach represented an additional incentive and bonus, and so it was agreed that three ratifications would be sufficient to bring the Convention into force.

1.5 *The Bright Star*

1.55. The importance of the Beijing Convention cannot be over-emphasised and there can be no better case to support this claim than the relatively recent case *The Bright Star*. It was decided by the Court of Appeal of Malta on the 12th January 2023,[30] confirming the judgment of the first tier court on the 27th May 2021.[31]

1.56. On the 9th January 2018, Bluefin Marine Ltd purchased the vessel *Trading Fabrizia* for the sum of US$10,300,000 in a judicial sale by auction in Jamaica. The vessel had been arrested in Jamaica by the mortgagee Jebmed Srl ("Jebmed"), followed by the vessel's judicial sale by auction in Jamaica. Subsequent to the sale the Jamaican courts ordered the sum of US$3,000,000 to be reserved in favour of Jebmed.

1.57. On the 19th June 2018 the vessel, now renamed "*The Bright Star*", was under charter passing through the Mediterranean en route from Kavkaz to Venezuela, fully loaded with a cargo of wheat. She stopped off at Malta to receive bunkers and was immediately arrested by Jebmed, the former mortgagee of the vessel prior to her sale in Jamaica.[32] The arrest was contrary to Article 37(D) of the Maltese Merchant Shipping Act which stated:

> Provided further that where a ship has been sold pursuant to an order or with the approval of a competent court within whose jurisdiction the vessel was at the time of the sale, the interest of the mortgagees as well as of any other creditor in the ship shall pass on to the proceeds of the sale of the ship.

1.58. Attempts to persuade Jebmed to withdraw the unlawful arrest failed. The *Bright Star* should not have been arrested by the vessel's former mortgagee following the sale of the vessel free and unencumbered six months previously. The mortgagee should have proceeded to seek payment from the proceeds of the judicial sale in Jamaica where the sum of US$3,000,000, later reduced to US$1,000,000, had been reserved to meet its claim.

---

29 Ibid. See also Appendix 2.

30 *Ann Fenech Nominee v Jebmed Srl – The Bright Star (Malta)* [2023] App. Civ. 846/18/2.

31 Ibid, 2021 846/2918.

32 Report of UNCITRAL, 51st session, A/73/17. It is somewhat ironic that the *Bright Star* was arrested in Malta by the initial mortgagee only a few weeks prior to the start of the 51st session of the Commission at UNCITRAL, which had agreed to assume responsibility for the Beijing Convention project.

1.59. The owners of the *Bright Star* had the ship under charter and full of wheat. They were consequently forced to confront the losses associated with the disruption of the charter and immediately mobilise assistance to ensure that the vessel could continue on its journey without undue delay. They had no option but to put up security in cash in the sum of Euro 778,000, to obtain the vessel's release from arrest and debate the merits later. This sum had to be put up in cash because Jebmed refused to accept a letter of undertaking from the vessel's P&I Club, Steamship Mutual, which, from the moment of the arrest, had become involved, lending support and guidance. In the meantime, the charterers were increasingly concerned about the delay to the voyage, with potential claims looming.

1.60. The financiers who had financed the purchase of the vessel in the judicial sale in Jamaica, were also concerned about the turn of events. They had agreed to finance the purchase on the understanding of an opinion given by the Admiralty Marshal in Jamaica. This indicated that the vessel was being sold free and unencumbered: and that the law of the vessel's registry, then Malta, fully recognised the transfer of a free and unencumbered title to the purchaser. This was understood to mean that the interests of former mortgagees and creditors would cease to attach to the vessel under new ownership and that their interests would transfer to the proceeds of the sale. They, therefore, financed the purchase of the vessel in the belief that all previous debts would fall away from the ship and that they, the new financiers, held the only mortgage on the vessel.

1.61. The unlawful arrest of the *Bright Star* commenced a judicial saga which lasted until the 12th January 2023 when the Court of Appeal of Malta handed down its final judgment.[33] The five-year period witnessed no less than 73 judicial proceedings. On the 27th May 2021, the first court declared the arrest unlawful and ordered Jebmed to pay damages. It declared that:[34]

> It is the Court's view that the proviso to article 37 D(1) ie that part which considers the consequence of the sale "with the approval of a competent court within whose jurisdiction the vessel was at the time of the sale" is clear enough to remove all doubt. There is no indication in the acts of this case that the sale was not ordered by a competent Court. The Jamaican Court conducted the sale process in terms of Jamaican law and in the process of recognizing the existence of a mortgage in favour of the defendant company, it reserved a sum of money from the proceeds to satisfy Jemed's credit once it proved its claim linked to the mortgage as required by Jamaican law.
>
> There is nothing in Maltese law which nullifies the effects of article 37D (1) to what has just been stated. Although the introductory part of article 37D(1) states that a mortgage continues to attach to the vessel until it is discharged, the said article imposes exceptions to this general rule including the sale pursuant to an order or with the approval of the Court as in this case. However this does not mean that the creditor loses his privileged right, rather his privileged rights are transferred from the ship to the proceeds of the sale. This means that whatever the sum constituting the proceeds may be, where there are various creditors expecting payment from those proceeds, the rules relating to the ranking of creditors come into play. According to Jamaican law Jebmed enjoyed the second highest preference by virtue of the mortgage once this claim was proved according to the laws of Jamaica.

---

33 Supra (n 30).

34 Supra (n 31).

> The Court considers that if this principle is hindered in its application it will constitute a big hindrance to international maritime trade which may stop entirely the transfer of ships pursuant to an order or with the approval of the Court if the title which is transferred in the sale is considered dubious, and notwithstanding the fact that as occurred in Jamaica the vessel was sold "free of all mortgages, liens and encumbrances.

1.62. The Court of Appeal in its final judgment confirmed the judgment of the first court.[35]

1.63. This case highlights the urgent need for the Beijing Convention on the International effects of judicial sales of ships and constitutes weighty evidence to counter those who are not convinced. It cannot be assumed that all jurisdictions will give proper effect to judicial sales of vessels sold free and unencumbered. And when they do not the case of *The Bright Star* illustrates the injustice and international commercial disruption that may result.

1.6 Conclusion

1.64. There is ample evidence to support the need for the Beijing Convention. The cases noted in this contribution and others which are on the record are not exceptional and remote. The Convention addresses a real contemporary problem and proposes a way forward. A financier, representing a consortium of German banks, in the seminar held in Malta in April 2023[36] declared that banks may well reach the stage, sooner rather than later, of extending finance for the purchase of ships in judicial sales *only* if such ships are sold or registered in state parties to the Convention.

1.65. Finally, the work of the CMI is not yet done. The Beijing project has shown very clearly that the CMI has a broader role than simply drafting international conventions with a view to contributing to the unification of international maritime law. It has a further and equally important role to facilitate, assist and pursue the signing and eventual ratification of the conventions it promotes. This Beijing project has amplified this role very clearly. It has shown that the CMI must continue to pursue matters with a view to ensuring that its national maritime law associations bring pressure to bear on their respective governments to encourage them to sign and ratify the Beijing Convention.

1.66. Conventions are only worth the time and effort applied to their drafting and subsequent deliberations, negotiations and adoption, if they are ultimately signed and ratified by states. It is to be hoped that the Beijing Convention will reward the intellectual labour that has been applied to its promulgation over a significant number of years.

---

[35] Supra (n 30).

[36] <comitemaritime.org/malta-symposium-on-the-convention-on-the-international-effects-of-judicial-sales-of-ships/>.

CHAPTER 2

A textual analysis of the Beijing Convention

*D. Rhidian Thomas**

2.1 Introduction

2.1. In this chapter the primary objective is to scrutinise the drafting and potential interpretation of the Beijing Convention.[1] The *raison d'etre* of the Convention has been described in the opening chapter.[2] In brief, it is to ensure that purchasers of ships under judicial sales acquire a title free of all encumbrances, in accordance with the intention of the sale.[3] Whether this declared goal has been successfully achieved depends not only on the structural formulation of the Convention but the skill of the draftsman in clothing the framework in appropriate and unequivocal language. This is not a straightforward task with the necessary skills not always appreciated.[4]

2.2. The Beijing Convention is an international convention: more particularly a private international law convention. It follows that the approach to its interpretation will in most jurisdictions follow the principles set out in the Vienna Convention on the Law of Treaties 1969.[5] This Convention has been widely adopted by nation states and the principles enshrined supersede the approach that might otherwise be adopted to questions of interpretation under municipal law.[6] These principles apply whether the convention is scheduled or given effect to by domestic legislation.[7]

---

* Emeritus Professor of Maritime Law and Founder Director of the Institute of International Shipping and Trade Law, College of Law, Swansea University, Wales, UK.

1 The UN Convention on the International Effects of Judicial Sales of Ships (The Beijing Convention) 2022. All quotes from this Convention, and from the Explanatory Notes, are reprinted with kind permission of the UNCITRAL Secretariat.

2 Chpt 1 written by Ann Fenech, President of the CMI.

3 See Preamble to the Beijing Convention.

4 See, generally, J Bell and G Engle (eds), *Cross on Statutory Interpretation*, 3rd edn. (1995, Lexis Nexis, Butterworths, UK); FAR Bennion, *Understanding Common Law Legislation (Drafting and Interpretation)* (2009, OUP, UK); D Bailey and L Norbury, *Bennion, Bailey and Norbury on Statutory Interpretation*, 8th edn. (2020, Lexis Nexis, UK). For a recent case of significance, see *Mints and Others v PJSC National Bank Trust and Another* [2023] EWCA Civ. 1132; [2024] 2 Lloyd's Rep 12.

5 Done at Vienna on 23 May 1969. Entered into force on 27 January 1980 and presently ratified by 116 states. See generally Chanh-fa Lo, *Treaty Interpretation under the Vienna Convention on the Law of Treaties* (2024, Springer Publishing); O Dorr and K Schmdenbach (eds), *Vienna Convention on the Law of Treaties (A Commentary)*, 2nd edn. (2020, Springer Publishing).

6 Cf. *Trafigura Pte Ltd v TKK Shipping Pte Ltd (The Thorco Lineage)* [2023] EWHC 26(Comm); [2023] 2 Lloyd's Rep 338; *Mints and Others v PJSC National Bank Trust and Another*, supra (n 4).

7 Cf. *Fothergill v Monarch Airlines Ltd* [1980] 2 Lloyd's Rep 295(HL). In the constitutional practice of the UK, an international convention which is adopted may be incorporated into national law by legislation

DOI: 10.4324/9781003499930-2

2.3. Articles 31–33 of the Vienna Convention indicate the general approach to be adopted to questions of interpretation.[8] The general rule is that a treaty "shall be interpreted in good faith in accordance with the ordinary meaning to be given to the terms of the treaty in their context and in light of its objects and purpose".[9] In the face of continuing ambiguity or the quest for confirmation, a supplementary rule permits recourse to "the preparatory work of the treaty and the circumstances of its conclusion".[10] This supplementary rule broadens the sources that may be drawn upon in aid of the process of interpretation, including *travaux préparatoires.*[11] This is of particular significance in the present context because it opens up the possibility of the *travaux préparatoires* of the Beijing Convention being referred to in appropriate circumstances as an aid to its interpretation.[12] This possibility, however, is limited by the express terms of the Vienna Convention to circumstances when "meaning continues to be ambiguous or to confirm the ordinary meaning".[13]

2.4. Anticipating the possible future adoption by states of the Convention, it is also a principle of interpretation that an international convention should be interpreted in a uniform manner. One implication of this principle is that regard be had to the way the convention is interpreted in foreign jurisdictions. The greater the emerging international consensus the weightier this principle.[14]

2.5. The reference to *travaux préparatoires* raises an initial question of definition. Strictly interpreted the words refer to preparatory materials but this is to cast the net too wide.[15] The potential range and nature of preparatory materials is extensive. Many, far from assisting the discovery of intention, may be of little or no assistance and even serve to muddy the waters. It follows that some qualification is essential. In English law, it appears that there are two operative criteria, one relating to the nature and the other to the potential effect of the material. First, as to its nature, the preparatory

---

or given effect by legislation. The former is considered to be the more accurate and desirable procedure. Under the UK constitution, an international convention is of no effect until incorporated or given effect to in English municipal law.

8 See, generally, *CMA CGM SA v Classica Shipping Co Ltd (The CMA Djakarta)* [2004] EWCA Civ 114; [2004] 1 Lloyd's Rep 460; *JTI Polska SP v Jakubowski (SC)* [2023] UKSC 19; [2023] 2 Lloyd's Rep 64; *MSC Mediterranean Shipping Co SA v Stolt Tank Containers BV and Others (The MSC Flaninia) (No 2)* [2023] EWCA Civ. 1007); [2024] 1 Lloyd's Rep 535.

9 Art 31.1.

10 Art 32. See, also, *Libya v Chad (Territorial Dispute Case)* [1994] ICJ 6 (3 February 1994).

11 *The same position was taken by the common law; see, Fothergill v Monarch Airlines Ltd [1980] 2 Lloyd's Rep 295 (HL).*

12 Some possible sources of *travaux préparatoires* are identified in Chpt 1 of this book. The *travaux préparatoirs* of the Hague and Hague-Visby Rules, both based on international conventions, are frequently referred to in the English Commercial Court and appellate courts when questions of interpretation arise. For a recent example, see *Fimbank Plc v KCH Shipping Co Ltd (The Giant Ace* [1923] EWCA Civ. 569; [1923] 2 Lloyd's Rep 457.

13 Art 32. Also, see, *Gard Marine & Energy Ltd v China National Chartering Co Ltd (The Ocean Victory)* [2017] 1 WLR 1793; [2017] 1 Lloyd's Rep 521; *Vinnlustodin HF v Sea Tank Shipping AS (The Aqasia* [2018] 1 Lloyd's Rep 530; *Glencore Energy UK Ltd v Freeport Holdings Ltd (The Lady M)* [2018] 1 Lloyd's Rep Plus; [2019] 2 Lloyd's Rep 109 (CA).

14 *Nautical Challenge Ltd v Evergreen Marine (UK) Ltd (The Alexandra 1* and *Ever Smart)* [2021] 1 WLR 1436 para 42; [2021] 1 Lloyd's Rep 299.

15 In the US legal system *travaux préparatoires* is interpreted to mean "legislative history": see *Fothergill v Monarch Airlines Ltd*, supra (n 7) per Lord Diplock at p. 304 col. 2.

material must be of a kind capable of being characterised as *travaux préparatoires.*[16] It must be a statement that relates to and describes the preparatory stage and governing intent or purpose of the material in question. This does not mean that the source must be published or come into existence in the course of the preparatory stage: it may appear later and speak retrospectively. But third-party commentaries are excluded.[17] Second, as to effectiveness, it must be determinative. Merely because material may be considered *travaux préparatoires* does not necessarily mean that it is or may be influential. For that to be the case the *travaux préparatoires* must, at least in the opinion of the English courts, "clearly and indisputably point to a definite legal intention. . . . Only a bull's eye counts. Nothing less will do".[18]

2.6. The ideal *travaux préparatoires* are probably reports or documents which give an account of the position or determination arrived at and accompanied by a direct and clear statement of the underlying policy and intent. Examples are explanatory reports that accompany proposals for new legislation or the reform of existing legislation[19]; and explanatory documents that accompany proposals for new or modified standard form contracts.[20] Of immediate interest, the Secretariat of UNCITRAL has prepared an Explanatory Note relating to the Beijing Convention the status of which is considered later in the text[21]

2.7. Less ideal is a record which traces the deliberations within an organisation over a period of time, with contributions, interventions and decisions noted in the same manner as minutes. And thereafter the absence of a decisive final report or statement bringing the entirety to a clear conclusion as to objective and intent. In this kind of circumstance it will often be challenging to identify a "settled consensus".[22] The procedure followed by some international organisations, including the CMI, typically lean, to varying degrees, in this direction.[23]

2.8. The *travaux préparatoires* of the Hague and Hague-Visby Rules published by the CMI provide a record of the evolution of the Rules, but again in the fashion of detailed minutes.[24] They record the diverse contributions made by individuals and committees, with outcomes often uncoordinated and imprecise. They have consequently proved to be of inconsistent assistance to the process of interpretation, crucially because of the

---

16 See, further, infra.

17 See infra (n 34).

18 *Effort Shipping Co Ltd v Linden Management SA (The Giannis NK)* [1998] AC 605; [1998] 1 Lloyd's Rep 337, 347–348 per Lord Steyn. See, also, *Alizw 1954 v Allianz Elementar Versicherungs AG (The CMA CGM Libra)* [2021] UKSC 51; [2021] 2 Lloyd's Rep 613. See, also, *Fothergill v Monarch Airlines Ltd*, supra (n 7) p. 302 col. 1, per Lord Wilberforce, who limited the use of *travaux préparatoires* to documents in the public domain and which "clearly and indisputably point to a definite legislative intention".

19 As are published by the Law Commission (England and Wales) and the Law Scottish Law Commission established by the Law Commissions Act 1965 for the purpose of promoting the reform of the law.

20 E.g. by shipping organisations of which BIMCO is a singular example.

21 Infra (n 36).

22 *Deepsea Maritime Ltd v Monjasa A/S (The Alhani)* [2018] EWHC 1495(Comm); [2018] 2 Lloyd's Rep 563, 575, per David Foxton QC.

23 Ibid. The methodology is revealed, by way of example, in the volumes published by the CMI on the international conventions promoted by the organisation: e.g. Berlingieri, *Berlingieri on Arrest of Ships Vol 1(2017) and Vol II (2017)* (Informa Law from Routledge); F Berlingieri (ed), *The Travaux Préparatoires of the LLMC Convention 1976 and of the Protocol of 1996* (CMI Publication – website – not dated).

24 *The Travaux Préparatoire of The Hague Rules and of The Hague-Visby Rules* (CMI Publication). See Annex 2.

absence of decisive clarity on the questions in issue.[25] Only on those occasions when the necessary clarity is identified may they exert a decisive influence.[26] Lord Bingham, revealing a familiarity with the procedure, expressed the resulting judicial caution in the following terms[27] –

> It must be remembered that in a protracted negotiation such as culminating in adoption of the Hague Rules there are many participants with differing and often competing objects, interests and concerns. It is potentially misleading to attach weight to points made in the course of discussion, even if they appear at the time to be accepted. In the present case I do not think that either party can point to such a clear, pertinent and consensual resolution of the issue before the House as would provide a sure ground of decision.[28]

2.9. In recent litigation relating to the interpretation of the one-year time limit in Article 111(6) of the Hague-Visby Rules, the question in issue was whether the time limit extended to a claim for misdelivery occurring after discharge of the cargo had been completed.[29] On the face of matters, there was no clear answer and informed opinion was divided. In the course of the submissions made, the court was referred to the plenary session of the CMI Stockholm Conference 1963, where the Report of the Sub-Committee on Bill of Lading Clauses was considered. It stated that the object of the amendment was to give the text a bearing as wide as possible, so as to embody within the scope of application of the one year period, even the claims grounded on the delivery of the goods to a person not entitled to them, ie even in the case of what we call a wrong delivery.

This statement was repeated when formal approval was sought. In the Court of Appeal, Males LJ considered that this amounted to providing the necessary "bull's-eye" and the court proceeded to interpret Article 111(6) in the way it had been presented to the delegates. The judge concluded that "there is no reason why effect should not be given to the clear intention of those who drafted the new rule . . .".[30]

2.10. The distinctive nature of the history of the Beijing Convention is that although initially launched and developed by the CMI, it was later consensually adopted by UNCITRAL which, with the continued involvement of the CMI, assumed responsibility for its further development and ultimate passage into international law as a UN convention.[31] The Beijing Convention, therefore, has been on the agenda of the CMI and UNICTRAL for many years, accompanied by sustained deliberation and discussion, copious minutes, reports and conference papers, by parties directly involved in its progress.[32] The procedural methodology of UNCITRAL is different

---

[25] *Fothergill v Monarch Airlines Ltd*, supra (n 7) per Lord Diplock at p. 305.

[26] See *FIM Bank plc v KCH Shipping Co Ltd (The Giant Ace)* [2023] EWCA Civ. 569; [2023] 2 Lloyd's Rep 457.

[27] *J MacWilliam Co Inc v Mediterranean Shipping Co SA (The Rafaela S)* [2005] UKHL 11; [2005] 2 AC 423[19].

[28] See, also, *Fothergill v Monarch Airlines Ltd.*, supra (n 7) per Lord Diplock, p. 305 col. 2: referred to by *Lord Hamblen in Alize 1954 v Allianz Elementar Versicherungs AG (The CMA CGM Libra* [2021] UKSC 51; [2021] 2 Lloyd's Rep 613 paras 34–42.

[29] *FIMBank Plc v KCH Shipping Co Ltd (The Giant Ace) (No 2)* [2023] EWCA Civ 569; [2023] 2 Lloyd's Rep 457 (CA).

[30] Ibid paras [73–75] and [83]. Affm. by Supreme Court [2024]UKSC 38.

[31] See Chpt 1.

[32] See Chpt 1.

from that of the CMI and potentially more effective. Its practice is to establish specialist Working Groups to consider specific subjects and publish reports that document the deliberations and explain proposals made.[33] This record, or at least material parts of it, may be identified as "official" commentary associated with the creative process and consequently *travaux préparatoires*. A court, at a future date, faced with ambiguity would be entitled to refer to it when in search of meaning and underlying intention. In the context of English law, it would appear to satisfy the test of characterisation but will be decisive only if it satisfies the "bull's-eye" test.[34]

2.11. In contrast, it appears to be settled that articles and analyses written by academics, lawyers and other informed commentators on the interpretation and impact of international conventions are not *travaux préparatoires*.[35] They are not part of the creative process but a response to it. Nonetheless, albeit not strictly *travaux préparatoires,* this does not mean that such sources are without potential influence. They may be of persuasive value with their potential impact relative to the relevance and cogency of the reasoning. They may be cited in support of legal argument or judicial reasoning, as may other categories of extraneous material. But beyond this have no greater claim to influence.[36]

2.12. This conclusion has implications for the contributions in this book save for the first chapter written by Ann Fenech. She is the current president of the CMI and played a leading role in the later development, drafting and promotion of the Convention within the CMI; and in the subsequent participation of UNCITRAL and the acceptance of the Convention by the UN. Although her contribution was written after the adoption of the Convention by the UN, and in that sense is a retrospective, it nonetheless draws on her direct participation in the evolution of the Convention of which she has a complete and intimate appreciation. This suggests that her contribution to this book satisfies the test of characterisation and qualifies as *travaux préparatoires*, but its influence will depend on the ability to provide clear and decisive answers to future issues that may come before the courts. In contrast, the other contributions are academic commentaries and do not satisfy the test of characterisation. At best they may have persuasive influence.

2.13. It has been noted that the Secretariat of UNCITRAL has published an Explanatory Note to accompany the Convention.[37] At a future date, a question may arise about its status.[38] It is a comprehensive and useful document which indicates the objectives and intent of the Convention, and analyses the individual articles. It expressly declares that it is not an official commentary but the Secretariat was requested

[33] See infra par 2.13.

[34] Supra (n 18).

[35] *Fothergill v Monarch Airlines Ltd*, supra (n 7) per Lord Diplock pp. 305, 306.

[36] The implication appears to be that in the face of ambiguity, if reference to the travaux préparatoires provides a clear and decisive answer, it will, in the absence of any wider consideration of public policy, be adopted by the court.

[37] UN Convention on the International Effects of Judicial Sales of Ships: with Explanatory Note Prepared by the UNCITRAL Secretariat (UN Publication). See Annex 2.

[38] In *Mints and Others v PJSC National Bank Trust and Another*, supra (n 4) the High Court and Court of Appeal accepted as admissible Explanatory Notes and a Government White Paper published in association with legislation imposing and implementing sanctions.

by UNCITRAL to prepare and disseminate a commentary on the Convention.[39] There is good reason to suggest that the Explanatory Note may be characterised as *travaux préparatoires*. It is clearly not a work of speculative third-party analysis. It records and explains the deliberations, intentions and conclusions of the IWG established to progress the Convention in draft.[40] A process to which the Secretariat was very close to and able to comprehend.

2.2 Relevant aspects of English admiralty practice

2.14. The Beijing Convention relates to a particular aspect of admiralty procedure and practice as developed in common law jurisdictions, and other jurisdictions with a maritime dimension, namely the judicial sale of arrested ships with purchasers acquiring a clean title.[41] It is proposed to analyse this aspect of practice and procedure in outline with particular reference to English admiralty practice.[42] This will be a helpful way to lead into an analysis of the corresponding provisions in the Beijing Convention which are considered later in the text.

2.15. The striking feature of maritime litigation is that in respect of many, probably most, claims against shipowners and operators there exists a right to arrest the ship in connection with which the claim arose or, alternatively, a related ship or even additional ships.[43] The precise jurisprudential basis of ship arrest may vary as between legal traditions, as also may the availability and practice relating to ship arrest.[44] A degree of uniformity, nonetheless, has been achieved by international conventions but ultimately matters of procedure and practice are governed by the *lex fori* (*lex loci arresti*).[45]

2.16. At its core the *raison d'etre* of ship arrest is that it establishes a security, to the maximum value of the ship, for claim(s) against the ship.[46] A substitute security

---

[39] See asterisked note to the title "Explanatory Note". The document is not an official commentary and was prepared for information purposes. Nonetheless, it was published at the request of the 55th session of UNCITRAL. The Secretariat had been directly involved with the passage of the Convention through UNCITRAL and its presentation for adoption by the UN.

[40] Working Group VI. See, further, Chpt 1.

[41] See, further, Chpts 3, 4 and 5. Also H Jessen and G Theocharidis, National Translations of the Arrest Conventions: European Civil Law, Chpt 10, in P Myrburgh (ed), *The Arrest Conventions: International Enforcement of Maritime Claims* (2019, Hart Publishing, UK); L Bleyan, *Judicial Sale of Ships (A Comparative Study)* (2016, Springer, Europe); Shao, Piñeiro and Mejia, 'Recognition of Foreign Judicial Sales of Ships and Private International Law' (2022) 28 JIML 166–185.

[42] The basis of English admiralty jurisdiction and practice is the Senior Courts Act 1981 ss 19–22 and Civil Procedure Rules (CPR) Part 61 and Practice Direction (PD) 61. See Chpts 4 and 6 for further accounts of English admiralty jurisdiction and practice. See, generally, SC Derrington and JM Turner, *The Law and Practice of Admiralty Matters*, 2nd edn. (2016, OUP, UK); A Tettenborn and F Rose, *Maritime Claims*, 2nd edn. (2023, Sweet & Maxwell, UK), N Meeson and J Kimbell, *Admiralty Jurisdiction and Practice*, 5th edn. (2018 Informa Law from Routledge, UK).

[43] The precise position will vary according to the international arrest convention a state has adopted or the provisions of national law. See, generally, D. Rhidian Thomas, Ship Arrest – Issues of Availablity, Fairness and Proportionality, Chpt 1, in P Myburgh (ed), *The Arrest Conventions: International Enforcement of Maritime Claims* (2019 Hart Publishing, UK).

[44] In the United States where the personification theory prevails ship arrest is perceived as a legal process against the ship herself as defendant; see Chpt 5.

[45] International Convention Relating to the Arrest of Sea-going Ships 1952, Art 6; International Convention on Arrest of Ships 1999, Art 2.4.

[46] See Arrest as Security and Security Arrest, Trichardt, Chpt 3, in Myburgh, supra (n 42).

may be provided to avoid or secure the release of the ship,[47] but in the absence of such substitute the ship may be sold by order of the court and the proceeds distributed to claimants in an established order of priority.[48]

2.17. In the English admiralty jurisdiction, an arrest is dependent on the issue of a warrant of arrest,[49] which is served by the Admiralty Marshal (an officer of the Admiralty Court) or his agent by attaching the warrant to the named ship.[50] Once arrested the ship is in the custody of the Admiralty Marshal and costs incurred in connection with the arrest and management of the ship may be recovered as a first charge in any subsequent distribution.[51] The Admiralty Marshal remains at all times subject to the control of the Admiralty Court.[52]

2.18. In the event that the claim succeeds but is not settled, the ship may be sold for the benefit of the claimant(s), a procedure which is commenced by the court issuing a "notice of sale".[53] The sale is conducted by the Admiralty Marshal who customarily instructs brokers to appraise the value of the ship and conduct the sale by public auction inviting sealed bids.[54] In exceptional circumstances, the court may approve a private sale.[55] The object of the appraisement is to indicate a value below which the ship ought not ordinarily to be sold.[56] Thereafter, the object of the auction is to obtain the best price that may be obtained.[57] A sale below the appraised value is only possible if the court consents.[58]

2.19. The Admiralty Marshal sells the ship to the highest bidder, with the proceeds paid into court. This procedure based on appraisement, advertisement and invitation to bid is considered an effective means to obtain the best price. Thereafter the proceeds are distributed to claimants in accordance with the priorities recognised under the *lex fori*.[59] In exceptional circumstances, a sale may be ordered before judgment.[60]

---

47 The most familiar form of security in maritime commerce is the Letter of Undertaking issued by Group P&I Clubs: see P Myburgh, 'P&I Club Letters of Undertaking and Admiralty Arrests' (2018) 24 JIML 201; D Rhidian Thomas, 'Letters of Undertaking (LOUs) and Shipping Litigation' (2023) 29 JIML 5.

48 The MV *Union Gold* & others [2013] EWHC 1696 (Admlty); [2014] 1 Lloyd's Rep 53, 54–55, where Mr Justice Teare summarises the procedure in admiralty.

49 Form ADM9 (Warrant of Arrest).

50 CPR Part 61.5, PD 61.5. The warrant of arrest is posted on the outer structure of the ship, most frequently by an officer of HM Customs acting as an agent on behalf of the Admiralty Marshal. This procedure may be avoided where the parties agree an alternative mode of service, as when security is volunteered in advance.

51 CPR Part 61.5, PD 61.5.

52 ADM10 (Standard Directions to the Admiralty Marshal).

53 CPR 61.10, PD 61.10. ADM14 (Order for sale of a ship).

54 There are brokers who are designated brokers for and who act regularly on behalf of the Admiralty Marshal.

55 See P Myburgh, 'Satisfactory for its own purposes' (2016) 22 JIML 355. For the rejection by the court of such a proposal, see, The M/V *Union Gold*, supra (n 47).

56 The M/V *Union Gold*, supra (n 47) p. 54 per Teare J.

57 Ibid.

58 *The Halcyon the Great (No 2)* [1975] 1 Lloyd's Rep 525.

59 CPR 61.10, PD 61.10.

60 *The Myrto* [1977] 2 Lloyd's Rep 243; *Dan-Bunkering (Singapore) Pte Ltd v The Ship "Yangtze-Fortune"* [2022] FCA 1556; [2023] 2 Lloyd's Rep 59; D Rhidian Thomas, 'Admiralty sales pendent lite' [1998] CJQ 409; P Myburgh, 'Admiralty sales pendent lite: reserve prices and broker appointments' (2018) 24 JIML 369.

2.20. In making an order for sale the Admiralty Court may specify (i) the period of time within which notice of claims must be filed, and (ii) the time and manner in which the specified time limit must be advertised.[61]

2.21. These important procedural matters fall to be decided by the court. All that is reasonable must be done to ensure that parties with claims against the arrested ship, which following sale are transferred to the proceeds of sale, are given reasonable notice of the sale and therefore fair opportunity to give notice of their claims.[62] What is reasonable depends not only on timing but also the way in which the sale is advertised, taking the assistance of appropriate modes of publication and transmission.

2.22. A party with a pre-existing claim who fails to give timely notice of claim loses the security of the ship because the purchaser from the court acquires a clean title, free of all encumbrances.[63] Consequently, the purchaser is protected against the risk of the ship being arrested again by any such pre-existing claimant. The justification for this consequence is the fact that the notice of sale has been publicised to the world at large and reasonable notice has been given to potential claimants to come forward and participate in the legal process.[64] Claimants who do not come forward continue to have the right to proceed in *personam*, but without the benefit of security.

2.23. The sale procedure also takes into count the interests of the arresting claimant and other claimants who have made claims. It would be unjust to keep them out of their entitlements for an excessive period of time. It is additionally possible that other factors might come into play that affect the value of the potential fund. The Admiralty Court in managing the sale must balance these competing considerations and endeavour to arrive at a determination which represents an equitable balance.

2.24. The "Order for sale of a ship" includes the statement that claimants have 28 days (or as may be) to make their claims against the proceeds of sale. Time begins to run from the date that payment of the proceeds into court is made and subsequently advertised as to the amount accrued and applicable time limit for claims against the fund.[65] The Admiralty Court Guide indicates that the applicant for an order of sale is expected to liaise with the Admiralty Marshal as to how and where notice of the time limit for making claims against the proceeds should be published.[66]

2.25. The Admiralty Marshal performs his role in relation to the sale of vessels as an officer of the court. He does not act for any of the parties. Any interference with the exercise of his duties may amount to contempt of the court.[67] The court appreciates that in this regard it occupies a sensitive position and is concerned to protect its reputation for impartiality.[68]

---

61 CPR 61.10; PD 61.10.

62 *The APJ Shalin* [1991] 2 Lloyd's Rep 62.

63 Infra (n 40).

64 *The Halcyon the Great (No 2)* [1975] 1 Lloyd's Rep 525, 527, per Brandon J, who refers to the vessel being offered "freely to the whole world".

65 ADM 14.

66 N.12.2. The Admiralty Court Guide is incorporated in the Commercial Court Guide 11th edn. (rev. 2023).

67 *The Ruth Kayser* (1925) 23 Ll L Rep 95; *The Jarvis Brake* [1976] 2 Lloyd's Rep 320; *The Cerro Colorado* [1993] 1 Lloyd's Rep 58.

68 The M/V *Union Gold*, supra (n 47) p. 54.

2.26. As previously observed, ship arrest is understood primarily as a means of securing maritime claims.[69] This is the function the international arrest conventions focus on and which is most consistently identified by judges.[70] In *The MV Alkyon*[71] Sir Terence Etherton MR observed[72]:

> the key purpose of arrest ever since the late 19th century is to prompt or compel the provision of security pending judgment in the action.

The security relates to the physical ship or substitute security provided to avoid or obtain the release of the ship from arrest. It follows that in admiralty proceedings the maximum security that may be demanded corresponds to the value of the arrested ship.[73]

2.27. In admiralty jurisdiction, the view prevails that the nature of the title of the purchaser of an arrested ship sold by judicial sale is governed by the *lex fori* (*lex fori arresti*).[74] Its own rule is that the purchaser of a ship sold by order of the Admiralty Court acquires a clean title, indicating a title free from all encumbrances.[75] This provides the purchaser with protection in relation to all pre-existing claims against the ship. In *The Stolt Kestrel* and *The Niyazi S*[76] Tomlinson LJ enunciated the rule in the following terms[77] –

> The action in rem is distinctive in that it enables a ship to be arrested to compel the provision of security and, if security is not forthcoming, to enable the Admiralty Court to sell the vessel free of all encumbrances to satisfy the claims against the ship.

The commercial significance of this rule is that the purchaser is protected against future claims against the ship arising from causes of action that originated prior to the judicial sale but not pursued in those proceedings. In this circumstance, the purchased ship is free of risk and this protection underpins the viability of the process. Without it commercial interest in this aspect of the ship sale market would probably decline materially.[78]

---

69 Supra (n 45). Also, Re Arco Co Ltd [1980] 1 All E R 1067, 1074, per L J Brightman, "The usual object of suing in rem is to obtain security". It may have other less frequently resorted to uses, such as to bring before the court a ship to which title and/or possession is disputed, or to enforce a security interest in a ship, such as a claim by a mortgagee, see Senior Courts Act 1981 s. 21(2).

70 International Convention Relating to the Arrest of Sea-Going Ships 1952, Art 1(2); International Convention on Arrest of Ships 1999, Art 1(2) and 2(3).

71 *NatWest Markets Plc (Formerly Known as The Royal Bank of Scotland Plc) v Stallion Eight Shipping Co SA (The MV Alkyon) [2018] EWCA Civ. 2760; [2019] 1 Lloyd's Rep 406.*

72 Ibid p. 420, para 82(ii).

73 CPR Part 61.6(3). There is nothing to preclude parties privately agreeing additional security different in nature.

74 The International Convention Relating to the Arrest of Sea-Going Ships 1952 and the International Convention on Arrest of Ships 1999 do not address this issue, just as they also steer clear of matters of procedure.

75 The contributions to this book support for this statement and also reveal the acceptance of the principle across legal traditions. See, also, Shao, Pineiro and Mejia, supra (n 40); Bleyan, supra (n 40).

76 *Owners of the Stole Kestrel v Owners of the Niyazi etc. [2015] EWCA Civ. 1035; [2016] 1 Lloyd's Rep 125.*

77 Ibid para [12].

78 The potential disadvantages are self-evident and have been consistently identified by the judiciary, see *The Tremont* (1841) 1 Wm Rob 163, *The Acrux* [1962] 1 Lloyd's Rep 405; *The Cerro Colorado* [1993] 1 Lloyd's Rep 58.

2.28. The sale does not immediately deny other claimants a remedy. Once an arrested ship is sold the fund held by the court represents the ship and claims may be brought against the fund.[79] In the words of Teare J[80] –

> When the vessel is sold by the Admiralty Marshal the purchaser acquires title free of all encumbrances and liens and so existing rights in rem against the vessel are transferred to the proceeds of sale.

This way of proceeding is only possible if, under the terms of the notice of sale, the claim against the fund is made within time.[81] If it is not, the claim may only be made in *personam*, should that be a feasible option.

2.29. The extent to which judicial sales of ships by foreign courts may be recognised as having the same legal effect as sales by the Admiralty Court has never been decisively determined. There are nonetheless dicta which suggest a favourable judicial disposition. In *The Acrux*[82] Hewson J said:

> This ship was sold under the proper process of this court whereby the purchaser was given a clean title. *This court recognizes sales by competent courts of other nations as giving a similar title.* The sale by this court extinguished all rights and liens against the ship and attached to the fund.[83]

And in *The Union Gold*[84] Teare J stated:

> The title which a sale by the Marshal confers on the purchaser, free of liens and encumbrances is recognised not only by the courts of this country but by the courts of all other countries. *Similarly, the courts of this country will recognize sales by competent courts of Admiralty in other jurisdictions.*[85]

2.30. These dicta do not amount to compelling authority.[86] At common law, it is established that a court may recognise a judgment in rem of a foreign court that determines the title to property located within its territorial jurisdiction.[87] Whether this principle applies by analogy to the judicial sale of a ship by a foreign court is undecided.[88] If it does, it may be anticipated that the same principles apply as those that govern the approach of the common law.[89] In more recent times there has also been developed a considerable corpus of international and regional jurisprudence relating to the recognition and enforcement of foreign judgments and questions might arise

[79] For the recognition of this principle in English admiralty law, see *The Acrux* [1962] 1 Lloyd's Rep 405, 409, per Hewson J.

[80] *Bank of Scotland Plc v The Owners of the M/V Union Gold*, supra (n 47) para 2.

[81] Supra (n 64).

[82] *[1965] P. 391.*

[83] Ibid p. 404. Italics added for emphasis.

[84] *[2014] 1 Lloyd's Rep 53.*

[85] *Ibid para 5. Italics added for emphasis: citing The Acrux [1962] 1 Lloyd's Rep 405; The Cerro Colorado [1993] 1 Lloyd's Rep 58.*

[86] See, further, Chpt 4, Myburgh.

[87] *Castrique v Imrie* (1870) LR 4 HL 414.

[88] Cf. *Air Foyle Ltd v Centre Capital Ltd* [2002] EWHC 2535 Comm; [2003] 2 Lloyd's Rep 753.

[89] See Chpt 4, P Myburgh, *International Recognition of Judicial Ship Sales: English Common Law and the Beijing Convention*; A Briggs, *The Conflict of Laws*, 5th edn., Chpt 3 (2024, OUP, UK).

about the potential impact of this development on the question under consideration.[90] This question is pursued by Professor Myburgh in Chapter 4.

2.3 Analysis of the Beijing Convention[91]

2.31. It is now proposed to address and analyse the provisions of the Beijing Convention.

2.4 Overriding objective

2.32. Article 1 declares that –

> This Convention governs the international effects of a judicial sale of a ship that confers clean title on the purchaser.

The particular "effect" in issue relates to the "recognition" of the judicial sale as conferring a clean title on the purchaser. The Convention is not further concerned with any question of enforcement or procedural matters, whether of form or in the nature of a review, relating to the judicial sale process. The Convention, also, does not specify which judicial sales, or in what circumstances, confer a clean title on the purchaser. This is left to the law of the State of judicial sale. The object of the Convention is to give international effect (recognition) to those judicial sales which under the lex fori fall within the Convention.

2.33. In the Preamble it is further declared that the Convention seeks[92] –

> to establish uniform rules that promote the dissemination of information on prospective judicial sales to interested parties and give international effects to judicial sales of ships sold free and clear of any mortgage or *hypothèque* and of any charge, including for ship registration purposes.

2.34. There are two wings to this declaration.

The first relates to the requirement of procedural fairness in connection with the judicial sale. It refers, in particular, to the dissemination of a notice of sale to interested parties. Thereafter, under the second wing, it is declared that the effect of a judicial sale must be to confer a "free and clear" title on the purchaser, with the security interests erased identified.[93] This suggests that procedural fairness, as defined, is to be considered a condition precedent to the effectiveness of a judicial sale that purports to confer a clean title on the purchaser.

---

[90] The position has been made additionally complex in English law following the departure of the United Kingdom from the European Union; see generally Briggs and Rees, *Civil Jurisdiction and Judgments*, 7th edn., Chpt 7 (2021 Informa Law from Routledge, London); D McClean and VR Abou-Nigm, *Morris The Conflict of Laws*, 10th edn., Chpt 10 (2021, Thomson Reuters, Sweet & Maxwell, England, UK).

[91] For an account of the historical development of the Convention, see Chpt 1. Also, Fenech, 'Draft Convention on the International Effects of Judicial Sales of Ships, Comparative Maritime Law', Croatian Academy of Sciences and Arts (2022) pp. 779–790. The General Assembly of the UN when adopting the Convention recommended that it be known as the "Beijing Convention on the Judicial Sale of Ships".

[92] 4th para.

[93] See, infra, under title "Clean Title".

2.5 Exclusions and limitations

(i) The Convention applies only to judicial sales ordered or approved after its entry into force in the State of judicial sale.[94]

(ii) The province of the Convention is limited and applies only as between State Parties.[95] It applies to judicial sales conducted in a State Party (State of judicial sale)[96] and to applications for recognition in a State Party (State of judicial recognition).[97]

(iii) The Convention applies to ship and security registrations in a State of registration which is also a State Party.

(iv) The Convention applies only to the judicial sale of ships in a State Party and which are physically within the territory of the State of judicial sale at the time of the sale.[98]

(v) Beyond stipulating the effect of a judicial sale, the Convention does not affect the procedure relating to judicial sales of ships; or the circumstance a judicial sale confers a clean title on the purchaser; or questions of priority in the distribution of the proceeds;[99] or the international effect of a decision of a court in the State of judicial sale in response to an application to decline jurisdiction or challenge the issue of certificate of judicial sale.[100]

(vi) The Convention does not apply to ship arrest and the procedure relating to the arrest of ships. But as an incident of its obligations under the Convention, a State of judicial recognition is vested with powers to refuse an application to arrest or to release a ship from arrest.[101]

(vii) The Convention does not affect claims *in personam* against the owner or person with proprietary rights in the ship prior to the judicial sale.[102]

(viii) The Convention does not apply to warships or naval auxiliaries, or other vessels owned or operated by a State and used, immediately prior to the time of judicial sale, only on government, non-commercial, service.[103]

2.6 International law framework

(i) The Convention enters into force 180 days after the date of the deposit of the third instrument of ratification, acceptance, approval or accession.[104]

---

94 Art 21.3.

95 Art 6.

96 Art 2(k).

97 Art 6.

98 Art 3.1. This is a rule of broad application. Most ships when arrested will be at anchor in a confined area such as a port, dock, harbour or bay. More exceptionally the ship may be at anchor or otherwise not underway in territorial waters. It continues to be the subject of debate whether a ship in the course of navigation in territorial waters may be arrested. The Arrest Conventions 1952 and 1999 are silent on this question.

99 Art 15.1(a). These matters continue to be governed by the *lex fori*.

100 Art 15.2 and Art 9.1.

101 Art 8.

102 Art 15.1(b).

103 Art 3.2. This follows the restrictive doctrine of foreign sovereign immunity.

104 Art 21.1. See, Chpt 1 for the position at the time of writing.

(ii) In relation to States, the Convention enters into force 180 days after the date of the deposit by the State of its instrument of ratification, acceptance, approval or accession.[105]

(iii) A State Party retains the right to give effect to a judicial sale in another State under some other international agreement, or by reference to applicable law.[106] A State Party, consequently, may embrace dual or multiple legal regimes relating to the recognition of the effect of foreign judicial sales of ships.[107]

(iv) The Convention may be signed, ratified, accepted, approved or acceded to by a regional economic integration organisation (REIO), to the extent it has competence over matters governed by the Convention.[108]

(v) With regard to States with two or more territorial units with different systems of law, the State may declare the extent to which the Convention shall apply.[109]

(vi) The Convention does not affect the application of the Convention on the Registration of Inland Navigation Vessels (1965) and Protocol No 2, concerning Attachment and Forced Sale of Inland Navigation Vessels, including any future amendment thereto.[110]

2.7 Basic concepts

2.35. The fundamental purpose of the Convention is crystal clear but it embodies a number of concepts which although familiar to maritime jurisprudence are often elusive to expound. The drafters of the Convention very sensibly isolated these key concepts and provided definitions. Although this approach is helpful, it has not always resulted in the avoidance of ambiguity.

2.36. There are two core concepts to be considered: (i) judicial sale of ships, and (ii) acquisition of a clean title by the purchaser.

2.7.1 Judicial sales of ships

2.37. The "Judicial sale" of a ship is a sale[111] –

(i) which is ordered, approved or confirmed by a court or other public authority either by way of public auction or by private treaty carried out under the supervision and with the approval of a court; and

(ii) for which the proceeds of sale are made available to the creditors.

---

105 Art 21.2.

106 Art 14.

107 The extent to which this possibility may actually arise is difficult to assess.

108 Art 18. The European Union is a significant example of a regional economic integration organisation (REIO). It, together with Belgium, signed the Convention at New York on 14 March 2024.

109 Art 19.

110 Art 13.1.

111 Art 2(a).

2.7.2 Nature of the sale

2.38. The essential nature of a judicial sale, in the first place, is that it is a sale ordered or approved or confirmed by a court or other public authority.

2.39. The definition is sufficiently wide to embrace constitutional and procedural variations in the law and practice of State Parties. The authority for the sale may be a "court" or "other public authority" which may "order, approve or confirm" the sale. It follows that in some jurisdictions the power to arrest may be vested not in a court but a public entity or person authorised to act on behalf of the State. The Convention embraces these possibilities.

2.40. The sale must have been "ordered, approved or confirmed" by the court or public authority. Beyond a sale ordered by a court or public authority, these words suggest that a court or public authority may "approve" a proposal by the owner that the ship be sold to a named purchaser. And, further, the court or public authority may "confirm" a sale, which suggests the confirmation of a sale already made by the owner. It is suspected that this last possibility would be exceptional and could in some instances be troublesome.

2.41. The sale may be conducted by public auction or private treaty, provided it has the approval and is subject to the supervision of the relevant court or public authority.[112] The concept of a "public auction" is not defined but it may be presumed that it extends beyond its traditional meaning of a public forum with bids made in person to include modern variations, such as an auction conducted by the submission of sealed bids and even online.[113]

2.42. Clearly a judicial sale is distinct from a sale by private treaty or made under a contractual or statutory power. The sale and purchase of a new or secondhand ship as between private parties is clearly not a judicial sale, nor is a sale by a mortgagee or other creditor of a ship under a default power contained in a mortgage or contractual instrument. The fact that a court might assist such procedures by granting an injunction or declaratory relief or otherwise does not change the characterisation. The same is true of a sale under statutory powers in the face of, for example, criminal conduct, breach of customs regulations and tax evasion.

2.43. It is improbable that a sale ordered or approved by an arbitrator acting within the scope of his authority would amount to a judicial sale.[114] Although the arbitral process must be conducted judiciously, an arbitral tribunal is not a court in the constitutional sense nor is it a "public authority".[115] This is the view adopted by the common law but it has to be recognised that a different analysis may prevail under other legal traditions.

---

[112] This follows the established practice of the English Admiralty Court which usually requires an arrested ship to be sold by public auction with bids presented in sealed envelopes. But the Court retains the right in exceptional circumstances to approve a privately negotiated sale; see, supra, "Relevant Aspects of English Admiralty Jurisdiction". For online auctions, see Chpt 6.

[113] Supra (n 53).

[114] This alludes to a sale ordered by an arbitrator acting within the scope of the jurisdiction conferred by the referring parties. The aim might be to establish pre-award security or funds to discharge an award.

[115] Of course, it is always possible that as a question of construction, a reference to "court" in a statute or contract could be construed in its prevailing context as including a reference to an arbitration tribunal.

2.7.2.1 Proceeds of sale available to creditors

2.44. Further, the object of the judicial sale must be that the proceeds are available not only to the claimant(s) who instituted the proceedings but to all creditors. "Creditor" is not defined by the Convention but, in the present context, it must allude to claimants (creditors) with pre-existing claims against the ship.

2.45. This requirement serves to constrain the definition of "judicial sale" significantly. Sales of this nature are familiar in admiralty and parallel maritime jurisdictions.[116] They are unlike an attachment of judgments generally which aim to assist the claimant(s) to take the full benefit of any victory in the litigation. Any such judicial sale is not within the meaning of the Convention. The sale of a ship ordered by a court to enforce a judgment or on the application of mortgagees or other parties with a security interest is not a judicial sale within the Convention: nor is the attachment of a ship in the United States under the applicable admiralty rules.[117]

2.46. There is also no indication that a judicial sale is a sale that follows judgment on the merits. In which case a sale *pendente lite* may be a judicial sale.[118]

2.7.2.2 Judicial sale of "ship"

2.47. A judicial sale relates to a "ship" and this raises a predictable question of definition.

Article 2(b) defines "ship" as follows:

> 'Ship' means any ship or other vessel registered in a register that is open to public inspection that may be the subject of an arrest or other similar measure capable of leading to a judicial sale under the law of the State of judicial sale.

2.48. "Ship" in the first place means a "ship or other vessel". It is notorious that the meaning of these words may vary with the context and there is no universally agreed definition to provide assistance. Most people will encounter little difficulty in identifying a 'ship' when they see it; and if the position is less obvious, the word "vessel" may prove propitious, to help include something different in structure and function. Should, for example, an autonomous vessel or offshore mobile vehicle not be a "ship" in the context of the Convention, each could be a "vessel".

2.49. The definition does not discriminate as between commercial and pleasure/leisure activities, nor as between sea-going and inland navigation.[119]

2.50. There are, however, additional criteria which render a detailed enquiry into the meaning of "ship or other vessel" less pressing. There are requirements relating to "registration" and "arrestability" which are significant limiting factors, particularly the former.

2.7.2.3 Registration

2.51. First, the "ship or other vessel" must be registered in a register open to public inspection. This refers to flag state or an equivalent registration which is a significant

[116] Supra (n 58) "Relevant Aspects of English Admiralty Jurisdiction".
[117] Rule B of the Supplementary Rules to the Federal Rules of Civil Procedure. See, further, Chpt 5.
[118] Supra (n 59).
[119] Cf. Art 13.1.

feature of shipping. Virtually all ships are registered with a state, customarily referred to as the flag state, with the registration details readily available to public examination. This system of registration also plays a crucial role in the attribution of nationality and registration of security interests.

2.52. The international system of ship registration has grown in complexity and sophistication. States may have separate registers for domestic and international fleets. Bareboat charters may be separately registered, not necessarily in the same register as the ship. And specific provisions may be made for vessels such as yachts and small craft. It is also possible for private associations connected to a specific category of vessel to establish a private registry.

2.53. The Convention does not appear to discriminate. It embraces both public and private registers subject to one key precondition. The register must be open to "public inspection" whether or not on payment of a charge. Flag state registers are open in this sense but private registers may be restricted, for example, to the membership and, if so, are excluded from the Convention.

2.54. It would be exceptional in contemporary times for a trading ship not to be registered with a flag state.[120] Rare exceptions may exist, for example, in relation to ships associated with the "dark fleet". This is a term coined to refer to vessels operating unlawfully outside the international regulatory regime of shipping in order to evade sanctions introduced to prohibit trading with specified countries.[121]

2.7.2.4 Subject to arrest

2.55. The ship or vessel must be capable of being subject to an arrest or equivalent procedure leading to judicial sale. This is self-evident given the nature of the Convention. Whether this capability exists will ultimately depend on the law of the State of judicial sale, where the arrest is made. The Convention is silent on the point. This may result in differences existing between State Parties.[122] It could, in some instances, have a narrowing effect on the application of the Convention by reducing the range of "ships and vessels" falling under the umbrella of the Convention.

2.56. In expressly referring to "ships and vessels" the Convention makes it clear that it does not apply to the arrest of cargo and/or freight, which may be subject to arrest in admiralty jurisdictions.[123] Nor, it would appear, does the Convention apply to a part of a ship, such as a designated share.[124]

[120] There is a current debate whether ship registration should be extended to include offshore mobile craft, typically used in the offshore maritime sector; see the records of the CMI Gothenburg Colloquium 2024, <comitemaritime.org>.

[121] G Theocharidis, 'The chronicle of the vexing problem of fraudulent registration',(2023) 29 JIML 135–137.

[122] In admiralty proceedings relating to England and Wales ship as defined, "includes any description of vessel used in navigation"; see Senior Courts Act 1981 s. 24(1).

[123] Derrington and Turner, supra (n 41) para 2.65; Tettenborn and Rose, supra (n 41) para 4–001.

[124] In UK law ships are divided into 64 shares, see Merchant Shipping Act 1995 s. 7(1).

2.7.3 Acquisition of clean title

2.7.3.1 Introductory note

2.57. This is a concept most familiar in the law of sale and purchase of personal and real property. In this context, it relates broadly to circumstances when a buyer acting in good faith acquires title to the property purchased free of all encumbrances, whatever may have been the position of the seller in possession. In other words, the property purchased is free of third-party claims or other interests in or against the property.[125] The same concept, although the legal basis is different, is embedded in the sale of ships in the admiralty jurisdiction of the common law.[126]

2.58. The concept of "clean title" is central to the purpose of the Convention. This is to ensure that judicial sales conducted in a State Party and which confer on the purchaser a clean title are recognised in all other State Parties.[127] In principle, whether a sale has the effect of conferring a clean title on the purchaser is determined by the law of the State of judicial sale. But where the Convention applies, for the clean title of the purchaser to be recognised by all other State Parties, the provisions of the Convention must be satisfied.

2.7.3.2 "Clean title"

2.59. The Convention defines "clean title" as –

> title free and clear of any mortgage or *hypothèque* and of any charge.[128]

2.60. Two broad categories of third-party interests are identified in this definition, "mortgages and *hypothèques*", and "charges". They are defined in some detail which is an indication of their significance. What is being identified are the security interests in or enforceable against the arrested ship which are extinguished when the ship is purchased from the court of judicial sale, by virtue of the purchaser acquiring a clean title.

2.7.3.3 Mortgages or hypothèques

2.61. They are defined as –

> any mortgage or *hypothèque* that is effected on a ship and registered in the State in whose register of ships or equivalent register the ship is registered.[129]

2.62. This provision does not define the nature of the security established by a mortgage or *hypothèque*, save to indicate that they must be effected on a ship and registered in the ship's flag state register or the equivalent. It follows that in the definition of "clean title" the allusion to "mortgage or *hypothèque*" is to be understood as a reference to "registered mortgage or registered *hypothèque*" Whether a security interest falls within

[125] See, generally, M Bridge et al., *The Law of Personal Property*, 3rd edn. (2021, Sweet & Maxwell, UK); D Sheehan, *The Principles of Personal Property Law*, 2nd edn. (2017, Hart Publishing, UK).
[126] Supra (n 79).
[127] Art 6.
[128] Art 2(c).
[129] Art 2(d).

either category is to be determined by the court of the State of judicial sale applying its applicable law.[130]

2.63. Under the common law, a mortgage is a security interest in a ship based on a redeemable transfer of title or a charge on the ship. In modern practice, the latter is the usual form of security.[131]

2.64. Under the Convention, mortgages are restricted to mortgages registered in the applicable ship's register. From the perspective of English law, this simplifies matters in so far as it makes it clear that the Convention applies only to what are described as statutory ship mortgages.[132] The Convention also makes it clear that the mortgage must be on a ship and not a share of a ship.[133] The effect and probable purpose of the provisions are to include only mortgages and *hypothèques* that are readily identifiable.[134]

2.65. Other categories of mortgage recognised in English law are excluded, such as equitable mortgages and legal but unregistered mortgages.[135] These might have been regarded as "charges" under the Convention but in the absence of registration, they are again excluded.[136]

2.66. *Hypothèques* are a civilian concept that are positioned parallel with mortgages in the Convention and other relevant international conventions.[137] They are, nonetheless, a distinct legal concept. The recognition and technical understanding may vary as between civilian jurisdictions. But for general purposes, they may be perceived as a security interest in a ship arising by operation of law which is conferred on a maritime claimant without the transfer of possession or title to the ship. In short, they are privileged claims.[138]

2.67. As with mortgages, *hypothèques* are within the Convention only if they are registered in the ship's register or the equivalent.

2.7.3.4 Charges

2.68. The concept of a "charge" arises frequently and in a range of different circumstances. It is an imprecise concept and may mean different things in different circumstances. It is, however, unnecessary to pursue the concept in the present context because the Convention provides a definition.

2.69. A "charge" is defined as[139] –

---

130 The status and priority of mortgages and *hypothèques* are addressed in the International Conventions relating to Maritime Liens and Mortgages 1926, 1967 and 1993.

131 D Osborne, G Bowtle and C Buss, *The Law of Ship Mortgages*, 2nd edn., Chpt 3 (2017, Informa Law from Routledge, UK).

132 Ibid.

133 In English Law ships are divided into 64 shares and individual shares may be mortgaged, see Merchant Shipping Act 1995, s. 7(1).

134 Typically, the mortgagee will be a prominent bank or financial institution.

135 Osborne, Bowtle and Buss, supra (n 130) Chpt 3, Security Interests in Ships.

136 See, infra, under "Charges".

137 Supra (n 129).

138 See, Osborne, Bowtle and Buss, supra (n 130) 89–93, where the response of the English courts to the position of the holder of a *hypothèque* is considered.

139 Art 2(e).

> any right whatsoever and howsoever arising which may be asserted against a ship, whether by means of arrest, attachment or otherwise, and includes a maritime lien, lien, encumbrance, right of use or right of retention but does not include a mortgage or *hypothèque*.

This is a very wide definition. It embraces in effect any claim or right that may be asserted against a ship by means of "arrest, attachment or otherwise". The range of possible rights identified is inclusive. The limitation is on the mode of remedy only, not the substantive claim.

2.70. A maritime lien is identified as a charge but mortgages and *hypothèques* are excluded from the definition.

2.7.3.5 Registered charges

2.71. The Convention having defined "charge" proceeds to identify and define "Registered charge". It is defined as –

> any charge that is registered in the register of ships or equivalent register in which the ship is registered or in any different register in which mortgages or *hypothèques* are registered.[140]

2.72. To be a "registered charge" the charge must be registered in the register of ships or its equivalent, or in a separate register maintained for mortgages or *hypothèques*. Any other form of registration will not suffice. The registration of mortgages or *hypothèques* is an established practice and a crucial factor in the finance of shipping. Beyond this, it would appear from the terms of the Convention that some states may also require or provide the opportunity for "charges" to be registered. This may be in the ship's register or equivalent or in a separate register maintained for mortgages or *hypothèques*. Again, it may be anticipated that state practice may vary.

2.73. With regard to "charge" the Convention adopts a different approach. "Charge" is not defined as meaning "registered charges", but there is the recognition that a charge, as defined in the Convention, may be "registered". And it will be seen later in the text that only "registered charges" are relevant to the precise objective of the Convention.

2.7.3.6 Maritime liens

2.74. The Convention defines "charge" as including a "maritime lien", but thereafter it functions differently from "charges" generally.

2.75. A maritime lien is defined as –

> any charge that is recognized as a maritime lien or *privilège maritime* on a ship under applicable law.[141]

This brief definition is full of contention.

2.76. There is debate whether a maritime lien is a charge on the relevant ship, as distinct from a privileged claim against the ship.[142] This debate is irrelevant to the

---

140 Art 2(f).

141 Art 2(g).

142 This debate is closely connected to the question of the applicable law relating to maritime liens, see infra (n. 147 et seq).

immediate context because a maritime lien or *privilège maritime* is defined as a "charge" for the purposes of the Convention.[143] But significantly registration is not required.[144]

2.77. Which claims are to be identified as maritime liens is not determined by the Convention. This begs the question, which system of law is to determine the question?[145] The Convention echoes the debate but refrains from providing an answer. It states that the question is to be determined by reference to the "applicable law".[146] In other words the decision is left to the court of judicial sale applying its rule of private international law.

2.78. The realistic choice is between the *lex fori* and *lex causae.*[147] The dominant historical choice is the *lex fori* and this probably continues to be the favoured approach. But the argument in favour of the *lex causae* has its supporters and has enjoyed limited judicial acceptance.[148] The international conventions relating to maritime liens do not make any direct contribution to this significant debate.[149]

2.79. There is also an absence of international harmony about the claims that may be identified as maritime liens or *privilège maritime*. There are significant differences between states in this regard and also in the approach taken by the international conventions.[150] It has long been appreciated in some states, notably in US Federal law, that most maritime claims are recognised as maritime liens.[151] By contrast, in common law admiralty jurisdictions, only a small number of claims are recognised as maritime liens.[152]

2.80. The common law, however, recognises a concept which is a close variant, namely the statutory right in rem. This right is viewed as distinct from a maritime lien but shares some of its characteristics.[153] The differences, however, are significant and relate primarily to the emergence of the right and priorities.[154] Nonetheless, it is not impossible that a claim in the nature of a statutory right in rem could be recognised as a maritime lien by a foreign court of judicial sale applying its applicable law.[155] A statutory right *in rem* appears to be a charge under the Convention but it is not required to be registered.[156]

---

[143] Whether it would be recognised as such in the broader maritime law is at least open to debate.

[144] See infra for circumstances when a maritime lien is expunged under the Convention.

[145] See, P Myburgh, Conflict of Laws and the Arrest Conventions, Chpt 7, in P Myburgh (ed), *The Arrest Conventions (International Enforcement of Claims)* (1999, Hart Publishing, UK).

[146] Art 2(g).

[147] For a summary of the debate, see Derrington and Turner, supra (n 41) paras 4.49–4.55; Tettenborn and Rose, supra (n 41) Chpt 12–034 et seq.

[148] See Myburgh, supra (n 144) Chpt 7(VI). Examples include *The Ioannis Daskalelis* [1974] 1 Lloyds Rep 174 (Canadian Supreme Court); *Reiter Petroleum Inc v The Ship "Sam Hawk"* [2015] FCA 1005 (Federal Court of Australia).

[149] The International Conventions on Maritime Liens and Mortgages 1926, 1967 and 1993, which have received only limited acceptance, do not address the issue.

[150] See W Tetley, *Maritime Liens and Claims*, 2nd edn. (1998, Blais, Montreal).

[151] TJ Schoenbaum, *Admiralty and Maritime Law*, 6th edn., Chpt 7 (2019, West Publishing, USA).

[152] D R Thomas, *Maritime Liens* (1980, Sweet & Maxwell, UK).

[153] Derrington and Turner, supra (n 41) Chpt 2; Tettenborn and Rose, supra (n 41), Chpt 4.

[154] Ibid. The emergence of the statutory right in rem is tied to the issue of the claim form and is again significant when priorities are in question. The statutory right *in rem* is inferior to a maritime lien.

[155] Art 2(g).

[156] There would be a documentary record in the form of a claim form and court record but it is unlikely this would be the equivalent to registration in the sense intended by the Convention.

2.81. Although maritime liens are not required to be registered,[157] nonetheless they acquire a relevance under the Convention only if their existence has been "made known" to the court of judicial sale.[158] How they might be "made known" is not indicated but would be determined by reference to the procedure and practice of the court of judicial sale.[159]

2.82. A final comment. In broad terms, most claims against an arrested ship are considered to be charges under the Convention. There is, however, a distinction to be drawn between identifying the charges defined by the Convention and the circumstances when such charges cease to be binding on a purchaser from the court of judicial sale. The key to the latter is "registration". In the case of mortgages and *hypothèques* the position is streamlined with "registration" incorporated in the definition. This is not the case with regard to "charges" where a separate registration is required. An exception is made in the case of a charge which is a maritime lien, but the lienor is required to make known the existence of the maritime lien to the court of judicial sale. Doubtlessly, this is a response to the fact that there is no general requirement that maritime liens must be registered. The points made in this comment are of crucial significance and are returned to later in the text.

2.8 Notice of judicial sale

2.8.1 Introduction

2.83. When the claim(s) made against the arrested ship has been determined in favour of the claimant(s) but the assessed compensation is not paid by the defendant in full or part, an application may be made to the Court of judicial sale that the ship be sold and the sale fund applied to the settlement of the claim(s). If the application is granted and proceeds, the sale fund is deposited with the court and applied to the settlement of the claim(s). Where the claim(s) in total exceed the deposited sale fund, the court distributes the fund in the order of priority prescribed by the *lex fori*.[160]

2.84. For the Convention to achieve its purpose of ensuring the international effectiveness of judicial sales of ships conferring a clean title on purchasers, it is an essential requirement of justice that the judicial sale follows a procedure which is fair and gives adequate advance notice of the sale to all relevant parties, the claimants before the court and other potential claimants.[161] The clear purpose is to alert the designated categories of claimants of the impending sale (as opposed to the public at large) and so provide them with a platform to protect their individual interests. The significance of the procedure is acknowledged by the Convention which in the Preamble expresses

[157] Nor are they in general. They spring into existence from the moment circumstances establish the underlying cause of action, *The Tervaete* [1922] p. 259 (CA).

[158] Art 4.3(c) and infra (n 169).

[159] Art 4.3(c). It appears that a notification of an informal nature which does not comply with the procedural rules would be regarded as inadequate.

[160] Art 15(1)(a). See, also, The M/V *Union Gold* [2014] 1 Lloyd's Rep 53, [2] per J Teare.

[161] The procedure followed by the Admiralty Court of England and Wales is considered Supra, under the title "Relevant Aspects of English Admiralty Practice".

the desire "to establish uniform rules that promote the dissemination of information on prospective sales to interested parties".[162]

2.8.2 Notice of judicial sale

2.85. The Convention provides that a notice of judicial sale must be given of the intended sale of the ship in accordance with the provisions of the Convention to the recipients identified in the Convention.[163]

2.86. A valid notice of sale is a condition precedent to the issue of a Certificate of Judicial Sale, the significance of which is considered later in the text.[164]

2.87. The method by which the notice is communicated (and most other matters relating to the notice) must be in accordance with the law of the State of judicial sale and contain, as a minimum, the information indicated in Annex I of the Convention.[165] This states the following information to be included[166] –

(i) that the notice is given for the purposes of the Convention
(ii) the identity of the State of Judicial sale,
(iii) the court or other public authority ordering, approving or confirming the judicial sale,
(iv) the reference identification of the judicial sale procedure,
(v) the name, registry details and IMO number of the ship or (if IMO number is not available) other identifying information,
(vi) the name, address or residence or principal place of business of the owner,
(vii) if a judicial sale by public auction, the anticipated date, time and place of the public auction,
(viii) if a judicial sale by private treaty, any relevant details including the time period for the judicial sale as ordered by the court or other public authority,
(ix) a statement either confirming that the sale will confer a clean title to the ship or, if this information is not known, a statement of the circumstances when the judicial sale would not confer a clean title,
(x) any other information required by the State of judicial sale, in particular, any information deemed necessary to protect the interest of the person receiving the notice.[167]

2.8.3 Recipients of the notice

2.88. The Convention divides the obligation to communicate a notice of sale into two categories, which may be identified as specific and general notice.

162 Para 4.
163 Art 4.2.
164 Art 4.2; infra, under the title "Judicial Sale and Certificate of Judicial Sale".
165 Art 4.4. See, also, Annex 1, infra.
166 The list as set out in the text is not a precise replication of the drafting in Annex 1 of the Convention but otherwise includes all the detailed provisions. Further information may be required by the State of judicial sale.
167 This para also does not follow the precise organisation of the requirements set out in Annex 1.

2.8.4 Specific notice

2.89 A notice of sale must be given to –

(i) The registry of ships or equivalent registry with which the ship is registered;[168]
(ii) All holders of a mortgage or *hypothèque* and of any registered charge, provided that the register and any registered instrument are open to public inspection, and extracts and copies are obtainable;[169]
(iii) All holders of any maritime lien, provided that they have notified the court or other public authority conducting the judicial sale of the claim secured by the maritime lien in accordance with the regulations and procedures of the State of judicial sale;[170]
(iv) The owner of the ship for the time being;[171] and
(v) If the ship is bareboat registered: (i) the person registered as the bareboat charterer; and (ii) the bareboat charter registry.[172]

2.90. It is to be observed that notice is to be given directly to persons/parties who are or ought to be readily identifiable or otherwise identifiable by resorting to accessible registered information. In the case of maritime liens notice must be given to lienors who have notified the court of their claim which is secured by a maritime lien. How this notification is to be made is not indicated. It may, presumably, be given as an incident of being a party to the court proceedings and the court in its rules may set out the procedure that is to be followed.[173]

2.91. Many of the notice obligations may be considered as administrative in the sense that the recipients are already on the record. Those relating to the holders of registered mortgages, *hypothèques* and charges, and maritime lienors who have disclosed their claims to the court of judicial sale, are the crucial notices, and central to the framework of the Convention.

2.92. In the event that an error arises in connection with the name or address of any person to whom notice is to be given, the Convention indicates that it is sufficient that reliance was placed on the information contained in the relevant or equivalent ship register or in the register in which the mortgage, *hypothèque* or charge is registered; or in the notification to the court provided by a maritime lienor.[174]

2.93. The use of the word "sufficient" is ambiguous but it appears to suggest that notwithstanding an error in the notice relating to the name and/or address of the intended recipient, the notice continues to be valid and effective. By implication, this rule suggests that it is the responsibility of parties who are potential recipients of notices of judicial sale to ensure that information that may be relied on by a court of judicial sale is accurate and maintained as such. The provision is limited to name

---

168 Art 4.3(a).
169 Art 4.3(b).
170 Art 4.3(c).
171 Art 4.3(d). "Owner" is a reference to the registered owner, Art 2(h); and the phrase "for the time being" refers to the time when the sale is notified, Art 4.2.
172 Art 4.3(d).
173 Art 4.3(c).
174 Art 3.7(a)–(c).

and/or address and does not have any wider application. The rule probably provides a degree of protection to the ultimate purchaser of the ship by limiting the possibility of the sale being rendered void on a technicality. A more significant error might be of greater consequence to the validity of a notice of sale.

2.94. It may be readily contemplated that many practical questions may arise about the validity and efficacy of a noticc, beyond the sparse details provided by the Convention. These may relate, for example, to the method, manner, form and procedure relating to service, such as proof of service, substitute procedures and international service. Ultimately all the possible issues and questions will fall to be determined by reference to the law of the State of judicial sale.

2.8.5 General notice

2.95. There are two broad obligations which run in parallel with the obligation to give notice to specific parties.

The notice of sale must be –

- (i) published by announcement in the press or other publication available in the State of judicial sale;[175] and
- (ii) transmitted to the Secretary General of the IMO who acts as repository under the Convention.[176]

2.96. These obligations are cumulative and, therefore in addition, to the obligation to give specific notice to designated parties. They do not serve to broaden the range of parties who are to be served with notice.

(i) Public announcement.

2.97. The announcement must be in the "press or other publication". These words are likely to be interpreted widely, relating to any form of public dissemination or communication, traditional or digital, including newspapers, specialist and trade journals, public media, internet and so on. The more international the reach of a publication, so much the better.

2.98. The only limitation is that the notice, whatever its form and reach, must be "available" in the State of judicial sale. This indicates that its source or derivation need not be in the State of judicial sale, provided it is available in that state, presumably in the sense of being accessible. At its simplest, a notice may be published abroad and yet available to purchase or otherwise access in the State of judicial sale.

2.99. Digital publications and notices would appear to readily satisfy these requirements. The wording appears not to exclude the application of digital platforms and communication systems. Traditional documentary materials are increasingly also available and accessible in electronic format. This is expressly acknowledged with regard to the Certificate of Judicial Sale.[177]

---

[175] Art 4.5(a).
[176] Art 4(5)(b).
[177] Arts 5.6 and 7.

2.100. There is nothing to preclude the State of judicial sale from stipulating further requirements, extending on the provisions of the Convention.[178] For example, the obligation to give a general notice in the "press or other publication" may be made more particular by naming specific publications and outlets.[179]

2.101. A question arises about the relationship between the obligation to give notices of sale to specific parties and the obligation to give public notice of sale in the "press or other publications".

A little surprisingly the obligation to give public notice is not an attempt to communicate with potential claimants beyond the specific groups identified. To the contrary, it builds up the obligation to communicate a specific notice of sale by stipulating an additional obligation.

To this extent it may be considered as a device aimed at compensating for any failure in the attempt to communicate a specific notice. This aspect of the Convention is considered further later in the text.

(ii) IMO as repository.[180]

2.102. The notice of sale must also be transmitted to IMO as the designated repository.[181]

2.103. How precisely this will be achieved is determined by the law of the State of judicial sale[182] and procedures developed by the Repository.[183]

The object is that the notice shall be published promptly by the Repository and made readily available to public access in the form and language in which it has been received, thereby assisting the process of communicating with the specified claimants. If that language is not a working language of the Repository it must be accompanied by a translation.[184]

The essential purpose of the Repository is that it protects against the risk that the obligation to give specific notice may fail for any reason. It also, more generally, provides the means for parties with a financial interest in a particular ship to maintain a continuous surveillance and respond quickly in the face of detrimental circumstances.

2.104. The position of IMO as Repository under the Convention is considered again under a discreet title later in the text.[185]

2.8.6 Notice across international boundaries

2.105. In relation to giving notice across international boundaries, where State parties are also parties to the Convention on the Service Abroad of Judicial and Extrajudicial Documents in Civil or Commercial Matters (1965), the notice of judicial Sale may

---

178 Arts 4.4. and 4.1.

179 Supra, "Relevant Aspects of English Admiralty Practice, for a Comparison with English Admiralty Practice".

180 Art 11 (Repository).

181 Art 5(b).

182 Art 4.4.

183 Art 11.

184 Art 4.6.

185 See infra, "IMO as Repository".

be transmitted abroad using channels other than those provided for in the 1965 Convention.[186]

2.9 Judicial sale and certificate of judicial sale

2.9.0.1 Judicial sale

2.106. The judicial sale of a ship within the meaning of the Convention is effected by order of a court or equivalent body in the State of judicial sale in accordance with the law of that State Party.[187]

2.107. The intention underlying the sale must be that the purchaser obtains a clean title.[188] And that the sale funds are applied to satisfying pre-existing claims against the ship.[189]

2.108. The procedure of the sale is governed by the rules and practice of the court of judicial sale, in other words, the *lex fori*. This is the clear policy underlying the Convention. The Convention specifies the occasional procedural rule, for example, the power to determine the time of the sale,[190] but any further aspect of practice and procedure not specifically addressed by the Convention is governed by the *lex fori*. This includes the precise procedure to be followed in effecting an arrest and subsequent sale, and in distributing the proceeds of sale.[191]

2.109. As previously observed, the ship must be physically within the "territory of the State of judicial sale" at the time of the sale.[192] The "territory of the State" probably includes the territorial sea. Although not expressly indicated, it may also be necessary that the ship is at anchor or otherwise stationary, so that the sale may be made immediately effective. This requirement will be readily satisfied when the ship continues to be under arrest at the time of the sale.

2.9.0.2 Certificate of Judicial Sale

2.110. Following a judicial sale which transfers a clean title to the purchaser of the ship, and which has been effected in accordance with the requirements of the Convention and the law of the State of judicial sale, the court is obliged to issue a certificate of judicial sale to the purchaser.[193]

2.111. The proper discharge of the obligation to give notice of sale in accordance with the terms of the Convention is a condition precedent to the obligation to issue a certificate of judicial sale.[194]

2.112. Whether the certificate is issued automatically following a sale or in response to an application by the purchaser is not addressed by the Convention. The question

---

186 Art 13.
187 Art 4.1.
188 Art 1.
189 Art 2(a)(ii).
190 Art 4.1.
191 Art 15.2.
192 Art 3.1(b).
193 Art 5.1. "Purchaser" is defined in Art 2(i).
194 Art 4.2.

may be governed by the rules of the court of judicial sale.[195] It also appears to be the case that there is no discretion vested in the court. If the sale and notice of sale have been properly discharged, a certificate of judicial sale must be issued.

2.113. Once issued the certificate of sale is required to be transmitted promptly to IMO as repository.[196]

2.9.0.3 Model Certificate of Judicial Sale

2.114. The certificate must be substantially in the form of the model certificate of sale in Annex II of the Convention. It must contain the following information:[197]

(i) A statement that the ship was sold in accordance with the requirements of the law of the State of judicial sale and the requirements of the Convention;
(ii) A statement that the judicial sale has conferred clean title to the ship on the purchaser;
(iii) The name of the State of judicial sale;
(iv) The name, address and the contact details of the authority issuing the certificate;
(v) The name of the court or other public authority that conducted the judicial sale and the date of the sale;
(vi) The name of the ship and registry of ships or equivalent registry with which the ship is registered;
(vii) The IMO number of the ship or, if not available, other information capable of identifying the ship;
(viii) The name and address of residence or principal place of business of the owner of the ship immediately prior to the judicial sale;
(ix) The name and address of residence or principal place of business of the purchaser;
(x) The place and date of issuance of the certificate; and
(xi) The signature or stamp of the authority issuing the certificate or other confirmation of authenticity of the certificate.

2.9.0.4 Form of the certificate

2.115. In the first place the Convention and Annex II contemplate that the certificate will exist as a traditional document, although there are few express statements made to this effect. It is, however, acknowledged that the certificate may be "transmitted" which suggests the contrary.[198]

2.116. It is indicated that the certificate may be issued by the court of judicial sale "in accordance with its regulations and procedures" which could include provisions relating to form, language and translation.[199]

---

195 Art 4.1.

196 Art 5.3. A State Party will probably impose this obligation on the court conducting the sale. The position of "IMO as Repository" is considered infra.

197 Art 5.2.

198 E.g. Art 11.2.

199 Art 5.1. Also, see, infra, "IMO as Repository".

2.117. It is also accepted that the certificate may be in the form of an electronic record provided that:

(i) the information it contains is accessible and usable for subsequent reference;
(ii) a reliable method is used to identify the authority issuing the certificate; and
(iii) a reliable method is used to detect any alteration to the record after the time it was generated, apart from the addition of any endorsement and any change that arises in the normal course of communication, storage and display.[200]

2.118. A certificate may not be rejected on the sole ground that it is in electronic form.[201]

2.119. The Convention further provides that the certificate of judicial sale and any translation of the same are exempt from "legalization or similar formality".[202] There is no further explanation of this statement but the object appears to be clear. It is to avoid the requirement of any formal or other legal authentication; or the signature and seal of an agency such as a notary.[203] It is a general indication that no formal affirmation of a certificate or any of its contents is required.

2.9.1 Comment

2.120. The certificate of judicial sale is the crucial document under the Convention, but many practical questions remain unanswered. It is a dynamic document: it is issued by the court of judicial sale to the purchaser; transmitted to the IMO repository; may be produced in another State Party court or to a ship or bareboat registry or transmitted to a subsequent purchaser. Throughout the Convention makes reference to "the" Certificate of Sale. The question arises whether the Certificate is a single document or may it be issued in multiples, with each a valid certificate? It is contemplated that copies and certified copies may be made and that translations may be directed. But what is the status of a copy? The Convention also speaks of the "production" and "transmission" of a certificate. In the case of a paper certificate, does this require the actual certificate to be produced or transmitted, or may a copy suffice; or is it sufficient to point to a source where the certificate may be examined, for example, the IMO repository? Parallel queries arise of a digital certificate. And where the certificate exists as an electronic record, are the conditions specified in the Convention adequate protection against unlawful intrusions?

---

200 Art 5.6. These rules are modelled on rules contained in the UN Convention on the Use of Electronic Communications in International Contracts 2005. "Electronic record" is not defined but the phrase is to be found and defined in the UNCITRAL Model Law on Electronic Transferable Records (2017).

201 Art 5.7.

202 Art 5.4.

203 The word "legalization" indicates what may be considered a cumbersome and time-consuming procedure aimed at confirming the authenticity of a signature, seal or stamp, or the capacity of the signor, by a diplomatic or consular agent in the state where the document is to be produced. It would appear that the reference to "similar formality" extends the exemption to an "Apostille" which is an authenticating certificate issued by the state in which the document is issued under the Hague Convention Abolishing Requirement of Legalisation for Foreign Public Documents (1961); UN Treaty Series, vol 527, No 7625: see Explanatory Note para 157 et seq.

2.9.2 Legal effect of the certificate

2.121. The fundamental effect of a certificate of judicial sale is that it is evidence of the sale of a ship by a court or equivalent body in a State Party which confers a clean title on the purchaser.[204]

2.122. Following its issue the certificate is binding on all other State Parties.[205] They are obliged to recognise the sale as "conferring clean title to the ship on the purchaser".[206] In other words, as between State Parties, a valid certificate of judicial sale is conclusive evidence of matters as to title in the subject matter to which it relates.

2.123. Article 6 is the key provision and provides –

> A judicial sale for which a certificate of judicial sale referred to in article 5 has been issued shall have the effect in every other State Party of conferring clean title to the ship on the purchaser.

Where this principle is or at risk of being ignored or rejected by a court or equivalent body in a State Party other than the State of judicial sale, the purchaser, on production of the Certificate of Judicial Sale, is in a position to incontrovertibly assert the acquisition of a clean title in the ship.[207]

This proposition raises the crucial question, what is meant by "clean title".

2.9.3 Clean title

2.124. The concept of a "clean title" is defined in the Convention as a –

> title free and clear of any mortgage or *hypothèque* and of any charge.[208]

This is an exceptionally wide statement and it is suggested it cannot be given a literal meaning. It must be understood in the context of the Convention in its entirety, the precise terms and underpinning principles.

2.125. The reference to any mortgage or *hypothèque* must be understood as meaning any "registered" mortgage and *hypothèque*. This is made expressly clear by the definition of these concepts in the Convention, as previously indicated in the text.[209]

2.126. The meaning to be given to "charge" is more convoluted. As previously discussed, a "charge" is defined very broadly to effectively include any right that may be asserted against a ship by means of an arrest, attachment or otherwise.[210] Thereafter, a definition of "registered charge" is introduced, indicating a charge which is registered in the ship's registry or equivalent, or in any different registry for mortgages and *hypothèques*.[211] Therefore, two definitions are provided, with "charge"

---

204 Art 6.
205 Ibid.
206 Ibid.
207 E.g. Art 8 (ship arrest).
208 Art 2(c), supra (n 127).
209 Art 2(d), supra (n 128).
210 Art 2(e), supra (n 138).
211 Art 2(f), supra (n 139).

not directly linked to "registered charge". The latter, it may be anticipated, will be a more restricted group numerically. It is also the case that notice of sale is only required to be transmitted to parties with "registered charges".

2.127. Taking these facts into account it is submitted that the reference to "any charge" in the definition of "clean title" must be understood as meaning "any registered charge". This submission is consistent with the broad approach of the Convention and to hold to the contrary would be unprincipled and manifestly unjust. It would result in parties losing rights against the arrested ship without the counter obligation to take reasonable steps to inform them in advance of the proposed sale and, therefore, also the opportunity to protect their interests.[212] Such an outcome would cut across a fundamental principle underlying the exercise of Admiralty and maritime jurisdiction.

2.128. The definition of "charge" appears to serve the purpose of defining the pool of claims out of which "registered charges" may emerge and be identified. It must also be borne in mind that the extent to which a "charge" may be required to be registered may be very limited, but the position may vary significantly as between different jurisdictions. Also, the requirement of registration is restricted to ships or equivalent registers or any different register where mortgages or *hypothèques* are registered. This gives "registered charges" the same degree of visibility and accessibility as registered mortgages and *hypothèques*, and they are similarly entitled to receive a specific notice of sale under the Convention.

2.129. Support for this analysis also derives from the way maritime liens are treated under the Convention. A maritime lien is defined as a charge but it is not required to be registered under the terms of the Convention.[213] There is no scheme of registration applicable to maritime liens. They are subject to a separate rule, with notice of sale only required to be given to maritime lienors who have "notified the court . . . conducting the judicial sale of the claim secured by the maritime lien".[214] It follows that it is only this category of maritime lien that is expunged by the judicial sale of the ship to the purchaser.

2.130. In summary, it is submitted that the concept of "clean title" is limited to registered mortgages and *hypothèques*, registered charges and maritime liens that have been made known to the court of judicial sale. The purchaser acquires a title free of claims that belong to any of these categories.

2.131. The implication of this line of reasoning is that the Convention does not guarantee a clean title relating to other claims against the ship that pre-existed the judicial sale to the purchaser. To this extent, with regard to these other pre-existing claims, there continues to be the risk that the ship may be arrested again in the possession of the purchaser. Under the Convention, "clean title" is a partial concept.[215]

---

212 Cf. Preamble para 4.
213 Art 2(e) and (g).
214 Art 4.3(c).
215 See infra, "Some Reflections".

2.10 Supervisory jurisdiction

2.132. Under the Convention, the procedure relating to judicial sales is governed primarily by the law of the State of Judicial Sale, including the determination of the time of the sale for the purposes of the Convention.[216]

2.133. The same law governs the supervisory jurisdiction.

It is provided that the law of the State of judicial sale shall "provide procedures for challenging the judicial sale prior to its completion".[217] By implication, this would appear to include a challenge to the notice of sale.

2.134. It is further expressly provided that the courts of the State of judicial sale possess exclusive jurisdiction to determine any claim or application –

(i) to avoid or suspend the effect of a judicial sale in that State Party, and
(ii) to challenge the issuance of a Certificate of Judicial Sale.[218]

2.135. If a court makes a positive order under (i) in respect of a judicial sale in connection with which a certificate of sale has been issued, it must be transmitted promptly to the IMO repository.[219]

2.136. It would appear that the jurisdiction under (ii) should be managed cautiously. It is unclear whether the jurisdiction is restricted to the "issue" of a certificate of judicial sale in a literal sense or, more widely, embraces any question relating to the validity and effect of a certificate that has been issued. The latter probably represents the more sensible interpretation. Once issued reliance may have been placed on the certificate by the purchaser and others who may be prejudiced by judicial orders made subsequently and adversely to their interests. To a degree, these possibilities are foreseen by the Convention and to be borne in mind.[220]

2.137. The effect of any decision made by the court is governed not by the Convention but the *lex fori*.[221]

2.138. The jurisdiction of the court of judicial sale is reinforced by the requirement that the courts of other State Parties must decline jurisdiction in respect of any claim or application to avoid a judicial sale that confers a clean title conducted in another State Party or suspends its effects.[222]

2.11 IMO as repository

2.139. The Convention provides that the Secretary-General of IMO or an institution identified by UNCITRAL is to act as repository in connection with the Convention.[223] IMO has accepted the role but assumes no legal responsibility.

2.140. Under the Convention a –

---

[216] Art 4.1.
[217] Ibid.
[218] Art 9.1.
[219] Art 9.3. See infra n. 2.11.
[220] Arts 9.1 and 9.3.
[221] Art 15.2.
[222] Art 9.2.
[223] Art 11.1.

(i) notice of judicial sale,[224]
(ii) certificate of judicial sale,[225] and
(iii) any decision of a court that avoids or suspends the effects of a judicial sale for which a certificate has been issued,[226] is required to be transmitted to the Repository. In the case of (ii) and (iii) the transmission is to be "promptly" made.[227]

2.141. Upon receipt by the Repository, the transmitted notice shall be made available to the public in a timely manner, in the form and language it is received.[228]

2.142. The Repository may also receive a notice of judicial sale emanating from a state that has ratified, accepted, approved or acceded to the Convention, but in which it has not yet entered into force, and make it available to the public.[229]

2.11.1 Comment

2.143. IMO assumes no legal responsibility for its role as repository. It provides no guarantee or assurance. Its duty as repository is to make the documents transmitted to it under the Convention "available to the public in a timely manner, in the form and in the language in which it is received". Beyond acting as custodian and making the information accessible, this is a passive duty. There is no obligation to publish, circulate or disseminate. The obligation is to make the information transmitted to it available "as received", confirming that there is no oversight responsibility. As a result, IMO is a bare repository and assumes no related responsibility. Even making a transmitted notice available to the public is to be done in a "timely manner" which is an imprecise responsibility. It appears also to be the case that transmitting information to the Repository does not represent an acceptable alternative mode of performing a specific notice of sale duty under the Convention.

2.144. Associated with the assumption of this role by the IMO is the development by the IMO of the Global Integrated Shipping Information System (GISIS). This is a platform that stores information relevant to international shipping provided to it by scrutinised sources. The information will now include notice of sales, certificates and other information transmitted to it under the Beijing Convention, to which the public will have unlimited access. This will make it possible to trace the position and circumstances relating to a ship with (it is indicated) the minimum of effort.

2.145. Significant reliance is based on this platform by the promoters of the Convention to function as an effective system for the international dissemination of notices of judicial sale, certificates of sale and related matters. Whether this confidence is justified awaits the judgment of time. But it continues to be the case that the onus is on individuals and their representatives to monitor the system.[230] Beyond making

[224] Art 4.5(b).
[225] Art 5.3.
[226] Art 9.3.
[227] Arts 5.3. and 9.3.
[228] Art 11.2.
[229] Art 11.3.
[230] See Chpt 1.

the information available, in other words accessible, there is no obligation to publicise and disseminate information received to any degree. The platform, doubtlessly, will be most helpful to those already in a state of alertness.[231]

2.12 Ancillary protective powers

2.12.1 Ship arrest

2.146. Given the purpose of the Convention, namely the protection of the clean title of the purchaser of a ship sold by judicial sale, it is clearly desirable that the Convention should include provisions that protect the purchaser from the risk of subsequent arrest or threat to arrest the purchased ship in a State Party, in connection with a pre-existing claim against the ship which has been expunged by the judicial sale.

This policy is adopted in Article 8.

2.147. Article 8.1 provides, in effect, that if an application is made in a State Party to arrest a ship (or take any other similar measure) for *a claim arising prior to the judicial sale of the ship* the court (or other judicial authority) is obliged upon production of the certificate of judicial sale dismiss the application.[232]

The court is obliged to dismiss the application: it is not a question of discretion.

2.148. The words in italics require a qualified interpretation: presumably they are to be given a meaning which is consistent with the terms and object of the Convention. This is to suggest that they are not as wide in their meaning as appears on their face. The claims arising prior to the judicial sale can only allude to those claims within the Convention that are expunged on the judicial sale to the purchaser. These are, as previously noted, registered mortgages and *hypothèques*, registered charges and disclosed maritime liens. This, it is suggested, gives the words a meaning which is consistent with the nature of the clean title of the purchaser.[233] Only to this extent may the purchaser claim the protection of Article 8.1.

2.149. Article 8.2 is a natural compliment. It provides, in effect, that when a ship has been arrested (or other similar measure taken) by a court (or other judicial authority) in a State Party *for a claim arising prior to the judicial sale of the ship* the court (or other judicial authority) shall, upon production of the certificate of judicial sale, release the ship.

2.150. Again, there is no discretion: if the terms of the article are satisfied the court is obliged to order the release of the ship. It is again submitted that the words in italics are to be construed as previously suggested when considering Article 8.1.

2.151. Although the point is not made expressly, the reference in sub-sections 1 and 2 to "a claim arising prior to the judicial sale of the ship" would appear to allude to a judicial sale in a State Party to the Convention. This interpretation would also appear to be implied from the fact that both sub-sections are triggered "upon production of the certificate of judicial sale" which is a core characteristic of the Convention. Also, the drafting of the sub-sections is based on the assumption of two distinct State Party

[231] See, further, infra, "Some Reflections".
[232] Italics are added to assist in the interpretation of the article.
[233] Supra, under the title "Clean Title".

courts, the court where the arrest or application to arrest is made and the preceding court of judicial sale. But the sub-sections appear to retain their relevance even when the two proceedings take place in the same State Party or even the same court.[234]

2.152. Further, in the event that the certificate of judicial sale has not been issued in an official language of the court, the court may request the producer of the certificate to produce a certified translation into such an official language.[235]

2.153. The obligations imposed on the courts of State Parties, as described, do not apply if the court considers that making the required order would be manifestly contrary to the public policy of that State.[236]

2.12.2 Ship registration

2.154. The Convention is concerned with not only ensuring that the purchaser acquires a clean title that is recognised by all State Parties but also with resolving administrative difficulties the purchaser may thereafter face with regard to ship registration and the registration of mortgages and *hypothèques*, and registered charges. The solutions provided by the Convention all derive from the production of the Certificate of Judicial Sale.

2.155. The purchaser may seek to remove or amend the details in the existing ship's register and register the vessel anew in that or another register. Concurrently, steps may be taken to remove registered mortgages, *hypothèques* and charges that predate the judicial sale. Without an acceptable measure of assurance, the registries in question may respond cautiously and hesitate, even refuse, to accommodate applications made by the purchaser. In an attempt to resolve these kinds of difficulties, curative obligations are imposed on registries in State Parties on production of a Certificate of Judicial Sale. These duties are owed to the purchaser and subsequent purchaser of the relevant ship.[237]

2.156. Article 7.1 provides that at the request of the purchaser or subsequent purchaser and upon production of the certificate of judicial sale, the relevant registry or other competent authority of a State Party must, as the case may be and in accordance with its regulations and procedures, but without prejudice to Article 6 –

- (i) Delete from the register any mortgage or *hypothèque* and any registered charge attached to the ship that had been registered before completion of the judicial sale;[238]
- (ii) Delete the ship from the register and issue a certificate of deletion for the purpose of a new registration;[239]
- (iii) Register the ship in the name of the purchaser or subsequent purchaser, provided that the ship and the person in whose name the ship is to be registered meet the requirements of the law of the State of registration;[240]

234 The principal theme of the Convention is to ensure that a judicial sale which confers a clean title conducted in a State Party is given effect to by all other State Parties.
235 Art 8.3.
236 Art 8.4, see infra, under "Public Policy".
237 The latter concept is considered infra, under the title "Subsequent Purchaser".
238 Art 7.1(a).
239 Art 7.1(b).
240 Art 7.1(c).

(iv) Update the register with any other relevant particulars in the Certificate of Judicial Sale.[241]

2.157. Where the ship is bareboat registered, at the request of the purchaser or subsequent purchaser and on the production of the Certificate of Judicial Sale, the registry or other competent authority must delete the ship from the register and issue a certificate of deletion.[242]

2.158. If the certificate of judicial sale is not in an official language of the registry or other competent authority, it may require the purchaser or subsequent purchaser to produce a certified translation into such an official language.[243]

2.159. The purchaser or subsequent purchaser may also be required by the registry or other competent authority to produce a certified copy of the certificate of judicial sale for its records.[244]

2.160. The obligation imposed on the registry or other competent authority is inapplicable if a court in the State of the registry determines under Article 10 that "the effect of the judicial sale" as prescribed by Article 6 would be manifestly contrary to its public policy, that is the State of registry.[245]

2.12.2.1 Subsequent purchaser

2.161. The obligations of registries and other competent authorities as set out in Article 7 relate to applications by the "purchaser" and "subsequent purchaser". The latter is defined as –

> the person who purchases the ship from the purchaser named in the certificate of judicial sale.[246]

2.162. A "subsequent purchaser" is a limited concept. It relates to the "purchaser" from the "purchaser named in the certificate of sale".[247] The latter alludes to the purchaser from the Court of judicial sale. Any later purchaser of the ship under a further on-sale is not a "subsequent purchaser" within the meaning of the Convention.

2.163. With regard to the rights and duties arising under Article 7 the purchaser under the judicial sale and "subsequent purchaser" from that purchaser occupy parallel positions. The duties imposed on registries and competent authorities are owed to each. Beyond this, the particular provision has no wider application in the Convention. This in turn creates a number of interesting questions.

2.164. The rule appears to address the situation where the purchaser of a ship under a judicial sale, who subsequently receives the certificate of judicial sale in which he is named as purchaser, sells the ship without taking any further steps with regard to the registration of the ship or securities. The parties also agree that the ship shall be registered by the subsequent buyer, who possesses all the rights of the purchaser under Article 7. It is understood that this kind of commercial arrangement may exist

---

241 Art 7.1(d).
242 Art 7.2.
243 Art 7.3.
244 Art 7.4.
245 Art 7.5. See infra, "Public Policy".
246 Art 2(j).
247 Art 2(j). Considered infra, "Some Reflections".

between companies in the same corporate group but on the drafting of the Convention it appears to be not strictly limited to this kind of situation.[248]

2.165. Although the point is not made expressly, by implication the provisions relating to "subsequent purchaser" appear to apply only when the purchaser under the judicial sale has not registered the ship or security. Following such registration, the provision appears to have no application.

2.166. The following analysis appears to apply. The purchaser under the judicial sale obtains a clean title under the *lex fori*. And thereafter the purchaser from the court receives a certificate of judicial sale in which he is identified as purchaser. Up to this stage the Convention does not apply. The on sale confers a clean title on the subsequent purchaser under the applicable law of the sale contract. At this stage the transaction continues to be outside the Convention.

2.167. The certificate of judicial sale is then transferred to the subsequent purchaser and the Convention is triggered. It has a consequential effect, but only with regard to the specific obligations set out in Article 7 in relation to ship and securities registries. What the certificate does in effect is guarantee the "subsequent purchaser's" root of title, namely the clean title of his seller, the purchaser under the judicial sale. The "subsequent purchaser" is otherwise outside the parameters of the Convention and takes no further benefit under it.

2.13 Public policy

2.168. The Convention contains the standard public policy limitation associated with private international law conventions.[249] It is set out in Article 10 in the following terms:

> A judicial sale of a ship shall not have the effect provided in article 6 in a State Party other than the State of judicial sale if a court in the other State Party determines that the effect would be manifestly contrary to the public policy of that other State Party.

2.169. The practical implication of this provision is that the functioning of the Convention must ultimately defer to the supervisory jurisdiction of the courts of State Parties other than the State of judicial sale. It is they that determine if to accept "the effect" of the Convention in "conferring clean title to the ship on the purchaser"[250] would be manifestly inconsistent with its domestic public policy. And if the question is answered affirmatively the court may refuse to give effect to the Convention rule.

2.170. The essential "effect" of the Convention as set out in Article 6 is that a judicial sale of a ship in respect of which a certificate of sale has been issued shall be recognised in every other State Party as conferring a clean title to the ship on the purchaser.[251] The precise test under art 10 is to ask the question of whether to give effect to the Convention rule in the particular context before the court "would be manifestly contrary to the public policy" of the State Party in question.[252]

---

[248] Fenech, 'Draft Convention on the International Effects of the Judicial Sale of Ships', pp. 787, 789–790, Comparative Maritime Law 2022, Croatian Maritime Law Association.

[249] See, generally, A Briggs, *Private International Law in English Courts*, 2nd edn. (2023, OUP, UK); Briggs and Rees, supra (n 89); McClean and Abou-Nigm, supra (n 89).

[250] Art 6.

[251] Supra, under "Clean Title".

[252] Art 10.

2.171. The constituent elements of "public policy" are not defined; they are to be determined by the municipal law of individual State Parties. Nonetheless, the requirement that the issue must be "manifestly" contrary to public policy does give an indication of the approach to be adopted. What is being indicated is a demanding standard, different from and more stringent than the elements of domestic public policy. By comparison the concept of public policy in the international context is narrow, to be cautiously approached and sparingly applied.[253] It suggests that to give effect to the Convention in the prevailing circumstances would be immoral, repugnant, offensive or highly objectionable to the population of the State Party in question.

2.172. This approach gives meaning to the word "manifestly" and echoes the approach taken in private international law to the concept of public policy in the commercial context.[254] It probably also represents the approach the framers of the Convention were seeking to endorse.

2.173. In the present context, it would appear that the scope of the public policy defence is limited. The Convention, having been accepted by State Parties, it is difficult to comprehend that objection could be raised, on grounds of public policy, to a circumstance which is a natural consequence of the effect of the Convention. It is suggested that something of much greater significance must be established to trigger the public policy defence, such as proof of fraud, bias, bribery, dishonest pleadings and evidence, or a material breach of the principles of natural justice in connection with the judicial sale and/or issue of the certificate of judicial sale.[255]

2.174. This general rule in relation to public policy is buttressed by two specific provisions relating to ship arrest[256] and the obligation of registries located in State Parties.[257]

2.13.1 Ship arrest

2.175. Following the issue of a certificate of judicial sale, State Parties are under an obligation to reject an application to arrest the ship or grant release of a ship from arrest under Articles 8.1 and 8.2.[258]

2.176. However, a court in a State Party may refuse to make such an order if "it would be manifestly contrary to the public policy" of that State Party.[259] In other words, if satisfied on the question of public policy, the court is free to order the arrest of the ship or, if already under arrest, not to order its release.

2.177. This is to present the test in a slightly different way. The issue of public policy does not relate directly to "the effect" of the Convention, as previously considered, but to the making of orders as set out in Articles 8.1. and 8.2. Nonetheless, the two approaches may be interconnected. The view a court takes on a question relating to the arrest or the release from arrest of a ship previously the subject of a judicial sale in another State Party may be influenced by the facts and circumstances surrounding the

---

[253] See infra, under "Some Reflections".
[254] Briggs and Rees, supra (n 89) Chpt 7.
[255] See infra, "Some Reflections".
[256] Art 8.4.
[257] Art 7.5.
[258] See supra, "Ancillary Protective Powers".
[259] Art 8.4.

judicial sale. And this may influence the assessment of the approach the court should take to the applications before it.

2.178. Although the point is not made expressly, the concept of public policy is probably to be approached in the same way as under Article 10.[260]

2.13.2 Registration

2.179. It has been observed that an obligation is imposed on a ship registry or other competent authority in a State Party to delete, amend or update existing registrations or enter a new registration, as the case may be, in relation to a purchased ship and registered securities.[261]

2.180. The obligation does not survive if a court or other competent authority in the State of the registry determines under Article 10 that "the effect of the judicial sale" would be manifestly contrary to its public policy.[262] In this regard, the public policy principle runs in parallel with Article 10.

2.181. The State of registry may be a different State Party and so a further tier of public policy is introduced to the application of the Convention. The meaning of the phrase "the effect of the judicial sale" in this context has been previously considered.[263]

2.182. Public policy in this regard relates to that of the State of registry, which must also be a State Party. Article 7.5 expressly indicates a common approach with Article 10 so that any question of public policy is to be determined by the application of the criteria relevant to that article.[264]

2.14 Some reflections

2.183. There can be no doubt that the Convention addresses an important principle of admiralty and maritime litigation. It is essential to the effective functioning of international maritime litigation that arrested ships should be judicially saleable, as is recognised in the Preamble to the Convention.[265] This will be achieved only if purchasers are secure in the knowledge that they acquire a clean title to the ship purchased from the court.

2.184. There are, however, contemporary instances of this principle being ignored or rejected by courts, which has emphasised in the minds of many the need for corrective intervention, of which the promotion of the Beijing Convention is an example. Although the instances identified are of concern it cannot be said that they highlight a problem of contagious proportions. There is, therefore, an initial question about the strategic appropriateness of the Convention. It also has to be recognised that the quality and experience of judges called upon to adjudicate international maritime

---

260 Supra (n 247).

261 Art 7. Supra, "Ship Registration".

262 Art 7.5.

263 Supra (n 243).

264 Supra (n 247).

265 The Preamble, para 3, states – "*Considering* that adequate legal protection for purchasers may positively impact the price realised at judicial sales of ships, to the benefit of both shipowners and creditors, including lienholders and ship financiers".

disputes vary significantly, and this probably represents a contributive cause of some vintage that cannot be cured by an international convention.

2.185. Paradoxically, a possible unintended consequence of the Convention is that it opens up the judicial sale of ships to the risk of increased challenges. Hitherto the broadly based and unqualified understanding has prevailed that the judicial sale of arrested ships confers a clean title on purchasers. A position consistently and confidently endorsed and rarely quizzed on matters of principle and detail. The strategic deficit of the Beijing Convention is that it gives only conditional acceptance to this understanding. It sets out explicitly in precise terms, procedural and technical, the circumstances when the judicial sale of a ship confers a clean title on the purchaser. The position thus exposed, a potential challenger is presented with a precise target by which to seek to undermine the purchaser's title, with challenges mustered or manufactured on procedural and technical issues.

2.186. The Convention addresses a small group of claims against ships, namely registered mortgages and *hypothèques*, registered charges and declared maritime liens. The first group is by far the most prevalent and significant, but otherwise, they are similar in that the associated parties are, or ought to be, readily identifiable. This range of claims is also significant in two interconnected regards. It defines the parties to whom notice of sale, specific and general, must be, or attempted to be, given. And secondly, it amplifies the meaning of "clean title" which, in the context of the Convention, it is suggested is a limited concept. If this is a correct interpretation, it adds to the difficulty of appreciating fully the approach taken to the giving of notices of sale.

2.187. It has been contended that "clean title" relates only to registered claims within the range covered by the Convention and to maritime liens made known to the court. Consequently, it does not necessarily indicate a title free of all pre-existing claims against the ship. The purchaser, therefore, continues to be at risk of the ship being arrested by claimants with pre-existing claims which are outside the range of the Convention. These, predominantly, may be maritime lienors who have not declared their claims to the court of judicial sale and, in the context of the common law, claimants with statutory rights *in rem*; and in the context of the civil law, claimants with rights to proceed against the ship. If this is a correct interpretation of the Convention, it represents an ominous limitation.

2.188. The position taken in relation to maritime liens is troublesome on several counts. To leave their recognition to the applicable law of the court of judicial sale is to invite contention and disparity in the functioning of the Convention. It also creates uncertainty with claimants unclear of their precise status and therefore also their obligations under the Convention. It further abandons parties who are not yet aware of their status as maritime lienors. To this extent, the Convention devalues maritime liens. Further, to limit the relevance to maritime liens which have been made known to the court of judicial sale may serve the functional design of the Convention, but it is inconsistent with the nature and practice associated with maritime liens.

2.189. There is, however, a surprising benefit to maritime lienors who fall outside the scope of the Convention and are not given a notice of sale. They are not prejudiced by the sale ordered by the court of judicial sale. As previously suggested, the clean title conferred on the purchaser by the court of judicial sale does not extend to undeclared maritime liens, and such lienors continue to be in a position to enforce their claims by arresting the ship.

2.190. The Convention is right to emphasise the need for effective notice of sale with the procedure made administratively straightforward by the requirement that notice is to be given only to "registered" security interests and "declared" maritime lienors. It may be anticipated that such identities may be fairly readily identified. This position is very different from that adopted by common law admiralty courts where notice of sale is given to the world at large because a judicial sale confers on the purchaser a clean title in the literal sense, as against all claims. This procedural difference assumes a profound significance to an understanding of the different approach taken by the Convention.

2.191. The role of IMO as repository serves to buttress the specific notice of sale obligations under the Convention, not to broaden the reach of the specific notice obligations. The acceptance by IMO of the role of repository is an exceptional development for that institution, and whether it will be functionally significant must await the judgment of time. Its role is very limited. It is confined to the storage and making accessible information received by it. It assumes no responsibility beyond this role. There is no legal guarantee of the validity or accuracy of the information stored, or that it is the most up-to-date information. It may, nonetheless, act as a useful and convenient backup for failures in the obligation to give specific notice and to provide affirmation of information obtained from another source. At the same time, doubt has previously been expressed about the necessity of this aspect of the Convention.

2.192. The ultimate Achilles heel of the Convention may well be the wide role ascribed to public policy. By reference to the public policy of a State Party or that of a State of registry, the obligations and powers established under the Convention may be set aside.[266] This position is consistent with a fundamental principle of private international law but which is also recognised as an unruly principle. It is often abused to favour domestic interests, with the decisions of national courts not open to review.[267]

2.193. The inclusion of the word "manifestly" clearly represents an attempt to counter this risk and encourage the concept to be applied narrowly and strictly.[268] There is, of course, no guarantee that this indication will be followed by the courts of State Parties. To the extent that public policy may become aligned with domestic interests, the core objective of the Convention will be seriously undermined. The risk is that courts whose practices are at the root of the problem which the Convention seeks to cure may, under the guise of public policy, continue to act in a way they consider to be fully justified when claimants with a domestic connection appear to be disadvantaged by the application of the Convention.[269]

2.194. The Beijing Convention feeds the truism that designing and drafting solutions to perceived problems at the international level can be a daunting task. It must also be borne in mind that on occasions inaction may be characterised as a strategic decision. As for the future prospects of the Beijing Convention, that is a question for the international community of maritime states.

[266] Art 10.

[267] Infra (n 255).

[268] *Kuwait Airways Corp v Iraqi Airways Co (Nos 4 and 5)* [2002] UKHL 19; [2002] 2 AC 883, per the speech of Lord Nicholls.

[269] *Loucks v Standard Oil Co* [1918] 224 N.Y. 99, 111; 120 N.E. '98, 202, per Justice Cardozo, "the courts are not free to refuse to enforce a foreign right at the pleasure of the judges, to suit the individual notion of expediency or fairness."

CHAPTER 3

The Beijing Convention on judicial sales of ships[1] from a comparative law perspective

*George Theocharidis**

3.1 Introduction

3.1. As approximately 80% of the goods are transported by sea (*res in transitu*), it would be no exaggeration to assert that shipment has become an integral part of most sale transactions, whether domestic or international. Transportation is connected to such extent with the sale of commodities so that performance of the transaction is executed predominantly with the aid of the cardinal "instrument" of the sea carriage contract, namely the bill of lading,[2] which serves as a tool in the fulfilment of the primary duty to deliver the goods[3] – notably the cargo – for the transfer of ownership.[4] Equally noteworthy is that, albeit no international uniform rule exists regarding the function of the bill of lading that it represents the object (*res*) – more precisely its possession[5] – the function is recognised internationally.[6] Further, national courts often ignore the

---

* Professor of Maritime Law and Policy.

[1] United Nations Convention on the "International Effects of Judicial Sales of Ships", hereinafter referred to as "Convention". The analysis takes into account the deliberations that took place at the 40th Session of UNCITRAL's Working Group VI in New York on 7–11 February 2022, the text approved by the Commission at the 55th Session of UNCITRAL in New York on 27–30 June 2022, the Resolution 77/100 of the UN General Assembly, which approved the Convention, and the final text signed in Beijing on 5 September 2023.

[2] Regarding the absence of definition of the bill of lading at the international level but also the lack of uniform law, governing the drawing up, the operation and the effects of the negotiable instrument, see, indicatively, WP Bennet, *The History and Present Position of the Bill of Lading as a Document of Title to Goods* (Cambridge UP, 1914) 3; I Rokas and G Theocharidis, *Maritime Law*, 4th edn. (Sakkoulas Publications, 2021) 695 ff. (in Greek).

[3] E.g. in German law, see s. 524 Handelsgesetzbuch (HGB), in Greek law, see Art 121 Law 5020/2023 Greek Code of Private Maritime Law (hereinafter "Greek KIND") in conjunction with Art 978 Greek Civil Code (hereinafter "Greek CC").

[4] *Inglis v Robertson* [1898] AC 616.

[5] *Sanders v Maclean* [1883] 11 QBD 327.

[6] According to ss. 433 et seq., Bürgerliches Gesetzbuch (hereinafter "German BGB") and Art 513 Greek CC, three are the substantive elements (*essentialia negotii*) of the sale contract, namely, the object, the price, and the agreement on those. With the valid conclusion of the contract, the seller undertakes the obligation to transfer the ownership and deliver the object while the buyer undertakes the obligation to pay the agreed price. In a cross-border transaction, where sea carriage is necessary, the fulfilment of the duty to deliver is executed by furnishing the bill of lading, in which possession of the *res* is "incorporated". While the transfer of ownership (ss. 929 et seq. German BGB and Art 1034 Greek CC) is governed by the law of the sale contract (*lex causae*), the proprietary effect, that is, transfer of the object, is determined by the law of the place where the bill of lading is surrendered (*lex situs cartae*). However, if the law of the latter ignores this function of the bill of lading, the transfer of ownership will not be perfected until the physical delivery of the cargo at the place of destination (*lex rei sitae*) is accomplished. The same principles apply in Anglo-common law jurisdictions, where no distinction is drawn between obligatory and proprietary effect.

DOI: 10.4324/9781003499930-3

question, from which applicable law, which is determined by the appropriate conflict rule,[7] the specific finding derives. This happens even in jurisdictions, where a distinction is drawn between the obligatory and proprietary effect in a sale transaction.[8]

3.2. At the same time, as the ship "lies" at the centre of all legal relationships arising from shipping, the question of its legal treatment becomes crucial, especially in view of the fact that during a commercial voyage, it crosses several jurisdictions and, consequently, it is exposed to the application of diverse regimes with a myriad of rules. The starting point of the present study is the legal treatment of the ship in general but particular attention shall be given to the enforcement proceedings against it, in order to expose the problematics relating to the recognition of the effects of a ship judicial sale, especially in light of the proposed regime by the Convention.

3.2 The *sui generis* nature of the ship

3.3. The ship is mobile[9] by nature (*res mobilis*).[10] Technically, it is a complex structure, which requires a prodigious capital for its construction, and it is exposed to a multitude of risks, inherent to the marine adventure. Further, the ship is constructed according to certain technical characteristics, which are integral parts of its scientific or technical concept,[11] and from which concepts its legal definition is forged.[12] The aforementioned attributes have led many jurisdictions to create a special legal status for the ship.

However, this causes no problem, as it is accepted that transfer of title is effected upon reception of the bill of lading by the consignee/endorsee, regardless if a different regime applies at the place of destination of the cargo.

[7] The first conflict rule that could apply would lead to the *lex contractus*, as the bill of lading "incorporates" a right stemming from the sea-carriage contract. The second option accords supremacy to the nature of the bill of lading, i.e. *lex cartae* applies, because the right that is exercised is based on the drawing up of the negotiable instrument and, more precisely, the right is exercised *from* the document but by virtue of a right *on* the document (legitimation). However, the cargo, until it reaches its destination, crosses the waters of several jurisdictions, therefore, both *lex expeditionis* and *lex destinationis* are only two of the many available applicable laws, which would in fact be displaced by the respective *lex situs*, which, in its turn, would set aside the *lex situs cartae*, except if the goods, due to an accident, would not arrive at the ultimate destination (P Lalive, *The Transfer of Chattels in the Conflict of Laws* (1955 (reprint 1977) 189, 192–193). It is submitted that the aforementioned options are not flawless and the quest for a uniform solution remains a *chimera* (D Markianos, Die Res in Transitu im Deustchen Internationalen Privatrecht (1958) 23 *RabelsZ* 21–43 (in German). That seems to be the reason that courts invariably ignore the particular private international law question.

[8] Lalive, supra (n 7) 4. In common law, the distinction between the obligatory and the proprietary effect is of no consequence, when it comes to the transfer of ownership of a tangible movable object (see s. 2(1) Sale of Goods Act 1979 "A contract of sale of goods is a contract by which the seller transfers or agrees to transfer"). This distinction, however, may ensue significant consequences, when a contractual breach has been committed and the matter has to be examined from a conflict of laws perspective (see *PST Energy 7 Shipping LLC v OW Bunker Malta Ltd (The Res Cogitans)* [2016] Lloyd's Rep 589, where the Supreme Court forced English law of sales to its limits in order to reach an acceptable solution for the validity of the transfer of ownership of bunkers in a Russian port by virtue of a contract governed by English law, see G Theocharidis, 'All About Freedom of Contract? Bunker Supply Arrangements Post-Res Cogitans in Global Context' [2018] JMLC 127–152).

[9] It is a chattel personal, see *Behnke v Bede Shipping Co Ltd* [1927] KB 649, 659.

[10] K Rokas, *Maritime Law*, vol A (1975) s. 11 (in Greek).

[11] A Antapasis and L Athanasiou, *Maritime Law* (2020) para 130 ff. (in Greek).

[12] In Greek law, see Art 1 Greek KIND and Art 3 Greek Code of Public Maritime Law (hereinafter "Greek KDND").

3.4. The first deviation from the regime that regulates tangible movables[13] according to many domestic laws is the requirement for registration of the vessel in a special book (ship register),[14] which also safeguards the valid exercise of certain rights *erga omnes*.[15] Further, in some countries, the transfer of ownership must be underpinned by an agreement,[16] which forms the valid cause (*causa*), much like immovable property,[17] and

[13] See Art 3 Greek KIND and 6 Greek KDND on ship registration. Registration serves the establishment of a nexus with a specific jurisdiction, which will confer nationality to the ship, so that the latter can legitimately perform transnational sea voyages.

[14] Ownership, as a proprietary right on a ship, includes the following powers in the various legal systems: physical use, collection of "fruits", administration and right of disposal (in English law, see *The Permina 3001* [1979] 2 Lloyd's Rep 327; in Greek law, see Art 12 Greek KIND, 973 and 1000 Greek CC). Especially in common law, ownership is manifested as dominance, ultimate control and ultimate title against third parties. Further, a distinction is drawn between legal and equitable ownership, depending on the interests of the beneficiary on the *res*, of which, in case of purchase, some are transferred *ex consenso* and others *ex lege*. The issue is not without consequences. The sale of a ship under English law triggers conveyance of certain proprietary interests but prior to the recording of the agreement in the register, it may be questioned whether the buyer acquires legal or beneficial ownership, see *The Evpo Agnic* [1988] WLR 1090. *Semble* registration is a substantive element for the transfer of title, Lord Collins of Mapesbury and Jonathan Harris (eds), *Dicey, Morris and Collins on the Conflict of Laws*, 15th edn., Chpt 13 (2018, Sweet & Maxwell) Rule 40, 13–017.

[15] So in English law, see *Hooper v Gumm* [1867] L.R. 2 Ch. App. 282, 290,

> A ship is not like an ordinary personal chattel; it does not pass by delivery, nor does the possession of it prove the title to it. There is no market overt for ships; In the case of American ships the laws of the United States provide the means of evidencing title to them.

According to the reasoning, the purchase was subject to English law but the transfer of title in the ship was subject to American law of the flag. In fact, the buyer should refer to the register for entries regarding charges. With that approach, the court distanced itself from *lex rei sitae* and chose *lex navis* for the examination of the validity of the proprietary right on the ship, see *The Jupiter (No. 3)* [1927] P. 122, 144; also, *The Nazym Khikmet* [1996] 2 Lloyd's Rep. 362. *Vostok Shipping Co Ltd v Confederation Ltd* [2000] 1 NZLR 37. Lord Collins of Mapesbury and Harris, supra (n 14) Rule 129 (3), Exception 1, arguing that recourse to *lex libri sitae* applies on a case-by-case basis. This approach has the following effect. If a third party challenges the shipowner's title in the vessel and the matter is brought before an English court, the latter will not review the judicial sale judgment, which was the shipowner's title, but the effect that it prompted according to *lex rei sitae*, in that case, the *lex fori executionis*, by virtue of which title in the ship was vested in the shipowner, see Lord Collins of Mapesbury and Harris, supra (n 14) Chpt 14, Rule 47, 14–110 and 14–111.

[16] In German law, see *Nöll* in Staudinger Kommentar zum BGB, Buch 3, Sachenrecht, 2009, s. 2 SchiffsRG para 1 (in German).

[17] In Greek law, see Art 12 Greek KIND and 1033 Greek CC. Cf. German law, G Schaps and HJ Abraham, *Das Seerecht in der BRD, Seehandelsrecht, Part I*, 4th edn. (1978) Vor s. 476, para 33 (in German). *Nöll* in Staudinger Kommentar zum BGB, s. 2 Schiffs RG paras 6 and 10, where equivalent effect is achieved based on knowledge *erga omnes*. Similarly in French, Spanish and Italian law, see F Berlingieri, *Arrest of Ships*, 3rd edn. (2000) 102–104.

the recording of that contract[18] in the register is a substantive element[19] for the acquisition of ownership[20] and not simply a record or evidence.[21]

3.5. The second characteristic concerns security, which is not exercised in the form of pledge, as in other tangibles, but in the form of ship mortgage,[22] a proprietary interest also relevant to immovable property.[23]

---

[18] In most jurisdictions the bill of sale serves the transfer of rights according to the sale agreement, see *The Sisters* [1804] 5 C Rob 155, 159–160,

> According to the ideas which I have always entertained on this question, a bill of sale is the proper title to which the Maritime Courts of all countries would look. It is the universal instrument of transfer of ships in the usage of all maritime countries; and in no degree a peculiar title-deed or conveyance known only to the law of England: It is what the Maritime Law expects, what the Court of Admiralty would in its ordinary practice always require, and what the Legislature of this country has now made absolutely necessary, with regard to British subjects, by the regulations of the Statute Law.

[19] In German law, see ss. 162 and 90 Gesetz über die Zwangsversteigerung und die Zwangsverwaltung (ZVG); in Greek law, see Rokas and Theocharidis, supra (n 2) para 77. This position ensues serious repercussions. The registrar will not register a foreign vessel in the Greek registry unless a deletion certificate is furnished from the previous flag within reasonable time. Further, the title obtained in a judicial sale of a Greek flagship in a foreign jurisdiction will not convey ownership to the purchaser unless it is entered in the Greek register or, in case the intention is to register the vessel in another flag, prior to its deletion from the Greek register.

[20] It would be an *absurdum* to apply *lex navis/lex rei sitae* for the ascertainment of title in a ship and *lex fori* to answer the question who is the owner for the purpose of ship arrest (cf. M Davies, *Choice of Law in Determining the Ownership of Ships, Essays in Honour of Francis Rose*, Bloomsbury (2020) 107, 114). If we were to accept the latter law for the arrest prior to the judicial sale, then it would be possible for an owner by virtue of *lex navis* to eschew the forced process by invoking that he is not the owner by virtue of *lex fori*.

[21] In Anglo-common aw systems, see Davies, supra (n 20) 107, 109. However, the position differs from jurisdiction to jurisdiction, see *Tisand Pty Ltd v The Owners of the Ship M/V Cape Moreton (ex 'Freya')* [2005] FCR 43 [127],

> For instance, in any given national law the register may play a role as an element in the title to, or ownership of, the ship, as opposed to its being only a record or evidence of the title to, or ownership of, the ship. Before the amendments contained in the MSA 1862, entry on the British Register was determinative of title. No legal or equitable interest of an unregistered party was recognised or enforced.... This role of title by, or by reference to, registration is to be contrasted with other systems, such as those of the United Kingdom and Australia in which the register substantially operates as a record of title, subject to the effect of provisions such as ss 39, 41 and 45 dealing with the order of registration, priorities and power of disposition.

But even in those jurisdictions, where registration merely reflects legal rights, the conferral of rights in a chain of interested parties could not be accomplished without entries in the ship register. According to this reasoning, the auction is a public sale with the safeguards prescribed by law, therefore the highest bidder could obtain title in the ship but unless registered, no third party would agree to purchase it. As will be shown, the complications start, when registration has to be executed in a jurisdiction different from the one, in which the judicial sale was executed.

[22] D Osborne, G Bowtle and C Buss, *Law of Ship Mortgages*, 2nd edn. (2016). In Greek law, see, Art 17 ff. Greek KIND.

[23] In the Civil law systems, the traditional view was against extending the mortgage to ships, see E Gold, A Chircop and Kindred, *Maritime Law*, Chpt 6 (2004). Conversely, Anglo-common law recognised chattel mortgage, which extended to ships, see W Tetley, *International Maritime and Admiralty Law* (2002) 474–475.

3.6. Third, in case of imposition of arrest[24] – provisional[25] or forced – on the vessel, specific provisions germane to immovable property[26] apply by extension to ships.[27] At this point, the following should be observed.[28] In the majority of civil law jurisdictions[29] a final unappealable decision or an enforceable notarial deed is a prerequisite for the imposition of a forced arrest, which serves as the starting point of the forced sale proceedings. After that act, the process continues without court intervention, unless a remedy is exercised to restrain the enforcement proceedings on grounds of invalidity of the title or defects in the process. In Anglo-common law jurisdictions,[30] on the other hand, proceedings are entertained by filing an *in rem* claim,[31] which is then served on the ship, while enforcement is entertained once an arrest warrant[32] is issued and served[33] on the ship.[34] The act of arrest will invariably exhort the owner[35] to appear in the proceedings. Then there are three paths; either judgment on the merits of the claim will be entered and the court will order appraisement and sale of the ship by the

---

24 The notion of arrest may be a cause of confusion. Anglo-Common Law jurisdictions have a single concept of arrest, which serves both protective and security functions, while civil law jurisdictions use the concept of forced arrest to describe the seizure of an object for the purpose of satisfying a claim by a forced sale, while provisional arrest is used when an object is seized (i.e. immobilised) temporarily for the satisfaction of a future judgment on the merits of the claim. In the latter case, once an unappealable judgment is awarded and if the object has not been released in the meantime with bail or other similar form of security, the provisional arrest is transformed into a forced arrest at the moment enforcement proceedings are entertained. English law recognised the provisional arrest some time ago (*Rasu Maritima SA v Perusahaan Pertambagan Dan Gas Bumi Negara (Pertamina)* [1978] QB 644, 658) but it was abandoned with the exception of ships in the form of *in rem* claim. At this point it must be stated that both provisional arrest and the *in rem* claim have a common feature, that is, they have *in rem* effect on the object, meaning that its transfer would be of no effect in favour of the person who imposed it (N Meeson and J Kimbell, *Admiralty Jurisdiction and Practice*, 5th edn., Chpt 4 (2017), 4.9). English law achieves an equivalent result with the freezing injunction with the difference that the effect is *in personam* and *not in rem* (*quaere* when the freezing injunction is served to a third party, in which case a *quasi-in rem* effect may be achieved).

25 In Greek law, see Art 713 Greek Code of Civil Procedure (hereinafter "Greek CCP").

26 For the position in English law, see Meeson and Kimbell, supra (n 24) Chpt 4. In German law, see J-E Pötschke J.-E., 'Judicial Sale of Ships in Germany' Paper submitted to CMI Conference, 2012. From a comparative law perspective, see L Hagberg, *Maritime Law, Vol. II, Enforced Sale of Ships* (1977).

27 See Art 992 s.1 Greek CCP "The provisions for the seizure of immovable also apply to the seizure of rights to which the rules relating to immovable property apply, as well as to the seizure of ships and aircraft".

28 See infra.

29 E.g. Greece, France, Germany, Belgium, Netherlands.

30 US law draws a distinction between Rule B attachment and Rule C arrest, the former involving an action *in personam* against the shipowner, the latter an *in rem* action against the ship (see, M Davies, "Recognition of foreign judicial sales in the United States" (2022) 28 (2022) JIML 425, 428).

31 An *in rem* claim has three aspects, the remedial, the jurisdictional and the security, the latter in the form of a preferred claim enforceable in priority to unsecured creditors, which are intermingled and not distinct (see DC Jackson, *Enforcement of Maritime Claims*, 4th edn. (2005) Introduction, 0.10).

32 Jackson, supra (n 31) 15.56.

33 It may be that the arrest warrant is served on the ship before the claim form is served on the ship (Jackson, supra (n 31) 15.57).

34 The *in rem* claim form can be issued even before the ship enters jurisdiction but it must be served on the ship within a period of 12 months, after which it expires (Jackson, supra (n 31) 10.68). On the other hand, if an *in personam* claim form is issued, the period is four months (*The Styliani Z* [2016] Lloyd's Rep 395).

35 Under US law, it is possible for the vessel to be held liable *in rem* when the owner was not held liable *in personam* (see, M Davies, 'In defense of unpopular values: personification and ratification', (2000) 75 Tulane Law Review 337).

Admiralty Marshal, or the admiralty proceedings may be stayed[36] in favour of foreign arbitration or litigation, in which case the *res* may be retained as security,[37] or a court order for sale *pendente lite* will be issued. In the latter case, if the judge is persuaded[38] that delay in time, pending trial, together with the inability of the debtor shipowner to furnish security, will cause significant depreciation of the ship's value, then it may order an immediate sale.[39]

3.7. Based on the aforementioned, it is evident that in the civil law systems, the process starts with an enforceable title, which may subsequently be challenged by a remedy before the court, in which case the latter may or may not restrain the enforcement proceedings. With the same remedy, the arrestee may also raise defects in the execution process. The picture is different in the Anglo-common law jurisdictions, as the court is vested with power over all steps of the process without the need of an enforceable title. It is the court that orders the sale of the ship, in which case it will also determine if defects have occurred in the arrest process, and it is the same that can set aside the order for sale.[40]

3.8. Fourth, as regards the legal treatment of the ship itself, in the civil law jurisdictions notable resemblance can be seen, as compared to the Anglo-common law jurisdictions, in which substantial discrepancies can be identified.[41]

3.9. Finally, the ship is subject to a plethora of regulations regarding its design, construction, maintenance, inspection and dismantling, attributed to its special nature, and which are rigorously implemented by the flag state, the port states and the classification societies (RO's).[42]

3.3 The significance of the legal treatment of the ship in relation to proprietary rights from a private international law perspective

3.10. The legal definition of the ship varies from country to country and this has repercussions on the private international treatment of proprietary rights recognised on a foreign ship. Thus, if the validity of the transfer of ownership of a foreign construction equipped with flotation arises in a national court, the judge, before applying the appropriate conflict rule, must decide whether the construction constitutes a ship, a determination to be made according to national law, albeit in a wider perspective.

---

36 See s. 26 Civil Jurisdiction and Judgments Act 1982. *Kallang Shipping SA Panama v AXA Assurances Senegal (The Kallang) (No 2)* [2009] Lloyd's Rep 124.

37 A Trichardt, Arrest as Security and Security Arrest, Chpt 3 in P Myburgh (ed), *The Arrest Conventions: International Enforcement of Maritime Claims* (2019).

38 See Civil Procedure Rules (CPR), Rule 61.10.

39 *The Myrto* [1977] 2 Lloyd's Rep 243, 260–261. D R Thomas, 'Admiralty sales pendente lite', [1998] CJQ 409.

40 *Qatar National Bank v The Owner of the Yacht Force India (The Force India)* [2020] 2 Lloyd's Rep 348 (QB, Adm. Ct: Teare J) on exceptional grounds.

41 See the analysis in the ship arrest context in Berlingieri, supra (n 17) paras I-408 to I-416.

42 G Rasmussen, *Maritime Governance and Control* (2016) 47 ff.

In supranational instruments the notion of the ship is often provided,[43] with the result that the activation of the application scope of the international substantive rule is uninfluenced from resembling national legal concepts. In the absence of definition,[44] however, the national notion may be invoked,[45] a solution that frequently exacerbates the problem of non-uniform application of international law.

3.11. In any case, the application of foreign law by virtue of the appropriate conflict rule presupposes a determination that the floating construction falls under the concept of ship according to the law of the forum (*lex fori*). To draw an example from Greek law; in the absence of a supranational notion and, in case, it is not encompassed by the relevant concept of Article 1 Greek KIND, the judge would treat the construction as a simple movable object, which would result in the application of the appropriate conflict rule.[46]

3.12. It may also be the case that the issue at hand is subject to a different legal characterisation.[47] Thus, if the transfer of title in the ship is perceived by the adjudicating court as a transfer of shares – shares in the ship – then the validity of the transaction would be determined exclusively by the law prescribed from the conflict rule, which regulates the promissory transaction, that is, *lex causae.*[48]

3.4 The private international law approach pertaining to security rights on the vessel

3.4.1 National level

3.13. The need for effective protection of maritime creditors due to the high risks involved in a maritime expedition led to the formulation of special tools, which would equip specific claims with a "security interest"[49] on the ship. Many countries devised

---

[43] E.g. Art 1 of Brussels 'International Convention on Civil Liability for Oil Pollution Damage' 1969, as amended and superseded by the London Protocol of 1992.

[44] The Arrest Convention 1952 does not provide a definition for the ship but the activation of the application scope necessitates one, which, inevitably, will be formulated according to domestic criteria, such as flotation, tonnage, purpose of activity, etc., see F Berlingieri, *Arrest of Ships*, 6th edn., vol 1 (2016) para 3.03 to 3.19. On the other hand, the *Supreme Court Act 1981*, which encapsulates rules derived from the Arrest Convention 1952, provides a definition but the debtor's ownership in the arrested ship has to qualify as beneficial and not as legal, see *The Nazym Khikmet* [1996] 2 Lloyd's Rep 362. This approach in conjunction with the application of *lex fori* for the determination of the notion of ownership does not promote uniformity but leads to "*forum shopping*", see P Myburgh, Conflict of Laws and the Arrest Convention, in *The Arrest Conventions: International Enforcement of Maritime Claims* (2019) 151, 162–163.

[45] See s. 313 Merchant Shipping Act 1995; similarly, see Arts 1–2 of the 8th Book of Dutch Civil Code.

[46] See Art 27 Greek CC; similarly in German law, see s. 929 ff. German BGB and 45 Einführungsgesetz zum Bürgerlichen Gesetzbuche (EGBGB).

[47] Regarding legal characterisation in general, see E Rabel, La problème de la qualification (1933) 28 *Revue de Droit International Privé* 1; AH Robertson, *Characterization on the Conflict of Laws* (1940); M Bogdan, Private International Law as Component of the Law of the Forum (2010) 348 *Recueil des Cours* 9.

[48] *Vostok Shipping Co Ltd v Confederation Ltd* [2000] NZLR 37. Critically to this approach, *Tisand Ltd v Owners of the Ship M/V Cape Moreton (ex 'Freya')* [2005] FCAFC 68, 80

> It would be similarly anomalous if the law of the country of domicile of the buyer or seller dealing with the registration of ships (if that were not the flag state's law) were treated as relevant to the ascertainment of rights passing or created in a transaction by way of assignment.

[49] Jackson, supra (n 31) Chpt 23; W Tetley, *International Encyclopedia of Comparative Law, Vol. XII, Law of Transport* (Loose-leaf Publication), Chpt 4, 4–307 ff.; G Theocharidis, 'The Relationship Between

legislative mechanisms to support the so-called *crédit maritime*.[50] The latter comprises special institutions, which, on one hand, underpin contractual interests, on the other, promote national policy values. As a result, there is disparity in the approach between countries,[51] although two institutions[52] prevail in all jurisdictions, namely the ship mortgage and the maritime lien,[53] on the impact of which the analysis endeavours to shed more light.

3.14. Two interacting parameters make the private international law approach to security rights on a vessel a vexing problem. Apart from the disagreement in the legal notion of the ship in many jurisdictions, as shown earlier, the legal treatment of the vessel as immovable, despite the fact that it is mobile by nature and should be subjected to different domestic regimes due to its motion, is one parameter, while the second is that any connecting factor, that could be deployed to crystallise the applicable law in a security right/interest on a ship, is inarguably "volatile". In particular, while immovable property is inextricably linked to a certain jurisdiction due to its territorial relationship,[54] the ship crosses the territorial waters of several states and, therefore, permanence and fixity are overridden. Even an attempt to link[55] the vessel to the *situm libri* which prescribes the conditions of nationality,[56] albeit with supranational conflict rules,[57] that can in no way override the right of other receiving states to treat the ship legally in a different manner. Further, even if it were accepted that there was consensus

"Forum Shopping" and Flag in the Satisfaction of Security Rights on a Vessel' [2013] END 388 ff. and footnote 5 (in Greek).

50 K Sourlos, *Security Rights in Maritime Law* (1939) 13 (in Greek). For the principles that govern *crédit maritime*, see L Georgakopoulos, *Maritime Law* (2006) 430–431 (in Greek).

51 In Greek law, after the introduction of the new Code of Private Maritime Law, *crédit maritime* is served by the following security interests: a) three types of ship mortgage, that is simple, preferred and of Art 13 Law Decree 2687/1953, and b) maritime liens. Before the introduction of the new Code, the fiduciary transfer of ship ownership, that is, transfer of ownership to secure a credit claim, was another available option but it was repealed because it became obsolescent. Another interesting institution is the *in rem scriptam* liability of the owner exclusively with the *res* towards a maritime creditor, who has a claim created from the operation of the vessel by the ship operator, see Rokas and Theocharidis, supra (n 2) para 140. Other tools with contractual nature serve the same purpose, such as the liability from the "acquisition" of a ship to the detriment of other creditors' interests, which is subject to abrogation by virtue of Art 939 ff. Greek CC (*actio pauliana*). In English law, the basic tools that serve the protection of security interests are: (i) common law mortgage; (ii) equitable mortgage; (iii) lease agreement in the form of demise charter or hire purchase arrangement; (iv) equitable charge; and (v) maritime liens, see Osborne, Bowtle and Buss, supra (n 22) 41 ff.

52 From a comparative perspective, see H Würdinger and P Sotiropoulos, *Schiffsgläubigerrechte und Schiffshypothek, eine rechtspolitische Untersuchung* (1961) (in German).

53 On the origin of the institution, see the treatise of W Tetley, *Maritime Liens and Claims*, 2nd edn. Chpt 1 (1998) 7 ff. There is no definition, not even in international conventions, and, as it has been aptly enunciated by in *The Father Thames* [1979] 2 Lloyd's Rep 364, 368 "[It is] . . . more easily recognized than defined".

54 As it has been emphatically pronounced, the *lex situs* for proprietary rights in immovable property constitutes a "sacred" conflict rule with "totemic" force, see A Ehrenzweig, Specific Principles of Private Transnational Law (1968) 124 *Recuil des Cours* 167, 270–271.

55 F Berlingieri, 'The 1952 Arrest Convention Revisited' [2005] LMCLQ 327, 334.

56 See Art 92 International Convention on the Law of the Sea, 1980 (UNCLOS).

57 See Art 2 Geneva 'International Convention on Maritime Privileges and Mortgages' 1993 on the applicable law in ship mortgages (hereinafter "Geneva International Convention 1993"). As it will be shown, despite ratification by a sufficient number of countries for its entry into force, the big maritime nations did not ratify it.

on the application of the law of the place of registration (*lex registrationis*),[58] the ship may justly and validly change registry (*flag hopping*), even without transfer of ownership. Therefore, the ship's flag[59] is a variable connecting factor (*conflit mobile*)[60] for the determination of the governing law in security rights on the ship.[61] Equally, the law of the place, where the ship is berthing (*lex rei sitae/lex loci*), or that of the court seized (*lex fori*), is subject to variation.

3.15. Furthermore, in view of the fact that security rights/interests on the vessel promote the domestic policy of a country, the law of which has a claim to be the governing law, it is evident that there is a genuine conflict. Nonetheless, in the absence of uniform law, it is far from clear that the values[62] of domestic law should be protected at the expense of the superior values[63] of private international law.[64]

3.16. As regards the ship mortgage, but for few exceptional grounds,[65] the various national laws are willing to acknowledge, first, the validity of the security right, and second, the powers it bestows to the holder, according to the law of the place of registration of the ship.[66] Consequently, the application of this law governs both creation and operation of the security right as well as the ranking order between rival claims. Thus, *lex navis* is prevalent for the vast majority of the countries and no point of friction is encountered.

3.17. This is not the case, as regards the maritime lien. The first problem arises from the legal characterisation of the right, which triggers the appropriate conflict rule. This determination, as previously stated, is performed according to the conceptual "arsenal" of the adjudicating court,[67] subsequent to the crystallisation of the attributes

[58] The law of the place of registration (*lex registrationis*) will coincide with that of the flag (*lex navis*), unless the vessel is registered in a registry, which accommodates bareboat charter agreements, in which case the law of that register (*lex libri sitae*) may prevail.

[59] S Bækhus, Choice of Law Problems in International Shipping (1979) 164 *Receuil des Cours* 251, 282 ff.

[60] Legal doctrine for a long time has asserted that flag change essentially means shifting the nexus of the vessel from one legal order to another, see G von Streit and P Vallindas, *Private International Law*, vol II (1937) 163 (in Greek).

[61] K Zweigert and U Drobnig, *Das Statut der Schiffsglaübigerrechte, VersR* (1971) 581, 587 (in German).

[62] E.g. the values upon which *crédit maritime* is founded.

[63] E.g. values upon which the closest link principle is founded.

[64] On this issue, see S Vrellis, *Methodological Problems on the Revision of Greek Private International Law, Nomiko Vima* (1989) 33, 38–39 (in Greek).

[65] Such grounds that could infringe public order would be, if the foreign legal regime would require no recording of the mortgage in a public book (in English law, see *The Shizelle* [1992] 2 Lloyd's Rep 444) or if the mortgage would take the form of a criminal measure or in case the ownership in the ship would be automatically transferred to the mortgagee on default of payment by the mortgagor and without any other prerequisite.

[66] *Iraqi Ministry of Defence v Arcepey Shipping Co SA (The Angel Bell)* [1979] 2 Lloyd's Rep 491, 495–496; S Carbone, Conflits de Lois en Droit Maritime (2009) 340 *Receuil des Cours* 63, 253.

[67] There is an antinomy in this. How can a judge delve into foreign law for the ascertainment of the substantive elements of the right under review, if it is not classified first, so that he is referred to the appropriate conflict rule? It is for this reason, that legal characterisation is performed with domestic institutions according to *lex fori*, a solution not free of flaws. The most significant is the "frivolous" exercise of categorisation of the foreign right by classifying it and treating it according to a resembling domestic right, which may, however, have a completely different nature and function. As regards the risks in using domestic notions in private international law, see K Zweigert and H Kötz, *An Introduction to Comparative Law*, 2nd edn. (1987) 31.

of the security right.[68] The majority of jurisdictions hold the position that the maritime lien[69] is created *ex lege* and it is a *jus in re*[70] with ancillary nature; it is inchoate,[71] "invisible",[72] indelible[73] and equipped with ranking force. In light of the aforementioned distinct characteristics, one would expect that the proprietary nature[74] of the right would be an incontestable assumption, as it is truly a security right/interest on the *res*. Consequently, the maritime lien should fall in the ambit of a commonly accepted conflict rule[75] for the determination of the applicable law. However, the reality is completely different.

3.18. Before examining the crux of the problem, it must be stated that the point of friction seems to lie in the relationship between the maritime lien and its antagonist, the ship mortgage. More specifically, as long as the secured claim can be satisfied without resorting to legal proceedings, it does not evince its privileged status, as the right is "dormant". Conversely, its force develops in its entirety, when it clashes with other security rights, in particular the ship mortgage, during enforcement proceedings, where ranking is required. That happens in the final stage of claim satisfaction and the more claims are secured with a maritime lien, ranking ahead of ship mortgage, the less the remainder from the sale proceeds for the satisfaction of the ship financier. It is at this point, that the judge becomes the catalyst in the protection of domestic policy values[76] by forging the catalogue of preferential claims of national law and by crystallising their ranking order[77] with *forum* tools. The paradigm of such tactics can be seen in English law,

---

[68] See the *ratio decidendi* of *"Sam Hawk" v Reiter Petroleum Inc* [2016] FCAFC 26 [104–105]

> Secondly, for the purposes of s 15 the identified foreign right must then be characterised by reference to Australian law to determine whether it is, or is sufficiently analogous to, a maritime lien recognised by Australian law. . . . It does not deny the recognition of a foreign law right. It merely requires that characterisation of the foreign right proceed by reference to Australian law. This is particularly important where, as we explain below, the essential function of attaching the label "maritime lien" to a foreign right (whether or not *in rem*) arising from the provision of necessaries is to afford additional priority to the right, a matter which has always been regarded as the province of the *lex fori*.

[69] *The Tolten* [1946] 1 Lloyd's Rep. 349; Schaps and Abraham, supra (n 17) Vor s. 754, paras 6–7. Rokas and Theocharidis, supra (n 2) paras 177–182.

[70] *The Ripon City [1897] pp. 226, 242 "jus in re".*

[71] *The Bold Buccleugh* [1851] Moore PC 267.

[72] It is perfected without registration.

[73] It is opposable even against a *bona fide* purchaser.

[74] R Marsden, 'Two Points of Admiralty Law' [1886] 2 LQR 357; PM Herbert, 'The origin and nature of maritime liens' [1929–1930] Tul LR 381.

[75] It is submitted that the conflict rule could not be drawn from Regulations (EU) 593/2008 (Rome I) and 864/2007 (Rome II), because the maritime lien is created *ex lege* and independently from the debt which secures, so their application would be incorrect. In English law, post-Brexit the matter will be regulated exclusively by *lex fori*.

[76] See *"Sam Hawk" v Reiter Petroleum Inc* [2016] FCAFC 26, [105]

> The priority that is afforded the maritime lien in Australian law is an expression of the circumstances (see s 15 (2)) in which a maritime lien arises by operation of Australian law and a product of the policy considerations that lead Australian law to safeguard the interests of the people the lien protects in those circumstances.

See M Davies, 'Choice of Law and US Maritime Liens', 83 Tul LR (2009) 1435 ff

[77] English courts have power to redetermine the order of priority of privileged claims pursuant to policy considerations, see *The Ruta* [2000] Lloyd's Rep 359, 364 "It is clear even from the restricted citation of authority set out above that questions of priority are not capable of being compartmentalized in the form of strict rules of ranking". *The Pickaninny* [1960] Lloyd's Rep 533. In legal doctrine, see R Thomas, *Maritime Liens* (1980) 418,

where the Privy Council in *The Halcyon Isle*[78] – despite the weak three to two majority – held that the maritime lien is a procedural remedy founded on the action *in rem,*[79] with the immediate consequence that the applicable law is governed predominantly by *lex fori,*[80] that is, always English law and the closed catalogue of maritime liens that it encompasses.[81] A thorough critique[82] of the majority's argument would exceed the scope of the present study, however, it is worth noting that the "obsession" to apply national law (*lex forism*) in the realm of maritime disputes, which invariably involve foreign elements, has aptly been described as particularly undesirable.[83]

3.19. The previously described "nationalistic" approach has not left unaffected the case law of other jurisdictions, although with variations.[84] Among them the Greek courts, which on the basis of a remarkable interpretative approach had accepted that the status and the scope of the maritime lien should be governed by the law of the flag (*lex navis*),[85] as prescribed by the conflict rule of Article 9 Greek KIND, but the ranking power should be determined by Greek procedural law (*lex fori*).[86] The main argument was

> the Admiralty and Appellate Courts have adopted a broad discretionary approach with rival claims ranked by reference to considerations of equity, public policy and commercial expediency, with the ultimate aim of doing that which is just in the circumstance of each case.

78 *Bankers Trust International Ltd v Todd Shipyards Corporation (The Halcyon Isle)* [1981] AC 221 (PC).

79 The remedy is catered for the claims listed in s. 20(2)(a–s) Senior Courts Act 1981, some of which are equipped with maritime lien, see Lord Collins of Mapesbury and Harris, supra (n 14) Chpt 13, Rule 40, 13–009 ff. Statutory rights of action *in rem* trigger proceedings between the plaintiff and the *res*, forcing the owner of the object to submit to the jurisdiction of the court, in which case parallel proceedings are activated, one concerning the action *in rem* and the other *in personam* (*The Anna H* [1995] 2 Lloyd's Rep 11, 18–19), which do not "merge" (*The Nordglimt* [1988] Q.B. 183)). If the defendant decides not to appear before the court, the judgment will be issued against the vessel, in which case the shipowner will not be personally liable (*The City of Mecca* [1881] 5 P.D. 106, 112). The action *in rem* seems to derive its origin from the *actio hypothecarea* of Roman law, as they share many common features, see O-W Holmes, *Common Law* (1881) 26.

80 By virtue of the principle *forum regit processum,* which prevails.

81 According to the *ratio decidendi*, in order for a foreign maritime lien to be recognised, the judge would examine, if, assuming the events that gave rise to the right took place in the English legal order, they would give rise to one of the maritime liens of domestic law. Recognition, therefore, is limited to those comprising the catalogue of English law.

82 *"Sam Hawk" v Reiter Petroleum Inc*. [2016] FCAFC 26. After expounding the English authorities since 1613, the minority judge argued that the Admiralty Court, which was vested with jurisdiction to settle maritime disputes outside the British territory, developed the *bottomry* as a form of security on the foundation of the Roman institution of *ship hypothecation*. Against that backdrop the court recognised maritime liens created by foreign law and accorded full priority to the claim of the creditor who provided the credit to the ship. Remarkably, at that time the ship mortgage had not yet been crystallised, while the *ship hypothecation* was concluded by the master of the ship without the shipowner's previous consent. The judge concluded that the leading speech of the majority in *The Halcyon Isle* had essentially "distorted" the content of the previous authorities with the aim of proving that the maritime lien was procedural in its nature.

83 Myburgh, supra (n 44) 151.

84 The Federal Court of Australia in *"Sam Hawk" v Reiter Petroleum Inc* [2016] FCAFC 26 deviated from the leading authority and accepted the application of *lex navis* for the recognition of a foreign maritime lien and *lex fori* for the ranking order with the following reasoning:

> "It does not deny the recognition of a foreign law right. . . . For the reasons elegantly explained . . . we agree that the status of a maritime lien in the priority system for maritime creditors is an integral feature of a maritime lien in Australian law. . . . We agree, for the reasons stated by their Honours, that the concept or description of a maritime lien in Australian law ought not be separated from the priority consequences of the lien and the circumstances in which the lien arises by operation of law.
> [104–105]

85 *Areios Pagos 284/1989* Efimeris Ellinon Nomikon 1990, 68 (in Greek). *Areios Pagos 295/2002* Epitheorisi Naftiliakou Dikaiou 30, 117 (in Greek).

86 Courts base their reasoning on Art 1012 s. 3 Greek CCP, which states: "The ranking order of creditors in the ranking list is determined primarily according to the provisions of the Code of Private Maritime Law".

that the ranking of creditors in a judicial sale of a foreign ship conducted in the Greek jurisdiction falls within the scope of procedural law and public order, therefore invocation of *lex fori* is appropriate. With the aforementioned interpretation, as a result, only the foreign maritime liens that corresponded to those of Greek law[87] were recognised and afforded priority, while the rest of the maritime lienors ranked *pari passu* after the ship mortgagees and before unsecured creditors.[88] Unsurprisingly, the new Article 47 Greek KIND[89] regulated the issue in alignment with the *ratio decidendi* of the courts.

3.20. In other jurisdictions,[90] as well as in international theory,[91] various arguments have occasionally been advanced[92] for the ascertainment of the governing law in a foreign maritime lien on the basis of a conflict rule that refers to the *lex causae* of the claim, the *lex navis* and *lex libri sitae* of the ship, the *lex situs* of the ship, the *lex domicilis* of the shipowner and the *lex fori,*[93] a position which clearly demonstrates the lack of uniformity in the field.

3.4.2 Supranational/transnational level

3.21. Attempts to address the problem of crystallisation of a widely accepted conflict rule pertaining to security rights on the ship were pursued at supranational levels as well.[94] Those transnational efforts, however, as will be shown, only indirectly tackled the problem. The first attempt was made by the framers of the Brussels "International Convention for the Unification of certain Rules of Law relating To Maritime Liens and Mortgages" of 1926,[95] which entered into force on 2 June 1931. Among the provisions worth mentioning are the following:

(i) recognition of ship mortgage by the law of the flag, subject to registration in a public register;[96]
(ii) acceptance of a closed catalogue of maritime liens[97] with partial reference to national substantive law;[98]

[87] *Areios Pagos 710/1992* Efimeris Ellinon Nomikon 1993, 540 (in Greek).

[88] *Piraeus Court of Appeal 1050/2001* Epitheorisi Naftiliakou Dikaiou 30, 26 (in Greek).

[89] The provision reads: "1. Maritime liens, ship mortgages and other proprietary rights on ship are governed by art. 16; 2. For the ranking of the preferred claims, *lex fori* is applicable".

[90] W Tetley, *Maritime Liens in the Conflict of Laws, Essays in Honour of Arthur von Mehren* (2002) 439 ff.; A Antapasis, *The Applicable Law in Maritime Liens* (1989) (in Greek).

[91] Schaps and Abraham, supra (n 17) Vor s. 754, paras 25–32 (in German). G Theocharidis, Issues relating to the election of applicable law in maritime liens, Epitheorisi Naftiliakou Dikaiou 31, 1 (in Greek).

[92] Even if *lex navis* would govern all security rights on the ship, the flag change, which entails change in the applicable law, would cause uncertainty in the protection of privileged creditors, so, to a certain extent, the *lex fori* assumes a "quasi-neutral" role, see K Kerameus, *Legal Opinion, Epitheorisi Naftiliakou Dikaiou* (2002) 1, 4 (in Greek).

[93] *Tisand Ltd v Owners of the Ship M/V Cape Moreton (ex 'Freya')* [2005] FCAFC 68, 80.

[94] See F Berlingieri and A Philip, *Essays on Maritime Liens and Mortgages and on Arrest of Ships, CMI* (1984) 15 ff., 51 ff. and 98 ff. Also, Tetley, supra (n 49) 4–334 ff.

[95] Hereinafter "Brussels International Convention 1926".

[96] See Art 1 Brussels International Convention 1926.

[97] See Art 2 Brussels International Convention 1926, listing claims for law costs, claims arising from employment contracts of the master and crew, remuneration for assistance and salvage, general average contributions of the vessel, compensation for collision or other accidents of navigation, indemnities for personal injury to passengers or crew, indemnities for loss of or damage to cargo or baggage and claims resulting from necessary acts and contracts made by the master of the ship, which were necessary for the preservation of the vessel or the continuation of its voyage.

[98] The relevant provision purported to deactivate the national conflict rules for the determination of the applicable law in maritime liens, while any domestic maritime liens, which were not included in Art 2 of the

(iii) determination of ranking order among the maritime liens;[99]
(iv) power of preference[100] of maritime liens over ship mortgages in case of judicial sale as well as indelibility (*droit de suite*)[101] in case of contractual sale of the vessel.

Not unsurprisingly, there was no explicit provision in respect of mutual recognition of judicial sales between Contracting States, leaving room for application of their respective *lex fori* mechanism.[102]

3.22. The second attempt culminated in the compilation of the framework of the Brussels "International Convention for the Unification of Certain Rules relating to Maritime Liens and Mortgages" of 1967,[103] which never entered into force. The regime introduced:

(i) validity of the ship mortgage and priority among several mortgages according to *lex navis* on the condition that the charges were registered in a public book;[104]
(ii) execution of the maritime mortgage in accordance with the respective *lex loci executionis*;[105]
(iii) exhaustive catalogue of maritime liens[106] with the option of expansion only for shipyard repair claims;[107]
(iv) ranking order of the maritime liens *inter se* and supremacy of the latter over ship mortgages.[108]

3.23. The principal contribution of this supranational regime, however, concerned the moot point of recognition of foreign judicial ship sales. In particular, if the judicial sale was completed in a contracting state with physical presence of the ship,[109] then all encumbrances[110] would be extinguished on the condition that the process was conducted in accordance with the *lex loci executionis* requirements[111] and with the supplemental duty to notify at least 30 days prior to the judicial sale the ship mortgagees, any existing maritime lienors, who were in any way announced in the forced sale proceedings, and the ship registrar, in respect of the location and time of the judicial sale.[112] On the condition that the afpre, emtopmed were complied with, the successful purchaser maintained a claim against the competent authority, which conducted the judicial sale, to issue a certificate of deletion of all mortgages and

Convention, would enjoy recognition, but in a ranking position below the ship mortgage.

99 See Arts 5–6 Brussels International Convention 1926.
100 See Art 3 of the Brussels International Convention 1926.
101 See Art 8 Brussels International Convention 1926.
102 See Art 16 Brussels International Convention 1926.
103 Hereinafter "Brussels International Convention 1967".
104 See Art 1 Brussels International Convention 1967.
105 See Art 2 Brussels International Convention 1967.
106 See Art 4 Brussels International Convention 1967.
107 See Art 6(2) Brussels International Convention 1967.
108 See Art 5 Brussels International Convention 1967.
109 See Art 11(1)(a) Brussels International Convention 1967.
110 Namely, ship mortgages and maritime liens.
111 See Art 11(1) Brussels International Convention 1967.
112 See Art 10 of Brussels International Convention 1967.

maritime liens on the ship, which could also be used for the de-registration of the vessel from the current registry and the re-registration in another.[113]

3.24. The final attempt to regulate the subject led to the Geneva "International Convention on Maritime Privileges and Mortgages" 1993, which came into effect on 5 September 2004. The provisions essentially reflected those of the Brussels Convention, 1967 with some changes, such as the removal of certain privileged claims from the list,[114] the imposition of formalities in the notice for execution of the judicial sale and the expansion of the list of recipients of the notice.[115]

3.25. None of the aforementioned supranational frameworks met the approval of the shipping community, while many reasons could be identified that led to that failure. It is noteworthy that in none of the attempts was consensus on the crystallisation of a conflict rule that would regulate the recognition and treatment of maritime liens. Instead, the crux of the problem was circumvented by two byways. The first, by prescribing a narrow and exhaustive list of maritime liens, a choice that obviously did not resolve the conflicting interests of the major shipping powers. The second, by "legitimising" the outcome of the judicial sale conducted under certain conditions with deletion of all charges from the existing registry and de-registration and registration of the vessel in a new registry, a choice that also did not reflect the expectations of the market.

3.5 The satisfaction of maritime creditors in the context of enforcement proceedings and the contribution of the Convention to the solution of existing problems

3.26. In light of the aforementioned analysis, two questions arise. What is the rationale[116] in assuming a new initiative for the creation of a new supranational regime? How is the Convention different from the previous endeavours at the international level?

3.27. Before commenting on the proposed provisions of the Convention, it is essential to explain the mechanism of a ship judicial sale and, in particular, against a ship flying a flag other than the state's, before which the enforcement proceedings are entertained.

3.28 The exercise of maritime activity by a ship-owning company gives rise to claims, which, on becoming due but not satisfied for reasons of impecuniosity or lack of liquidity, they will invariably be pursued by legal means. Occasionally, resort may be had to enforcement proceedings (*processus executivus*), frequently outside the country of origin of the judgment on the merits,[117] with the activation of a domestic execution mechanism against the debtor's asset. As the most apparent asset of a ship-owning company will be the ship, many countries have forged special legislative regimes[118]

---

[113] See Art 11(3) Brussels International Convention 1967.

[114] See Art 4 Geneva International Convention 1993.

[115] See Art 11 Geneva International Convention 1993.

[116] See paras 10–13 of the Explanatory Note (hereinafter "Explanatory Note") prepared by the Secretariat of UNCITRAL for information purposes after the 55th session in New York.

[117] Regarding the methods of enforcement, see K Kerameus, Enforcement in International Context (1997) 264 *Recueil des Cours* 179, 215 ff.

[118] E.g. Art 277 Greek KIND and its predecessor Art 214 KIND, which introduced the system of multiple arrests (Rokas, supra (n 10) s. 38 III 2), before its introduction into general procedural law by Art 997 s. 5

to assist maritime creditors in the quest for claim satisfaction against the *res mobilis*. However, this panspermia of national rules in conjunction with the lack of uniform international law for the resolution of the clash between rival claims at the final stage of enforcement, especially those with a privileged character, unavoidably instigate tactics in the behaviour of litigants. More specifically, the "eternal" movement of the vessel requires vigilance on the side of the creditor as well as thorough knowledge of the legal "arsenal" of the various jurisdictions, which are located at the preferred trading routes of ships, in order to achieve the optimum result in the satisfaction of its claim. The phenomenon is called *forum shopping* and afflicts severely this area of disputes.[119]

3.29. To make things more complicated, there is another problem in interaction with the above. Although it is common ground in many jurisdictions for the *lex executionis* to prescribe a "cleansing" effect for the vessel[120] after the execution of a judicial sale,[121] this outcome is imperilled by the actions of creditors on the basis of two action paths. First, albeit the judicial sale should constitute valid *causa* for the enrichment of the announced creditors from the sale proceeds, so as to prevent redetermination of priority and redistribution of the sale proceeds by another court, in some jurisdictions unjust enrichment provisions are available,[122] "enticing"[123] unsatisfied creditors to disturb the priority crystallised by the *lex executionis*. The problem arises in its most acute form, when such provisions are invokable at the place of registration, in which case the purchaser's attempt to record the awarding title in the register could be imperilled from counter measures by the unsatisfied creditors. The second path could be characterised as "trench warfare". It is a form of "harassment" against the vessel, post-forced sale, with the aid of "immobilisation" remedies by virtue of a court order, so that the purchaser would surrender by paying the unsatisfied creditor. Obviously, both action paths are sub-categories of *forum shopping*.

Greek CCP; also Art 2 Law Decree 2927/1954. Similarly, the *in rem scriptam* action introduced by Art 63 Greek KIND, see *Court of Appeal of Piraeus 746/2003* Epitheorisi Naftiliakou Dikaiou 31, 365. Antapasis and Athanasiou, supra (n 11) para 803 ff.; Rokas and Theocharidis, supra (n 2) para 203 ff.

[119] F Jünger, *Choice of Law and Multistate Justice* (1993). For a more detailed analysis in the field of security rights, see G Theocharidis, Relationship Between *Forum Shopping* and Flag in Satisfaction of Security Rights on a Ship [2013] *Epitheorisi Naftiliakou Dikaiou* 388 ff. (in Greek).

[120] The proceeds of sale represent the auctioned ship, which is released from all charges, see *The Acrux* [1962] Lloyd's Rep 405, 46 USC §31326, Art 37(D) Maltese Marchant Shipping Act.

[121] G Mavros, *Maritime Liens in International Maritime Law* (1937) 115–116 (in Greek).

[122] This was the position in German law before the latest revision of the rules of private international law with Gesetz zum Internationalen Privatrecht für außervertragliche Schuldverhältnisse und für Sachen vom 21 May 1999.

[123] English courts express disapproval for creditors announced at the auction and then, because they failed to satisfy their claim, attempt to set aside the outcome of the proceedings in other jursidictions (*The Acrux*) [1962] Lloyd's Rep 405, 409

> It would be intolerable, inequitable and an affront to the Court if any party who invoked the process of this Court and received its aid and, by implication, assented to the sale to an innocent purchaser, should thereafter proceed or was able to proceed elsewhere against the ship under her new and innocent ownership. Court recognizes proper sales by competent Courts of Admiralty, or Prize, abroad-it is part of the comity of nations as well as a contribution to the general well-being of international maritime trade, making at the same time an insinuation of discontent about foreign courts that tolerate such practices.

3.30. Based on the previous analysis of the private international approach of security rights on a vessel and the issues described, can the new supranational legislative endeavour tackle effectively those complicated problems?

The first step is to outline the main provisions of the instrument.

3.5.1 Framework

3.31. The Convention establishes a mechanism for "uniform" embedment of specific legal consequences stemming from a ship judicial sale[124] conducted in a Contracting country to the other Contracting countries.[125] The execution of the process by the prescribed mechanism[126] ensures, first, effortless registration and de-registration of the ship by the purchaser, second, unfettered enjoyment of the acquired ownership *erga omnes*.[127]

3.32. Despite the title of the instrument, it is not only the "judicial sale" that is regulated, as the process can also be conducted before a public authority[128] vested with power to sell a ship.[129] The sale can be executed by public auction[130] or by private sale. Therefore, the scope covers also a *court approved private sale,*[131] in a jurisdiction[132]

[124] In the present analysis the terms "forced sale" and "forced auction" will be ascribed to the definition of "judicial sale".

[125] Art 1 prescribes "This Convention governs the international effects of a judicial sale" The adjective "international" was added at the 55th Session. However, it does not describe precisely the range of effects introduced by the Convention, despite the comment included in the Addendum, A/CN.9/LV/CPR.1/Add.1, para 5 (hereinafter "Addendum"). As will be shown, these are national effects (e.g. the safeguards of Art 4 and the actions of Art 7, in case the domestic legislation of the ratifying country does not cater for them). That was acknowledged by the drafters in para 25 of the Explanatory Note.

[126] By virtue of Art 21 para 3 the regime governs only judicial sales of ships that have been ordered or approved after its entry into force in respect of the State of judicial sale. Further, Art 11 para 3 caters for the case, where a notice will be validly transmitted to the Repository by a country that ratified the Convention before its entry into force. For Civil law jurisdictions, which follow a different path of enforcement, it is submitted that the provision may be problematic and it would have been more appropriate to prescribe that the regime applies to judicial sales that were completed after ratification and entry into force of the regime by the country. See also the analysis in the Report of Working Group VI, 12 February 2022, A/CN.9/1095, paras 81–85 (hereinafter "Report").

[127] See the preamble of the "Beijing Draft" as approved in Hamburg in 2014 "Considering that once a ship is sold by way of a judicial sale, the ship should in principle no longer be subject to arrest for any claim arising prior to its judicial sale".

[128] See the definition in Art 2(a)(i). For example, before a notary public, as it is prescribed by Greek and Belgian law.

[129] For the mechanisms of forced/judicial sale in various jurisdictions, see CMI Yearbook (2010) 248–255.

[130] According to the Draft Explanatory Report, the public auction encompasses both the sale by auction and by tender, see Addendum, Add. 1, para 7.

[131] See Addendum, Add. 1, para 8.

[132] See Art 359 Maltese Code of Civil Procedure, see J Scerri-Diacono, 'Private, Court-Approved Sales of Vessels and Aircraft in Malta' [2012] LMCLQ 356; also Art 279 Greek KIND, which recently introduced the specific mechanism, see A Alapantas, The court approved ship sale under the new Code of Private Maritime Law and the relevant International Convention of Beijing of 5 September 2023, Volume in honour of Prof Pelagia Yessiou-Faltsi, Lex and Fori (2023) 1 (in Greek). In the Netherlands the mechanism is judicially created by extending the procedural enforcement regime applicable to immovable property in ships. Similarly, English courts have upheld this practice (*The Everilda* (1927–28) 29 1 Lloyd's Rep 238. Osborne, Bowtle and Buss, supra (n 22) 14 April 2013) although certain scepticism has been expressed, that the practice should be allowed only under special circumstances (*Bank of Scotland Plc v Owners of the MV*

where such option is offered on specific grounds.[133] In fact, from the wording of the relevant provision, it could be argued that the term encompasses also a sale in the context of a bankruptcy or other reorganisation process. Necessary conditions, in order for the process to fall within the scope of the Convention, are: (i) the compilation of a priority list of announced creditors to be satisfied from the sale proceeds,[134] (ii) the issuance of "clean title",[135] so that the ship is free and clear of any interests (i.e., mortgages, hypothèques) and other charges.[136] *E contrario*, if the issued title does not extinguish all encumbrances, the sale is not governed by the international regime. As will be shown, the *lex executionis* determines if the title is clean[137] and the local court is vested with competency for the challenge of the issuance of the certificate on that ground.[138] As a result, the title may not be reviewed by the receiving country on the grounds that it is not clean. But in case it is not clean, then the application scope could not be triggered and, therefore, any *forum*, including that of the receiving country, may determine the issue.[139]

Union Gold [2014] Lloyd's Rep 53; A Basu Bal, 'Ontological Turn in Judicial Sales of Ships' (2022) 28 JIML 434, 438–440).

133 P Myburgh, '"Satisfactory for Its Own Purposes": Private Direct Arrangements and Judicial Vessel Sales' (2016) 22 JIML 355, 366. It should not be confused with the private sale of a ship, which is executed by a mortgagee-lender with power granted by the deed of covenants (C Buss, Ship Mortgagees: Enforcement and Remedies, in B Soyer and A Tettenborn (eds) *Ship Building, Sale and Finance* (2016, Informa) 152; Rokas and Theocharidis, supra (n 2) para 168) and the purchaser acquires title *cum onere*, such type of sale not falling in the ambit of the Convention (see Explanatory Note, para 37). The essential difference is that the court-approved private direct sale is executed after arrest proceedings have been entertained and the sale is approved by the Admiralty Court, a safeguard which justifies acquisition of title by the purchaser free of charges.

134 See Art 2(a)(ii).

135 In most cases, it will be straightforward, when a title has a "cleansing" effect. Almost invariably, an obligatory right (e.g. a time charter) on a ship would be nullified after the forced process. However, there are rights with special characteristics (e.g. a demise/bareboat charter), which, in some legal systems (e.g. Germany, Spain), could be asserted even after the completion of a forced sale. Further, there are legal systems, in which a judicial sale will only extinguish pre-existing property rights in the ship that are vested in lower-ranking creditors according to applicable priority rules, i.e. it will not extinguish property rights that have priority over the right of the creditor who commenced judicial sale proceedings. Also, it may be that the ship is sold by the court but with no effect on other claims (see Rule B attachment of US law, *Belcher Co v M/V Maratha Mariner* 724 2d 1161). The drafters correctly point out that a sale that preserves pre-existing property rights does not confer "clean title" according to the meaning of the Convention (Draft Explanatory Note, para 47, p. 10). At the same time, there are jurisdictions, in which the outcome, i.e. whether there is a full "cleansing" effect, is not known before the judicial process is accomplished. It is for this reason that the regime will be triggered and notice shall comply with the requirements of Art 4 paras 3–4, including the transmission to the Repository, but if it transpires that title is not clean at the end, the international effects of those sales, if any, shall not be governed by the Convention. However, in case the country of judicial sale wrongly asserts that the title is clean and the "cleansing" effect is recorded in the certificate, how would the registrar of the receiving country rectify the anomaly?

136 See Art 2(c–g) and 5(1). "Clean title" transfers to the purchaser title in the auctioned ship free of mortgages or *hypothèques* and any other charge, whether registered or invisible. The definition "charge" encompasses the arrest, attachment, maritime lien, lien, encumbrance, right of use and right of retention of the ship. However, the thorny question, which proper law shall determine the genesis of a maritime lien at the place of execution, is not answered categorically, because the reference to the relevant applicable law (see Art 2(g)) leaves room for arbitrary results based on domestic interpretations.

137 See draft Explanatory Note, A/CN.9.1110, para 24, p. 5 (hereinafter "Draft Explanatory Note").

138 Art 9 para 1.

139 P Myburgh, 'International Recognition of Judicial Ship Sales: English Common Law and the Beijing Convention' (2022) 28 JIML 410, 419–420.

3.5.2 Scope of application

3.33. The supranational framework applies only to judicial sales conducted in Contracting countries,[140] provided the auctioned ship was physically present at the *locus executionis* at the time of the sale[141] and, in any event, at the time the ship will be awarded[142] to the highest bidder.[143] Not surprisingly, this condition is also prescribed in Article 4 Arrest Convention 1952 to ensure that the court will not order the material detention of a vessel unless it is within the territorial reach of the *forum arresti.*[144] However, in order for the certificate to produce its full effect, the receiving state of registration must also be a contracting country.[145]

3.34. The mechanism applies to "ship", without the Convention giving a technical definition of the type of floating construction that qualifies as such, provided it is not a warship or a state-owned vessel,[146] that operated as such immediately prior to the forced sale.[147] However, it must be registered[148] in a register that is open to public inspection and it should be the subject of an arrest or other similar measure, capable of leading to a judicial sale by virtue of the *lex loci executionis.*[149] Based on the above, the term must be interpreted autonomously, however, it must meet cumulatively[150] the criteria of the *lex executionis* and the *lex registrationis* for the scope to be triggered.

3.35. *Ratione materiae*, all[151] procedural issues of the enforcement process prior to its completion[152] are excluded from the international regime.[153] The Convention also excludes matters, which are incidental to the sale process, such as the "procedure for or priority in

---

[140] The wording in the scope of the Convention does not preclude application of the regime on ships flying non-Contracting countries flags. However, any attempt to de-register the latter on the basis of the judicial sale certificate would not be fruitful, as it would be required to submit the original title of the forced sale to the non-Contracting country registry.

[141] See Art 3(a-b). The remark made by the drafters is as follows,

> The physical presence requirement is not intended to prevent existing practices by which (a) proceedings for the arrest of a ship or other proceedings leading to a judicial sale can be commenced before the ship enters territorial waters, or (b) the ship is released from arrest pending its judicial sale. Draft Explanatory Note, para 85, p. 117 (may be problematic).

The imposition of forced arrest immobilises the ship, which is restrained from sailing, unless the court grants permission on exceptional grounds and on the condition that it will return until the date of the sale to the original *situs*. It is submitted that many receiving countries may consider the imposition of ship arrest before its entry within the jurisdiction of the *forum executionis* or its release before the completion of the process as a manifest contravention to public policy by virtue of Art 10.

[142] Meaning the physical delivery of the auctioned vessel.

[143] See Explanatory Note, para 87.

[144] On that issue, see H Jessen and G Theocharidis, National Translations of the Arrest Conventions: European Civil Law Jurisdictions, Chpt 10, 231, 248–251 in the volume P Myburgh (ed.), *The Arrest Conventions: International Enforcement of Maritime Claims* (2019).

[145] See Explanatory Note, para 85.

[146] Draft Explanatory Note, paras 42–44, p. 9.

[147] Draft Explanatory Note, Add.1, para 6, p. 3.

[148] A forced sale of an unregistered ship falls outside the scope of the international regime.

[149] See Art 2(b) and 3(2).

[150] Draft Explanatory Note, para 41, p. 9. See also Explanatory Note, para 44.

[151] With the exception of one, i.e. the notice of the judicial sale according to Art 4 para 2, for which see below.

[152] See Art 4 para 1 " which shall also provide procedures for challenging the judicial sale prior to its completion".

[153] They are referred to *lex executionis* by virtue of Art 4 para 1.

the distribution of proceeds of the judicial sale"[154] as well as "any personal claim against the person who owned or had proprietary rights in the ship prior to the judicial sale".[155] The former is a thorny problem, which is linked to the controversial issue of the legal characterisation of security rights on the vessel, while the latter, as already shown, is associated with the former, as non-satisfied creditors often seek to set aside the outcome of the judicial sale by pursuing the ship post-auction in the hands of the new owner.

3.36. More importantly, the crucial issue of the consequences from the avoidance of the judicial sale[156] is excluded from the application scope, which, inescapably, is governed by the *lex executionis*, but the unconditional reference of the matter to the domestic law of that country could prove extremely problematic. As a legislative choice, the total lack of safeguards could undermine the structural integrity of the Convention, as the avoidance of the judicial sale ensues the consequence of elimination of the foundation, that is the certificate, by virtue of which the purchaser enjoys protection of his interests in the ship.

3.5.3 Main provisions

3.37. The framers[157] of the Convention seek to extend[158] specific consequences[159] deriving from the judicial sale – more precisely "effects" – which are founded on the clean title and have occurred in the country of origin to the receiving Contracting countries. However, does *lex executionis* have exclusive[160] competency to confer clean

---

[154] See explicit reference in Art 15 para 1(a).

[155] See Art 15 para 1(b).

[156] See Art 15 para 2.

[157] Circumvention of the mandatory path of recognition of the forced sale judgment in the receiving countries seems to be an intentional choice by the drafters. Equivalent force is conferred to the certificate of judicial sale, transforming it into an "enforceable" title with the aim to attain two goals; first, entry of specific information in the ship register, second, protection of the ship from creditors of the previous registered owner.

[158] Regarding that issue in general, see Tetley, supra (n 53) Chpt 29.

[159] The most significant consequence is the elimination of existing charges, especially those having the nature of a maritime lien, albeit this is already confirmed by English (*The Cerro Colorado* [1993] Lloyd's Rep. 58, 60–61), American (*The Trenton* 4 F. 657, 661), Canadian (*Krochenksi v Galaxias* [1989] 1 F.C. 375), German (*BGH*, NJW 1961, 1672) and French law (*Tribunal de Commerce de Rouen,* 4, 6, 11 June 1969, DMF 1970, 90). However, when a vessel was sold by an Egyptian court in insolvency proceedings, the English court refused to recognise the extinguishment of a maritime lien for salvage, insisting that such effect could only be accommodated by an *in rem* court sale, see *The Goulandris* [1927] 182, 189,

> but it was not a sale by the Court in the sense that it was a sale on a judgment in rem, which would be a sale of the thing as it stood, and not merely a sale of such interests as the parties to whom it belonged had in it. I cannot think there is any doubt about that. It was a sale such as any other trustee in bankruptcy would make – namely, a sale of the interest of the debtor, such as it was. In other words, it was a sale *cum onere*.

[160] *Cammell v Sewell* 5 Hurl & N 728 (1860) 744–745. The position promoted by English courts does not enjoy wider acceptance, see *The Tremont* (1841) 1 W Rob 163

> The jurisdiction of the Court in these matters is confirmed by the municipal law of this country and by the general principles of the maritime law; and the title conferred by the Court in the exercise of this authority is a valid title against the whole world, and is recognised by the Courts of this country and by the Courts of all other countries;

see also the reasoning in *The Phoenix* [2014] Lloyd's Rep 449. Cf. the position under German law, C Hermanussen, *Anerkennung von ausländischen Zuschlagsbeschlüssen, RdTW* (2016) 407 ff. (in German).

title in a foreign ship[161] or does *lex registrationis* also share competency[162]? While the ship is physically present in the territorial waters of the country, where the forced sale is conducted,[163] it is subject to the jurisdiction of the local court. However, the transfer of the auctioned right, as well as the "cleansing" of the ship, especially the extinguishment of the registered charges, is subject[164] also to the power of the country of registration[165] – or bareboat registration[166] – because, as was shown, the ship is treated as immovable property. The significance of this distinction is manifested at the moment the purchaser seeks to register/deregister the purchased ship.[167] If updates are conditional on an act of entry according *to lex registrationis,*[168] then it could be argued that the title is not[169] clean. By a different interpretation, one could argue that, if the title is clean in accordance with *lex executionis*, then the country of registration should be obliged to lift any obstacles in the registration/deregistration if it has chosen to ratify the international regime and become a Contracting country. In any event,

---

[161] In English law, see *Dornoch Ltd v Westminster International BV (The WD Fairway)* [2009] 2 Lloyd's Rep 191, 220

> In relation to ships, the choice between the law of the place of registry and the "actual" situs may often be academic. In circumstances where there is likely to be dispute between those with competing interests, ships will often be transferred by judicial sale in proceedings in rem. There is the high authority of the House of Lords in *Castrique v Imrie* (1870) LR 4 HL 414 for the proposition that such a judgment will be recognized in this court. In such a case the law of the place of registry has no part to play. If the ship was so situated as to be within the lawful control of the state under the authority of which the relevant court sits, and if the sovereign authority of the state has conferred on that court jurisdiction to proceed in rem rather than simply inter partes, then the adjudication is regarded by this court as conclusive against all the world, irrespective that application of either the law of the place of registry or English law might produce a different result.

[162] Myburgh, supra (n 139) 410, 413; Myburgh, supra (n 133) 355, 362.

[163] Very characteristic is the concern of the English court on the recognition of the effects of legal acts performed outside the place of registration, see *Castrique v Imrie* [1870] LR 4 HL 414, 439

> No doubt the proposition seems to be rather startling, that by the comity of nations a British ship putting into a French port in the ordinary course of navigation may be seized and sold under the judgment of a French tribunal adjudicating upon an English contract, though misconceiving or disregarding the English law, so that the property of an English shipowner may be thus sold to pay the debt of another person in pursuance of an erroneous judgment upon its face, and that without even notice being necessarily given to him of the proceedings.

[164] A title issued on the basis of a foreign judicial sale requires no enforcement at the place, where the ship chances to be registered, but it will invariably need recognition of the incidents of the title prior to making entries in the register (Myburgh, supra (n 133) 355, 364). That is so, because no enforcement can be pursued against a state entity, as the registry is.

[165] This is precisely the *ratio* of Art 24(3) reg 1215/2012 (hereinafter "Brussels I-bis"), which prescribes that for entries in public registers, exclusive jurisdiction shall be vested in the court, where the registry is situated, see V Lazic and P Mankowski, *The Brussels I-bis Regulation* (2023) 4.073.

[166] Remarkably by virtue of Art 7(2) the clean title terminates the bare boat/demise charter and the certificate ensues the consequence of revocation of permission by the State of bare boat charter-in registration to fly its flag (Draft Explanatory Note, Add. 2, para 10, p. 4). However, can the *lex executionis* set aside a demise charter agreement and vest in the purchaser possession and right of use in the ship vis-à-vis the demise charterer?

[167] L Bleyen, *Judicial Sale of Ships* (2015) 154–157.

[168] According to Art 86 para 6 Presidential Decree 913/1978, which constitutes a breach in the system of universal satisfaction of creditors from a forced sale, the Greek ship registrar demands evidence of payment of seafarers' contributions from the purchaser, before title in the ship is recorded (registration) or a deletion certificate for it is issued (deregistration).

[169] Draft Explanatory Note, Add. 2, para 14, p. 5.

the Convention[170] aspires to determine the "cleansing" effect of the title solely in accordance with the provisions of the *lex executionis*[171] and uninfluenced by the *lex registrationis* of the receiving country, a legislative choice not without consequences.[172]

3.38. But what is the effect of a judicial sale, by which it is not full ownership in the ship that is sold but another right[173] or if the *lex executionis* transfers an "overarching" right[174] in the ship and not the interest that the debtor shipowner had in it?[175] Furthermore, what if the arrestee was not the owner of the ship, such as it had no valid title in the ship, and after court proceedings at the *locus registrationis* it is proved that another person had title in it? As long as the awarding title prescribes the elimination of all charges, then according to the most logical interpretation, this process should fall within the scope of the Convention, an interpretation not free of risks.[176] But no foreign law or international rule could rectify the defect of lack of ownership in the

---

[170] Cf. the statement in the Draft Explanatory Note, para 48, p. 10 "As the convention does not address the transfer of ownership, whether a judicial sale confers "clean title" within the meaning of the convention does depend on whether those additional formalities are taken".

[171] Argument from Art 7 para 1, which reads "the registry or other competent authority of a State party shall, as the case may be and in accordance with its regulations and procedures, without prejudice to article 6". Deletion of charges is binding on the registrar, who will execute it according to the regulations and procedures of the place of registration, but the "cleansing" effect by virtue of Art 6 is a premise (Report, paras 23–26, pp. 5–6).

[172] Arguably, in the legal systems, where registration of a right is a substantive element of the transaction and not merely a record, the transfer of ownership subsequent to a judicial sale could not be accomplished solely with the issuance of the court judgment without entry of the title in the register. Ratification of the Convention would entail a shift from that legal position, as the entry of the particulars of the certificate would need to be executed automatically without review of possible flaws. Cf. the position under English law, *The Tremont* (1841) 1 Wm Rob 163, 165

> As regards the interest of the American purchaser, it would, I conceive, be altogether unnecessary for I am clearly of opinion that the register is not required, and that his title is sufficiently established by the document issued by the Court in decreeing the sale under which the purchase has been made.

[173] E.g. a percentage of ownership (in German law, *Miteigentumsanteil*), shares in the ship (in English law, Merchant Shipping Act 1995, s. 7(1)) or a mortgage on a share in the ship. According to the drafters, such type of sale does not fall within the scope of the Convention, as no full title in the ship is awarded. Conversely, if the sale involves *usufruct* (in German law, *Nießbrauch*) or other proprietary right in the whole vessel, it will be subject to the provisions of the international regime but the registrar will be unable to discern the exact nature of the sold right, as no such reference would be made in the certificate according to Appendix II.

[174] Can the principle "*nemo dat quod non habet*" be displaced by the enforcement process, so that the highest bidder will be awarded ownership from a non-owner?

[175] Under English law, the sale of a vessel by an action *in rem* awards the ship as a whole, without regard to the right that the shipowner had in it, see *Castrique v Imrie* (1870) LR 4 HL 414, 428

> But when the tribunal has jurisdiction to determine not merely on the rights of the parties, but also on the disposition of the thing, and does in the exercise of that jurisdiction direct that the thing, and not merely the interest of any particular party in it, be sold or transferred, the case is very different,

and 436

> The judgment of the French Court decreeing the sale of the vessel was not, according to the view of the facts which we take, a judgment that only the interest of Claus, if any, in the ship should be sold, but that the particular ship itself should be sold.

The Convention is not cognisant of this fundamental distinction.

[176] It will be shown that the registrar will proceed with the appropriate entries in the register without getting hold of the sale judgment except for the certificate, from which it will not be possible to ascertain the nature of the right sold to the purchaser. Consequently, legal flaws may ensue.

ship,[177] as that would amount to an infringement of a fundamental human right[178] and contravene the public order of the receiving country.

3.39. We now come to the hallmark of the mechanism established by the Convention. As will be shown, the framers underpin the extension of the "effect" of the forced sale not on the judgment/court order, which confers title to the purchaser, but on the certificate[179] of judicial sale, which must be issued by the court or the competent authority of the country of the judicial sale[180] in the form reflected in Appendix II of the Convention. Also, it must be transmitted promptly to the Repository.[181] One of the reasons for this choice is to eliminate the controversy in identifying between the plethora of titles that may exist in the Contracting countries, those that should fall within the ambit of the Convention. But the cardinal reason lies in the very nature of the awarding title, which constitutes a judicial decision, and for its effect it ought to be subjected to the cumbersome process of recognition[182] according to the domestic procedural mechanism of the receiving country.[183] Things are even more complicated in case the title has the nature of a notarial deed, in which case the conditions for recognition are invariably stricter. So, according to the Convention, the title of the purchaser in the auctioned ship would be the certificate of judicial sale, issued in

177 It is questionable if the certificate could assist the purchaser in a dispute with the real owner at the court of the place of registration, despite the intention of the framers (Explanatory Note, para 173).

178 See Art 1 Protocol to the Convention for the Protection of Human Rights and Fundamental Freedoms 20 March 1952 "No one shall be deprived of his possessions except in the public interest and subject to the conditions provided for by law and by the general principles of international law".

179 Remarkably, the mechanism contrived by the framers is identical to that for the recognition of a judgment, i.e. *ipso jure* force of the matters decided (*quasi res judicata*) subject to the defence of infringement of public policy. If that is so, then the following questions require a reasoned response. What is the rationale behind the substitution of the judgment by the certificate? Can the certificate constitute valid title for proprietary rights without the rest of the safeguards inherent to a judgment? Is this a justifiable circumvention of the domestic mechanism for judgment recognition?

180 See Art 5 para 1. According to para 6, under certain requirements the electronic version of the certificate enjoys functional equivalence (Explanatory Note, para 166. Draft Explanatory Note, Add. 1, para 66–70, p. 16) by virtue of the Electronic Communications Convention or the UNCITRAL Model Law on Electronic Transferable Records.

181 Art 5 para 3. What if the certificate is not transmitted to the Repository? Could it be argued that no international effect can ensue? Probably not, as Art 6 is not conditional on the compliance of all requirements for the issue of the certificate but it suffices that the latter has been issued.

182 In Greek law, see Art 905 Greek CCP. In German law, see s. 328 ZPO. Interestingly, in English law, if a ship has been sold in a foreign judicial sale abroad and the previous owner brings proceedings in England for wrongful interference against the purchaser, the latter will rely on his title, i.e. the ownership stemming from the *in rem* sale, and not the source of it, i.e. the court sale order itself. That is so, because foreign judgments *in rem* are freely recognised in England (Lord Collins of Mapesbury and Harris, supra (n 14) Chpt 14, Rule 47, 14–110).

183 Art 278 new Greek KIND regulates the issue according to previous administrative practice followed by the Greek Ship Registry. It displaces the recognition mechanism and title of the purchaser, subsequent to a judicial sale conducted outside Greece, can be recorded after filing with the registrar the following documents: (i) foreign executory title (court order or title awarded by public authority), (ii) certificate, either from the foreign consulate or from a law firm based on the *locus executionis*, stating that the forced process was accomplished, it is no longer subject to appeal and the purchaser acquires clean title on the vessel, and (iii) public document evidencing that the proceeds of sale were, either deposited with the court or were set off.

accordance with the regulations and procedures of the country in which the judicial sale was conducted,[184] and would certify, among others, the following:

(i) that the ship was sold in accordance with the requirements of the law of the country of judicial sale and the requirements of the Convention;
(ii) that the purchaser acquired clean title to the ship;
(iii) the name of the court or public authority that conducted the judicial sale;
(iv) the name of the ship and the registry;[185] and
(v) the signature or seal of the issuing authority and the place and date of issue.

3.40. Based on the above, it is submitted that the certificate is not an "authentic" judicial act in respect of the right awarded by the judicial sale but a mere acknowledgement document. Nor is it bestowed with *res judicata*.[186] This begs the following question; is it sufficient for the acquisition of title on the ship in the receiving country and, if yes, what guarantees does it provide?[187]

3.41. Regarding the first part of the question, two conditions would need to be fulfilled. First, ratification of the international framework by the country, when it enters into force, and second, compulsory expansion of the domestic closed catalogue of enforceable titles, in order to enable registration as well as protection of the purchaser *erga omnes*. The latter would be unavoidable, because foreign certificates[188] cannot modify proprietary relationships recorded in public books. In fact, it would be imperative to do so, because if the registrar were to refuse entry of the awarded right on the ship by virtue of the certificate, its decision would be upheld before the competent local court. *Mutatis mutandis* applies when the certificate is submitted before a Contracting country court for the purpose of setting aside an application for

[184] See Art 5 para 1 " in accordance with its regulations and procedures". As regards those conditions (e.g. time frame of issuance), see Draft Explanatory Note, Add. 1, para 45, p. 11.

[185] There is no provision in the Model Certificate about the flag of the auctioned vessel, which in two cases might prove crucial. Tanzania has one flag but two ports of registration, namely Dar-es-Salaam and Zanzibar, which function independently. In case the IMO number of the Tanzanian flag vessel is not available (see para 4.4 of the Model Certificate), confusion might ensue about the identity of the ship. The second case involves vessels under bare boat registration, because the flag together with the name of the registry will ensure proper identification of the sold ship.

[186] This is the reason that Art 5 para 5 prescribes that the certificate shall be sufficient evidence – not conclusive evidence as initially proposed (Report, para 112, p. 19) – of the matters contained therein with an option of consideration of other information outside the certificate (Explanatory Note, para 163). But if proof to the contrary in respect of inaccuracies in the document is allowed, under what process will they be rectified? What about the reliance placed by the purchaser on its force? Of what avail would the certificate be, when the framers have prescribed that it shall only be issued once? For the aforementioned reasons, it has aptly been said that the status of the certificate is "unusual" (see D Rhidian Thomas, 'The United Nations Convention on the International Effects of Judicial Sales of Ships: The Beijing Convention – A Textual Analysis' (2022) 28 JIML 367, 378).

[187] As will be shown, the certificate is not a decision fulfilling the requirements of Art 2(a) Brussels I-bis but probably a public document according to Art 2(c), in which case the special mechanism of recognition and enforcement could be invoked.

[188] Even if it were accepted that the certificate is a public document falling under Art 2(c) Brussels I-bis and it would be recognised unconditionally, to the extent that entries in the register of the receiving state are ordered, it would be doubtful, if the registrar would be compelled to comply, in view of the effect of Art 24(3) Brussels I-bis, even if the certificate of judicial sale would be accompanied by the certificate of enforceability according to Art 60 Brussels I-bis.

ship arrest, filed by a creditor of the previous owner of the ship,[189] or to release it in a port, where the ship chanced to sail after the judicial sale.

3.42. As regards the second part of the question, a reasoned response would require a comparative analysis of the various domestic regimes pertaining to safeguards for the protection of fundamental substantive and procedural rights, in order for a foreign judgment to be recognised in the receiving country. Those safeguards would apply equally for the certificate. Such endeavour would exceed the scope of the present study. Suffice it to say, however, that the crux of the above-described problem lies in the everlasting clash between "comity" and "reciprocity" and the division of opinion[190] regarding mutual recognition of judgments and their ensuing effects.

3.5.4 Express and implied procedural guarantees

3.43. The Convention aptly accords supremacy to the *lex executionis,*[191] which governs the pre-sale stage, the process of the forced sale and the conditions for issuance of the "clean title". Indicatively, this applies in respect of the qualifications for the title to be enforceable,[192] the service of the order for payment below the enforceable title, the issuance and service of the *in rem* claim form, the imposition of the forced arrest, the issue and service of the warrant of arrest, the service and period of notice to persons with an interest in the process, including the publicity of the judicial sale, the conduct of the auction process *stricto sensu,* together with the entry bid, in case the ship is sold by auction, and the conferral of title to the highest bidder, the settlement of the awarding price and the right to the awarding title, as well as the legal remedies and means for challenging[193] the procedural acts of the process[194] prior to the completion

[189] In case the certificate is issued by an EU authority, and on the assumption that it qualifies as a public document under Art 2(c) Brussels I-bis, and the receiving court is situated within the EU, then, it is submitted, that the latter would be bound to recognise the international effect of the certificate and reject the application for ship arrest or lift the ship's material detention according to Art 8.

[190] D Vagts, Dispute Resolution Mechanisms in International Business Law (1987) 203 *Recueil des Cours* 9, 55 ff.

[191] See Art 4 para 1. The title of the provision reflects only partially the content. It is submitted the para 1 should stand on its own under the title "Law of the Judicial Sale".

[192] It was already stated that in the majority of the Continental law jurisdictions an enforceable title is required before sale proceedings are entertained and the process continues without court intervention, as opposed to Anglo-Common Law systems, in which, due to the peculiar nature of the *in rem* proceedings, the arrest is imposed without enforceable title and the sale is ordered by the court, either *pendente lite* or after the claim is heard on its merits (see Diagram 1).

[193] The *carte blanche* afforded to the *lex executionis* in respect of the existence of such remedies may prove fatal for the judicial sale in the receiving country on the ground of manifest contravention to public policy (Myburgh, supra (n 139) 410, 422).

[194] In the 55th Session of the Commission of UNCITRAL a proposal was submitted by the European Union for the inclusion of a safeguard pertaining to an effective remedy for challenging the judicial sale by an aggrieved party. That proposal was a result of compromise between the EU Member State representatives. According to that, Art 9 para 1 would read: "The State of Judicial Sale shall provide procedural remedies to challenge a judicial sale before its completion under the law of the State of Judicial Sale". During the deliberations, which were partially held behind closed doors, a compromise was reached, which, unfortunately, failed to achieve the intended objective. As stated, para 1 not only was misplaced, more importantly, the phraseology is so moderate, that it leaves the matter to be determined freely by the domestic law of every Contracting country. In fact, the disdain on that matter was so apparent that the Commission decided to avoid any mention about remedies for the avoidance of the judicial sale in Appendix I (Addendum, Add. 2, para 4 in conjunction with Addendum, Add. 1, para 22). The main argument of

of sale.[195] For a reason not so obvious the drafters decided to exclude from the scope of application the announcement of claims, when the matter would have to be referred to *lex executionis* in any case.[196]

3.44. On an exceptional basis, the Convention imposes a supplemental[197] obligation[198] of publicity[199] in the form of service[200] of notice of the judicial sale to the following interested persons; the registrar[201] of the ship registry,[202] the holders[203] of mortgage or hypothèque and of any registered charge, the holders[204] of any maritime lien,[205]

---

the opposers was that coercive wording would amount to "intrusion" in the domestic procedural regime. However, as will be shown, the imposition of safeguards secures proper balance between conflicting interests.

[195] According to the drafters, Art 4 para 1 refers to *lex executionis* for all procedural matters until the completion of the forced sale, while Art 9 para 1 refers to the same law for remedies post-sale (see Explanatory Note, para 205). The distinction is made for the purpose of ensuring that only in the second case can the court decide the suspension of issuance of the certificate of judicial sale.

[196] Art 15 para 1(a) prescribes that the procedure for the distribution of the sale proceeds, which includes announcement of claims, falls outside the scope of the Convention. Therefore, *lex executionis* will apply for the formalities of the announcement, the particulars of the security right, the invocation and proof of the material facts that trigger the maritime lien, the interested parties, the limitation period for filing oppositions against the list of priorities, etc. (for those formalities, see *Antapasis A.*, Claims enjoying maritime lien status, 1976, 39 (in Greek)).

[197] In the sense that, if the procedural rules of the *forum* do not prescribe these actions, then the Contracting country would be obliged to promulgate relevant legislation.

[198] If not complied with, it will not be possible to issue a valid certificate of judicial sale under Art 5 para 1 (see Draft Explanatory Note, Add. 1, para 5, p. 2).

[199] Art 4 para 2 and 4 para 3(a–e).

[200] Art 13 para 2 prescribes that service can be executed according to *lex fori* or the "Convention on the Service Abroad of Judicial and Extrajudicial Documents in Civil and Commercial Matters" 1965.

[201] The proposed provision does not prescribe what action the registrar should take upon receipt of the notice. A proposal was submitted for the registrar to make notation of the prospective sale, so that third parties, including holders of registered rights in the register, would obtain knowledge of the impending sale (see Compilation of Comments, A/CN.9/1109, p. 19–20). The imposition of arrest on a ship is a legal act with territorial effect and extension of other related effects to a foreign jurisdiction would cause serious problems. In fact, the drafters of the Arrest Convention 1952 were faced with those in the case of provisional arrest. The outcome was that the instrument would deal only with the material and not the legal detention of the vessel. The rationale was obvious. No country would accept to record in its register the legal detention of a vessel ordered by a foreign court. This applies more for the notation of a forced arrest, which would prohibit the private sale of the ship as well as the recording of mortgages. Based on the above, it is preferable that the matter is not regulated by the Convention.

[202] The framers submit that the notice should be communicated, even if the ship registry does not reside with a Contracting country (Explanatory Note, para 107). Such statement could be accepted only on the basis that the *lex executionis* itself prescribes the service, because if the place of registration does not reside with a Contracting country, then the Convention would be to no avail for the registration/deregistration of the auctioned ship by virtue of the certificate.

[203] On the condition that their right is recorded in a register, which is open to public inspection (Art 4 para 3(b)), even if legitimate interest needs to be proved before access is granted by the registrar (Explanatory Note, para 109).

[204] Let us suppose that certain creditors announce their claims in the pending enforcement proceedings and assert that they are maritime lien holders. According to which law will the genesis of the lien be determined, so that they can properly be served with notice? It seems that the problem will be resolved by the conflict rules of the *forum executionis* (argument from Art 2(g) "under applicable law"). If that were so, however, then it is questionable, whether the Convention achieves the intended protection of lien holders, as proclaimed in the preamble, and *forum shopping* is combatted.

[205] Due notice of the enforcement process to privileged maritime creditors had traditionally been an issue of controversy. In case those persons had announced their claims in the pending process, as envisaged by the Convention (see Art 4 para 3(c)), then, one could validly argue, there is no need to serve them with notice, as they are already alert to the impending forced sale. Contrariwise, if they were not privy to the enforcement proceedings, then it would not be possible to serve them with notice, simply because they would

the registered[206] owner of the ship[207] "*for the time being*"[208] and, where applicable, the bareboat charterer and the registrar of the bareboat charter registry. The provision regulates the issue *ratione personae* but not *ratione tempore*.[209] Further, it does not require confirmation of receipt of the notice,[210] which may prove fatal for the validity of the certificate in the receiving country.

3.45. The prescribed notice should be performed according to the *lex fori* of the place of the judicial sale[211] but the determination of the identity and address of the above-interested persons will be carried out by reliance[212] on the information entered in the register or the particulars submitted to the court or other public authority conducting the judicial sale. The notice must also be published by press announcement[213] at the place of the judicial sale and transmitted[214] to the Repository of the International

---

be of unknown identity to the arrestor. In this *circulus vitiosus*, the key question is, whether it is fair, just and reasonable to extinguish those charges according to the prescriptions of the Convention.

206 The restriction for service only to the registered (Art 4 para 3(d) and 2(h)) and not to the beneficial owner, may prove problematic for the valid execution of judicial sales in civil law jurisdictions for ships flying flags of common law countries (Myburgh, supra (n 139) 410, 420–421).

207 As service of the notice will be given according to *lex fori*, it is doubtful, if under English law, there will be a need to serve the document to the shipowner itself, or it would suffice to serve the writ in *rem* on the ship.

208 The expression may be subject to different interpretations and the framers have not thrown sufficient light on the intended goal. It is submitted that the person who has the capacity of "owner" for the purpose of a forced sale is the one that appears in the register at the moment the arrest is imposed, regardless of the time that it has received the notice. However, the Convention accommodates no mechanism for the notation of the forced arrest in the foreign ship register, therefore the owner may transfer ownership at any time, even after the imposition of the arrest. Further, even if the *lex executionis* would attempt to impose such effect, it could not apply *erga omnes*. No one can exclude the hypothetical case, where the "owner", who received notice, files an objection to the court of the forced sale on the ground that it had sold the vessel prior to receiving the notice, with the result that the transfer was executed *bona fide*, and no notice was extended to the real "owner", therefore, the whole arrest process would have to be restarted. Obviously, the specific matter could be the source of many frictions, including the validity of physical delivery of the vessel after the completion of the sale at the *locus executionis*.

209 During the deliberations there were proposals to prescribe a specific minimum period for service or to be executed "in due time". Both were disapproved, with the result that the *lex fori* will have the last word. It is submitted that a minimum period, with power vested in the court to shorten it, after the publication of the notice in the Repository should have been prescribed, so that due process is guaranteed. It is anticipated that courts in many receiving countries will strike down the certificate of judicial sale for that reason on the ground of manifest contravention to public policy.

210 See Explanatory Note, para 125.

211 See Art 4 para 4. Also, Draft Explanatory Note, Add. 1, paras 2 and 23–28. If the notices are to be served in EU Member States, then Regulation 1393/2007 "on the service in the Member States of judicial and extrajudicial documents in civil or commercial matters" may be selected as a valid alternative.

212 See Art 4 para 7 "it is sufficient to rely". The amendment introduced at the 55th Session, which abandoned "exclusivity", has merits, as it provides an option for cumulative service to another address, in case such address is verifiable, so as to avoid fictitious and defective services of the notice. An outcome not improbable, as there is no requirement for confirmation of receipt. One needs to be mindful of the fact, that address details are subject to change, while failure to update relevant records is not infrequent. Moreover, such option is crucial for maritime lien holders, who were not announced in the process, but for whom there is knowledge of their domicile. A valid service of notice to them would, arguably, deprive them in future proceedings of the argument, that they were not notified about the impending sale. Whether the presumption of valid service as "sufficient" could be contested on the basis of stronger contrary evidence, would depend on the *lex fori* and, in any event, at the court of the receiving country by virtue of Art 10.

213 See Art 4 para 5(a).

214 Art 4 para 5(b) provides no hint for the identification of the authority, which would be responsible for communicating the notice to the Repository, a deliberate choice, as one may infer from the deliberations (see

Maritime Organization (IMO).[215] To avoid discrepancies in the wording of the notice, a standard text with minimum content is reflected in Appendix I of the Convention.[216]

3.46. Regarding the nature and the function of the prescribed notice, there is support that it is not a formal requirement, which complements those of the *lex executionis*, but it has merely a declaratory effect. It is submitted that such a view is not persuasive.[217] It was shown previously that the title, which will be issued according to the provisions of the Convention, shall be respected by the receiving countries, principally the place of registration. On the assumption that the notice is assigned to strike a balance in the conflicting interests of purchaser, debtor shipowner and creditors in a judicial sale, then, no less, it should assume a substantial role[218] in the enforcement process. In fact, the notice aims to impose a minimum guarantee of publicity. Such measures will prevent contravention to the respective provisions of the public policy of the receiving country on the grounds of insufficient publicity of the process. Moreover, publicity via the GISIS repository of IMO may signify preclusion in the exercise of rights of other interested persons, such as unannounced creditors.[219] Therefore, the notice is an essential supplement[220] of the publicity of the forced sale process.

Report, para 51, p. 11). In case of non-compliance, one could argue that the certificate should not be issued, as the sale was not conducted according to the requirements of the Convention.

[215] Electronic database with the acronym GISIS (Global Integrated Shipping Information System), which publishes primarily information on ships of IMO member States. As regards entries, the IMO has immunity under its 1948 Founding Convention and the 1947 New York "International Convention on Privileges and Immunities of the Specialized Agencies".

[216] The content of the notice encompasses, *inter alia*, the place and date of the judicial sale, the specific details of the ship to be auctioned, the identity of the registered shipowner and a statement, that the acquired title is clean. It also empowers the competent authority to include any other information deemed necessary for the protection of the interests of the recipients of the notice.

[217] Argument can be derived from Art 2 para 2 "a certificate of judicial sale under article 5 shall only be issued if a notice of judicial sale is given prior to the judicial sale of the ship", making the issuance of the certificate conditional on due notice. But since the court or other public authority that conducted the judicial sale or other competent authority of the *locus executionis* will issue the certificate upon completion of the forced sale, is there room to review whether the notice requirements were respected? Even if that issue was raised before the *forum executionis* during the enforcement proceedings, but the process was not restrained, pending decision, how effective would that condition be, in view of no competent body and no specific remedy to hinder the issuance of the certificate? *Ultimum refugium* would be the invocation of Art 10 in the receiving country.

[218] See Draft Explanatory Note, Add. 1, para 3, p. 2

> the primary purpose of the notice requirements in the convention is to alert creditors to the impending sale and eventual distribution of proceeds. The requirements are designed to strike a fair balance between due process towards creditors and the expediency required in judicial sale proceedings.

[219] This had always been a vexing problem. Should creditors, especially with maritime liens, without notice of the judicial sale, be precluded from asserting their claims against the purchaser? In the Anglo-Common Law jurisdictions the prevailing view was that they had constructive notice according to *Rolimpex Centrala Handlu Zagranicznego v Owners of Motorship Prins Bernhard (The Prins Bernhard)* [1964] P. 117, 131–132

> This method of service prescribed . . . for giving notice to all interested parties is a rule of the court. It has been firmly established by many years of usage. It may not be a perfect way of informing all interested parties that an action in rem is laid against the ship; but no other method has yet been suggested or devised. This method is well-known throughout the maritime countries of the world. It is based upon experience for the protection of all interested parties.

[220] According to Art 4 paras 2, 5, paras 1 and 6, no international effect can ensue, unless notice is given in accordance with the provisions of the Convention.

3.5.5 "International effects"[221] of the judicial sale

3.47. On the condition that the *lex executionis* was applied, including the supplementary obligation to provide notice for the forced sale, the "outcome"[222] extends to the other Contracting countries ("international effect of the judicial sale"). However, the embedment of those effects at the national level, which includes the perfection[223] of transfer of the awarded right, requires an act from the receiving country. One option would be to submit the judicial sale judgment for recognition in accordance with the national procedural mechanism.[224] For reasons already explained, the international regime abandons[225] this option and, instead, offers the effortless method of "circulation" of the judicial sale certificate, which purports to achieve the effects in the other Contracting countries.[226]

3.48. In particular, the intended effects have two manifestations. One concerns the "production"[227] of the certificate[228] of the auctioned vessel by the purchaser to the registrar.[229] At its request the ship will be registered in its name,[230] as the lawful

221 As shown, the national effects are multiple and are addressed to Contracting countries, which are bound to execute the certificate (e.g. register ownership of the purchaser in the ship register, release of the ship from an arrest based on a claim arising prior to the judicial sale, etc.) However, the "international effect" is single, that is the extension of the outcome of a judicial sale conducted in one contracting country to other Contracting countries. It is submitted that the singular form, i.e. "international effect of judicial sale", would reflect the gloss more appositely.

222 The "outcome" of a forced sale is manifold and derives from four legal frameworks: (i) procedural law (*lex fori arresti* and *lex fori executionis*), which determines the assumption of jurisdiction for the material detention of the ship, the conduct of the judicial sale and the issuance of title; (ii) law, according to which the list of priorities will be compiled, that is, if national procedural law (*lex fori*) prevails or foreign substantive law will also be applied (e.g. *lex navis*, *lex causae*, etc.), especially on the crystallization of preferred claims; (iii) law of registration/deregistration (*lex registrationis*) in the implementation of the foreign sale judgment; and (iv) law for the recognition of the effects of the forced/judicial sale in countries, other than the *locus executionis* and the *locus registrationis*. It will be shown that the Convention attempts to forge rules pertaining exclusively to the first, third and fourth frameworks.

223 Argument from Art 6, which reads: "A judicial sale . . . shall have the effect . . . of conferring clean title".

224 Regarding the problem of recognition of forced auctions in other countries, see MN Shaw, *International Law* (2008) 697–701.

225 See Draft Explanatory Note, Add. 1, para 74, p. 17 "To emphasize that it is not concerned with the recognition and enforcement of foreign judgments, the convention avoids the term 'recognition'".

226 See Art 6 "A judicial sale for which a certificate of judicial sale . . . has been issued shall have the effect in every other State Party".

227 Art 7 requires production of the certificate and request by application for the recordings in the register, unless the registrar acts *ex officio* (Draft Explanatory Note, Add. 2, para 15, p. 5).

228 It should be stressed that nowhere in the Convention is there a duty to attach the original title to the certificate.

229 What if the vessel was provisionally registered in more than one registry? That seems to be a loophole in the global system of ship registrations. If the vessel was judicially sold flying flag A under provisional registration but, at the same time, it was provisionally registered in country B, the purchaser would need to produce the certificate before both registries. However, it is questionable if *lex executionis* would be the only competent to resolve the issue of ownership (Davies, supra (n 20) 107, 113).

230 According to the *travaux préparatoires*, the right enures also to the benefit of the first subsequent purchaser (Draft Explanatory Note, Add.2, para 8, p. 3; cf. para 16, p. 6), because it may be that the *lex executionis* prescribes that title in the ship from the auction by the purchaser should be asserted with a domestic special purpose company, in which case the purchaser's initial company would need equal protection. Also, in case the country, in which reflagging would be pursued, might require a domestic company to register the vessel. However, according to the deliberations (see Report, paras 4–5, pp. 18–21), it was agreed to include in the explanatory report that the registrar would be obliged to accept submission of the certificate from other successors in the chain of transfers, a solution that may entail serious risks. At the end, the wording adopted reflects discretionary power, which is the correct approach (see Explanatory Note, para 192).

beneficiary,[231] and all the encumbrances that were registered before completion of the judicial sale will be deleted.[232] Alternatively, if the intention would be to register its property right in another registry, the request to the previous registrar would be twofold; removal of all encumbrances and production of a certificate of deletion,[233] so that together with the judicial sale certificate[234] the new registration process would be accomplished. In any case, according to the Convention, the clean title will ensue the elimination of all charges, registered and "invisible", in all Contracting countries.[235] The action of the registrar will be precluded, if the effect is found to be manifestly contrary to the public policy of the receiving country. That will be determined, either by the local court or the registrar itself,[236] which would save time and cost.

3.49. The second manifestation relates to the protection of the purchaser from hostile measures that could be assumed by non-satisfied creditors of the previous registered owner of the ship in various ports situated in contracting[237] countries. But should the purchaser enjoy such protection prior to registering ownership in the register? Since the type of protection offered by the provision stems from ownership, it should not be available before the perfection of the transfer, which, as shown earlier, is conditional on the act of registration in the receiving country. The problem evinces its dimension, when the judicial sale is conducted in a contracting country but the registry lies in a non-contracting country. As already exposed,[238] the framers encourage the application of the Convention in such case with service of notice according to Article 4. But since the registrar will not be bound by the certificate and will not need to make an entry in

---

231 The Convention deliberately abstains from characterising the auctioned right as ownership (Draft Explanatory Note, para 68, p. 14). However, as already mentioned, it is not obvious, what the registrar will do, in case the existing registered right differs from that, which was awarded to the purchaser under *lex executionis*. It may be possible for full ownership to be have been sold in the judicial sale, while the arrestee had only *usufruct*. As the issued certificate does not require denomination of the right conferred (see Preamble to Appendix II under "(b) The judicial sale has conferred clean title to the ship on the purchaser"), failure to register the correct right in the register, as prescribed by an international convention, would be a legal inconsistency, if not an error. On the other hand, the registrar will in principle be presumed to have acted lawfully in accordance with the content of the certificate.

232 See Art 7 para 1(a) and (c). The text gives support for the position that deletion may also be executed on a charge that is not recorded in the ship register, such as the *floating charge* of English law, which is entered in a different register. Whether that would be attainable, it will depend on the receiving country.

233 See Art 7 para 1(a) and (b).

234 If the purchaser applies for deletion from the current register and, at the same time, triggers the process for new registration to another registry, then there is a question whether the registrar of the latter can validly register the vessel, even temporarily, or it should wait for the deletion certificate. It must be recalled that the certificate of judicial sale is not a judgment nor enforceable title. To complicate things more, what if proceedings have been entertained at the place of the forced sale for its overturn as well as the place of initial registration according to Art 10? Moreover, how can the previous owner ascertain the place of new registration to pursue proceedings in that court according to Art 7 para 5? He could only suspect the scenario by the application for the issuance of a deletion certificate but then how could he identify the new place of registration? By that time, it could well be that the ship has been transferred further, especially if the new registry would not require the certificate of deletion to be submitted prior to executing the new sale transaction. It is submitted that the correct approach would be to prohibit registration in a registry other than the initial, unless the deletion certificate is issued and submitted together with the certificate of judicial sale to the new registry.

235 See Art 2(c), (e) and 6.

236 See Explanatory Note, para 196.

237 Obviously, the intended result could not be achieved in non-Contracting countries and domestic remedies would need to be invoked to achieve equivalent protection there, if any.

238 See fn. 202.

the change of ownership upon presentation of the certificate, how could the purchaser invoke protection from arrest in other Contracting countries? It is submitted that the drafters should have made Article 8 conditional on the fulfilment of the requirements of Article 7.

3.50. Regarding substance, the purchaser invariably feels vulnerable due to the possibility that the acquired ship may be detained by previous creditors who, either *bona fide* of the execution of the judicial sale failed to announce their claim, or *mala fide* refused to accept the "cleansing" effect of the judicial sale, are in search of a convenient jurisdiction that would assist them in displacing the outcome of the forced sale.[239]

3.51. The repercussions for the purchaser are substantial; not only the financial loss from the claim, in case it is settled but also the damage sustained from the detention of the vessel, which may be under charter. Evidently, the non-satisfied creditors are exhorted to commit the abovementioned acts by the tolerance of *forum shopping*, which results in the decomposition of the "core" of the forced sale. In the vast majority of cases, the creditors will assume the drastic measure of material detention, to force payment of the debt, as featured in the Arrest Convention 1952.

3.52. However, there is nothing in the text to suggest that the provisions could not also apply in case a forced arrest[240] is imposed by virtue of an enforceable title. That is the alleviating effect of the certificate of the judicial sale, which may be used as a "shield", either to set aside an application for ship arrest or similar measure or to lift a provisional or forced arrest already imposed.[241] The decision by the court is subject to the determination that the effect does not manifestly contravene the domestic public policy.[242]

3.5.6 Remedial action against the enforcement proceedings and the issued certificate

3.53. The approach of the drafters to "channel" the legal remedies pertaining to effects after the completion of the forced sale to the *forum executionis*, by granting exclusive jurisdiction[243] to that court, is appropriate. According to the wording of Article 9 paragraph 1, the jurisdiction extends to both avoidance of the forced sale and suspension of its effects, as well as the challenge of the issuance of the judicial sale certificate.

[239] To provide an example, the Maltese flagged M/V *The Bright Star* was judicially sold in Jamaica in 2018 but the status of the ship mortgage was not recognised according to *lex navis*, which prescribed higher priority. Instead *lex fori* applied. After the completion of the forced sale, the vessel sailed to Malta, where the mortgagee arrested it on the ground that the Maltese conflict rule was not respected by the court of Jamaica in the compilation of the ranking list. The Maltese court arrested the vessel and the purchaser had to deposit security for its release. An application of the latter to set aside the arrest was rejected. After a five-year battle with 73 proceedings, the Court of Appeal upheld the first instance court, which held that the Jamaican enforcement proceedings should be respected, including priority of the mortgagee, who would need to satisfy its claim from the sale proceeds.

[240] See Explanatory Note, para 199.

[241] See Art 8 para 1–2.

[242] See Art 8 para 4.

[243] Art 9 para 1 incorporates a safeguard, according to which all courts of other Contracting countries ought to decline their jurisdiction in favour of the *forum executionis* under Art 9 para 2.

3.54. Many critical questions arise from the aforementioned legislative choice. When it comes to contesting enforcement proceedings, how wide should the scope be, so that the result is "admissible" in the other Contracting countries? Is it pertinent to challenge the process of the forced sale as well as its substance, that is the sold right[244] in the ship, and which class[245] of aggrieved persons should be admitted to contest the proceedings? Should the *forum* provide a legal remedy[246] for the suspension of the sale process or would avoidance be considered adequate[247] to safeguard the rights of the interested persons? What if no remedy, even for the avoidance, exists at all?

3.55. Closely related is the following question. The Convention has a provision[248] for the challenge of the issuance of the certificate post-sale, but it does not provide a *locus standi*, as it is merely declaratory.[249] But how justifiable is the total absence of grounds for the restraint of the force of the certificate at the *forum executionis*? The latter becomes crucial for maintaining "balance of interests" in the mechanism devised. Indeed, once the issued certificate is made available to the public via the IMO repository and changes are entered in the register, in case of avoidance[250] of the

---

244 See supra.

245 *The Trenton* 4 F. 657, 661

> Such sales, however, may be impeached, by the owner or other person interested by showing (1) that the court or officer making the sale had no jurisdiction of the subject-matter by actual seizure and custody of the thing sold. . . . (2) That the sale was made by a fraudulent collusion, to which the purchaser at such sale was a party. . . . (3) That the sale was contrary to natural justice.

246 See Addendum, Add. 2, para 16

> It was understood that the provision did not require a State Party to introduce or devise new legislation providing specific procedures for challenging a judicial sale, and that it would be sufficient for the State to point to procedures under existing law, whether provided for in legislation, rules of civil procedure, or case law, and whether or not specific to judicial sales.
>
> (and Explanatory Note, para 206)

The argument of the drafters was that more compelling wording would constitute intolerable "invasion" in the *lex executionis*.

247 The drafters avoided to touch the issue of "adequacy", at any cost, see Report, para 64 "In response, the view was reiterated that the convention should avoid as much as possible intruding into procedural matters in the State of judicial sale and therefore should not deal with the availability of remedies" and Addendum, Add. 2, para 14 "In response, it was pointed out that notion of 'adequacy' was vague and that the provision went against the objective of the convention to leave matters of procedure related to judicial sales to domestic law".

248 The relevant part of Art 9 (1) reads "which shall extend to any claim or application to challenge the issuance of the certificate of judicial sale".

249 By another reading, it may be argued that the remedy for the challenge of the issuance of the certificate is freely available, as long as the applicant can prove before the local court that the certificate should not be issued, because restoration to the *status quo ante* would be impossible. Let us provide an example. The arrestee files an opposition against the enforcement process together with a petition for the restraint of the process. If the latter is rejected, the process will continue until the completion of the forced sale. Under the circumstances, an application to challenge the issuance of the certificate could not be excluded so as to prevent deregistration and sale of the ship by the purchaser. The only obstacle to such interpretation would be the position of the remedy in Art 9 para 1, which regulates matters after the completion of the sale, instead of Art 4 para 1, which deals with procedural issues before completion of the sale. Certainly, the national courts will have the last word on which is the preferable reading.

250 The Draft Explanatory Note, Add. 2, para 31 reads "In practice, avoidance of a judicial sale is exceedingly rare". It is submitted that the argument is not convincing. The legislator ought to deal with all possible scenarios no matter if they may occur rarely.

forced sale, to what extent is it expected to reverse the international effects, that is, how imperative is it for the international regime[251] to introduce a "reversal mechanism"? Undoubtedly an intractable problem, but it is submitted that it should.

3.56. To leave the matter to be determined at the place, which will arise,[252] is not a satisfactory solution. After the entry of the awarded right in the highest bidder's name and the deletion of all charges from the register, if the purchaser sells the vessel to a third person and the latter reflags it in a new registry, how will the reversal to the *status quo ante* be possible? It should be stressed that the publicity of the certificate via the GISIS[253] system will provide an incontestable ground for legal certainty in respect of subsequent legal acts[254] concerning the ship. In any event, justice and certainty would be served more efficiently, if the initially published valid certificate is marked as "revoked" in the Repository subsequent to a successful hearing on the avoidance of the judicial sale, as compared to the mere transmission to the Repository of the judgment only.[255]

3.57. Based on the aforementioned findings, it seems expedient to examine, if more safeguards need to be accommodated by the Convention.

3.58. First, the issuance and circulation of the certificate of the judicial sale should be conditional on the maturity of the enforcement proceedings according to the *lex executionis*.[256]

3.59. Secondly, automatic suspension of the international effects of the judicial sale, so that the certificate cannot be issued until the judge examines the application of the previous shipowner on the validity of the grounds for the avoidance of the judicial sale. The remedy should be filed within three days from the issuance of the clean title. Adjudication could be carried out in adversarial summary proceedings with preponderance. In case of rejection of the application, the certificate would be issued, even if the hearing on the merits for the avoidance of the judicial sale would not have been concluded.

---

[251] See Art 15 para 2. The framers were categorical that such type of relief fell outside the application scope as being an "extraneous matter" (see Draft Explanatory Note, Add. 2, para 54, p. 16). Therefore, it is the *lex fori* that will determine this crucial matter (Draft Explanatory Note, Add. 2, para 32 "The convention does not seek to find an answer to the international effect of avoidance or suspension, which is left to the law applicable in the State in which the issue arises, as provided for in article 15(2)") But how appropriate is for the host country to give extraterritorial effect to the consequences from the avoidance of the judicial sale?

[252] See Explanatory Note, para 208.

[253] During the deliberations at the 40th UNCITRAL Meeting in New York there was a proposal to introduce a provision with a duty to submit to the GISIS repository the judgment for the avoidance of the judicial sale, which was adopted. Dogmatically this is correct, as it serves legal certainty, although it contributes insignificantly in the restoration to the *status quo ante*. To provide an example. If the auction is set aside, all proceeds of sale will have to be returned, but how will the mortgagee be able to record his mortgage, especially if the ship has been sold to a *bona fide* purchaser, who was financed by another financier?

[254] Such as a sale contract, a bareboat charter, as well as the creation of security interests on the vessel.

[255] See Explanatory Note, para 209. It is submitted that the transmission cannot achieve reversal of the effects of the certificate, as there is no duty on the registrar to act upon the court decision that avoided the sale.

[256] The enforcement proceedings culminate in the execution of the forced sale, which, unless challenged, will become unappealable. The drafters not only considered unfit to prescribe a certain degree of maturity in the proceedings, they also refused to impose availability of adequate remedies by the Contracting countries, leaving the matter to be determined by *lex fori* (see Diagram 1 for an understanding of the function of the remedies during the process).

3.60. Thirdly, if the *lex executionis* does not offer to the announced creditors a remedy against the judicial sale process, assuming that their intervening role should be limited to the impeachment of the list for the distribution of the sale proceeds, they should also be permitted to intervene[257] during the previously described adversarial summary proceedings by invoking a closed catalogue of grounds.[258]

3.61. Fourthly, a copy of the court order/notarial award of the judicial sale should be attached to the certificate, so that the registrar will discern the nature of the awarded right in the sold vessel before entries are executed in the register.

3.62. Now the crux of the problem will be exposed. It is no coincidence that the international framers failed to achieve the consensus required for the ratification of a regime that would deal satisfactorily with the treatment of creditors in need of preferential protection. This failure is manifested in the non-entry into force of two of the three supranational regimes on maritime liens and mortgages, as shown earlier. Inevitably, the problem was treated at the national level, a solution that exacerbated the phenomenon of forum shopping.

3.63. However, it is one thing for a creditor to pursue its ambitions by invoking "convenient" remedies available in a specific jurisdiction and accepting the risk of reversal by the mechanism of recognition of judgments in another or for the purchaser in the registry due to supremacy of prevailing policy grounds, and totally different to establish an international regime for the "legitimisation" of the "fruits" of the *forum executionis* shopping.[259] But that is exactly, what the Convention is attempting to attain.[260]

3.64. Since the vexing problem of priority in the satisfaction of creditors cannot be resolved in a direct manner and according to pre-agreed and commonly accepted criteria, it is bypassed with a detour path, which is the "legitimisation" of "whatever" outcome occurs from the judicial sale in "whichever" jurisdiction. But that entails approval even of "fraudulent" solutions for the sake of uniformity, so as to achieve "legal certainty".

3.5.7 Limits to the "effects" of the judicial sale

3.65. It was shown earlier that the "outcome" of the judicial sale is not recognised unconditionally, and the embedment of the consequences aspires to be accomplished

257 The immunity offered to the title by the Convention has aptly been acknowledged that it "goes too far". Indeed, it would be unacceptable to allow a title, tainted with fraud between seller and purchaser in a judicial sale, to enter the register and provide ground for valid subsequent transfers (Myburgh, supra (n 133) 355, 367–368).

258 E.g. creditor is given no chance to participate in the satisfaction process by announcement, collusion of arrestor and arrestee shipowner against whom the judicial sale is enforced, with the aim to exclude a specific class of creditors (e.g. mortgagees).

259 Regarding the problematic of refusal of recognition of a foreign judgment issued on the basis of *forum shopping*, see P Mayer, *Droit International Privé*, 4th edn. (1991) paras 384, 251.

260 See Draft Explanatory Note, para 23, p. 5, where it is stated that the Convention is concerned only with the effects of "judicial sales" and not with the effects of judgments in respect of such sales. But how are the receiving countries to accept in their jurisdiction "certificates", which are based on judgments ruling on the fate of proprietary rights on registered ships without sufficient safeguards? This applies especially in respect of remedies that ensure balance of interest as well as protection of rights of specific interested persons.

with the certificate. Free circulation of the certificate endeavours to achieve unimpeded registration of the awarded right in the *res*, valid execution of sale agreements of the ship and unfettered enjoyment of its use. At the same time, the framers of the Convention[261] attempt to draw limits to the extraterritoriality of the effects by granting a sole[262] ground[263] of refusal of those in case they are manifestly[264] contrary to the public policy[265] of the receiving country.[266]

3.66. The first limit is marked at the place of registration of the sold ship. After receiving the application from the purchaser with the certificate issued in accordance with the provisions of Appendix II,[267] the registrar is bound to execute the actions prescribed in Article 7, without power to review the substance of the title incorporated in the certificate. Even if, as previously stated, the *lex executionis* awarded a right of a different nature compared to the one registered in the register, the registrar cannot reject the request for registration, especially because the certificate will provide no such evidence. However, Article 7 paragraph 5 prescribes that registration of the awarded right and deletion of the charges from the register will not be executed, either if the

---

261 One cannot but notice that the structure of the mechanism of the Convention has its origin in English law. Recognition of a foreign judgment is not denied (see *Castrique v Imrie* [1870] LR 4 HL 414, 428–429

> In Story on the Conflict of Laws (3), it is said that the principle that the judgment is conclusive 'is applied to all proceedings in rem as to moveable property within the jurisdiction of the Court pronouncing the judgment. Whatever it settles as to the right or title, or whatever disposition it makes of the property by sale, revendication, transfer, or other act, will be held valid in every other country where the question comes directly or indirectly in judgment before any other foreign tribunal. This is very familiarly known in the cases of proceedings in rem in foreign Courts of Admiralty, whether they be causes of prize or bottomry, or salvage or forfeiture, of which such Courts have a rightful jurisdiction founded in the actual or constructive possession of the subject matter. . . . We apprehend the true principle to be that indicated in the last few words quoted from Story. We think the inquiry is, first, whether the subject matter was so situated as to be within the lawful control of the state under the authority of which the Court sits; and, secondly, whether the sovereign authority of that State has conferred on the Court jurisdiction to decide as to the disposition of the thing, and the Court has acted within its jurisdiction. If these conditions are fulfilled, the adjudication is conclusive against all the world',

unless the content infringes public order (Lord Collins of Mapesbury and Harris, supra (n 14) Chpt 5, Rule 2, 5–001 ff.

262 See Explanatory Note, para 210.

263 Traditionally the catalogue with the grounds for refusal of recognition of judgments is longer (e.g. see Art 45(1)(a–e) Brussels I-bis. B Hess, *EU-Zivilprozessrecht*, 5th edn. (2021) para 2 ff.; W Tetley, *International Conflict of Laws* (1994) 834–846), albeit the traditional grounds are four: (i) lack of international jurisdiction, (ii) violation of public policy of the *forum*, (iii) fraud/*fraus legis* (*Cammell v Sewell* 3 Hurl & N 617 (1858). W Wylie-Spicer, Court-Ordered Sale of Vessels (1979–1980) 11 *JMLC* 239, 245–249) and (iv) breach of natural justice (Lord Collins of Mapesbury and Harris, supra (n 14) Rule 55, paras 14R–158 et seq.)

264 According to the drafters, the term is adopted to set a high threshold and avoid an overly and expansive application by courts, see Explanatory Note, para 212.

265 In the Civil law systems, the term appears as "*public order/ordre public*".

266 On the distinction between domestic public order, domestic public policy and international public order/policy, see Tetley, supra (n 265) 100–101.

267 According to Art 7(3), if the certificate has been issued in a language other than the official language in which the register is kept, the registrar has a right to request its production in an official translation. No new certificate shall be issued in the requested language from the authority that conducted the judicial sale, as it is issued only once. Therefore, an official translation according to the provisions of the *lex loci actus* of the place of registration will suffice (Draft Explanatory Note, Add. 2, para 17, p. 6).

registrar[268] or the local court, determines that the effect of the judicial sale is manifestly contrary to its public policy.

3.67. Public policy is a legal concept[269] embodied in many national[270] and international[271] regimes. Its meaning is developed by judicial interpretation, which inevitably gives ground for divergent approaches.[272] If the challenge of the effects of the judicial sale by contesting the certificate would be paralleled with the refusal of recognition of a judgment according to Article 45 paragraph 1(a) Brussels I-bis[273] on the ground that it is manifestly contrary to public policy of the receiving state, then, as regards the meaning of public policy, the approach taken by the Court of Justice of the European Union (CJEU) could prove useful.[274] In *Krombach v Bamberski* the court found that,

> the infringement would have to constitute a manifest breach of a rule of law regarded as essential in the legal order of the State in which enforcement is sought or of a right recognised as being fundamental within that legal order.[275]

3.68. Thus, in the aforementioned example, where the application for registration according to the certificate relates to a right, which differs from the right recorded in the register, the answer would probably be negative in terms of manifest contravention to public policy. On the other hand, in the extreme case of execution proceedings without pre-enforcement formalities and publicity or without notice to the arrestee[276] or on

---

[268] As mentioned above, the determination at the *locus registrationis* can be carried out, either by the registrar or by the court, and from that perspective, Art 7 para 5 is an exception to the exclusive court review introduced by Art 10.

[269] F Mosconi, Exceptions to the Operation of Choice of Law Rules (1989) 217 *Recueil des Cours* 9–214; A Mills, 'The Dimensions of Public Policy in Private International Law' (2008) 4 Journal of Private International Law 201.

[270] In English law, see *Kuwait Airways Corp v Iraqi Airways Co (Nos 4 & 5)* [2002] 2 AC 883. In Greek law, see *Areios Pagos (plenary) 9/2016* Chronika Idiotikou Dikaiou 2016, 747. *Areios Pagos (plenary) 17/1999* Nomiko Vima 48, 461. *Vrellis* in Civil Code (Commentary) of Georgiadis and Stathopoulos, *General Principles*, vol I, Art 33 (in Greek); K Simantiras, *General Principles of Civil Law*, 4th edn. (1988) paras 71–74 (in Greek). Public order comprises a set of primary and fundamental principles and perceptions, of moral, political, social or economic nature that regulate every-day life in Greece at a given time period (*Areios Pagos 203/1963* Nomiko Vima 11, 1114). According to Art 33 Greek CC, the foreign provision must contravene public order in its application, so that consequently it will be displaced. However, not every mandatory rule of Art 3 Greek CC falls in the ambit of public order of Art 33 Greek CC. In the field of maritime law, see S Vrellis, The Protection of Maritime Creditors and Greek Private International Law [1994] *Proceedings of the 1st International Conference on Maritime Law Under the Auspices of Piraeus Bar* 106, 124 (in Greek).

[271] See Art 45(1)(a) Brussels I-bis. On the origins of this ground of refusal of recognition, see Brussels Convention 1968 "on jurisdiction and recognition of decisions in civil and commercial disputes" and the Jenard Report [1979] OJEC C59/1, 44. Also Art 7(1)(c) Hague International Convention 2019 "on the recognition and enforcement of court decisions in civil and commercial cases" (hereinafter "Hague Convention 2019").

[272] Bleyen, supra (n 167) 171.

[273] Lazic and Mankowski, supra (n 165) 7.301 et seq.

[274] The drafters also provided few examples in the Explanatory Note, para 213. See also *C-302/13 flyLAL-Lithuanian Airlines AS v Starptautiskā lidosta Rīga VAS and Air Baltic Corporation AS* EU:C:2014:2319 para 77 et seq.

[275] *C-7/98 Krombach v Bamberski* [2000] ECR I-1956 para 37. S Leible in T Rauscher, *Europäisches Zivilprozess- und Kollisionsrecht EuZPR/EuIPR*, vol I, 5th edn. (2021) Art 45, para 5 ff (in German).

[276] *Areios Pagos 1038/1973* Nomiko Vima 1974, 639 (in Greek). *Quaere*, in English law service of the writ *in rem* on the ship suffices for arrest purposes, without need for service to the shipowner (Myburgh, supra (n 133) 355, 365).

the basis of forged and falsified documents, the invocation of manifest contravention would probably succeed. Similarly, if the enforceable title was issued against the time charterer and execution was levied on the ship, as if judgment was also pronounced against the shipowner.[277] In view of the aforementioned examples, it is apparent that contravention to public policy according to Article 7 paragraph 5 will not occur often.[278]

3.69. Moreover, the Convention does not determine the holders[279] of the right, apparently, because the issue in question is contingent on the *lex fori* of the receiving country, a solution that may produce unsatisfactory consequences, especially in case of collusion between arrestor and arrestee.

3.70. The second limit is placed at the ports that the vessel visits post-sale, in which various unsatisfied creditors may pursue its detention by virtue of a provisional[280] arrest or other similar measure. If the purchaser seeks relief by invoking the effects stemming from the certificate, then the creditor may, in defence, raise the ground of manifest contravention to public policy before the adjudicating court.[281] Apart from the difficulty in adducing sufficient evidence to substantiate the ground, this path could exacerbate forum shopping, as it is undoubtable that the creditor would entertain proceedings only in a *forum* where he would have positive knowledge in advance that the specific ground would be upheld.

3.71. The third limit is marked in the rest of the receiving countries according to Article 10. *Ex officio* power is conferred to every contracting country court[282] but the fact that the provision, neither prescribes the type of remedial relief *ratione materiae* nor the scope *ratione personae,*[283] makes it vestigial. On the other hand, it obviously aims to "absorb" the adverse repercussions from the circulation of the certificate outside the boundaries of the *locus executionis*. It is submitted that the court could determine the point, either as a main or as an incidental issue.

3.72. It may safely be concluded from the aforementioned analysis, that the finding by a national court of manifest contravention to public policy could only have

---

[277] Bleyen, supra (n 167) 22–23.

[278] Draft Explanatory Note, Add. 2, paras 36–37, p. 11; Myburgh, supra (n 139) 410, 417.

[279] E.g. arrestee, announced creditor, holder of charge in the register, etc. See Art 25 Belgian Code of International Private Law, which empowers the ship registrar with the right to examine grounds -not only contravention to public policy – for refusal of recognition of the judgment submitted to the registry. The same power is vested in the Belgian court on adjudication of recognition, whether as principal or incidental issue (Bleyen, supra (n 167) 63–64). Under Dutch law, the mechanism of recognition of judgments has been developed by courts. Moreover, the registrar shall refuse the deletion from the register of a Dutch flag ship sold abroad (Art 195 Book 8 of Dutch Civil Code) unless a local court approves the sale (Bleyen, supra (n 167) 93–97).

[280] Reference is made to the explanatory notes of the Arrest Conventions. Therefore, it is not accurate that the similar measure should be capable of leading to a judicial sale (Draft Explanatory Note, Add. 2, para 23, pp. 7–8), as in the Continental law systems it would suffice for the application to have been pursued so as to force the shipowner to place security.

[281] See Art 8(4).

[282] Argument from the wording of Art 10, which reads "in a State Party other than the State of judicial sale".

[283] See Explanatory Note, para 214.

territorial effect,[284] because in the rest of the Contracting countries, the presumption of its validity would survive, especially at the place of registration of the ship.

3.73. Contrariwise, should the registrar or the court of the *locus registrationis* determine contravention to public policy with the consequence of invalidation of the certificate and re-enrolment of the initial ownership and other charges in the register, such outcome would have "*quasi-extraterritorial effect*" in the sense that the purchaser would be divested of his substantive rights in the ship due to lack of title, especially if registration in the register is a substantive element for the acquisition of rights.

3.5.8 Relationship of the Convention with existing international treaties and national law

3.74. In spite of the problematic wording in Article 14,[285] the drafters are correct in proclaiming that any legal duties of the ratifying Contracting countries stemming from previous international treaties on recognition of judicial sale of ships would remain unaffected.[286]

3.75. Regarding countries, which were parties to a previous treaty on the subject but, now, only one is a contracting party to the Convention, the provision reflects the self-evident,[287] that supremacy should be accorded to the provisions of the predating international instrument.[288] In case both countries have ratified the new regime, the only logical construction of Article 14 would be to accept that it "gives way" to the domestic mechanism,[289] on the condition that no infringement of the Convention would occur.[290]

3.76. The provision also seems to encourage the Contracting countries to retain their domestic mechanism, in case the judicial sale is conducted in another contracting

---

[284] See Explanatory Note, para 210. It is also reinforced by the non-imposition of a duty on the national court to convey its decision to the GISIS repository, a duty which rests only with the *forum executionis* upon avoidance of the judicial sale by virtue of Art 9 para 3.

[285] When one reads the provision in light of the Explanatory Note, it seems that the term "Party" next to "State" is missing from the text of the provision. As it stands, it gives the impression that it deals with non-Party States.

[286] See Explanatory Note, para 227.

[287] See Art 30 para 4(b) Vienna Convention on the Law of Treaties 1969 (hereinafter "Vienna Convention").

[288] See Explanatory Note, para 228. The comment of the framers that Art 14 should not "give way" to a previous treaty, which provides grounds for denial of the effect of a foreign judicial sale according to the Convention, is questionable.

[289] As already shown, the domestic mechanism of judgment recognition is distinguishable from the embedment of consequences of the foreign judicial sale by virtue of the Convention (Draft Explanatory Note, Add. 1, para 74, p. 17

> Article 6 and other provisions of the convention purposefully refer to 'giving effect' to a foreign judicial sale and not to the 'recognition' of that sale. As noted in the remarks on article 1, the convention is concerned with the effects of judicial sales and not with the recognition of judgments).

As such, nothing should prevent the purchaser from recognising the sale decision/order by virtue of the domestic regime, in case it would prove to be a more favourable option.

[290] Argument from Art 30 para 3 Vienna Convention. Draft Explanatory Note, Add. 2, para 59, p. 17.

country but somehow[291] the Convention could not apply. More so, to accommodate the recognition of judicial sales conducted in non-contracting countries.[292]

3.77. Regarding the position in EU Member States, the following should be observed. By virtue of Council Decision (EU) 2024/414, the Council authorised its President to designate a person to sign the Convention on behalf of the European Union and make the declaration, annexed in the Decision, in accordance with Article 18 paragraphs 2 and 20 and paragraphs 1–2 of the Convention. The signing act was executed on 14 March 2024. As a result, no conflict should ordinarily occur with the framework introduced by Brussels I-bis regarding the outcome of a judicial sale from one EU Member State to another or from a third country[293] and an EU country.

However, in view of the previous analysis, the following should be exposed.

3.78. First, it is submitted that the judicial sale certificate does not fall in the ambit of Article 2(a) Brussels I-bis,[294] because, as was shown, it does not have the attributes required to qualify as "judgment". A problematic situation, therefore, could be faced, if, concurrently with the attempt of the purchaser to execute the certificate in an EU Member State ship registry, the previous shipowner would entertain proceedings for the suspension of the effects of the judicial sale judgment, either according to Article 36(2) by analogy or according to Article 45 Brussels I-bis,[295] supported by an application for interim relief to enjoin the registrar from taking action according to the provisions of the Convention. In that case, the registrar would be bound by the provisional decision of the local court, if it would order suspension of registration until adjudication of the application for non-recognition on the merits. Under those circumstances, should the relevant rules of Brussels I-bis be displaced, even subsequent to ratification by EU Member States?

3.79. Second, would ratification of the Convention prevent occurrence of a similar problem, in case the application for non-recognition or non-enforcement would assert that the certificate qualifies as a "public document"?[296] Following the previous line of reasoning, and on the hypothesis that the certificate could qualify as a "public document" by virtue of Article 2(c) Brussels I-bis, there is a question that requires a reasoned response. Would it be possible for an EU Member State to issue a certificate of judicial sale for use in the ship registry of another Member State, without violating the exclusive jurisdiction base of Article 24(3) Brussels I-bis? The counterargument, that a court decision following a forced sale, which underpins the issuance of the

---

291 E.g. the title was not clean, the certificate could not be issued because notice was not given according to the requirements of Art 4 paras 3 to 7.

292 See Explanatory Note, para 228.

293 If the judgment originated from a non-EU country, then the matter would fall within the scope of the Hague Convention 2019 (see I Revolidis, From the Ashes We Will Rise – Recognition and Enforcement of International Judgments After the Revival of the Hague Convention [2021] *Lex & Forum* 1025 ff. (in Greek)). But, since public documents fall outside the scope of recognition and enforcement of the latter instrument, a problem may occur from the prevention of the effects of the certificate by invoking denial of recognition of the forced sale judgment.

294 Lazic and Mankowski, supra (n 165) 1.168 et seq.

295 Lazic and Mankowski, supra (n 165) 7.097–7.099.

296 Lazic and Mankowski, supra (n 165) 7.419. If the certificate qualifies as public document, then would ratification of the Convention set aside Art 58(1)(b), 46 and 45 Brussels I-bis?

certificate, does not have a ruling for entries in the register but rather on the auctioned right, is unpersuasive because the issued certificate will generate an equivalent effect, that is, by a backdoor, the court of one Member State will order the registrar of another Member State to make entries in the records that it keeps.

3.80. Third, for EU Member States, in which registration is a substantive element for the acquisition of proprietary rights in a ship, the mechanism of the Convention would seem problematic and a breach of the exclusive jurisdiction base of Article 24(3) would also constitute an obstacle for recognition and enforcement according to Article 45(1)(e)(ii) Brussels I-bis.[297]

3.81. Now, according to the declaration annexed to Decision 2024/414, the Council, on behalf of the EU, proclaimed:

> To the extent that they may affect common rules or alter the scope of the legal acts referred to in points a and b, the matters governed by provisions of the Convention in respect of which the Member States of the European Union have transferred competence and in respect of which the European Union has exclusive competence within the meaning of Article 3(2) TFEU are the following:
>
> (a) Article 9 of the Convention ('Jurisdiction to avoid and suspend judicial sale') with regard to the rules on jurisdiction in Regulation (EU) No 1215/2012 of the European Parliament and of the Council of 12 December 2012 on jurisdiction and the recognition and enforcement of judgments in civil and commercial matters (OJ L 351, 20.12.2012, p. 1); and
>
> (b) Article 4 of the Convention ('Notice of judicial sale') with regard to the rules on the service of judicial and extrajudicial documents in civil or commercial matters (service of documents) in Regulation (EU) 2020/1784 of the European Parliament and of the Council of 25 November 2020 on the service in the Member States of judicial and extrajudicial documents in civil and commercial matters (OJ L 405, 2.12.2020, p. 40).

In consideration of the aforementioned declaration, two remarks need to be made.

3.82. First, it is submitted that Articles 4 and 9 are not the only provisions that clash with Brussels I-bis. Should we accept that the certificate is a "public document" – if not a simple document – then substantial tools and devices of the latter instrument need to be set aside for the Convention to function. More importantly, a fundamental principle in Brussels I-bis that public books of Member States should not be amended by legal acts originating from other EU organised-courts would be infringed.

3.83. This brings us to the second remark. What is the ambit of power of the Council in the "deactivation" of a regulation? Are there limitations and restrictions? Can a "particular matter" decompose the "core" of a fundamental legal instrument, such as Regulation 1215/2012, which aims at the development of judicial cooperation in civil matters with cross-border implications based on the principle of mutual recognition of judgments and of decisions in extrajudicial cases?

3.84. The issue is extremely complicated and exceeds the scope of the present Article but the following thoughts should be submitted. On the premise that the Convention qualifies as a specialised instrument, it must be observed that Brussels I-bis is not dealing with future instruments, albeit certain principles could be extracted from

[297] Lazic and Mankowski, supra (n 165) 7.369–7.370.

Article 71 – comprising a "coordinating provision"[298] or a "disconnection clause"[299] – and apply *per analogiam*.[300]

3.85. First, the CJEU has held that the application of international conventions preceding the Regulation,

> cannot compromise the principles which underlie judicial cooperation in civil and commercial matters in the European Union, such as the principles, recalled in recitals 6, 11, 12 and 15 to 17 in the preamble to Regulation No 44/2001, of free movement of judgments in civil and commercial matters, predictability as to the courts having jurisdiction and therefore legal certainty for litigants, sound administration of justice, minimisation of the risk of concurrent proceedings, and mutual trust in the administration of justice in the European Union. Observance of each of those principles is necessary for the sound operation of the internal market, which, as is apparent from recital 1 in the preamble, constitutes the raison d'être of Regulation No 44/2001.[301]

3.86. More importantly, the application of the specialised legal instruments that had been concluded prior to the Regulation cannot lead to results, which are less favourable for achieving sound operation of the internal market than the results to which the regulation's provisions lead.[302]

3.87. Therefore, the relevant provisions of the previous conventions can be applied in the European Union only to the extent that they are highly predictable, facilitate the sound administration of justice and, in the case of recognition and enforcement of judgments, the relevant principles are free movement of judgments and mutual trust in the administration of justice (*favor executionis*.)[303]

3.88. It is submitted that the aforementioned principles extend *per analogiam*, restraining the Council's power in the ratification of future international instruments, as the present Convention.

3.89. Further, Regulation (EU) 662/2009, albeit dealing with the authorisation by the Council of a Member State to conclude an agreement between the latter and a third country on particular matters concerning the law applicable to contractual and non-contractual obligations, could be of assistance in the development of principles that could apply for the signature of a specialised convention by the Council itself.

3.90. Of relevance may be Article 4(b), by which the Commission is required to assess whether the envisaged agreement appears not to render community law ineffective and not to undermine the proper functioning of the system established by that law.

3.91. However, as was shown, there may be pure intra-EU cases, where the judicial sale was conducted in a Member State and the recordings need to be entered in another Member State ship registry. Also, the forced sale process may be performed outside the European Union but the entries are requested in an EU ship registry.

3.92. It is questionable if the Convention should be accorded supremacy over the recognition and enforcement mechanism and remedies of Brussels I-bis in view of the

298 *C-406/92 The Tatry*, Opinion of Advocate General Tesauro, ECR- I 7442, para 8.

299 M Pauknerova, *International Conventions and Community Law: Harmony and Conflicts, Liber Fausto Pocar, vol. II, Nuovi strumenti del diritto internazionale Private* (2009) 793, 802.

300 U Magnus and P Mankowski, *Brussels I Regulation*, 2nd edn. (2012) Art 71, para 5.

301 *C-533/08 TNT Express Nederland BV v AXA Versicherung AG* [2010] ECR I-4107 paras 49–50.

302 Ibid, para 51.

303 Ibid, paras 53–54.

inferior protection afforded to the arrestee by the Convention, especially in case of avoidance of the judicial sale. That may be so, due to lack of a specific remedy for the elimination of the effects of the judicial sale that was avoided. Also, because there is no requirement for the certificate to be submitted with the underpinning judgment, which may be problematic in case of discrepancy between the awarded and the registered right or in case the sale order was issued *ex parte* subsequent to a contentious summoning method of the arrestee.

3.93. A final remark about Article 14. It is submitted that there is a dogmatic contradiction in the assertion that the Convention is only dealing with the effects of a judicial sale and not with the recognition of judgments, but when it comes to a domestic mechanism which deals with that subject and gives grounds for refusal of the effect of a foreign judicial sale,[304] it should be displaced so as to avoid collision.[305]

3.6 Final remarks

3.94. The special nature of the ship, which is *res mobilis* but it is treated as immovable property for specific purposes, together with the special nature of the charges on it, especially from a private international law perspective, render the recognition of a judicial sale process an extremely complicated issue.

3.95. What exacerbates the problem is also the disparate nature of the forced proceedings on a ship,[306] *in rem* for the Anglo-common law jurisdictions and *in personam* for the civil law systems. The three failed attempts to unify the law on recognition of ship security rights at supranational level also demonstrate the inefficiencies ensuing. Consensus between countries is still a desideratum.

3.96. The Convention endeavours to address the issue but, regrettably, does not tackle the "core" of the problem, as it finally creates a "detour". This is because it does

---

[304] Draft Explanatory Note, Add. 2, para 53, p. 16

> As such, article 14 would not give way to the application of grounds for refusal under another treaty beyond the public policy exception in article 10 of the present convention. In that case, the provisions of the convention, notably article 6, would apply to their fullest extent, in accordance with the general principle stated in article 30(3) of the Vienna Convention on the Law of Treaties (1969).

[305] Draft Explanatory Note, Add. 1, para 74, p. 17

> Article 6 and other provisions of the convention purposefully refer to 'giving effect' to a foreign judicial sale and not to the 'recognition' of that sale. As noted in the remarks on article 1, the convention is concerned with the effects of judicial sales and not with the recognition of judgments

and Draft Explanatory Note, Add. 2, para 53, p. 16

> As such, article 14 would not give way to the application of grounds for refusal under another treaty beyond the public policy exception in article 10 of the present convention. In that case, the provisions of the convention, notably article 6, would apply to their fullest extent, in accordance with the general principle stated in article 30(3) of the Vienna Convention on the Law of Treaties (1969).

[306] See the pertinent comments in *The Mary* 9 Cranch, 126 (US 1815)

> Where these proceedings are against the person, notice is served personally, or by publication; where they are in rem, notice is served upon the thing itself. This is necessarily notice to all those who have any interest in it, to guard that interest by persons who are in a situation to protect it. Every person, therefore, who could assert any title to THE 'MARY', has constructive notice of her seizure, and may fairly be considered as a party to the libel.

not solve the problem on the basis of substantive law. Instead, the solution is based on procedural tools with the aim to "clean" the sold ship from charges, but in a way which "legitimises" the results of *forum executionis* shopping practices.

3.97. Is this "*finis rerum*"? Definitely not,[307] and the quest for uniformity in this controversial field of law continues.

[307] See the scepticism expressed by Myburgh, supra (n 139) 410, 423.

CHAPTER 4

The Anglo-common law approach to foreign judicial ship sales and the Beijing Convention

*Paul Myburgh**

4.1 Introduction

4.1. The judicial sale of a ship[1] is the usual *terminus ad quem* of an admiralty proceeding *in rem*, at least where no satisfactory alternative security has been provided, which will usually be the case where the shipowner is insolvent or has no P&I Club cover for some other reason.[2]

4.2. Most jurisdictions draw a fundamental distinction between private and judicial ship sales, with the latter category having the important legal consequence of conferring clean title on the purchaser in a judicial sale[3] – a protection not afforded to purchasers in private ship sales, who must take the vessel subject to all existing claims and encumbrances.[4] The obvious advantage of a title-cleansing judicial imprimatur has led to the development of a rather more controversial "hybrid" judicial ship sale process, the court-approved private direct sale,[5] which has been enthusiastically embraced by courts and legislators in some jurisdictions, but treated with significantly more circumspection in others.[6]

---

* Professor, Auckland University of Technology Law School; Adjunct Research Professor, Centre for Maritime Law, National University of Singapore.

1 On which, see generally, Lief Bleyen, *Judicial Sales of Ships: A Comparative Study*, Hamburg Studies on Maritime Affairs, vol 36 (2016, Springer).

2 See, generally, Paul Myburgh, 'P&I Club Letters of Undertaking and Admiralty Arrests' (2018) 24 JIML 201.

3 See *The Union Gold* [2013] EWHC 1696 (Admlty), [2014] 1 Lloyd's Rep 53 [2]–[6]; *Natwest Markets Plc v Stallion Eight Shipping Co SA (The MV Alkyon)* [2018] EWHC 2033 (Admlty) [2018] 2 Lloyd's Rep 601 [51]; and the cases discussed in Part 4.2.

4 See *The Spermina* [1923] 17 Ll L Rep 52: "Mr Justice HILL pointed out that the Canal Company, in any sale which they effected, could not give a title free from maritime liens, whereas the Marshal could give an absolutely clean title if he sold". But see *The Blitz* [1992] 2 Lloyd's Rep 441 (Sheen J).

5 On which, see Paul Myburgh, "Satisfactory for Its Own Purposes": Private Direct Arrangements and Judicial Vessel Sales (2016) 22 JIML 355; *The Union Gold*, supra (n 3); *The Margo L* [1997] HKCFI 776, [1988] 1 HKC 217; *The Turtle Bay* [2013] SGHC 165, [2013] 4 SLR 615; *The Sea Urchin* [2014] SGHC 24, [2014] 2 SLR 646.

6 While there has been a noticeably more wary, or even hostile, attitude towards court-approved private direct ship sales in the United Kingdom, Hong Kong SAR and Singapore in recent years (see cases in n 5 above), other countries have deliberately moved in the opposite direction: see, e.g. Sub-title V of the Code of Organization and Civil Procedure of Malta, Arts 358–364, introduced in 2006, which allows the Maltese Courts to "approve a private sale of an aircraft, ship or vessel, in favour of an identified buyer and in consideration of a determined price": <https://legislation.mt/eli/act/2006/14/eng/pdf>. These starkly differing domestic law approaches to private direct ship sales will undoubtedly fuel judicial sale forum shopping.

DOI: 10.4324/9781003499930-4

4.3. For the creditors and original owner of the ship, the judicial sale process and distribution of sale proceeds by the court represents the determination and conclusion of the causes of action which gave rise to the *in rem* proceedings. For the new owner of the ship, judicial sale and its conferral of clean title are supposed to provide a clean break, a fresh start and a safe *terminus a quo* from which the ship's new operations can commence. Where the law of the vessel's place of registration (the law of the flag) and the *lex fori* under which the judicial sale took place (the *lex executionis*) are the same, there are unlikely to be any serious legal or practical complications – the local ship register should be amenable to the local selling court's instructions to transfer registered title to the purchaser in the judicial sale;[7] and any attempts by creditors to re-arrest the vessel for unsatisfied claims (even if they enjoyed a maritime lien prior to the judicial sale) in the local jurisdiction should receive short shrift from that court on the basis of judgment estoppel.

4.4. However, the globalised nature of the shipping industry and the rise of forum shopping in the context of judicial sales means that, more often than not, the law of the flag of the ship being sold and the *lex executionis* will not coincide. That raises an obvious problem for the purchaser in a judicial sale – will the ship registry of the purchased ship and the courts of its flag state recognise and enforce, or at least assist to uphold the consequences of, the foreign judicial ship sale? Unwillingness to do so may result in significant legal and practical problems for the purchaser, both in terms of getting its foreign court-approved title registered or transferred in the relevant ship registry system and avoiding re-arrest of the vessel by creditors who had claims against it prior to the (unrecognised) foreign judicial ship sale.

4.5. By contrast to the key substantive parameters of ship arrest, which have been harmonised to a significant degree by the Arrest Conventions 1952 and 1999, the issue of judicial ship sales and their recognition and enforcement have largely been left to national law and domestic private international law rules, which has occasionally caused problems. An initiative by the Comité Maritime International (CMI), subsequently taken up by the United Nations Commission on International Trade Law (UNCITRAL), however, has resulted in a new Convention tackling these issues directly: the United Nations Convention on the International Effects of Judicial Sales of Ships, colloquially referred to as the Beijing Convention on the Judicial Sale of Ships (the Beijing Convention).[8] The purpose of this chapter is to analyse the approach in Anglo-common law legal systems to judicial ship sales and their recognition and enforcement, and to compare that with the proposed Beijing Convention framework. The chapter concludes with an evaluation of the benefits and drawbacks of the Beijing Convention from an Anglo-common law perspective.

[7] Although not invariably – see *The Ruby (No 2)* [1898] P 52, 58 (PDA), where the Registrar of Shipping refused to recognise the full effect of an appraisement and sale by the high bailiff of the Bow County Court exercising jurisdiction under the County Courts Admiralty Jurisdiction Act 1868, on the basis that that Act did not give the County Courts jurisdiction in rem to extinguish a registered ship mortgage by judicial sale. This argument was rejected by Jeune P, who found that "the sale was good, and the ship must be registered in the name of the purchaser' free from encumbrances".

[8] See Part 4.

4.2 The English approach

4.2.1 The judicial ship sale process

4.6. The usual process in England and Wales[9] is for an order to be made upon judgment or (in the case of a sale *pendente lite*, before judgment)[10] that the vessel be surveyed, appraised and sold by the Admiralty Marshal.[11] Appraisal involves an official valuation by a court-appointed broker or brokers to ascertain a fair market price for the vessel.[12] This appraisal value, in the normal scheme of things, represents the minimum price at which the Marshal may sell the vessel, and therefore acts as a protection against judicial "fire sales".[13] If the bids fall below the appraisal value, or indeed if there are no bidders, the Admiralty Court will then have to do what it can to act in the best interests of all the parties involved.[14]

4.2.2 The legal effect of English judicial ship sales

4.7. The most significant hallmark of a judicial ship sale in English law is that it confers a clean title, free of any claims or encumbrances, on the purchaser of the vessel. This is significant for at least two reasons: first, it ensures legal finality, in that all existing claims against, and encumbrances on, the sold vessel are automatically transferred to the sales proceeds held by the court. This means that the sold vessel should, in theory at least, no longer be a target for the enforcement of any existing maritime liens or statutory rights of action *in rem*, and the purchaser in a judicial sale should enjoy a cast-iron confidence in its title to the vessel that a purchaser in a private sale cannot. Secondly, the clean title conferred by the judicial ship sale should, again in theory at least, ensure the most favourable price for the vessel in the judicial sale, or at least a more favourable price than might be achieved in a private direct sale.[15]

---

9 For the practice in Scotland, see Duncan MacLean, Ship Arrest in Scotland [2010] LMCLQ 579.

10 On which, see D Rhidian Thomas, Admiralty Sales Pendente Lite (1998) 17 Civil Justice Quarterly 409; Paul Myburgh, Admiralty Sales Pendente Lite: Reserve Prices and Broker Appointments (2018) 24 JIML 369; *The Commercial Court Guide (Incorporating the Admiralty Court Guide)*, 11th edn. (2022) para N12.2 <www.judiciary.uk/wp-content/uploads/2022/06/Commercial-Court-Guide-11th-edition-1.pdf>.

11 CPR r. 61.10(1) and PD 61.10.

12 In England and Wales, Kellocks, now a member of the Eggar Forrester Group, has acted as the Admiralty Marshal's broker for over 150 years (but cf *Deutsche Bank Trust Co Americas v The Owners of the Motor Vessel Sertão* [2018] EWHC 1013 (Admlty), [2018] Lloyd's Rep 275, where the mortgagee insisted on its own specialist broker being involved in the judicial sale). In Singapore, the Supreme Court has appointed a panel of three shipbrokers to provide appraisal services in the context of judicial sales: see <www.judiciary.gov.sg/services/sheriff-services-admiralty-actions>.

13 See the ADM14, which provides that "the Admiralty Marshal sell the vessel on his conditions of sale for the highest price that can be obtained for it, but not for less than the certified value without an order of court". See, also, *The Halcyon the Great (No 2)* [1975] 1 Lloyd's Rep 525.

14 By, e.g. sanctioning a private direct sale if that is the only way to achieve a sale (see *The Union Gold*, supra (n 3)), or postponing the judicial sale in the hope that economic conditions will improve (see *The Sertão*, supra (n 12)).

15 An assertion disputed by proponents of court-approved private direct sales, who argue that the hybrid process produces the best of both worlds: the speed and efficiency of a private sale, and the price maximisation of clean title: see, e.g. Buss, supra (n 133) 152, 154, who argues that judicial sales tend to achieve depressed "forced sale" prices, and that a private directed sale is a more effective mechanism for achieving a full market price.

4.8. The classic authority on this point is *The Tremont*,[16] in which the High Court of Admiralty was called upon to decide the legal effect of the judicial sale of a US vessel in Liverpool in a bottomry case. Doctor Lushington held that:[17]

> In all cases of bottomry and salvage, and also in claims for wages, which are brought before it, this Court possesses an undoubted power to decree a sale of the vessel proceeded against, unless the demand of the successful suitor be satisfied. The jurisdiction of the Court in these matters is confirmed by the municipal law of this country and by the general principles of the maritime law; and the title conferred by the Court in the exercise of this authority is a valid title against the whole world, and is recognised by the Courts of this country and by the Courts of all other countries.

4.9. However, the fact that the relevant vessel was registered in the United States caused a complication. The US purchaser refused to go through with the sale without a copy of the ship's register and sought a monition against the US Consulate to produce the register. The Judge refused this application, stating that this was unnecessary – the purchaser's title was "sufficiently established by the document issued by the Court in decreeing the sale under which the purchase has been made".[18] In fact, the Judge was concerned that requiring the ship's register to be produced might undermine the Admiralty Court's perceived legal authority to sell the vessel and to give clean title:[19]

> The result would be, that a distrust of the title conferred by the Court might be raised in future cases, and a serious injury be inflicted upon property of this kind sold under the jurisdiction of the Court, by inducing an alarm in the minds of purchasers that something was necessary to confer a valid title beyond the document issued by decree of the Court.

4.10. Despite Doctor Lushington's references to "the general principles of the maritime law", and his confident assertion of universal recognition of the court's judgment, the facts in *The Tremont* clearly illustrate the potential Achilles' heel of the Anglo-Common Law approach to judicial ship sales. While any judgment *in rem* and judicial ship sale by any admiralty court is, of course, effective within the territorial limits of its own jurisdiction,[20] where the ship sold is registered in another jurisdiction, there are inevitably going to be subsequent legal and practical issues that require the co-operation of the registry where that ship is flagged, as well as recognition by foreign courts.

4.11. The theme of confidence in the clean title conferred by judicial ship sale was further developed in *The Acrux*,[21] a case involving the court-ordered sale of an Italian

---

[16] [1841] 1 Wm Rob 163, 166 ER 534.

[17] Ibid.

[18] Ibid 165, 535.

[19] Ibid.

[20] See *Deputy Marshal, Federal Court v The Galaxias* [1989] 1 FC 375, 20 FTR 141, 1989 AMC 348 [11] (Rouleau J):

> Where a ship is sold by a judicial sale pursuant to a Court order in Canada, I do not see that any conflict of laws problem arises with respect to the sale itself, (the disposition of the proceeds is a different question). The sale of the *Galaxias* has occurred as a result of the recognition of substantive rights held by the parties before this Court, and as a judicial sale is a remedy attaching to such rights, it is governed by the laws of Canada, the *lex fori*.

See also the rather carefully worded r. 490(3) of the Canadian Federal Courts Rules (SOR/98–106): "Property sold under subsection (1) is free of any liens under Canadian maritime law".

[21] [1962] 1 Lloyd's Rep 405. For an attempt to apply the reasoning in *The Acrux* by analogy to a Dutch court sale of an aircraft, see *Air Foyle Ltd v Center Capital Ltd* [2002] EWHC 2535 (Comm), [2003] 2 Lloyd's Rep 753.

vessel, where Hewson J was alerted by the Admiralty Marshal to the fact that the purchasers were having difficulties deleting the vessel from the Italian register because there was doubt as to the efficacy of the English judicial sale at Italian law and that there was a risk that the mortgagees might pursue the ship again in Italy or other countries to recover the unsatisfied balance of their claims.

Hewson J was deeply unimpressed by this situation:[22]

> So far as all claimants against this ship before her arrest are concerned, their claims are now against the fund in this Court and not against the ship properly sold to an innocent purchaser free of incumbrances. Were such a clean title as given by this Court to be challenged or disturbed, the innocent purchaser would be gravely prejudiced. Not only that, but as a general proposition the maritime interests of the world would suffer. Were it to become established, contrary to general maritime law, that a proper sale of a ship by a competent Court did not give a clean title, those whose business it is to make advances of money in their various ways to enable ships to pursue their lawful occasions would be prejudiced in all cases where it became necessary to sell the ship under proper process of any competent Court. It would be prejudiced for this reason, that no innocent purchaser would be prepared to pay the full market price for the ship, and the resultant fund, if the ship were sold, would be minimized and not represent her true value.
>
> I cannot believe that ships' creditors keep themselves so ill-informed of the movements of the ship in which they are interested that they are unaware when that particular ship has been arrested and sold under an order of a Court of Admiralty, or unaware that such a sale gives and, so far as I can discover, always has given a clean title.
>
> It would be intolerable, inequitable and an affront to the Court if any party who invoked the process of this Court and received its aid and, by implication, assented to the sale to an innocent purchaser, should thereafter proceed or was able to proceed elsewhere against the ship under her new and innocent ownership. This Court recognizes proper sales by competent Courts of Admiralty, or Prize, abroad – it is part of the comity of nations as well as a contribution to the general well-being of international maritime trade.

Hewson J therefore sought an undertaking from the mortgagees that they would not bring any further proceedings against the relevant ship.

4.12. An appeal to the international comity of nations was similarly made by Sheen J in the *Cerro Colorado*,[23] where the efficacy of an English judicial sale of a Spanish vessel was brought into question by an advertisement in Lloyd's List suggesting that the sale might not be recognised at Spanish law. After emphatically confirming that the Admiralty Marshal's sale of the ship would indeed confer clean title, free of all liens and encumbrances,[24] Sheen J said:

> I can only express the hope that the Spanish Court will, as a matter of comity, recognise the decrees made by this Court, which endeavours to give effect to the International Arrest Convention. From time to time almost every ship-owner wants to borrow money from his bank and to give as security a mortgage on a ship. The value of that security would be drastically reduced if, when it came to be sold by the Court there was any doubt as to whether the purchaser from the Court would get a title free of encumbrances and debts.

4.13. The obvious difficulty with both "hope" and "comity" is that they provide a relatively fragile foundation for the worldwide recognition and enforcement of judicial

---

22 [1962] 1 Lloyd's Rep 405, 409.
23 [1993] 1 Lloyd's Rep 58.
24 Ibid 60.

ship sales. A cynic might suggest that comity is merely one of those weasel words which judges employ to justify their accommodation (or non-accommodation) of foreign elements in conflict of laws.[25] Even those academic commentators who are well-disposed towards the notion of comity as the basis for the recognition and enforcement of foreign judgments would have to acknowledge its lack of teeth. It has been obvious from as early as 1841 in *The Tremont* that not all foreign jurisdictions are going to play ball in the aftermath of an English judicial ship sale. That said, the relative paucity of reported English judgments on problems arising from judicial ship sales suggests that international comity, whatever that might mean in the eye of the beholder, provides a sufficient stimulus for practical international co-operation in most judicial ship sale cases.

4.2.3 Recognition and enforcement of foreign judicial ship sales by the English courts

4.14. As Dicey, Morris and Collins point out, foreign judgments *in rem* "are freely recognised in England, but rarely call for enforcement".[26] Where the foreign judgment in rem[27] is in respect of immovable property situated overseas, the English courts will have no jurisdiction, thanks to the *Moçambique* rule.[28] The situation is more complex, however, where the foreign judgment in rem concerns movable property, like ships. Even in these cases, however, the courts are unlikely to be dealing with an issue of direct enforcement of the foreign judgment in rem. Instead:[29]

> if a claimant entitled under a foreign judgment in rem vesting in it the title to some movable thing brings an action for wrongful interference in England against a person who denies that title, it is in reality relying on its title rather than the source of it – the judgment. It is, in other words, relying on the foreign judgment qua an assignment rather than qua a judgment. So also is the purchaser of a ship sold by foreign judicial sale who sets up the foreign judgment by way of defence to the original owner's proceedings for wrongful interference. All that is involved is, at most, recognition of the foreign judgment, and, at that, recognition qua an assignment.

4.15. In other words, the main issue from a private international law perspective is who owns the vessel following a foreign judicial sale, and whether that alleged owner's title is clean. However, the resolution of that issue invariably turns on the incidental question of whether the foreign judgment in rem was valid in the first place.

[25] On the inherent ambiguity of the notion of comity, see, e.g. JR Paul, 'Comity in International Law' (1991) 32 Harvard Int LJ 1; A Watson, *Joseph Story and the Comity of Errors: A Case Study in Conflict of Laws* (1992, U of Georgia P). For a more sympathetic analysis of the practical advantages of comity, see Thomas Schultz and Jason Mitchenson, 'Navigating Sovereignty and Transnational Commercial Law: The Use of Comity by Australian Courts' (2016) 12 JPIL 344.

[26] Lord Collins of Mapesbury and Jonathan Harris (eds), *Dicey, Morris, and Collins: The Conflict of Laws*, 16th edn. (2022, Sweet & Maxwell) paras 14–110.

[27] As broadly conceived in terms of private international law categories: where the foreign country's concept of in rem jurisdiction does not coincide with the English version, characterisation questions may arise: Lord Collins of Mapesbury and Harris, supra (n 26) paras 14–109. The prevailing view is that the legal effect of the foreign judgment matters more than the label which the foreign court attaches to it.

[28] See *British South Africa Co v Companhia de Moçambique* [1893] AC 602.

[29] Lord Collins of Mapesbury and Harris, supra (n 26) paras 14–110.

4.16. In *Cammell v Sewell*,[30] the Court of Exchequer had to determine the validity of the judicial sale of a Prussian ship, *The Augusta Bertha*, and its cargo, which was underwritten by English insurers, by a Norwegian court following its grounding near Molde in Norway. Martin B held that the Norwegian judgment was "in the nature of a judgment *in rem*, and such a judgment finally determines the question".[31] The plaintiff underwriters argued that the Norwegian judgment should be avoided by fraud, an argument which was rejected by the Court:[32]

> This is so if there were fraud found to affect it, but there is none. It is impossible to say there was any fraud in the Court. Indeed we see no reason to believe that the judge was not perfectly *bonâ fide*. If the defence to the suit, by the master or his agent and Mr Clausen [the purchaser of the cargo], can be said to be fraudulent, that is not the species of fraud to affect the judgment. Such fraud must be a fraud in the procuring of the judgment, such as collusion or the like, or fraud in the Court itself. It was also said that the judgment ought to have been pleaded. But this is not so. If it be a judgment in rem, it is conclusive evidence upon the plea that the goods were not the plaintiffs', and there is no necessity to plead it.

The plaintiffs' complaint of error was rejected by a majority[33] of the Exchequer Chamber,[34] with Crompton J affirming Martin B's general principle that "if personal property is disposed of in a manner binding according to the law of the country where it is, that disposition is binding everywhere".[35]

4.17. The reasoning in *Cammell v Sewell* was further developed in the landmark case of *Castrique v Imrie*,[36] which involved *The Ann Martin*, owned by Claus and registered in Liverpool, which was supplied with necessaries in the port of Melbourne. The master of the ship, Benson, drew a bill of exchange on Claus to cover the cost of the necessaries. This bill was subsequently dishonoured. Claus executed an English mortgage over the ship with Harrison, who subsequently sold the ship to Emley, who in turn sold it on to Castrique. The bill of exchange had meanwhile been endorsed to a French company, Trotteux & Co, who had the ship seized and sold in Le Havre to enforce their *privilége sur ce navire* (maritime lien over the ship) under French law. The French Tribunal appears to have disregarded the English ship mortgage and the subsequent transfers of the ship in England:[37]

> Whereas the nature of the deed which has been called 'mortgage' according to the English law, is of little importance in the case; whether it constitutes a real sale or only an apparent

30 3 H & N 617, 157 ER 615.

31 Ibid 627, 646.

32 Ibid 627–628, 646–647.

33 Cockburn CJ, Wightman, Williams, Crompton, and Keating JJ; Byles J dissenting.

34 *Cammell v Sewell* 5 H & N 728, 157 ER 1371.

35 *Cammell v Sewell* 5 H & N 744–745, 157 ER 1378. The majority doubted whether the Norwegian judgment was a judgment in rem or generated a judgment estoppel: "It is not, however, necessary for us to express any decided opinion on these questions, as we think that the case should be determined on the real merits as to the passing of the property". (*Cammell v Sewell* 5 H & N 742, 157 ER 1377). By contrast, Byles J partially based his dissent on his view that the Norwegian judgment was *not* a judgment *in rem* (*Cammell v Sewell* 5 H & N 751, 157 ER 1381).

36 [1870] LR 4 HL 414, HL(E).

37 [1870] LR 4 HL 417, HL(E) (n 2). The original French text is given at *Castrique v Imrie* 8 CB (NS) 10, 141 ER 1066.

> sale, or a security surrounded by certain peculiar privileges derived from the foreign law under the authority of which it was executed, the decision must be the same.

Imrie purchased the vessel in the judicial sale and registered his ownership in Liverpool. When the *Ann Martin* subsequently arrived in England, Castrique formally demanded possession of it, and brought an action in the Court of Common Pleas to recover it, on the ground that the judicial sale in France was illegal and void as against his earlier title. The Court of Common Pleas found in Castrique's favour.[38] The Court of Exchequer reversed.[39] Castrique appealed to the House of Lords, which affirmed the judgment of the Court of Exchequer.

4.18. In the House of Lords, Blackburn J quoted *Story on the Conflict of Laws* to the effect that a foreign judgment in rem is conclusive when it concerns:[40]

> moveable property within the jurisdiction of the Court pronouncing the judgment. Whatever it settles as to the right or title, or whatever disposition it makes of the property by sale, revendication, transfer, or other act, will be held valid in every other country where the question comes directly or indirectly in judgment before any other foreign tribunal. This is very familiarly known in the cases of proceedings in rem in foreign Courts of Admiralty, whether they be causes of prize or bottomry, or salvage or forfeiture, of which such Courts have a rightful jurisdiction founded in the actual or constructive possession of the subject matter.

Focusing on the last clause of this quotation as providing the "true principle", Blackburn J set out two fundamental requirements for recognition of foreign judicial ship sales:[41]

> We think the inquiry is, first, whether the subject matter was so situated as to be within the lawful control of the state under the authority of which the Court sits; and, secondly, whether the sovereign authority of that State has conferred on the Court jurisdiction to decide as to the disposition of the thing, and the Court has acted within its jurisdiction. If these conditions are fulfilled, the adjudication is conclusive against all the world.

Applying this legal test to the facts, Blackburn J had no doubt that the relevant judgments of the French Tribunals should be recognised, even though he might, "without arrogance",[42] say that they had misunderstood the legal effect at English law of the English ship mortgage to Harrison, and subsequent transfers of the ship to Emley and Castrique in England. However, a mistake regarding foreign law was not equivalent to fraud,[43] and it "would be peculiarly ungracious to assert this doctrine in a case where the English Courts below have differed on the question what the French law is".[44]

4.19. The first limb of the test in *Castrique v Imrie* is relatively unproblematic, but the second requirement regarding the foreign court's jurisdiction is more slippery. The issue is whether "a foreign judgment in rem, in order to be recognised in England, must have been pronounced by a court having local competence as well as international

38 *Castrique v Imrie* 8 CB (NS) 1, 141 ER 1062.
39 *Castrique v Imrie* 8 CB (NS) 1, 405 ER 1222.
40 (1870) LR 4 HL 414, 428–429.
41 Ibid 429.
42 (1870) LR 4 HL 414, 433.
43 See, also, *Godard v Gray* (1870–71) LR 6 QB 139.
44 (1870) LR 4 HL 414, 434.

jurisdiction".[45] In other words, does one assess the foreign court's jurisdiction in respect of a judicial ship sale against the yardstick of jurisdictional competence at the relevant foreign domestic law, or will it suffice if the foreign court had international jurisdiction according to English private international law principles? Dicey, Morris and Collins prefer the latter view: a foreign judgment should be regarded as unimpeachable in England when it meets the minimum criteria of international jurisdiction according to English conflicts rules, even if there were issues of jurisdictional competence under the local law.[46]

4.20. The primary ground on which a foreign judgment in rem will be refused recognition at English law is fraud, either on the part of the party in whose favour the judgment is given, or on the part of the court pronouncing the judgment.[47] This general rule must be adapted to the circumstances of foreign judicial ship sales by also focusing on the knowledge and conduct of the ship purchaser. Where the ship purchaser has colluded with creditor(s) and/or the shipowner in achieving a fraudulent judicial ship sale or has bribed the court directly, for example, there can be little doubt that the foreign judgment and subsequent transfer of ownership will be void. However, if the ship purchaser was not involved in, and had no knowledge of fraud perpetrated by the creditor(s), shipowner, or court, it would appear to be insulated from these vitiating factors. In the words of Blackburn J:[48]

> Fraud will indeed vitiate everything; though we may observe that there is much force in what [counsel] suggested in the course of his argument in this case, that even if there had been fraud on the part of the litigants, or even of the tribunal, it would be very questionable whether it could be set up against a bona fide purchaser who was quite ignorant of it.

4.21. Public policy may provide another basis for English courts to refuse to recognise a foreign judgment in rem and consequent judicial sale,[49] but this remains rather woolly. It is unlikely that an argument that the foreign judgment in rem and subsequent judicial ship sale process is, per se, punitive or contrary to human rights legislation, will succeed, as ship arrest and its legal and proprietary consequences are internationally recognised and sanctioned by the Arrest Conventions.[50]

4.22. A more interesting question is whether an English court will be willing to recognise a foreign judgment in rem and subsequent judicial ship sale effected in defiance of the issuance of an English anti-suit injunction. This question is rendered more complex by the position of the bona fide purchaser, who would typically be a

---

45 Lord Collins of Mapesbury and Harris, supra (n 26) paras 14–131.

46 Ibid paras 14–132. See further *Public Joint Stock Co ('Rosgosstrakh') v Starr Syndicate Ltd* [2020] EWHC 1557 (Comm), [2022] 1 Lloyd's Rep 74 [81].

47 Lord Collins of Mapesbury and Harris, supra (n 26) paras 14R–134 (R 53).

48 (1870) LR 4 HL 414, 433. See Lord Collins of Mapesbury and Harris, supra (n 26) paras 14–144.

49 Lord Collins of Mapesbury and Harris, supra (n 26) paras 14R–148 ff (Rule 54).

50 See, e.g. *Baltic Shipping Co Ltd v Pegasus Lines SA* [1996] 3 NZLR 641, 650 where the New Zealand Court of Appeal dismissed an argument based on s. 21 of the New Zealand Bill of Rights Act 1990, which provides that everyone has the right to be secure against unreasonable search or seizure, whether of the person, property, or correspondence or otherwise. McKay and Henry JJ observed:

> There is no doubt that the writ in rem and the arrest of a vessel is a very strong and effective remedy, but that does not make it unreasonable. It is a seizure by judicial process, to ensure that the ship or some alternative security is available to satisfy a claim which has still to be substantiated.

third party to the litigation, and not subject to the English court's anti-suit injunction. Even if the English court were unwilling to give effect to the foreign judgment in rem, it would seem to be deeply problematic to deny the bona fide purchaser's clean title to the vessel.

4.23. A lack or breach of natural justice is the other usual basis for attacking recognition and enforcement of foreign judgments.[51] Again, there would seem to be slim scope for this argument in the context of foreign judicial ship sales, given the *ex parte* nature of ship arrest and the universal acceptance of default admiralty judgments.[52] However, it must be conceivable that a lack of natural justice argument might come into play, for example, where foreign proceedings are held in secret, the ship is expropriated without any legal basis or process, or the judicial sale is not advertised, or advertised adequately. Such extreme cases, however, are already highly likely to fall at the second hurdle of the *Castrique v Imrie* test, as an abuse or excess of the competent jurisdiction of the selling court.

4.3 The Commonwealth approach

4.24. The English legal rules on the effects of judicial ship sales and recognition of foreign judicial ship sales have been readily received and applied by the courts of other Anglo-Common Law jurisdictions across the current and former Commonwealth.

4.25. In 1862, the Upper Canada Court of Queen's Bench adopted the reasoning in *Cammell v Sewell*[53] and the Court of Exchequer decision in *Castrique v Imrie*[54] in *Van Every v Grant*,[55] several years before the House of Lords decision in *Castrique v Imrie*.[56] *Van Every v Grant* involved an ownership dispute over the steamboat *Kaloolah*. The plaintiffs' claim to title arose from their purchase of the vessel in a judicial sale conducted by the Michigan Admiralty Court "for the satisfaction of certain claims which by the laws of that country constituted a lien upon the boat".[57] The Canadian jury held for the plaintiffs. The defendant in the original Michigan litigation interpleaded, arguing for a nonsuit or new trial on the basis that the Canadian jury had been misdirected as to the ownership of the vessel prior to its arrest and judicial sale in Michigan. Robinson CJ held that this issue was irrelevant, given the effect of the foreign judgment in rem and judicial sale in conferring clean title on the plaintiffs:[58]

> But if they were undecided on that point, or were even convinced that the steamer had really belonged to Alexander, and not to John, before she was sold in the state of Michigan, under the attachment law there, then their verdict should still have been in favour of the

---

[51] Lord Collins of Mapesbury and Harris, supra (n 26) paras 14R–158 ff (Rule 55).

[52] Myburgh, supra (n 5) 365.

[53] *Above (n 30).*

[54] *Above (n 39).*

[55] (1862) 21 UCQB 542, [1862] OJ No 78.

[56] Above (n 36).

[57] Above (n 55) [12].

[58] Above (n 55) [11]. See also *Meagher v Aetna Insurance Co* 1873 [1873] OJ No 175, 20 Gr 354 [46]:

> I should . . . not feel safe in deciding the question of the jurisdiction of the District Court, if I had to decide it upon American authorities; but I may safely proceed upon a principle enunciated in *Castrique v Imrie*.

> plaintiffs, for it did not signify to which of the two, or to what other person, she might have belonged at the time of her being attached, for she became beyond doubt, we think, the property of Moore [the plaintiffs' agent], by virtue of the sale made under the proceedings in the Court of Admiralty there in December 1859.

4.26. In full accordance with the rule in *Castrique v Imrie*, Canadian courts have held that a foreign judgment in rem handed down by a competent foreign court, and a subsequent judicial sale based on that judgment, will be respected as conferring clean title, even if they disagree with the reasoning of the foreign court's judgment.[59] As a logical corollary, a judgment of a foreign court lacking competency to exercise jurisdiction in rem will not be recognised.[60]

4.27. In Australia, the rule in *Castrique v Imrie* has also been received into Australian common law, first in the context of criminal res judicata,[61] and subsequently in forfeiture[62] and judicial sale cases. In the significant decision of *Readhead v Admiralty Marshal, Western Australia District Registry*,[63] the Federal Court of Australia was called upon to decide the status of the fishing vessel *Aliza Glacial* which was seized for fisheries offences in Australia under the Fisheries Management Act 1991 (Cth). The vessel was detained by the Australian Fisheries Management Authority. It was subsequently arrested in execution of a warrant issued under the Admiralty Act 1988 (Cth). Ryan J ordered summary judgment in the admiralty proceedings and the judicial sale of the ship in accordance with the Admiralty Rules. This squarely raised a fundamental conflict between the Australian fisheries forfeiture regime and the Australian admiralty judicial sale regime.

In attempting to resolve this conflict, Ryan J observed:[64]

> I accept, in the light of the ancient statements of principle as recently endorsed, for example, by Sheen J in *The 'Cerro Colorado'*, that a sale by the Marshal pursuant to an order of a Court of Admiralty made within jurisdiction confers on the purchaser an unencumbered title which is good against the whole world. See also *Castrique v Imrie*.

4.28. Singapore has also adopted the rule in *Castrique v Imrie*. In *WestLB AG v Philippine National Bank*[65] Andrew Ang J was called upon to decide whether a foreign judgment was *in rem* or *in personam*. He referred to *Castrique v Imrie* in detail

[59] *Michado v The Hattie and Lottie* (1904) 9 Ex CR 11 (McLeod LJ): "Under these circumstances I do not think I can interfere to undo what was done in the court at Providence, although that court may have taken a course which I would not have taken".

[60] *Burn v Bletcher* [1863] OJ No 60, 23 UCR 28.

[61] See, e.g. *Davis v Gell* [1925] VLR 8, (1924) 35 CLR 275, (1925) 31 ALR 49 (HCA); *Nassoor v. Nette* (1937) 58 CLR 446, [1937] ALR 585, (1937) 11 ALJR 189.

[62] See *McGovern v State of Victoria* [1984] VR 570: "[A] judicial decision which creates title to or affects property in a thing in possession is a decision that determines the status of that thing and, to that extent, is conclusive in rem".

[63] (1998) 87 FCR 229, (1998) 157 ALR 660.

[64] (1998) 87 FCR 229, 242F.

[65] [2012] SGHC 162, [2012] 4 SLR 894.

and with approval.[66] In *The Turtle Bay*,[67] Belinda Ang J explained that conferral of clean title, a "unique and important legal consequence of an admiralty judicial sale is an ancient in rem doctrine recognised in most admiralty jurisdictions".[68] *Castrique v Imrie* has also been followed in Fiji,[69] Hong Kong,[70] Malaysia,[71] South Africa[72] and Tonga.[73]

4.29. Finally, in *BCEN-Eurobank v Vostokrybporm Co Ltd (The Phoenix)*,[74] the Eastern Caribbean Supreme Court, sitting as the Court of Appeal of St Vincent and the Grenadines, was called upon to decide a complex case involving multiple foreign judicial ship sales. *The Phoenix* was registered in St Vincent and the Grenadines and was subject to a registered ship mortgage in favour of the appellant bank, BCEN-EuroBank. In 2003, the vessel was arrested in Rajin, North Korea, and was sold by the North Korean Court.

In 2005, the vessel entered the port of Tianjin, People's Republic of China, where it was arrested by the appellant bank. The then-owner successfully applied to the Tianjin Court to release the vessel from arrest on the basis that the prior North Korean judicial sale had freed the vessel from all encumbrances.

The vessel was subsequently sold on to the first respondent, Vostokrybporm Co Ltd (Vostok), in 2006. Vostok unsuccessfully sought to deregister the vessel from the St Vincent and the Grenadines Shipping Registry.

In 2009, the vessel was arrested again in the Qingdao Maritime Court, China, upon the application of the company that had sold the vessel to Vostok. The Qingdao Maritime Court made an order for the judicial sale of the vessel. The appellant bank applied to the Qingdao Maritime Court to stop the auction. That application was refused.

In 2010, the vessel was sold at auction and purchased by the second respondent, Apex Luck Business Ltd (Apex).[75]

4.30. At first instance, Thom J granted a declaration that Apex was the owner of the vessel free from all encumbrances and ordered the Registrar of Ships of Saint Vincent and the Grenadines to terminate the vessel's registration.[76] This decision was unanimously upheld on appeal:[77]

---

[66] Ibid [48]–[54]. See also *The Republic of the Philippines v Maler Foundation* [2013] SGCA 66, [2014] 1 SLR 1389; *Desert Palace Inc (trading as Caesars Palace) v Poh Soon Kiat* [2008] SGHC 144, [2009] 1 SLR(R) 71; *Payna Chettiar v Maimoon bte Ismail* [1997] SGHC 95, [1997] 1 SLR(R) 738 (fraud as an exception to recognition of foreign judgments *in rem*); *Payna Chettiar v Low Meng Seng* [1998] SGCA 18, [1998] 1 SLR(R) 657.

[67] Above (n 5).

[68] Above (n 5) [11]–[13].

[69] *Cong Yu Qin v The Owners of the Motor Vessel 'Ping An 6'* [2003] FJHC 59.

[70] *Re Law Kin Man; Anwide Co Ltd v Attorney General* [1994] 2 HKC 118, 139: "in relation to in rem proceedings, where a judgment affects not just the party but the whole world, the English or Hong Kong courts will investigate whether the foreign court had local competence and jurisdiction".

[71] *The Ka Wah Bank Ltd v Low Chung Song* [1998] 6 MLJ 384; see, also, *PT Sandipala Arthaputra v Muehlbauer Technologies Sdn Bhd* [2021] 9 CLJ 484.

[72] *Wayland v Transvaal Government* (1904) 3 TS 753, 755.

[73] *Valeusa v Mate* [2020] TOSC 79.

[74] [2014] 1 Lloyd's Rep 449.

[75] Ibid [5]–[8].

[76] Ibid [9].

[77] Ibid [34]–[35], [40]. Footnotes omitted.

> At common law the legal effect of judicial sales has been long recognised. A judicial sale extinguishes not only the lien which led to the arrest and sale but all other liens attached to the property. The liens are transferred to the fund created by the proceeds. In *The Tremont* Dr Lushington said: 'The jurisdiction of the Court in these matters is confirmed by the municipal law of this country . . . and the title conferred by the court in the exercise of this authority is a valid title against the whole world, and is recognised by the courts of this country and by the courts of all other countries'. These principles were restated by Hewson J in *The Acrux (No 2)* and by Mr Justice Sheen in *The Cerro Colorado*. The legal effect of a judicial sale in a state not party to the Convention is governed by the common law and not by the 1993 Convention [on Maritime Liens and Mortgages].
>
> Thom J was correct in holding that at common law the judicial sales should be recognised as having transferred ownership of the vessel free of the appellant's mortgage. The judicial sale in North Korea should be recognised as having that effect as it satisfies both of the two common law conditions specified by Lord Blackburn in *Castrique v Imrie* . . .
>
> In conclusion, a foreign judicial sale is to be recognised and given effect qua assignment/transfer of title unless it is invalid under the law of the country where the sale took place. There was no plea or evidence that such was the case in respect of either of the judicial sales at issue at the trial. The prime consideration is whether the transaction was valid under local law.

4.31. This brief survey of selected Commonwealth cases suffices to demonstrate that the rules of English common law relating to the conferral of clean title in competent judicial sales and the recognition and enforcement of foreign judicial sales in accordance with the *Castrique v Imrie* test have been widely and uniformly embraced by and applied in Anglo-Common Law jurisdictions without, seemingly, any doubt or difficulty.

4.4 The Beijing Convention

4.4.1 Introduction

4.32. The possibility of a Convention dealing with judicial sale of ships was first mooted in a paper presented by Professor Henry Hai Li to the CMI Athens Conference in 2008.[78] Professor Li's paper noted that the Executive Council of CMI had decided in 2007 to explore the topic of judicial ship sales. After discussing a dozen case studies, his paper concluded:[79]

> While ships are being arrested in one country or another, and some of the ships are sold by court for enforcement of maritime or non-maritime claims, problems in relation to judicial sale of ships have been encountered by the international shipping industry and are calling for consideration and solutions.

4.33. This inevitably involved the establishment of a CMI International Working Group (IWG). The usual draft questionnaire was circulated to national Maritime Law

[78] Henry Hai Li, *A Brief Discussion on Judicial Sales of Ships* <www.comitemaritime.org/wp-content/uploads/2018/05/A-Brief-Discussion-on-Judicial-Sales-of-Ships.pdf>. See, also, Juan Pablo Rodriguez Delgado, The Scope of Application of the UNCITRAL Instrument on the Judicial Sale of Ships [2022] *Poredbeno Pomorsko Parvo* 705, 708–711 <www.hrcak.srce.hr/file/419988>, for a useful summary of the historical development of the Convention.

[79] Li, supra (n 78) 20.

Associations in 2010.[80] This preparatory work led to the drafting of several iterations of the proposed instrument, namely the First Draft Instrument, Second Draft Instrument, Beijing Draft and Revised Beijing Draft. The final version of the Beijing Draft was approved at the CMI Conference in Hamburg in 2014.[81]

4.34. The approved Beijing Draft was subsequently submitted to the Legal Committee of the International Maritime Organization (IMO) in 2015 for its sponsorship and as an addition to its work programme.[82] However, the Legal Committee of the IMO decided in June 2016 "not to pursue the proposal at this time".[83] An advance made to the Hague Conference on Private International Law was equally unsuccessful.

4.35. CMI sought to revive the fortunes of the Beijing Draft in the following year with an invitation to the United Nations Commission on International Trade Law (UNCITRAL) to take over the work instead.[84] The initial response by UNCITRAL might be described as a lukewarm demurral, with concern being expressed that the Beijing Draft, while addressing a legitimate concern, might not command broad enough support among UNCITRAL members. UNCITRAL also noted that the CMI proposal had already been submitted without success to the IMO and the Hague Conference on Private International Law, which had passed the parcel back to UNCITRAL.[85]

4.36. Further support and evidence for the need for a Convention were sought in a "High Level Technical Colloquium on a Draft International Instrument on Foreign Judicial Sales of Ships and their Recognition" held by CMI in Malta in 2018.[86] Following the Malta colloquium, Switzerland made a second proposal to UNCITRAL to adopt the Beijing Draft.[87] This time, UNCITRAL agreed to allocate the topic to Working Group VI.[88]

4.37. UNCITRAL Working Group VI subsequently met several times from 2019–2022 in New York and Vienna to work on a Convention draft, even though progress was disrupted by the Covid pandemic.[89] On 7 December 2022, the UN

[80] Henry Hai Li, *A Brief Introduction to the Topic on Recognition of Foreign Judicial Sales of Ships* <www.comitemaritime.org/wp-content/uploads/2018/05/A-Brief-Introduction-to-the-Topic-by-Henry-Hai-Li.pdf>.

[81] See *Report of the International Working Group on the Preparation of the Proposed Draft International Convention on Recognition of Foreign Judicial Sales of Ships* <www.comitemaritime.org/wp-content/uploads/2018/05/Beijing-Draft-approved-at-plenary.docx>. There were 24 votes in favour: Argentina, Australia, Belgium, Canada, People's Republic of China, Denmark, Finland, France, Germany, Greece, Ireland, Italy, Japan, Malta, the Netherlands, New Zealand, Nigeria, Norway, Republic of Korea, Spain, Sweden, Switzerland, Turkïye, the United Kingdom and the United States; and two abstentions: Brazil and Poland.

[82] See <www.imo.org/en/MediaCentre/MeetingSummaries/Legal/Pages/LEG-102nd-session.aspx>.

[83] See <www.imo.org/en/MediaCentre/MeetingSummaries/Pages/LEG-103rd-session.aspx>; Patrick Griggs, IMO Legal Committee: 103rd Session (2016) 22 JIML 237, 240.

[84] A/CN.9/923, 13 April 2017, reproduced at <www.comitemaritime.org/wp-content/uploads/2018/05/CMI-proposal-to-UNCITRAL-2017.pdf>.

[85] A/72/17, para 461 f, reproduced at <www.comitemaritime.org/wp-content/uploads/2018/05/UNCITRAL-Report-2017.pdf>.

[86] <www.comitemaritime.org/wp-content/uploads/2018/05/CMI-Colloquium-Final-Programme.docx>.

[87] A/CN.9/944/Rev.1, 22 June 2018, reproduced at <www.comitemaritime.org/wp-content/uploads/2018/05/Swiss-proposal-to-UNICTRAL-2018.pdf>.

[88] A/73/17, para 252, reproduced at <www.comitemaritime.org/wp-content/uploads/2018/05/UNCITRAL-Report-2018.pdf>.

[89] The relevant documents <www.uncitral.un.org/en/working_groups/6/sale_ships>.

General Assembly adopted the final text of the United Nations Convention on the International Effects of Judicial Sales of Ships.[90] A signing ceremony was held in Beijing on 5 September 2023.[91]

4.4.2 Scope and definitions

4.38. Article 1 of the Beijing Convention sets out its general purpose, providing that: "This Convention governs the international effects of a judicial sale of a ship that confers clean title on the purchaser". This general article, which was not included in the Beijing Draft, appears to limit the scope of the Convention to the "international effects" of judicial ship sales. "International effects", which, it must be said, is not a common term of articles in private international law, would seem to encompass such issues as recognition and enforcement of foreign judicial ship sales, as well as consequential administrative matters, such as amending the relevant ship register to reflect the outcome of a foreign judicial ship sale. Logically, the wording of Article 1 means that the Convention does not apply to any "domestic effects" of judicial ship sales. Where the relevant vessel is registered locally and sold by the local court, any legal incidents and issues will continue to be governed by domestic local law, rather than by the Convention regime.

4.39. Article 1 retains a problematic aspect of the Beijing Draft, in the sense that it provides that the Convention will only govern "a judicial sale of a ship *that confers clean title on the purchaser*".[92] As I have previously noted in respect of the Beijing Draft, which defined judicial sale in Article 1.8 as

> any sale of a Ship by a Competent Authority by way of public auction or private treaty or any other appropriate ways provided for by the law of the State of Judicial Sale *by which Clean Title to the Ship is acquired by the Purchaser and the proceeds of sale are made available to the creditors,*

there is a fundamental logical circularity at play here, in the sense that claimants' arguments in favour of non-recognition and/or non-enforcement of foreign judicial ship sales invariably involve an allegation that the foreign judicial sale has *not* conferred

[90] UNIS/L/335, 8 December 2022 <www.unis.unvienna.org/unis/en/pressrels/2022/unisl335.html>. For the final English text, see A/C.6/77/L.8, 27 October 2022 <www.documents-dds-ny.un.org/doc/UNDOC/LTD/N22/659/27/PDF/N2265927.pdf>.

[91] See <https://uncitral.un.org/sites/uncitral.un.org/files/media-documents/uncitral/en/info_brochure_bjss_and_signing_ceremony_en.pdf>.

[92] Emphasis added. See *UNCITRAL Report of Working Group VI (Judicial Sale of Ships) on the Work of Its 35th Session (New York, 13–17 May 2019)* A/CN.9/973, 24 May 2019, para 35 <www.documents-dds-ny.un.org/doc/UNDOC/GEN/V19/037/78/PDF/V1903778.pdf>:

> It was noted that, in some jurisdictions, a judicial sale did not have the effect of extinguishing all rights and interests in the property being sold. For instance, it was noted that the law may preserve the rights of a registered leaseholder, or provide for the continued registration of unsatisfied creditors despite a judicial sale. It was noted that these judicial sales could be considered beyond scope as they did not result in the acquisition of clean title, and therefore fell outside the definition of 'Judicial Sale' in article 1(h). The view was expressed that the instrument should not apply to these judicial sales.

All quotes from this Report in its 35th and 36th sessions are reprinted with kind permission of the UNCITRAL Secretariat.

clean title on the purchaser.[93] If that argument is accepted by the reviewing court, the foreign judicial sale will automatically fall outside the Convention, and the court will therefore be forced back to square one and an application of domestic law.

4.40. In my view, it is rather unfortunate that the drafters of the Convention retained the Beijing Draft's concept of treating conferral of clean title as a constituent defining element, rather than as a separate legal consequence, of the foreign judicial ship sale, as defined.[94] The loophole created by this logical fallacy is reminiscent of the problematic drafting of Article 4 of the United Nations Convention on Contracts for the Sale of Goods (the CISG) which states that the "Convention governs only the formation of the contract of sale and the rights and obligations of the seller and the buyer arising from such a contract", but not the prior question of the contract's validity, which has encouraged numerous attempts by claimants to bypass the CISG with legal arguments as to whether there was a valid sales contract in the first place.[95]

4.41. Possible complications caused by the wording of Article 1 of the Beijing Convention are likely to play out in a similar way, although there is more wiggle room in Article 4(a) of the CISG because of its proviso "except as otherwise expressly provided in this Convention", which has led to ingenious (and sometimes tortuous) arguments in favour of retaining the application of the CISG to contract validity issues. In respect of the Beijing Convention, if a party argues that the foreign judicial sale in question did *not* confer clean title on the purchaser, the reviewing court will be forced to address the issue of the application of the Beijing Convention squarely.

4.42. The obvious questions will be which law should determine whether or not the foreign judicial sale conferred a clean title: the *lex fori* of the reviewing court, or the *lex causae* (presumably the *lex fori* of the selling court)? Which legal test should the reviewing court apply to determine this conflicts question? Is it enough that the selling court complied with the notice requirements under Article 4 of the Beijing Convention and produced a certificate of judicial sale under Article 5? A literal interpretation of Article 6 of the Beijing Convention might suggest that the issuance of such a certificate is binding evidence that clean title was conferred on the purchaser in any other State

---

93 Emphasis added. See Myburgh, supra (n 5) 366.

94 This appears to have been a deliberate choice on the part of the drafters: see *UNCITRAL Report of Working Group VI (Judicial Sale of Ships) on the Work of Its 36th Session* (Vienna, 18–22 November 2019), A/CN.9/1007, 2 December 2019, para 43 <www.documents-dds-ny.un.org/doc/UNDOC/GEN/V19/114/57/PDF/V1911457.pdf>:

> There was wide agreement to limit the scope of the instrument to judicial sales that (already) provided clean title under the domestic law of the State of judicial sale (i.e., 'option A' described in para. 5 of document A/CN.9/WG.VI/WP.84). It was observed that, as a consequence, judicial sales for which clean title was not conferred on the purchaser under the law of the State of judicial sale would fall outside the scope of the instrument. . . . As such, it was emphasized that a provision limiting the scope of the instrument should allow an assessment of whether a judicial sale fell within scope to be carried out on a case-by-case basis.

See, also, *UNCITRAL Report of Working Group VI (Judicial Sale of Ships) on the Work of Its 37th Session* (Vienna, 14–18 December 2020) A/CN.9/1047/Rev.1, 29 December 2020, paras 39 ff <www.documents-dds-ny.un.org/doc/UNDOC/GEN/V21/005/89/PDF/V2100589.pdf>.

95 See, e.g. Ulrich G Schroeter, Contract Validity and the CISG (2017) 22 Uniform Law Review 47; Helen Elizabeth Hartnell, 'Rousing the Sleeping Dog: The Validity Exception to the Convention on Contracts for the International Sale of Goods' (1993) 18 Yale Journal of International Law 1.

Party but Articles 9 and 10, which allow for avoidance, suspension or nullification of judicial sales in certain circumstances, mean that the issue cannot be quite as simple as that.

4.43. It could, of course, be argued that this is a non-issue, as Article 9(1) provides:

> The courts of the State of judicial sale shall have exclusive jurisdiction to hear any claim or application to avoid a judicial sale of a ship conducted in that State that confers clean title to the ship or to suspend its effects, which shall extend to any claim or application to challenge the issuance of the certificate of judicial sale referred to in article 5.

The intention behind Article 9(1) was clearly to channel all challenges away from the reviewing court and back to the selling court but the difficulty with that is that Article 9(1) suffers from the same logical bootstrapping problem as Article 1, in that it only applies to avoidance or suspension of "a judicial sale of a ship conducted in that State *that confers clean title to the ship*". If the core claim is that clean title was *not* conferred by the foreign judicial sale, an argument can again be made on the literal wording of the Convention that Articles 1 and 9 are not applicable, even in the courts of a State Party, until the prior issue of conferral of clean title has been resolved.

4.44. It may be that this circularity can be cured by purposive interpretation to preserve the integrity and efficacy of the Convention's reach but the drafters arguably did themselves few favours by defining "judicial sale" in Article 2(a) by reference to court or other public authority order, approval, or confirmation and distribution of proceeds to creditors, but without reference to clean title. This confirms that the Convention acknowledges a category of valid judicial sale which does not confer clean title, which is a highly peculiar notion for an Anglo-Common Law lawyer at least.[96]

4.45. Article 2(b) defines "ship" as meaning,

> any ship or other vessel registered in a register that is open to public inspection that may be the subject of an arrest or other similar measure capable of leading to a judicial sale under the law of the State of judicial sale.[97]

This differs from the Beijing Draft definition of ship, which covered "any ship or other vessel capable of being an object of a Judicial Sale under the law of the State of Judicial Sale". Although the drafters of the Beijing Convention thought it necessary to exclude unregistered or deregistered vessels, and it must be acknowledged that this is not a situation which is likely to occur frequently, it is still not inconceivable that a foreign judicial sale of an unregistered vessel will give rise to conflict of laws issues.[98]

4.46. It is also worth noting that Article 2(h) defines the "owner" of a ship as meaning "any person registered as the owner of the ship in the register of ships or equivalent

[96] The fudging of this issue would seem to have to do with the possibility that in certain Civil Law jurisdictions, such as Spain, Japan, and Germany, the interest created by a bareboat charter party may survive judicial ship sales: see Delgado, supra, (n 51) 733 ff. It would have been preferable for UNCITRAL to grasp the nettle and deal with this problem directly and decisively.

[97] On the discussion of this issue, see *UNCITRAL Report of Working Group VI (Judicial Sale of Ships) on the Work of Its Thirty-Sixth Session*, supra (n 94) para 28 ff. The concern seems to have been not to tread on the toes of the Convention on the Registration of Inland Navigation Vessels 1965, in particular Protocol No 2 Concerning Attachment and Forced Sale of Inland Navigation Vessels. In that case, it might have been more prudent to exclude all inland navigation vessels from the scope of the Beijing Convention, and to leave unregistered seagoing/commercial vessels within its purview. See also Delgado, supra (n 78) 717–718.

[98] Cf., e.g. *The WD Fairway* [2009] EWHC 889 (Adm), [2009] 2 Lloyd's Rep 191.

register in which the ship is registered", which excludes owners of unregistered ships, as well as beneficial owners of ships. This is of particular significance when one considers the additional notice of judicial sale requirements imposed by Article 4(3) of the Beijing Convention, which will be interpreted as only referring to the registered owner. That said, Article 4(1) provides that the "judicial sale shall be conducted in accordance with the law of the State of judicial sale", which should allow for involvement of beneficial owners in Anglo-Common Law systems as appropriate.

4.47. Article 3 provides that:

1. This Convention applies only to a judicial sale of a ship if:
    (a) The judicial sale is conducted in a State Party; and
    (b) The ship is physically within the territory of the State of judicial sale at the time of that sale.

This largely reflects the first limb of the test for recognition of foreign judicial sales set out by Blackburn J in *Castrique v Imrie*, albeit substituting physical presence for 'lawful control' by the State in which the judicial sale is held. However, it omits the second limb of the test as to whether "the sovereign authority of that State has conferred on the Court jurisdiction to decide as to the disposition of the thing, and the Court has acted within its jurisdiction". This omission will have been deliberate, as the drafters intended by Article 9 to channel any jurisdictional challenges back to the original selling court in the interests of certainty and protection of the bona fide purchaser.

4.48. It may be questioned, however, whether this final drafting gets the balance right between protecting the interests of the ship purchaser and the parties who had claims against, or interests in, the ship prior to its judicial sale. It represents a significant watering down of the Beijing Draft, which originally included a version of both limbs of the *Castrique v Imrie* test in Article 4.

4.4.3 Effect of judicial sales

1. Subject to:
    (a) the Ship being physically within the jurisdiction of the State of Judicial Sale, at the time of the Judicial Sale; and
    (b) the Judicial Sale having been conducted in accordance with the law of the State of Judicial Sale and the provisions of this Convention, any title to and all rights and interests in the Ship existing prior to its Judicial Sale shall be extinguished and any Mortgage/*Hypothèque* or Charge, except as assumed by the Purchaser, shall cease to attach to the Ship and Clean Title to the Ship shall be acquired by the Purchaser.

4.49. The effect of Article 3(1) of the Beijing Convention, on the face of it, would seem to be to remove the ability from the reviewing court of investigating an excess of jurisdiction (whether viewed through the reviewing court's private international law lens or not) perpetrated by the selling court. However, it is unlikely that this will be the practical effect of the Convention. Articles 7(5), 8(4) and 10(1) all provide safety valves, in the sense that the reviewing court does not have to release a vessel from arrest (even where there is an Article 5 Certificate of Judicial Sale) or recognise a prior foreign judicial sale if this would be "manifestly contrary to the public policy of that State".

4.50. In that sense, the most likely practical effect of the Beijing Convention will be the substitution of the existing discrete Anglo-Common Law grounds to vitiate recognition of foreign judicial ship sales discussed previously in Part 2 (excess of jurisdiction, fraud, public policy and lack of natural justice) for the amorphous catch-all of public policy. Whether that achieves greater certainty is debatable.[99]

4.4.4 The judicial sale process under the Convention

4.51. In accordance with the usual deference to the domestic *lex fori* on procedural matters, Article 4(1) of the Beijing Convention provides:

> The judicial sale shall be conducted in accordance with the law of the State of judicial sale, which shall also provide procedures for challenging the judicial sale prior to its completion and determine the time of the sale for the purposes of this Convention.

4.52. The second part of Article 4(1) is interesting in that it seems to import notions of natural justice, but the wording is (necessarily) rather general and vague, and it is unclear what the legal consequences are for a failure to comply – as with many other international instruments, "shall" is ultimately hortative rather than mandatory. Presumably, a lack of any real opportunity to challenge the foreign judicial sale prior to its completion will provide grounds for a refusal to recognise it as being manifestly contrary to public policy under Article 10.

4.53. As a supplement to the judicial sale procedure under the *lex fori*, the Beijing Convention sets out additional notice of judicial sale requirements in Articles 4(3)–(7). Article 4(2) provides that "a certificate of judicial sale under Article 5 shall only be issued if a notice of judicial sale is given prior to the judicial sale of the ship in accordance with the requirements of paragraphs 3 to 7". However, given that it is the selling court which is in charge of both the notice requirements and the issuing of the certificate and, given that Article 3 has ostensibly removed the reviewing court's right to investigate the selling court's excesses of jurisdiction, it is not clear how these requirements will be policed effectively.

4.54. The notice requirements set out in Article 4 are largely unremarkable and would not require major changes to current Anglo-common law admiralty practice. The two main additional requirements are that the selling court must provide notice

---

[99] This issue was acknowledged by the drafters: *UNCITRAL Report of Working Group VI (Judicial Sale of Ships) on the Work of Its 36th Session*, supra (n 94) para 84:

> It was noted that public policy was a vague notion that varied from jurisdiction to jurisdiction. Concern was expressed that the ground could expose the judicial sale to unwarranted challenge and be used to harass good faith purchasers. In response, it was noted that the words 'manifestly contrary' set a high threshold. It was also noted that the public policy ground was a common feature in conventions establishing recognition regimes, and that including the ground would assist in gaining acceptance of the instrument.

of judicial sale to the registry where the ship is registered[100] and the Repository (the Secretary-General of the IMO, or an institution named by UNCITRAL),[101] who will publish the notice of judicial sale.[102]

4.55. These are welcome developments. Most Anglo-common law jurisdictions already make use of local trade newspapers and Lloyd's (*Informa*) international news publications to ensure that judicial sales are adequately advertised to all maritime creditors and interested parties. The involvement of the IMO, or another appropriate international organisation, in publicising an internationally available register of judicial ship sales can only enhance transparency,[103] as well as ensuring that all maritime creditors bring their claims to the judicial sales process in a timely fashion. The requirement to inform the relevant foreign ship registry will also hopefully enhance the likelihood of practical co-operation or at least flush out any major legal disagreements prior to the conclusion of the judicial ship sale.

4.56. Article 7, which deals with the practicalities of amending the ship register following a foreign judicial sale, is also a welcome development. It reflects what should already happen, and does happen in most cases, but provides a logical and formal process to assist a purchaser in a judicial sale to ensure that the relevant ship register reflects its clean title. Again, Article 7 is framed in mandatory terms but sets out no sanctions for non-compliance. Article 7(5) also provides for the usual escape of public policy. While it provides administrative clarity, it may be argued that Article 7 does not add much to existing Anglo-common law admiralty practice.

4.4.5 Recognition of foreign judicial ship sales under the Convention

4.57. Article 6 of the Convention provides:

> A judicial sale for which a certificate of judicial sale referred to in Article 5 has been issued shall have the effect in every other State Party of conferring clean title to the ship on the purchaser.

4.58. On the face of it, this provides a clear and absolute statement of judgment estoppel, but Article 6 must be read in conjunction with the articles of the Beijing Convention previously discussed, and especially the safety valves regarding public policy in the Convention. While the Convention should be effective in prohibiting State Parties from making bald assertions that other states have no right to sell "their" ships, the ultimate utility of the Convention is likely to rest on how restrained States Parties are in unleashing the "unruly horse" of public policy.[104]

---

[100] Art 4(3)(a).

[101] Art 11(1).

[102] Arti 11(2).

[103] Cf., e.g. the Cape Town Convention on International Interests in Mobile Equipment and its Protocol on Matters Specific to Aircraft Equipment, which has implemented a very successful international electronic register of international security interests.

[104] *Richardson v Mellish* [1824] 2 Bing 229, 303, 130 ER 294, 252.

4.4.6 Evaluation

4.59. I am on the record as stating (no doubt uncharitably) that the Beijing Draft was "an international unification solution in search of a largely non-existent problem".[105] There is undoubtedly *a* problem, in that a small number of jurisdictions have routinely refused to recognise foreign judicial sales of ships flagged in their countries, which has caused difficulties for bona fide purchasers. However, questions about the extent of the international problem, and whether it warrants the solution of an international convention, remain.

4.60. It is interesting to note that in the early stages of the development of the Beijing Draft, it was acknowledged that there were only isolated instances of refusals to recognise foreign judicial ship sales. For example, at the CMI Beijing Conference in 2012, Lawrence Teh noted:[106]

> Although it would appear that in many Associations an exhaustive review of the case law was not undertaken, our comment is that there are surprisingly few instances where the consequences of judicial sales have been challenged and in none of the examples provided was a single challenge successful.

4.61. The CMI has routinely referred to the same dozen or so international case examples,[107] which must represent a minuscule fraction of the total number of successful international ship judicial sales in any given period,[108] and an even smaller fraction of all worldwide admiralty litigation. By the time the Beijing Draft needed sponsorship by an international organisation to translate it into a convention, it must be said that the perceived problem of uncertainty surrounding recognition of foreign judicial ship sales seems to have grown somewhat exponentially.[109]

4.62. If the yardstick to be employed is market confidence in the integrity of the judicial ship sale system worldwide, this is incredibly difficult to gauge objectively. Likewise, it is difficult to get an accurate sense of whether judicial ship sales are indeed maximising the prices paid by bona fide purchasers, particularly given the challenging international economic conditions of the past decade or so. If one proceeds by the number of reported international judgments alone, the problem seems currently to be confined to litigation involving a relatively small number of outlier maritime jurisdictions worldwide.[110] Ironically, the introduction of the Beijing Convention may

---

[105] Myburgh, supra (n 5) 369.

[106] Lawrence Teh, *The CMI Questionnaire in Respect of Recognition of Foreign Judicial Sales of Ships: Commentary on Answers to the 5th Group of Questions* <www.comitemaritime.org/wp-content/uploads/2018/05/Paper-of-Lawrence-Teh.pdf>.

[107] See, e.g. 'Judicial Sales: Case Summaries' <www.comitemaritime.org/wp-content/uploads/2018/05/List-of-Case-Summaries.docx> presented at the Malta Colloquium in 2018. It should also be noted that not all of these cases concerned lack of recognition of foreign judicial ship sales.

[108] Myburgh, supra (n 5) 366.

[109] See the rather more alarmist language in the 2018 Swiss proposal to UNCITRAL: A/CN.9/944/Rev.1, 22 June 2018, reproduced <www.comitemaritime.org/wp-content/uploads/2018/05/Swiss-proposal-to-UNICTRAL-2018.pdf>, noting that "the lack of certainty in recognition of judgment affected a broad spectrum of industries and States".

[110] For case examples, see Bleyen, supra (n 1) 154–157: *Goldfish Shipping SA v HSH Nordbank AG* 2010 377 Fed App 150, 2010 AMC 1210 (3rd Circ) (Türkiye refusing to recognise US judicial sale); *Bridge Oil Ltd v Fund Constituting the Proceeds of the Sale of the MV Mega S (formerly the MV Aksu)* [2003] ZAWCHC 24 (Turkïye refusing to recognise Danish judicial sale); *Deputy Marshal, Federal Court v The Galaxias* [1989]

well encourage, or at least result in, increased litigation, because it provides a high profile, internationally public and "precise target" to potential challengers to attack titles afforded by judicial ship sales.[111]

4.63. In my view, the success of the Beijing Convention will depend, crucially, on whether these outlier jurisdictions sign up to the Convention, and then whether there is widespread international acceptance of the Convention. The fact that Türkiye voted in favour of the Beijing Draft is encouraging, as it was one of the main jurisdictions opposed to foreign judicial sales of its ships, but it is unclear whether Türkiye, Greece and Panama, the habitual offenders in this regard, will eventually be enticed into ratifying and faithfully applying the Convention.[112]

4.64. For the rest of the world that already routinely recognises clean title conferred by foreign judicial ship sales, provided that the vessel was within the physical and legal sphere of jurisdiction of the selling court and that the selling court abided by the rules of international jurisdiction, it might reasonably be suggested that the Beijing Convention is a bit of a damp squib. There is little in it that is harmful or dangerous (except perhaps, from an Anglo-common law perspective, for the undermining of the notion that a judicial ship sale will invariably confer clean title on the purchaser) but it is difficult to see any massive changes, advantages, or improvements in the Convention, apart perhaps from the enhanced international notice and publicity requirements around international judicial ship sales.

4.65. One of the main aims of the Beijing Convention is to bring clarity and certainty to this area and to increase stakeholders' confidence in the efficacy and integrity of the international judicial ship sales system. Judged against these criteria, the Convention is a decidedly mixed bag. While setting out a more uniform system, and clarifying and tidying up administrative matters to do with notice requirements and registry amendments, it also injects more uncertainty by introducing the notion of a judicial ship sale which does *not* confer clean title, and by muddying the waters around challenges to suspect foreign judicial sales, which will now be tested against the more amorphous metewand of public policy, as opposed to focusing on hard evidence of fraud. In this regard, it could be argued that the decision in *Castrique v Imrie*, which has stood the test of time and been adopted throughout the Commonwealth, provides rather more clear guidance, and inspires rather more confidence, than the Beijing Convention regime.

---

1 FC 375, 20 FTR 141, 1989 AMC 348 (Greece attempting to place conditions on recognition of Canadian judicial sale); *Vrac Mar Inc v Demetries Karamanlis* [1972] FC 430 (Panama refusing to recognise the effects of a Canadian judicial sale). But cf *UNCITRAL Report of Working Group VI (Judicial Sale of Ships) on the Work of Its 35fth Session*, supra (n 92) para 16:

> It was suggested that more data on the scale and the scope of the problems to be addressed by the Working Group would be useful in terms of the number of cases in which a foreign judicial sale had not been recognized and the reasons for such non-recognition. In response, several court cases from a variety of jurisdictions were described, including ongoing proceedings. However, it was also stated that the number of cases would not be indicative of the economic impact because the legal uncertainty in general had a far-reaching impact on the market as a whole.

[111] D Rhidian Thomas, 'The United Nations Convention on the International Effects of Judicial Sales of Ships: The Beijing Convention – A Textual Analysis' (2022) 28 JIML 367, 377.

[112] At the time of writing, only Greece has signed the Convention as a Member State of the EU.

4.66. It will be interesting to see what uptake the Beijing Convention enjoys, particularly amongst Anglo-common law jurisdictions.[113] The Convention only requires three states to ratify, accept, approve or accede before it enters into force[114] – hardly an arduous threshold requirement. The deliberate decision of the drafters to make the Convention a closed legal framework which only applies to State Parties means that widespread international acceptance will be crucial for its success.[115] Failure to gain widespread international approval of the Convention will result in the worst of both worlds, with both domestic law and Convention regimes for recognition of foreign judicial ship sales co-existing untidily.

4.67. At the time of writing, the Convention has 31 signatories and one ratification.[116] The most likely outcome seems to be that the Beijing Convention will enter into force at some stage. The real litmus test is whether the Convention will gain sufficiently widespread international acceptance amongst major maritime jurisdictions, particularly those in the Anglo-Common Law family.[117] One suspects that, if those jurisdictions apply a pragmatic cost-benefit analysis in deciding whether to accede to the Convention, the answer may well be no – not because the costs are huge, but because the benefits are not self-evident.

4.68. In this regard, the sage advice provided by Patrick Griggs in his Nicholas J Healy lecture on maritime law in 2002 would seem particularly apposite to the genesis and development of the Beijing Convention project:[118]

> [The] issue of 'compelling need' is often glossed over in the early stages of discussion of a new harmonising instrument. By the time the issue is addressed, the forward momentum that the project has developed meanwhile cannot be checked. An unwanted, unloved and therefore unratified convention may then be the result.
>
> What should we conclude from this? In analysing the success or failure of a convention, we may be forced to conclude that the area of the law covered by the instrument was not suitable for harmonisation because there was no 'compelling need', and that time, in consequence, has probably been wasted. . .. The message: if you want a convention that will be widely accepted, 'compelling need' must be a precondition to starting work.

---

113 There is a loose nexus between the Beijing Convention and the Convention on Maritime Liens and Mortgages 1993, in that the Beijing Convention adopts the same Civil Law terminology in referring to *hypothèques* and *privilèges* maritime and conceptualises maritime liens as charges: see Art 2(c), (e) and (g). It is not clear whether this will put off Anglo-Common Law countries, who have stayed well away from the various iterations of the Maritime Liens and Mortgages Convention: see Yingfeng Shao, Laura Carballo Piñeiro, and Maximo Q Mejia Jr, 'Recognition of Foreign Judicial Sales of Ships and Private International Law' (2022) 28 JIML 166, 168.

114 Art 21.

115 See *UNCITRAL Report of Working Group VI (Judicial Sale of Ships) on the Work of Its Thirty-Seventh Session*, supra (n 94) paras 16–18.

116 For the treaty's status, see <www.treaties.un.org/Pages/ViewDetails.aspx?src=TREATY&mtdsg_no=X-21&chapter=10&clang=_en>.

117 To date, Kiribati and Singapore are the only Anglo-Common Law signatories.

118 Patrick JS Griggs, Obstacles to Uniformity of Maritime Law, *CMI Yearbook 2002*, 158, 165–166 <www.comitemaritime.org/wp-content/uploads/2018/06/YBK_2002.pdf>.

CHAPTER 5

Recognition of foreign judicial ship sales in the United States

*Martin Davies**

5.1A Introduction

5.1. Private international lawyers often use the composite phrase "recognition and enforcement of foreign judgments" to describe a subset of their area of study but in practice, most legal proceedings of that kind are concerned with enforcement in one country of a judgment obtained in another. Disputes about judicial sales of ships fall into the less-often-litigated category of *recognition* of foreign judgments. The typical situation is where a claimant seeks in one country to enforce a pre-existing maritime claim against a ship that has been sold as a result of judicial proceedings in another country. The question for the court in which the claim has been brought is whether, and how, to recognise the effect of the foreign court-ordered sale of the ship so as possibly to preclude the claimant from continuing with its claim in the local proceedings.

5.2. Section B of this chapter gives a general overview of the law relating to recognition of foreign judgments in the United States. Because the US law of recognition of foreign judicial sales is firmly grounded on the domestic American distinction between arrest pursuant to true *in rem* proceedings and attachment pursuant to *in personam* admiralty proceedings, Section C gives a brief description of that distinction. Section D describes the rules of general maritime law (such as they are) that US courts apply in the admiralty jurisdiction when considering whether to recognise foreign judgments and, in particular, whether to recognise judicial sale orders made by foreign courts. Section E considers to what extent ship sales made by order of US courts would be eligible for recognition in other countries under the UN Convention on the International Effects of Judicial Sale of Ships (the Beijing Convention),[1] and what effect that Convention might have on recognition of foreign judicial sales by US courts.

* DCL (Oxon), FAAL; Admiralty Law Institute Professor of Maritime Law, Tulane University Law School, New Orleans; Director, Tulane Maritime Law Center.

[1] UNCITRAL, *UN Convention on the International Effects of Judicial Sale of Ships* (2023, UN, Vienna), <uncitral.un.org/sites/uncitral.un.org/files/media-documents/uncitral/en/united_nations_convention_on_the_international_effects_of_judicial_sales_of_ships.pdf>

DOI: 10.4324/9781003499930-5

5.2B Recognition and enforcement of foreign judgments in the United States

5.3. In most cases concerned with recognition or enforcement of foreign judgments, US federal courts have jurisdiction because of diversity of citizenship of the parties,[2] which is one of the limited bases of the subject-matter jurisdiction of federal courts.[3] When sitting in its diversity jurisdiction, a federal court must apply the law of the state in which it sits.[4] In the case of enforcement of foreign judgments, that is typically the state where enforcement is sought.[5]

5.4. Most (but not all) US states have enacted one of two similarly-named uniform statutes relating to recognition and enforcement of foreign judgments: either the Uniform Foreign Money Judgments Recognition Act (UFMJRA), which was drafted by the Uniform Law Commission in 1962 and which is still in force in nine states and one territory; or the Uniform Foreign-Country Money Judgments Recognition Act (UFCMJRA), which was drafted by the National Conference of Commissioners on Uniform State Laws in 2005 and which has been adopted by 29 states and the District of Columbia.[6]

5.5. These state statutes are surprisingly generous in their willingness to grant recognition and enforcement of foreign judgments, even when the foreign country in question does not reciprocate by recognizing or enforcing American court judgments. However, neither uniform statute applies in relation to recognition and enforcement of foreign *admiralty* judgments, where the relevant law is federal, not state, law. Federal courts have subject-matter jurisdiction in "any civil case of admiralty or maritime jurisdiction",[7] but (unlike when they exercise their diversity jurisdiction), they must apply federal maritime law when sitting in admiralty.[8]

---

[2] 28 USC s. 1332. The diversity jurisdiction of federal courts is properly called "alienage" jurisdiction when it involves an action between an American party and a foreign party, but that terminology is seldom used in practice. If both plaintiff and defendant are foreigners, a federal court does not have diversity/alienage jurisdiction, even if the foreigners are citizens of different foreign countries, because the diversity required by the statute is between an American and a foreigner: see, e.g. *Hakan Agro DMCC v Van Son Service Agriculture Co Ltd* [2018] WL 6822639 (ND Cal, 2018) (federal court had no jurisdiction to hear claim by a UAE-based corporation to enforce an English judgment against a Vietnamese defendant).

[3] A claim that does not fall within one of the limited bases of the subject-matter jurisdiction of federal courts can only be brought in a state court.

[4] *Erie R Co v Tompkins*, 304 US 64, 58 S Ct 817 (1938).

[5] *Ohno v Yasuma,* 723 F 3d 984, 990 (9th Cir 2013); *De Joria v Maghreb Petroleum Exploration SA*, 804 F 3d 373 (5th Cir 2015); *De Fontbrune v Wofsy*, 39 F 4th 1214 (9th Cir 2022).

[6] UFCMJRA has been enacted in: Alabama, Arizona, California, Colorado, Delaware, Georgia, Hawaii, Idaho, Illinois, Indiana, Iowa, Maine, Michigan, Minnesota, Montana, Nebraska, Nevada, New Mexico, New York, North Carolina, North Dakota, Oklahoma, Oregon, Rhode Island, Tennessee, Texas, Utah, Virginia, Washington and the District of Columbia. UFMJRA is still in force in Alaska, Connecticut, Florida, Maryland, Massachusetts, Missouri, New Jersey, Ohio, Pennsylvania and the US Virgin Islands. See Uniform Law Commission, *Foreign-Country Money Judgments Recognition Act* <www.uniformlaws.org/committees/community-home?CommunityKey=ae280c30-094a-4d8f-b722-8dcd614a8f3e> accessed 25 June 2024.

[7] 28 USC s. 1333(1).

[8] *East River Steamship Corp v Transamerica Delaval Inc*, 476 US 858, 864, 106 S Ct 2295, 2298–9 (1986) ('With admiralty jurisdiction comes the application of substantive admiralty law'). When state courts exercise admiralty jurisdiction (as they are permitted to do by 28 USC s. 1333(1)), they, too, must apply federal maritime law. This is sometimes referred to as the "reverse *Erie*" principle (see *Offshore Logistics Inc v Tallentire*, 477 US 207, 223 (1986)), because it is the reverse of the *Erie* rule, supra (n 4) that federal courts must apply state law when sitting in diversity.

5.6. Thus, when the foreign judgment to be recognised or enforced is to be characterised as an admiralty judgment, the relevant substantive law must come from federal maritime law and not from the generous, statute-based, law of the state in which the court sits, as would be the case if the court were exercising its diversity/alienage jurisdiction. As a result, any federal court that is asked to recognise or enforce a foreign judgment must first consider the preliminary question of whether its jurisdiction to make the order sought derives from its admiralty jurisdiction (in which case, federal maritime law must be applied), or its diversity/alienage jurisdiction (in which case, state law must be applied).

5.7. The (federal) US Courts of Appeals for the Second and Fourth Circuits have held that the preliminary question whether the foreign court order should properly be regarded as an admiralty judgment must be determined by the law of the forum (*lex fori*), meaning US federal maritime law, rather than by the law of the country where the order was made or the judgment was rendered.[9] That is so because the question is essentially one of the subject-matter jurisdiction of the federal court to hear and decide the claim: foreign law cannot determine the subject-matter jurisdiction of an American court.[10] Thus, for example, in *Flame SA v Freight Bulk Pte Ltd*,[11] the US Courts of Appeals for the Fourth Circuit held that an English judgment about a forward freight agreement (FFA) should be characterised as an admiralty judgment under American notions of what constitutes a maritime contract, even though it would not be so characterised under English law.[12] This is the first of several ways in which US maritime law views foreign proceedings through the lens of its own domestic concepts shaping admiralty proceedings.

5.8. The most profound way in which American decisions about recognition of foreign judicial ship sales are shaped by domestic concepts is in the distinction between foreign judicial proceedings that are truly *in rem* and those that are not. That distinction is explained in further detail in Section D but in order for non-American readers to make sense of the distinction, it is first necessary to give a brief explanation of the difference in US admiralty procedure between arrest (truly *in rem* proceedings) and attachment (an adjunct to *in personam* proceedings).

5.3C American admiralty proceedings: arrest and attachment distinguished

5.9. In admiralty proceedings in countries that derive their procedure from the United Kingdom's, one of the central legal questions in determining whether a ship can be arrested is whether the person who would be liable *in personam* (called the "relevant person" in the legislation of many countries) is the beneficial owner of the ship to be arrested.[13] In contrast, the American doctrine of personification regards

---

[9] *D'Amico Dry Ltd v Primera Maritime (Hellas) Ltd*, 756 F 3d 151, 2014 AMC 1539 (2d Cir 2014); *Flame SA v Freight Bulk Pte Ltd*, 762 F 3d 352, 2014 AMC 2014 (4th Cir 2014); *D'Amico Dry Ltd v Primera Maritime (Hellas) Ltd*, 886 F 3d 216, 220, 2018 AMC 666 (2d Cir 2018).

[10] *Seismic Reservoir 2020, Inc v Paulsson*, 785 F 3d 330, 335 (9th Cir 2015), citing *Flame SA v Freight Bulk Pte Ltd*, 762 F 3d 352, 363, 2014 AMC 2014 (4th Cir 2014) (Wilkinson J concurring).

[11] 762 F 3d 352, 2014 AMC 2014 (4th Cir 2014).

[12] An FFA would not be the one of the kinds of contract defined by statute as coming within an English court's admiralty jurisdiction: see Senior Courts Act 1981 (UK), s. 20(2).

[13] See, e.g. Senior Courts Act 1981 (UK), s. 21(4) ("beneficial owner"); High Court (Admiralty Jurisdiction) Act (Singapore), Cap 123, 2001 rev edn., s. 4(4) ("beneficial owner"); High Court Ordinance (HK), Cap 4, s. 12B(4) ("beneficial owner"); Admiralty Act 1973 (NZ), s. 5(2)(b) ("beneficially owned as respects all shares

the ship itself as a separate legal person for purposes of *in rem* liability, capable of acquiring legal obligations even when its owner would not be personally liable.[14] Thus, the potential *in personam* liability of the owner or other "relevant person" and that person's relationship to the offending ship is, literally, irrelevant so far as American ship *arrest* is concerned. An *in rem* action in the United States is not merely a means of obtaining security and forcing the appearance of the shipowner, as it is in the UK-based systems:[15] it is an action against the ship itself. Thus, the ship may be held liable *in rem* when the shipowner would not be liable *in personam*.[16] If the shipowner does come before the court to defend the claim against the ship, it does so not by entering an appearance because it is not (and cannot be) party to the *in rem* proceeding.[17] If an arrested ship is sold (either after judgment or *pendente lite*, pending decision on the merits) to satisfy the arresting party's claim, then *all* claims against the ship are transferred to the proceeds of sale; the ship is sold by the court free of all existing maritime claims.[18] The result is that no other claimant can bring an *in rem* claim against the ship itself after the judicial sale; any subsequent claimant must bring its claim against the proceeds of sale.

5.10. As well as the procedure for ship *arrest* pursuant to genuinely *in rem* proceedings against the ship itself, the Supplemental Admiralty and Maritime Claims Rules to the Federal Rules of Civil Procedure also make provision for *attachment* of assets, which may include ships as well as other assets. The two procedures are typically called by the name of the rule in the federal Supplemental Admiralty and Maritime Claims Rules that govern them – Rule C arrest[19] and Rule B attachment.[20] Although they seem similar in many respects – each permits seizure of assets to satisfy the plaintiff's claim – they are conceptually distinct in important respects. The key difference between Rule C

therein"). The Australian legislation refers simply to "owner" (see Admiralty Act 1988 (Cth), ss. 17(b), 19(b)), but it has been held that "owner" in this context means "beneficial owner": *Malaysia Shipyard v Iron Shortland as Surrogate for the Ship Newcastle Pride* (1995) 131 ALR 738, 747–8 (J Sheppard); *Kent v SS Maria Luisa (No 2)* (2003) 130 FCR 12 [17] (Tamberlin and JJ Hely); *Shagang Shipping Co Ltd v Ship Bulk Peace* [2014] FCAFC 48, (2014) 314 ALR 230 [20] (Allsop CJ).

14 See Martin Davies, 'In Defense of Unpopular Virtues: Personification and Ratification' (2000) 75 Tul L Rev 337.

15 *Republic of India v India Steamship Co Ltd (The Indian Grace) (No 2)* [1998] AC 878; *Ocean Industries Pty Ltd v M/V Steven C* [1994] 1 Qd R 69.

16 For example, the carrying ship may be held liable *in rem* on a bill of lading issued by a time charterer as contracting carrier, even though the shipowner would have no liability itself: *United Nations Children's Fund v S/S Nordstern*, 251 F Supp 833 (SDNY, 1966); *Tube Products of India v S/S Rio Grande*, 334 F Supp 1039, 1971 AMC 1629 (SDNY, 1971); *Demsey & Associates, Inc. v S/S Sea Star*, 461 F 2d 1009, 1972 AMC 1440 (2d Cir, 1972); *British West Indies Produce Inc v S/S Atlantic Clipper*, 353 F Supp 548, 1973 AMC 163 (SDNY, 1973); *Cavcar Co v M/V Suzdal*, 723 F 2d 1096, 1984 AMC 609 (3d Cir, 1983); *Cactus Pipe & Supply Co v M/V Montmartre*, 756 F 2d 1103, 1985 AMC 2150 (5th Cir 1985).

17 The procedure by which a shipowner (or other party) could appear to defend the claim against a ship was formerly called a "claim of owner". Now, the shipowner must file a verified statement asserting "a right of possession or any ownership interest: see FRCP, Rule C(6)(b)(i). This entitles it to argue on behalf of the ship, but it does not thereby become party to the proceedings.

18 46 USC s. 31326.

19 FRCP Supp Admlty r C. It is only necessary to consider the federal rules here, as ships can be arrested only under the jurisdiction of federal courts: see *The Hine v Trevor*, 71 US 555, 18 L Ed 451 (1866). Although state courts have concurrent jurisdiction to hear matters coming within the federal courts' subject-matter jurisdiction in admiralty (28 USC s. 1333), they are not constitutionally permitted to order *arrest* of wrongdoing ships: ibid.

20 FRCP Supp Admlty r B(1)(a).

arrest and Rule B attachment is that the latter is an adjunct to an *in personam* claim, whereas the former is the means of giving effect to a true *in rem* claim against the ship itself.

5.11. Terminology is important here. Strictly speaking, a ship can only be *arrested* pursuant to *in rem* proceedings, which must be against the ship itself, not its owner or operator, according to Rule C. In order to arrest a ship under Rule C, the claimant's claim must be secured by a maritime lien over the ship, although it should be noted that almost all maritime claims are secured by a maritime lien under US law.

5.12. Only the "wrongdoing" ship itself may be arrested under Rule C, as it is the only legal person that has (allegedly) caused loss to the plaintiff. Thus, there is no surrogate ship *arrest* in the United States, although there may be *attachment* of other ships owned by the owner of the wrongdoing ship, in much the same way that surrogate ship *arrest* is sanctioned by the international Arrest Convention 1952.[21] A ship may be *attached* under Rule B of the Supplemental Admiralty Rules to the Federal Rules of Civil Procedure pursuant to an action *in personam* against the shipowner. A Rule B attachment order has much the same practical and physical effect as a Rule C arrest, in that it prevents the ship from moving unless security for the ship's release is given but there is a profoundly important conceptual difference between Rule B attachment and Rule C arrest.

5.13. Rule B provides that *any* property of the *in personam* defendant, tangible or intangible, may be attached if the *in personam* defendant is not "found within" the federal district in which the property is attached.[22] Thus, assets as diverse as bank accounts of the defendant,[23] bunkers aboard a ship,[24] "order" bills of lading conferring the right to possession of valuable cargo,[25] and debts owing to the defendant,[26] may be attached under Rule B, as may any other ships owned by the *in personam* defendant.[27] Furthermore, there is no equivalent of the "one ship, one arrest" rule enshrined in the Arrest Convention 1952;[28] a plaintiff can continue to attach the defendant's property until it has sufficient security for its claim.[29]

---

[21] International Convention Relating to the Arrest of Seagoing Ships, 10 May 1952, 439 UNTS 6330 (1962) Art 3(1) (hereafter "Arrest Convention").

[22] FRCP Supp Admlty r B(1)(a).

[23] See, e.g. *Aurora Maritime Co v Abdullah Mohamed Fahem & Co*, 85 F 3d 44, 1996 AMC 1755 (2d Cir 1996); *Royal Swan Navigation Co v Global Container Lines Ltd*, 868 F Supp 599, 1995 AMC 1266 (SDNY, 1994). Electronic funds transfers (EFTs) passing through intermediary banks are not subject to Rule B attachment: see *Shipping Corp of India Ltd v Jaldhi Overseas Pte Ltd*, 585 F 3d 58, 2009 AMC 2409 (2d Cir 2009).

[24] *Schiffahrtsgesellschaft Leonhardt & Co v A Bottachi SA de Navegacion*, 773 F 3d 1528, 1986 AMC 1 (11th Cir 1985) (*en banc*); *Malin International Ship Repair & Drydock Inc v Oceanografia SA de CV*, 817 F 3d 241, 2016 AMC 1084 (5th Cir 2016).

[25] *Thypin Steel Co v Certain Bills of Lading Issued for a Cargo of 3017 Metric Tons, More or Less, of Hot Rolled Steel Plate Laden on Bard the MV Geroi Panfilovsky*, 1996 AMC 2014 (SDNY, 1996).

[26] See, e.g. *Reibor International Ltd v Cargo Carriers (KACZ-Co) Ltd*, 759 F 2d 262 (2d Cir 1985); *Engineering Equipment Co v S/S Selene*, 446 F Supp 706 (SDNY, 1978); *Day v Temple Drilling Co*, 613 F Supp 194 (SD Miss, 1985). Strictly speaking, debts are "garnished" under Rule B, not "attached".

[27] See, e.g. *Nassau Maritime Holdings Designation Activity Co v Riverside Navigation Ltd*, 508 F Supp 3d 65 (MD La, 2020), among many other examples.

[28] Arrest Convention, supra (n 21) Art 3(1).

[29] FRCP Supp Admlty r B(1)(a): "a verified complaint may contain a prayer for process to attach the defendant's tangible or intangible personal property—*up to the amount sued for*—in the hands of garnishees

5.14. Any property that has been attached under Rule B may be sold by the court to satisfy the plaintiff's *in personam* claim if that claim is not satisfied by other means.[30] However, if the court sells a ship that has been attached under Rule B, it does so only to obtain funds to satisfy the attaching plaintiff's individual *in personam* claim against the shipowner. The sale has no effect on any other claims against the ship or its owner, just as the sale of any other (non-maritime) attached property would not. In contrast, if the court sells a ship that has been *arrested* under Rule C, the sale is effective in relation to any and all claims that are outstanding against the ship, because all maritime liens against the ship are then transferred to the proceeds of sale.[31]

5.15. The significance of this distinction between the effect of sales under Rule B and Rule C was explained succinctly in the following way by the US Courts of Appeals for the Fifth Circuit in *Belcher Co v M/V Maratha Mariner*:[32]

> 'An execution sale pursuant to a writ of attachment is not, however, the equivalent of a judicial sale in admiralty. The ship is not sold free of all liens; instead only the owner's interest, whatever it may be, is adjudicated.'
>
> It is this fundamental distinction between Rule C sales and Rule B sales that colours the attitude taken by US courts to recognition of foreign judicial sales, as the next section shows.

5.4D Federal maritime law on recognition of foreign judicial sales

5.16. Because federal general maritime law about recognition and enforcement of foreign admiralty judgments is entirely judge-made, it is less detailed and precise than its statutory state-law counterparts, UFMJRA and UFCMJRA, which were considered in Section B. Furthermore, admiralty-jurisdiction cases on the precise question of recognition of the effect of foreign judicial ship sales are few and far between. What few cases there are often begin by quoting one or both of the following dicta of the notorious (for other reasons) Judge Henry Billings Brown[33] from the late nineteenth-century case *The Trenton*:[34]

> The doctrine that the sale of a vessel by a court of competent jurisdiction discharges her from liens of every jurisdiction, is the law of the civilized world.[35]
>
> That the sale of a vessel, made pursuant to the decree of a foreign court of admiralty, will be held valid in every other country, and will vest a clear and indefeasible title in the purchaser, is entirely settled, both in England and America.[36]

---

named in the process" (emphasis added). See, e.g. *Central Hudson Gas & Electric Corp v Empresa Naviera Santa SA*, 56 F 3d 359 (2d Cir, 1995) (Rule B attachment permitted to "top up" amount secured by Rule C arrest).

[30] FRCP Supp Admlty r E(9).

[31] 46 USC s. 31326.

[32] 724 F 2d 1161, 1165 (5th Cir 1984).

[33] Judge Brown's notoriety stems from the fact that, as a Justice of the US Supreme Court later in his career, he wrote the opinion of the Supreme Court in the case of *Plessy v Ferguson*, 163 US 537, 16 S Ct 1138 (1896), which affirmed the constitutionality of racial segregation under the "separate but equal" doctrine. Perhaps deservedly, Judge (later Justice) Brown has been described as "[O]ne of the most forgotten men who ever sat on the United States Supreme Court": see Robert J Glennon Jr, 'Justice Henry Billings Brown: Values in Tension' (1973) 44 U Colo L Rev 553, 553. *Plessy* was eventually overruled by the Supreme Court in *Brown v Board of Education of Topeka, Kansas*, 347 US 483, 74 S Ct 686 (1954).

[34] 4 F 657 (ED Mich, 1880).

[35] Ibid 661.

[36] Ibid 662.

5.17. Sonorous and generous sounding though these dicta are, they give a misleading impression of the willingness of US admiralty courts to recognise foreign admiralty judgments. The surprisingly few cases that have been decided are firmly grounded on the domestic American distinction between Rule C arrest pursuant to true *in rem* proceedings and Rule B attachment pursuant to *in personam* admiralty proceedings: foreign sales similar to the former are recognised, foreign sales similar to the latter are not. To put the same point another way, when deciding recognition cases, US courts project admiralty law concepts of the domestic American *lex fori* onto foreign judicial proceedings that result in ship sales.

5.18. If the foreign court's sale sells the ship "free of all liens", it will be recognised by a US court as having the same effect as a Rule C sale, thus precluding any subsequent efforts by claimants to satisfy pre-sale claims by arrest of the ship within the United States. If, however, the foreign sale is equivalent to "an execution sale pursuant to a writ of attachment", it is regarded as having no effect on the right of other claimants to proceed against the ship in the United States (under either Rule C or Rule B) after the foreign sale has taken place. Thus, the court must first characterise the nature of the foreign proceedings and ensuing sale.

5.19. Readers in some common law countries might shrug and feel unmoved by the information that American courts apply this distinction because it is axiomatic in their legal systems that a judicial sale *does* transfer title free of all liens and encumbrances, with the result that US courts should always and necessarily recognise any such sale. Nevertheless, closer inspection might prompt such readers not to be so sanguine. Some countries, such as India and South Africa, have passed legislation that specifically provides that a judicial sale transfers the ship free of all liens and encumbrances.[37] The legislation in other countries, such as Canada, does so less clearly and completely.[38] In many other common law jurisdictions, including Australia,[39] Hong Kong,[40] New Zealand,[41] Singapore[42] and the United Kingdom,[43] there is no legislation that specifically provides that a judicial sale transfers title to the buyer free of all liens or claims; that result follows only as a matter of judge-made (albeit well-established) law.[44] However, where the rule is judge-made, it is not absolute, as it is in countries where it derives from

[37] Admiralty (Jurisdiction and Settlement of Maritime Claims) Act 2017, s. 8 (India); Admiralty Jurisdiction Regulation Act 1983 (S Africa), s. 9(3). *See* Damien Cremean, *Admiralty Jurisdiction*, 5th edn. (2020, Federation Press) 374–375.

[38] Federal Courts Rules (SOR/98–106) r 490(3) provides that property sold by the Court "is free of any liens under Canadian maritime law", which at least arguably might not apply to liens arising under the law of other countries.

[39] *Readhead v Admiralty Marshal, Western Australia District Registry* (1998) 89 FCR 229; 157 ALR 660.

[40] *The Margo L* [1998] 1 HKC 217, 218 (J Waung).

[41] *All-Weather Investments Ltd v Sealord Charters Ltd* (1997) NZPC 808 (CA).

[42] *The Turtle Bay* [2013] SGHC 165, [2013] 4 SLR 615, [11]–[13] (Belinda Ang Saw Ean J); *The Sea Urchin* [2014] SGHC 24; [2014] 2 SLR 646, [8] (J Belinda Ang Saw Ean).

[43] *The Tremont* (1841) 1 Wm Rob 163, 164; 166 ER 534, 534 (Dr Lushington); *The Acrux* [1962] 1 Lloyd's Rep 405, 409 (J Hewson); *The Cerro Colorado* [1993] 1 Lloyd's Rep 58, 60 (J Sheen); *Bank of Tokyo-Mitsubishi UFJ Ltd v Owners of the MV Sanko Mineral (The Sanko Mineral)* [2014] EWHC 3927 (Admlty); [2015] 1 Lloyd's Rep 247, [41] (J Teare).

[44] It is a mystery how this judge-made rule can possibly thought to be consistent with the doctrine established in *Republic of India v Indian Steamship Co Ltd (The Indian Endurance and Indian Grace) (No 2)* [1998] AC 878, that an action *in rem* is, in effect, merely a means of bringing an *in personam* action against the shipowner, but that is a topic for a different time.

legislative provision. Thus, for example, in countries without an affirmative legislative rule about the transfer of clean title, judicial sale of a ship pursuant to *in rem* proceedings may yet be found to be subject to pre-existing statutory rights of forfeiture.[45]

5.20. Perhaps more importantly for present purposes, many civil law legal systems have no concept of a pure *in rem* proceeding that treats the seized ship as the means for satisfying the claims of *all* claimants, not just the particular one whose claim led to the ship's seizure by the court. Civil law concepts such as *saisie conservatoire* (conservatory attachment) are much closer to Rule B attachment than they are to Rule C arrest.[46]

5.21. Axiomatic though the effect of court-ordered sales might seem to some readers, it should be stressed that the truly *in rem* nature of the foreign proceedings will not be presumed in the United States but rather must be established by the party seeking recognition of those proceedings. The possibility that a foreign judicial sale might not clear the ship of all maritime liens was confronted squarely by the US Courts of Appeals for the Fifth Circuit in *Belcher Co v M/V Maratha Mariner*.[47] Although the particular issue decided by the Fifth Circuit was the extra-territorial effect of security given for release of a ship from seizure ordered by a foreign court, the case also shows clearly how US courts analyse the effect of foreign judicial sales.

5.22. In *The Maratha Mariner*, an American necessaries supplier (Belcher) sued the ship's Indian owner (Chowgule) in the Netherlands and had the ship seized by process of the Dutch court, claiming that it had not been paid for bunkers provided to the ship in the United States on the order of the ship's Danish time charterer (Armada). The owner, Chowgule, secured the release of *Maratha Mariner* by posting a letter of undertaking. While the Dutch litigation was still pending in Rotterdam, Belcher proceeded *in rem* against the ship *Maratha Mariner* and had the ship arrested under Rule C in the port of Houston, Texas, claiming that it had a statutory maritime lien for the supply of necessaries.[48] The US District Court for the Southern District of Texas dismissed the plaintiff's claim on *lis alibi pendens* grounds, holding that the American proceedings should not be allowed to continue because they essentially duplicated the Dutch proceedings.[49] The US Courts of Appeals for the Fifth Circuit reversed that dismissal, holding that the plaintiff was entitled to continue with its *in rem* action in the United States, notwithstanding the release of the ship in return for security in the Netherlands. The *in rem* proceedings against *Maratha Mariner* in Texas were not proceedings between the same legal persons in relation to the same legal issues, so the doctrine of *lis alibi pendens* had no application. The defendant in the Dutch proceedings was the owner, Chowgule, but the defendant in the US proceedings was the ship *Maratha Mariner* itself. The Dutch claim turned on the

---

45 *Readhead*, supra (n 39); *Debis Financial Services (NZ) Ltd v Cray Fishing Vessel Stryker (The Stryker)* [2005] NZAR 385. Nigel Meeson and John Kimbell, *Admiralty Jurisdiction and Practice*, 5th edn. (2017, Informa) [6.10]–[6.20].

46 William Tetley, *Maritime Liens and Claims*, 2d edn. (1998, Blais) 962–971.

47 Above (n 32).

48 At the time *The Maratha Mariner* was decided, the relevant statute was referred to as the Federal Maritime Liens Act and the provision granting necessaries suppliers a maritime lien was codified at 46 USC s. 971. The statute is now referred to as the Commercial Instruments and Maritime Liens Act (CIMLA) and the relevant provision is now codified at 46 USC s. 31342.

49 *Belcher Co v M/V Maratha Mariner*, 1983 AMC 2089 (SD Tx, 1983).

contractual liability of Chowgule to pay for the bunkers but the American claim turned on the interpretation of the terms of the US statute conferring a maritime lien on necessaries providers.

5.23. The decision shows the full force of the projection of American *lex fori* concepts when characterizing foreign judicial proceedings. The Fifth Circuit stated:[50]

> If American law had been applicable when the vessel was attached in the Netherlands, the supplier of fuel would have had a lien on the vessel and an action *in rem* could have been brought to enforce the maritime lien. The Netherlands action was, however, based on contract principles because Dutch law does not recognize the concept of maritime lien and, therefore, provides no mechanism by which such a lien can be enforced. The fact that an *in rem* action could not be brought in the Netherlands does not convert the attachment there filed into an *in rem* proceeding.

5.24. In *Gulf and Southern Terminal Corp v SS President Roxas*,[51] the US Courts of Appeals for the Fourth Circuit came to the opposite conclusion from the *Maratha Mariner* court on the facts of the case but applied an identical analysis, scrutinizing the nature of the foreign court proceedings that led to the sale before deciding whether to permit American proceedings to go ahead. In *The President Roxas*, an American stevedoring company provided stevedoring services on credit to a ship then called *Rio Aqui*, which was owned at the time by a Mexican corporation. The Mexican shipowner subsequently opened bankruptcy proceedings in Mexico and *Rio Aqui* was sold by the bankruptcy court to a purchaser who renamed the ship *The President Roxas*. The stevedoring company proceeded *in rem* against *The President Roxas* when it next visited the United States, claiming a maritime lien for the sums owed for the stevedoring services previously provided to the ship.[52] The new owners of *The President Roxas* moved for the plaintiff's claim to be dismissed, arguing that the plaintiff's maritime lien had been extinguished by the sale ordered by the Mexican court. The district court granted the motion to dismiss, and the US Courts of Appeals for the Fourth Circuit affirmed. Importantly for present purposes, however, the motion to dismiss was granted only after the court had satisfied itself that the sale by the Mexican bankruptcy court was similar in effect to true *in rem* proceedings, transferring the rights of all claimants to the proceeds of sale, as would be the case with *in rem* proceedings in the United States:[53]

> [The plaintiff] urges this court to refuse to recognize the Mexican court's decision because its proceedings were *in personam* and it lacked personal jurisdiction over the appellant. While Mexican law does not provide for an explicit *in rem* proceeding, it is apparent that the Mexican court's judicial sale of the vessel employed procedures virtually identical to those which are denominated as an *in rem* proceeding under American law. . . . The vessel having been under the jurisdiction and control of the Mexican bankruptcy court, and that court's proceedings being proper and regular so far as the record shows, we find that

---

50 *Belcher*, supra (n 32) 1164.

51 701 F 2d 1110, 1983 AMC 1521 (4th Cir, 1983).

52 See above (n 48) for a description of the statute conferring a maritime lien on American necessaries providers.

53 *President Roxas*, supra (n 51) 1112.

court's order entitled to recognition and binding on American courts, as a decree which would in this country be denominated as an *in rem* decree.

5.25. Similarly, in *Atlantic Ship Supply Inc v M/V Lucy*,[54] the US District Court for the Middle District of Florida held that a ship sale ordered by a court in Costa Rica in foreclosure proceedings brought by the ship's mortgagee had the effect of extinguishing pre-existing maritime lien rights of American necessaries suppliers but only after the court had first asked itself whether the proceedings were "truly *in rem*": that is, whether the effect of the court-ordered auction sale was that the purchaser "receive[d] title to [the ship] free and clear of all liens and encumbrances".[55]

5.26. Before leaving this description of the approach taken by US courts to the recognition of foreign court-ordered sales, it is worth noting that there is an (apparently little-cited)[56] English case that employs exactly the same process of reasoning as that used in *The Maratha Mariner*, *The President Roxas* and *The Lucy*. In *The Goulandris*,[57] the plaintiff provided salvage services in the Bosphorus to a ship then named *The Carston* under the terms of a Lloyd's Open Form (LOF) contract signed by the master. *The Carston* was later arrested in the port of Constantinople (now Istanbul), its owners having failed to provide the plaintiff salvors with acceptable security. *The Carston* was, however, allowed to leave Constantinople on the basis that it could be rearrested in Alexandria, in Egypt, its next scheduled port of call. The plaintiff obtained a saisie conservatoire order from an Egyptian court for *The Carston* to be detained on arrival in Alexandria. Unfortunately for the plaintiff salvors, the owner of *The Carston* became bankrupt after the ship left Constantinople and when the ship arrived in Alexandria, it was seized by the trustee in bankruptcy (or syndic, as he was known in Egyptian legal terms).

5.27. The plaintiff salvors instituted arbitration proceedings in London as agreed in the LOF contract, but only the cargo owners participated in the arbitration, the bankrupt shipowner making no appearance. The arbitrator made an award in the salvors' favour. Shortly afterwards, *The Carston* was sold to the defendants by the syndic/trustee-in-bankruptcy, with the approval of the Egyptian Mixed Tribunal of Commerce. The plaintiff later arrested *The Carston*, now named *The Goulandris*, in the port of Hull, England, seeking to enforce its maritime lien for the amount of salvage reward that had been awarded by the salvage arbitrator. The new owner of *The Carston/Goulandris* moved to set aside the plaintiff's writ *in rem* on the basis that it (the new owner) had acquired clean title to the ship as a result of the court-approved sale in Egypt. Bateson J refused to set aside the writ, stating:[58]

> The [defendant's] next contention was that the sale by the syndic under the authority of the Court in Egypt was as good as a sale in an action in rem. The action of the syndic, however, had nothing whatever to do with an action in rem and the sale does not purport to be by the Court; it is a sale by the syndic with the approval of the Court. . . . I do not think the sale in this case has any resemblance to a sale in an action *in rem*.

---

54 392 F Supp 179 (MD Fla, 1975).

55 Ibid 182.

56 Cf. Jeremy Browne, 'The extinction of maritime liens' [2003] LMCLQ 360, 366, which contains a brief description of the effect of the case.

57 [1927] p. 182.

58 Ibid 194.

5.5E The UN Convention on the International Effects of Judicial Sales of Ships (the Beijing Convention)

5.28. As the Fifth Circuit pointed out in *The Maratha Mariner*, an attachment sale is not the equivalent of a judicial sale under US law,[59] and it would not qualify as one under the Beijing Convention on the Judicial Sale of Ships[60] either. The Convention provides that the "competent authority" of a contracting state shall issue a certificate of judicial sale if the sale "conferred clean title to the ship",[61] and that any such certificate shall be recognised in all other contracting states as conferring clean title.[62] "Clean title" is defined to mean "title free and clear of *any* mortgage or hypothèque and of *any* charge" (emphases added).[63] Similarly, the Convention defines "judicial sale" to mean any sale of a ship ordered, approved or confirmed by a court, "For which the proceeds of sale are made available to *the creditors*" (emphasis added).[64] The phrase "the creditors" is not otherwise defined, but to be consistent with the definition of "clean title" it must surely mean *all* creditors.

5.29. As has been explained above, a court-ordered sale of a ship that has been attached under Rule B makes the proceeds of sale available to the attaching plaintiff, but only the attaching plaintiff. Only a judicial sale pursuant to a Rule C arrest makes the proceeds of sale available to *all* creditors whose claims are secured by a maritime lien, because the maritime liens are then transferred to the proceeds of sale.[65] It follows that a US court following the scheme of the Convention could only issue a certificate of judicial sale for court-ordered sales made pursuant to Rule C arrest. A Rule B "attachment sale" in the United States would not qualify for recognition in other Convention countries because it would not confer "clean title" (as that is defined in the Convention) and would not make the proceeds of sale available to *all* creditors.

5.30. The need to distinguish between different types of court-ordered sales before issuing a Convention-compliant certificate might be reason enough in itself for the United States not to ratify the Convention when (and if) it is actually made. In any event, unfortunately, it is very unlikely that the United States will ratify the Convention immediately when (and if) it comes into force. The President cannot ratify a treaty on behalf of the United States (thus making it "the supreme law of the land", meaning that it becomes both federal law and the law of all states and territories)[66] without the "advice and consent" of the Senate, which requires a majority of two-thirds of the Senate.[67] The present political polarisation in the United States makes it unlikely that there can be "advice and consent" by a two-thirds majority of anything even remotely controversial.

5.31. Although the Senate often gives "advice and consent" to bilateral treaties or protocols to existing conventions (particularly treaties on such matters as extradition

---

59 Above (n 32).
60 Above (n 1).
61 Ibid, Art 5(1).
62 Ibid, Art 6.
63 Ibid, Art 2(c).
64 Ibid, Art 2(a).
65 46 USC s. 31326.
66 US Const, Art VI(2).
67 Ibid, Art II, s. 2, cl. 2.

or recognition of maritime boundaries),[68] "advice and consent" to new multilateral treaties affecting individual rights is rare (but not unknown). The last time that the Senate gave "advice and consent" by a two-thirds majority to a new multilateral treaty was in 2019,[69] recommending ratification of the UN Convention on the Assignment of Receivables in International Trade,[70] a multilateral treaty in no immediate danger of coming into force internationally.[71] Before that, it was in 2013,[72] recommending ratification of two international conventions on the conservation and management of high seas fisheries resources in the Pacific Ocean.[73] Neither of the conventions ratified in 2013 was "self-executing", meaning that neither imposed any binding obligations on individuals (as opposed to ratifying countries) by its terms. Bluntly put, "advice and consent" from the Senate for ratification of a multilateral convention affecting individual rights is unlikely.

5.32. Nevertheless, even if the United States does not ratify the Beijing Convention (which unfortunately seems likely), a proliferation of Convention-compliant certificates of judicial sale issued by ratifying countries would presumably have at least some impact on recognition by US courts of foreign judicial sales. As noted above, the key question affecting recognition by a US court of a foreign judicial sale is whether that sale has the same effect as a sale incident to *in rem* proceedings in the United States – that is, whether it transfers all claims against the ship to the proceeds of sale, leaving none enforceable against the ship itself. A Convention-compliant certificate of judicial sale issued by a ratifying country would not be *conclusive* evidence of that effect (as it would if the United States itself were to become party to the Convention) but it would obviously have significant probative effect if a *Maratha-Mariner*-like question about the effect of foreign judicial proceedings were to arise in a US court about the effect of a foreign judicial sale.

5.6F Conclusion

5.33. Like all instruments that have been considered at length by both CMI and UNCITRAL, as this one has, the Beijing Convention on judicial sales is a well-crafted

---

68 US Congress, *Treaty Documents* <www.congress.gov/search?q=%7B%22source%22%3A%22treaties%22%7D> accessed 25 June 2024.

69 Senate Consideration of Treaty Document 114–7, *UN Convention on the Assignment of Receivables in International Trade* <www.congress.gov/treaty-document/114th-congress/7?s=1&r=21&overview=closed> accessed 25 June 2024.

70 *UN Convention on the Assignment of Receivables in International Trade* (opened for signature 12 December 2001) <treaties.un.org/pages/ViewDetails.aspx?src=TREATY&mtdsg_no=X-17&chapter=10> accessed 25 June 2024.

71 The convention will not come into force internationally until five countries ratify it: ibid Art 45(2). To date, Liberia and the United States are the only two countries to have ratified it.

72 Senate Consideration of Treaty Document 113–2, *Convention on the Conservation and Management of High Seas Fisheries Resources in the North Pacific Ocean* <www.congress.gov/treaty-document/113th-congress/2?s=1&r=32&overview=closed>; Senate Consideration of Treaty Document 113–1, *Convention on the Conservation and Management of High Seas Fisheries Resources in the South Pacific Ocean* <www.congress.gov/treaty-document/113th-congress/1?s=1&r=33&overview=closed> accessed 25 June 2024.

73 *Convention on the Conservation and Management of High Seas Fisheries Resources in the North Pacific Ocean* (opened for signature 24 February 2012, entered into force 19 July 2015) <treaties.un.org/Pages/ViewDetails.aspx?src=IND&mtdsg_no=XXI-7&chapter=21&clang=_en>; *Convention on the Conservation and Management of High Seas Fisheries Resources in the South Pacific Ocean* (opened for signature 1 February 2010, entered into force 24 August 2012) 2899 UNTS 211, accessed 7 October 2022.

legal framework for international uniformity. Unfortunately, for good or ill, it is unlikely that the United States will ever become party to the Convention. If that prediction proves to be correct, US courts will have no formal obligation to recognise certificates of judicial sale issued in contracting states. Conversely, of course, contracting states will have no formal obligation to recognise sales ordered by courts in the United States. As this chapter has tried to show, not all ship sales ordered by US courts qualify as "judicial sales", either as defined in the draft Convention or under domestic US law.

CHAPTER 6

Online sales of ships

Prospects and challenges

*Abhinayan Basu Bal**

6.1 Introduction

6.1. During the past two decades, advances in digital technology have allowed for tremendous growth in the use of online auctions through digital platforms. Despite this growth, courts in most traditional maritime states, with the notable exception of China, have failed to specify whether a ship could be sold online through an auction conducted on a third-party digital platform. This silence leaves creditors, debtors and platform owners unsure about whether online judicial sales of ships would confer "clean title" to the purchaser. Interestingly, since 2016, the Chinese courts have embarked on auctioning ships through a third-party digital platform called *Taobao*.[1] While no comprehensive empirical evidence exists detailing the percentage of online judicial sales of ships in China, experts in the field assert that most auctions are held on *Taobao*.[2] However, practitioners have raised concerns about the court's lack of "control and administration" on such online sales.[3]

6.2. The noticeable lack of reported disputes in this area suggests that the vast majority of debtors do not pursue litigation following online judicial sales, possibly because both debtors and creditors themselves are capitalising on the efficiencies and benefits associated with these sales. In general, the efficiencies and benefits associated with online auctions may include their expedience, inexpensive nature, higher prices relative to traditional auctions, and the potential to sell to a vastly large worldwide

---

* Reader in Law, School of Business, Economics & Law, University of Gothenburg.

1 sf.taobao.com.

2 C Wang, I Wei Chong and R Hong, *Purchase of Vessels via Online Judicial Auction – A Foreign Buyer's Guide* (29 November 2017, Clyde & Co LLP) www.lexology.com/library/detail.aspx?g=ba3ed26a-fcdb-43d9-b762-c1a08ba75c98 asserts that "nine of the ten maritime courts of China (excluding the Qingdao Maritime Court) have chosen Taobao as their first option for arranging the judicial auction of ships". Note that in 2018, a new maritime court was established in Ningbo, China. Therefore, at present, there are eleven maritime courts in China. Also, the Qingdao Maritime Court eventually chose *Taobao* for arranging judicial sale of ships.

3 E J Cheng, 'Judicial Sale of Arrested Vessels: The Suitability of Taobao as a Platform for Singapore Judicial Sale' (2019) 31 Singap Acad Law J 72, 75. In addition to arguing about reduced control and administration, Cheng presents several other deficiencies in online judicial sale, namely, that – (i) there are no interlocutory proceedings to advance the sale process; (ii) there is lack of uniform rules governing the online sale in China thereby causing uncertainty for potential buyers; (iii) the bids and appraised values on *Taobao* are not kept a secret, thereby opening the bids and sale prices to manipulation; (iv) a sale on *Taobao* may not ensure that the highest sale price because advertisements are not targeted to prospective ship buyers; and (v) ships sold "offline" are not sold below market value and there is no guarantee that a sale on *Taobao* would yield a better price as compared to a traditional judicial sale.

DOI: 10.4324/9781003499930-6

audience.[4] Be that as it may, with the adoption of the Beijing Convention,[5] it is instructive to examine whether online judicial sales of ships through third-party digital platforms[6] would confer clean title to the purchaser.

6.3. The chapter proceeds in two parts. The first part provides a brief review of judicial sales of ships primarily from an English and wider common law perspective with particular focus on the requisite "control and administration" of the court for granting clean title. The second part examines online judicial sales of ships by commencing the discussion with the specific example of *Taobao* and then progressing to draw evidence from information systems and strategy literature to highlight the "digital first" strategy resulting from platformisation.[7] This part also discusses the conceptualisation of ecosystem orchestration in online judicial sales and then goes on to review selected provisions of the Beijing Convention to draw conclusions as to how the instrument suggests that online judicial sales could be made. The role of the International Maritime Organization (IMO) through the proposed creation of a separate module under its existing Global Integrated Shipping Information System (GISIS) platform is discussed in this context.[8] The chapter concludes by synthesising the positive signals about online sales, and it asserts that the Beijing Convention has the potential to support the digital-first strategy.

6.2 Judicial sales of ships

6.2.1 The in rem proceedings and ship arrest

6.4. Judicial sale of a ship is generally considered as the last phase of an *in rem* admiralty proceeding.[9] Under English law, an admiralty claim *in rem* is commenced by issuing a claim form in the prescribed form by invoking *in rem* jurisdiction under the Senior Courts Act (SCA) 1981.[10] The *in rem* claim form is served within the jurisdiction on the ship named in the claim form. The ship may be arrested by the Admiralty Marshal and when judgment is given, or *pendente lite*,[11] the ship can be sold by the Admiralty Court

---

[4] SS Gilstrap, 'Refreshing the Page on Online Collateral Auctions' (2010) 120 Yale Law *J* 679, 680.

[5] The Beijing Convention on Judicial Sale of Ships, Which is Formally Known as the United Nations Convention on the International Effects of Judicial Sales of Ships, adopted on 7 December 2022 UNCITRAL Doc A/77/17 (documents-dds-ny.un.org/doc/UNDOC/GEN/221/088/8E/PDF/2210888E.pdf?OpenElement), Annex I. Currently, the Convention has received 20 signatures (treaties.un.org/pages/ViewDetails.aspx?src=TREATY&mtdsg_no=X-21&chapter=10&clang=_en).

[6] Hereinafter referred to as "online judicial sales of ships" or "online judicial sales" or "online sales".

[7] In information systems literature, "digital first" or "digital first, physical later" strategy refers to organising in a digital environment. This strategy is also referred to as "ontological turn". While "ontology" refers to the study of reality as constructed in both human and non-human worlds, the term "ontological turn" describes the change in theoretical orientation according to which differences are understood not in terms of differing world views, but a difference in worlds and all these worlds are of equal validity. This chapter discusses the digital first strategy in the context of judicial sales in section 3.2 below.

[8] gisis.imo.org/Public/Default.aspx.

[9] On judicial sale of ships generally see N Meeson and JA Kimbell, *Admiralty Jurisdiction and Practice*, 5th edn. (2018, Informa) paras 4.111–4.139.

[10] Ibid, para 4.1.

[11] Sale *pendente lite* is a special feature afforded by courts in common law jurisdictions. It is a departure from the standard judicial sale process where an Admiralty Court may at its discretion order appraisement and the sale before judgment *in rem* is given. Sale *pendente lite* is not available in civil law jurisdictions, because enforceable title arising from a judgment or arbitration award is a precondition to judicial sale.

and the judgment satisfied from the proceeds of sale.[12] Thus, a distinctive feature of maritime law is the possibility of arresting the ship connected with the litigation,[13] which places maritime claimants in favourable position as it establishes jurisdiction and provides security for the claim.

6.5. Ship arrest is the most common way in which maritime claims are enforced worldwide.[14] It is a form of pre-trial remedy and is governed by national law or the *lex fori* with both substantive[15] and procedural features.[16] In practice, most ships are released from arrest following the provision of security, and courts exercise supervisory jurisdiction over the process.[17] However, if the shipowner does not submit to the jurisdiction of the court, or does not provide security either because it does not want to or cannot do so, or the ship is a wasting asset,[18] a judicial sale is ordered and the claimants are paid out of the sale proceeds.[19]

6.2.2 Harnessing the procedural advantage of judicial sale

6.6. The judicial sale process comprises three important elements, namely, (i) provide sufficient notice to all creditors of the ship, (ii) to fetch the best possible price for the ship and (iii) to grant a clean title to the purchaser of the ship.[20] The emphasis on

Sale *pendente lite* is ordered where the ship is dangerous, perishable, or deteriorating rapidly under arrest, or where the costs of maintaining the arrest are greatly disproportionate to the value of the ship. See, e.g. *The Myrto* [1977] 2 Lloyd's Rep 243, 260. For a comprehensive discussion on sale *pendente lite* generally see DR Thomas, 'Admiralty Sales Pendente Lite' [1998] CJQ 409; C Buss, Ship Mortgagees: Enforcement and Remedies, in B Soyer and A Tettenborn (eds), *Ship Building, Sale and Finance* (2016, Informa) 152–153.

[12] In a recent case, *The Styliani Z* [2016] 1 Lloyd's Rep 395 [20], the Admiralty Judge Sir Nigel Teare refers to the peculiar characteristic of the admiralty *in rem* claim and provides an excellent summary to this age-old procedure.

[13] Pursuant to s. 21(4) of the Senior Courts Act (SCA) 1981, *in rem* claims can not only lead to the arrest of the ship involved in the claim but also another ship which is under the same ownership, usually called a sister ship.

[14] On ship arrest generally see F Berlingieri, *Berlingieri on Arrest of Ships*, vol 1, 6th edn. (2016, Informa).

[15] The substantive law of ship arrest is mainly governed by the 1952 Arrest Convention to which over 70 states are parties. Under the 1952 Convention, a ship can only be arrested for a claim listed under Art 1(1)(a)–(q). This list is virtually the same as the list in s. 20(2) of the SCA 1981, the predecessor of which was enacted in 1956 to give effect to the 1952 Convention. A later regime, namely, the 1999 Arrest Convention, which entered into force in 2011, failed to gain popularity and is not followed by leading maritime States. The Convention has so far received 13 ratifications and accessions. For a discussion on the 1999 Arrest Convention see F Berlingieri, *Berlingieri on Arrest of Ships*, vol 2, 6th edn. (2016, Informa).

[16] The procedures vary from one jurisdiction to another although there are some common denominators. As mentioned above, in the United Kingdom and other common law jurisdictions, arrest is a way to found jurisdiction for the prosecution of a maritime claim and provide security for the claim. However, in civil law jurisdictions, the only purpose of arrest is to afford security for the claim. For a detailed discussion on the differences in common and civil law jurisdictions see, W Tetley, 'Arrest, Attachment, and Related Maritime Law Procedures' (1998–1999) 73 Tulane Law Rev 1895.

[17] A ship is usually released from arrest if the shipowner posts security for the claim, which could be in the form of a bail bond, a payment of money into court, a bank guarantee, or a letter of undertaking from the protection and indemnity club (P&I Club) of the shipowner. Meeson and Kimbell, supra (n 9) 4.31.

[18] *The Sertao* [2018] EWHC 1013 (Admlty); [2018] 2 Lloyd's Rep 275.

[19] Caution must be exercised by a claimant when arresting a ship as wrongful arrest may result in a condemnation of the claimant for damages. Meeson and Kimbell, supra (n 9) 4.35. To conclude that an arrest is wrongful the court has to be satisfied that the arrest was motivated by bad faith or gross negligence. *The Evangelismos* (1858) 12 Moo PC 352 (PC).

[20] For a brief discussion on these three elements see section 2.3 below. See, also, P Myburgh, 'Satisfactory for its Own Purposes: Private Direct Arrangements and Judicial Vessel Sales' (2016) 22 J Int Mar Law 355, 358–362.

these three elements makes the judicial sale process fundamentally different from a private sale.

6.7. Before a court orders a judicial sale, a private sale may be organised by the shipowner or a claimant.[21] The private sale allows the owner or claimant promptly to recover the price of the ship in a cost-effective manner. This is because the private sale need not be widely publicised, and the sale proceeds vest in the seller alone. A judicial sale, however, may take anything from six weeks to two years or more, and the costs of the court procedure and of maintaining arrest ranks ahead of the claimants' debt.[22] While promptness and cost-effectiveness are advantages of a private sale, the process does not allow for finality of litigation for all parties with real or potential claims against the ship. Therefore, the purchaser through a private sale acquires title *cum onere*, that is, subject to any existing liens, encumbrances and claims against the ship.[23]

6.8. The struggle between the "quest for promptness and cost-effectiveness of a private sale" versus "clean title of a judicial sale" has resulted in the development of a hybrid solution known as the court-approved private treaty sale.[24] There, the private treaty is with the court, rather than with the owners or the bank which lent money to purchase the ship.

6.9. Under a private treaty sale, the court determines through independent valuers that the proposed sale price is equal to or greater than the current value of the ship and the buyer is not connected to the claimant.[25] The court would then be prepared to effectuate a sale by court order, hence giving a clean title to a party identified by the claimant as a potential buyer without going through an auction sale. The avoidance of public auction is possible because the Admiralty Marshal, by virtue of century-old case law, has the flexibility to sell by private treaty as well.[26] In 1999, this flexibility was stretched further in the *Edinburgh Castle* when the court was satisfied that the best

[21] On private sale generally see Meeson and Kimbell, supra (n 9) 4.119–4.122.

[22] For example, under English law, the proceeds are first distributed to satisfy paramount priority claims such as *custodia legis*, Admiralty Marshal's costs, court costs and statutory dues. Thereafter, the following ranking is followed to satisfy the claimants: maritime liens, possessory liens, mortgages and statutory rights *in rem*. Any remaining funds would go to the shipowner. See Tetley, supra (n 16) 1910.

[23] Myburgh, supra (n 20) 356. In addition to lack of clean title, private sales have several other disadvantages which usually tip the balance against such sale. For example, when a mortgagee bank arrests a ship and executes a private sale, the bank can incur liability to the mortgagor shipowner or other claimants if it does not act in good faith and take reasonable care to obtain a genuine market price. Also, the bank may not sell to itself or to its nominee or agent although it is permitted to sell to a company in which the bank is interested, but the closeness of the relationship may be scrutinised. In the aforementioned examples, mortgage law principles are applied in a maritime context. For a detailed discussion on ship mortgages see Buss, supra (n 11).

[24] These sales are also known as "fast-track" sales, "*ex parte*" sales, or "court approved direct" sales. Such sales allow banks to save ship operating expenses, which may potentially run into hundreds of thousands of dollars. In addition, the banks avoid liability for the court-appointed brokers' fees which is around 1 per cent of the purchase price: see Buss, supra (n 11) 153. Some jurisdictions such as Gibraltar and Malta recognise private treaty sale through their domestic legislation. The sale can be achieved with great speed if certain criteria can be satisfied, most important among them being that a third party is prepared to buy the vessel for an amount which can be demonstrated to the satisfaction of the court to be at least as much as would be realised by public auction: see J Scerri-Diacono, 'Private, Court-Approved Sales of Vessels and Aircraft in Malta'[2012] LMCLQ 356, 356.

[25] Generally, the claimant in a private treaty sale is a bank and the bank cannot sell to itself but can sell to a shipowner who has borrowed money form the bank to finance the purchase.

[26] See, for example, *The Everilda* (1927) 29 Ll L Rep. 238.

price would be obtained from one or other of two parties interested in the ship and two other ships arrested in separate actions.[27] The court directed the parties to submit sealed bids for all three ships *en bloc* within twenty-four hours. The court then effected the sale to the highest bidder without a public auction.

6.10. Private treaty sale is preferred by banks as it reduces the time taken for enforcement and sale to a mere couple of weeks.[28] That lowers the very significant costs and loss of freight or hire earnings associated with keeping a ship under arrest for months. However, Myburgh presents a critical view highlighting that the bank's "preferred purchaser obtains the vessel, without either having to provide the purchaser with an indemnity that the vessel is unencumbered and free from existing debts or liabilities, or exposing itself to liability for a negligent valuation of the vessel".[29] Indeed, the purchaser is often another customer of the bank, whom the bank finances to purchase the ship.[30] Buss, on the contrary, argues that courts found this arrangement suitable as in most cases the sale price of the ship would be above its market price.[31] This is particularly so because banks do not mind financing above-market purchases and roll forward the old borrower's loan debt (which may exceed ship's open market value) into a loan to the purchaser.[32]

6.11. While these advantages made private treaty sale to be the preferred choice for disposing debt-ridden ships in England and Wales for almost fifteen years,[33] the practice was brought to a grinding halt in 2013, in *The Union Gold*.[34] In this case, Teare J ruled that private treaty sale would be permitted if there were "special circumstances", for example, loss of a particularly valuable employment fixture, to justify such an order.[35] Soon thereafter, in Singapore, in *The Turtle Bay*,[36] and *The Sea Urchin*,[37] Ang J followed and approved *The Union Gold* and also referred to *The Margo L*[38] from Hong Kong, emphasising that "powerful special features or special circumstances" have to be identified before allowing a private treaty sale.

6.12. While these decisions are based on legitimate concerns of the judges about the cursory brokers' valuation, they seem to have closed a pragmatic enforcement

---

27 [1999] 2 Lloyd's Rep 362. Note, this case was reported in a different context and the private treaty sale aspects is unreported: see D Osborne, G Bowtle and C Buss, *Law of Ship Mortgages*, 2nd edn. (2016, Information) 361, footnote 164.

28 For example, in Malta, within ten days from the filing of application for court-approved, privately arranged sales, the court appoints a hearing: see Scerri-Diacono, supra (n 24) 356; see also Buss, supra (n 11) 153.

29 Myburgh, supra (n 20) 357.

30 Buss, supra (n 11) 153.

31 Conversely, Myburgh argues that private treaty sale may result in 'market distortion': see Myburgh, supra (n 20) 358.

32 Buss, supra (n 11) 153.

33 Since the *Edinburgh Castle*, court sales without auction accounted for a sizeable chunk of sales conducted by banks. For example, 23 of 31 mortgagee led sales in England in 1999–2000 were private treaty sales: see Buss, supra (n 11) 153.

34 *The Union Gold* [2013] EWHC 1696 (Admlty); [2014] 1 Lloyd's Rep 53.

35 *The Union Gold* decision brought to fore the approach taken long ago, in 1998, in Hong Kong, in *The Margo L* [1998] 1 HKC 217 where J Waung held that there must exist "powerful special features" to justify a private treaty sale.

36 [2013] SGHC 165; [2013] 4 SLR 615.

37 [2014] SGHC 24; [2014] 2 SLR 646

38 *See (n 35).*

procedure in several important admiralty jurisdictions.[39] Keeping up with this judicial trend and other legislative strictures, banks nowadays increasingly lean towards consensual restructurings rather than hostile mortgage enforcements or private treaty sales.[40]

6.13. Be that as it may, this chapter continues to explore the tensions between admiralty procedures and private treaty sales to flesh out the finer points, with an objective to facilitate the ensuing discussion of online judicial sale of ships.

6.2.3 Tensions between admiralty procedures and "special circumstances"

6.14. Although English law allows flexibility to the Admiralty Marshal to sell either by public auction or private treaty, the admiralty procedures established through case law predating *The Edinburgh Castle* create tensions in delineating the "special circumstances" as highlighted in *The Union Gold*. These tensions relate to best possible price, fairness to all parties, the impartiality, independence and integrity of the court and clean title.[41]

6.2.3.1 Best possible price

6.15. As discussed above, Buss argues that private treaty sales are preferred by courts as they fetch higher sale prices above the market price. However, Myburgh argues that private treaty sales distort the market. Myburgh's view resonates with the view expressed by the judge in *The Margo L* where private treaty sale negotiations were considered as inherently anti-competitive, especially when compared with the ordinary judicial sale process, which provides not only the 'floor protection' of an independent appraisal, but also the incentive for potential purchasers to submit their best possible prices through an internationally publicised competitive tender or auction process.[42]

6.16. In the same vein, Teare J, in *The Union Gold*, relied on *The Halcyon Isle (No. 2)*[43] to emphasise that the timing of an auction should be decided by the Admiralty Marshal even if that meant further costs being incurred to maintain the ship; and *The APJ Shalin*[44] to highlight that once an order for appraisal and sale has been made, it would be contempt of court for parties to market ships for private sale, even if done under the Admiralty Marshal's supervision.[45]

---

39 See Buss, supra (n 11) 155.

40 For example, the ability of institutional lenders to offer favourable finance for a 'preferred' bid, usually in an amount at or exceeding the ship's market value, to other customers, has been heavily curtailed by the new regulatory environment in which such lenders operate. See Osborne, Bowtle and Buss, supra (n 27) 379.

41 For a comprehensive discussion on these tensions see Myburgh, supra (n 20) 358–362. In this chapter, the tensions are presented in summary form to connect with the discussion on platforms in section 3 below.

42 Myburgh, supra (n 20) 359.

43 *[1975] 1 Lloyd's Rep 525.*

44 *[1991] 2 Lloyd's Rep 62.*

45 Buss, supra (n 11) 154.

6.17. Adopting a similar approach to that of the English courts, the Singaporean High Court in *The Turtle Bay*[46] held that utilising major local newspapers, the Government Gazette and trading magazines to advertise the sale to the world at large to be the normal and usual mode of advertising a judicial sale to fetch the best possible price.[47]

6.2.3.2 Fairness to all parties

6.18. The perception of a judicial sale by an admiralty court is that it is a process which is fair to all parties. What matters is that the judges have made an effort to protect all creditors, both high-ranking maritime lien holders and mortgagees, as well as creditors with ordinary maritime claims.[48]

6.19. However, as Buss points out, the legitimate concerns of judges are sometimes dwarfed by how the facts play out in reality.[49] For example, in *The Margo L*, the judge had already awarded US$12 million to the bank, over three times the sum offered by the direct purchaser.[50] In addition, Buss points out that in *The Sea Urchin*, the claim of the bank "exceeded the price offered several times over". So, if the auction generates a higher price, then the bank would receive a higher amount. However, if the auction generates a lower price, then the bank would lose and other creditors remain unaffected, resulting in an unfair outcome for the bank.[51]

6.20. Myburgh highlights that even when a private treaty sale would have the same economic outcome as an ordinary judicial sale, a court may be reluctant to choose the former as that would "blur the lines between private commercial self-interest and public judicial administration".

6.2.3.3 Impartiality, independence and integrity of the court

6.21. When a private sale is organised by a single creditor and the court gives its seal of approval to make it a judicial sale, then that may undermine the reputation of the Admiralty Court as to its impartiality, independence and integrity in the eyes of the other creditors.

6.22. To address this concern, Teare J in *The Union Gold* highlighted that "[t]he Marshal is an officer of the court whose role is essential to the administration of justice in the Admiralty Court".[52] *The Turtle Bay* and *The Sea Urchin* resonate this public administrative process by highlighting that the court must have "entire control over the sale process".[53]

---

46 *[2013] 4 SLR 615 [17] and [20].*

47 Cheng, supra (n 3) 86.

48 *The Margo L* [1997] HKCFI 776, [1998] 1 HKC 217 [5].

49 Buss, supra (n 11) 155.

50 Myburgh, supra (n 20) footnote 36, points out that in *The Margo L* [1997] HKCFI 776, [1998] 1 HKC 217 [7] J Waung indicates: "In my judgment, even if valuation is done in the most convincing way, it cannot persuade the Court to sanction private sale. This is because valuation and appraisement is only able to perform "the floor protection" function".

51 Buss, supra (n 11) 155.

52 *The Union Gold*, supra (n 34) [20].

53 *The Turtle Bay* [2013] 4 SLR 615, [2013] SGHC 165 [17]; *The Sea Urchin* [2014] 2 SLR 646, [2014] SGHC 24 [8].

6.2.3.4 Clean title

6.23. The fairness and impartiality in the judicial sale process is not just an ethical responsibility but is a critical component of the Admiralty Courts' ability to confer clean title to the purchaser of a ship.[54] This responsibility has been highlighted in several court decisions across jurisdictions.[55]

6.24. The emphasis on the administrative process gains further significance because the judicial sale orders are made under and subject to national law, and is given effect to by comity of nations.[56] Therefore, a cautious approach to private treaty sale becomes imperative, so that the "fragile and nebulous concept of comity" in recognition of judicial sale is preserved.[57]

6.2.3.5 Special circumstances

6.25. The "special circumstances" which Teare J referred to in *The Union Gold* to justify a private treaty sale have been exemplified in that case itself. The judge allowed the sale of one out of the four ships, namely, *The Union Pluto*, because the evidence showed that a delay in the sale would cause the loss of a particularly valuable employment fixture.[58] Therefore, finding "special circumstances" to justify a sale outside the ordinary judicial sale procedure will be grounded on the facts of each case.

6.2.3.6 Recognition and enforcement

6.26. The recognition of a private treaty sale and conferment of clean title is generally respected worldwide based on domestic conflict rules, purportedly derived from the foreign judgment *in rem* and judicial sale.[59] This recognition can be gleaned from the decision of *Castrique v Imrie*[60] where it was held that a decision of a foreign court confers a clean title good against all third parties, if

> [t]he subject matter was so situated as to be within the lawful control of the State under the authority of which the Court sits; and . . . the sovereign authority of that State has conferred on the Court jurisdiction to decide as to the disposition of the thing, and the

[54] The expression "clear title" is also used to describe the notion of "clean title"; see e.g. WM Sharpe, 'Towards an International Instrument for Recognition of Judicial Sales of Ships: Policy Aspects' [2013] CMI Yearbook 166–181.

[55] *The Tremont* (1841) 1 W Rob 163, 166 ER 534; *The Acrux* [1962] 1 Lloyd's Rep 405, 409; *The Cerro Colorado* [1993] 1 Lloyd's Rep 58, 60; *The Turtle Bay* [2013] 4 SLR 615, [2013] SGHC 165 [11]; and *The Phoenix* [2014] 1 Lloyd's Rep 449 [34].

[56] See *The Acrux* [1962] 1 Lloyd's Rep 405, 409; *The Cerro Colorado* [1993] 1 Lloyd's Rep 58, 61; *Adams v Cape Industries Plc* [1990] Ch 433 (CA), 552

[57] Myburgh, supra (n 20) 362.

[58] The *Union Pluto* was 20 years old, valued at €315,000, and would be operated under a long-term contract, saving the jobs of 21 crew members: see Osborne, Bowtle and Buss, supra (n 27) 362.

[59] According to Myburgh, "courts in a few jurisdictions do seem to regard any foreign judicial sales of their registered ships as illegal or contrary to public policy, but these are outliers". For a comprehensive discussion on recognition of judicial sales see Myburgh, supra (n 16) 564–566.

[60] *(1869–70) LR 4 HL 414, 428–429.*

Court has acted within its jurisdiction. If these conditions are fulfilled, the adjudication is conclusive against the world.

6.27. The approach of *Castrique v Imrie* was later applied in *The Acrux*.[61] There, in discussing the basis of the clean title bestowed upon the purchaser of a ship sold via a judicial sale, Hewson J refers to three points – (i) that a judicial sale cannot be impeached by third parties if a court had competent jurisdiction in the matter; (ii) exercised its powers honestly; and (iii) delivered the relevant orders in an *in rem* proceeding.

6.28. Therefore, the most important consideration on which recognition of private treaty sale and conferment of clean title hinges is the Admiralty Court's reputation for impartiality and integrity. The recent developments in case law in major maritime jurisdictions such as England, Singapore and Hong Kong – by laying emphasis on permitting private treaty sales only in "special circumstances" – may be seen as an attempt to preserve the Admiralty Courts' reputation by not allowing reduced "control and administration".

6.3 Online judicial sales of ships through third-party digital platforms

6.29. Online judicial sales of ships using third-party digital platforms is a relatively recent phenomenon.[62] The concern of the court's lack of "control and administration", which is usually raised in context of private treaty sales, has already been transposed on online judicial sales.[63]

6.30. However, bearing in mind the dynamics of digital platforms and ecosystems, this chapter deems it necessary to investigate whether online judicial sales actually reduce the control and administration of the courts, and if yes, under what circumstances. The investigation is carried out based on the chosen example of *Taobao*, as it is one of the forerunners in online judicial sales of ships.

6.3.1 Online judicial sale on Taobao

6.31. The main steps involved in an online judicial sale in China are similar to an "offline" sale in England, or any other admiralty jurisdiction, that is, the ship to be sold is advertised, bids are accepted, reviewed and matched against one another, and the highest bidder wins.[64] Unless any bid reaches the reserve price, the ship is barred from being sold and the auction process is repeated.[65] The process of bidding, auction rules and transfer of title is briefly summarised next.[66]

[61] [1962] 1 Lloyd's Rep 405.

[62] An electronic platform operated and managed directly by the courts to sell ships may not be a viable option economically: see Cheng, supra (n 3) 90–92.

[63] Cheng, supra (n 3) 75.

[64] Ibid 73.

[65] Ibid.

[66] This summary is based on a guide published by a leading London based law firm with comprehensive practice: see Wang, Wei Chong and Hong, supra (n 2). See, also, Cheng, supra (n 3) 81–82.

6.32. In Chinese practice, a Chinese company or citizen with a *Taobao* account can participate in the auction by registering as bidder after remitting a deposit.[67] A foreigner may participate in the auction by registering a *Taobao* account through a Chinese company or citizen, appointed as its "bidding agent". According to the standard auction rules authorised by the Chinese courts, a *Taobao* account holder would automatically be deemed as bidder and obtain title to the ship if it wins the auction. If a foreigner wants to obtain the title to the ship directly from the court, it must disclose to the court, before the auction begins, its identity and the *Taobao* account used for the auction as well as authorisation documents in favour of the bidding agent. Anyone can register as a bidder before the end of the auction.[68]

6.33. The auction rules stipulate that the auction lasts for twenty-four hours; and the time is automatically extended by five minutes if a bidder places a bid within the last two minutes before the end of the auction. If a bidder wins the auction, the deposit is automatically remitted to the court's account, and the bidder must pay the balance of the auction price directly to the court, usually within ten days. The deposits of unsuccessful bidders are automatically returned to their *Taobao* accounts, usually within five days from the date of the auction. The purchaser is required to submit a confirmation of the auction to the court within three days after the end of the auction. Upon receipt of full payment, the court issues an order declaring clean title to the ship in favour of the purchaser and issues a certificate.[69]

6.3.2 Platform economy results in digital-first strategy

6.34. *Taobao's* role in the judicial sale transaction must be appreciated in the context of the power of the digital platform which is a new business model that uses technology to connect people, organisations and resources in an interactive ecosystem in which vast amounts of value can be created and exchanged.[70] The platform provides an open, participative infrastructure for these interactions and sets governance conditions for them.[71] Therefore, the role of *Taobao* or any other digital platform in digitalising judicial sales of ships cannot be ignored. Indeed, today's biggest platform businesses resemble states.[72]

6.3.2.1 The concept of digital-first strategy

6.35. Conceptually, digital innovation is the driver of digital platforms and ecosystems. A digital platform uses digital technology to radically reshape the nature, process and outcomes of digital innovation. Digital innovation is defined

[67] The deposit, which is generally announced 30 days before the auction, can be remitted to *Taobao* before the end of the auction. The deposit amount is fixed by the court and is generally set around 30% of the starting auction price. The deposit must be paid in Renminbi (RMB) due to China's foreign exchange control policy: see Wang, Wei Chong and Hong, supra (n 2).

[68] Wang, Wei Chong and Hong, supra (n 2).

[69] Ibid.

[70] GG Parker, MW Van Alstyne and S Paul Choudary, *Platform Revolution*, 1st edn. (2016, Norton) 3.

[71] Ibid 5.

[72] For example, *Alibaba* which owns *Taobao* handles trillions of yuan worth of transactions each year and accounts for more than two-thirds of all commercial shipments in China: see ibid 4.

as "the creation of and consequent change in market offerings, business processes, or models that result from the use of digital technology".[73] Digital innovation can be conceived as nested in three layers.[74] The outermost layer is digital innovation, inside which lies digital technology, and inside that lies the digital object. This digital object could be data or algorithm which facilitates automated processes in new information systems.

6.36. With traditional information systems, all digital representations are the reflection of the physical world that exist beforehand. An example of traditional information system is electronic data interchange (EDI) which is used for exchanging shipping data in the supply chain. However, with new information systems, digital objects represent an existing and expected reality; and increasingly, with digital innovation, digital technology shape the reality, which leads to a digital-first, physical later strategy.[75]

6.37. With digital-first, digital objects are not just as real as physical objects; they are more real.[76] A classic example of digital-first strategy is the airline ticket. Fifteen years ago, an airline would issue a physical ticket, and a digital record of the transaction would be stored in the airline's data centre as evidence of the transaction. However, in 2008, when the airline industry achieved 100% electronic ticketing through a coordinated industry approach under the auspices of the International Air Transport Association (IATA), all airlines stopped issuing physical tickets.[77]

6.38. Currently, the real tickets exist in cloud storage. When a passenger needs physical evidence of the real ticket, which in reality is not a physical ticket, they can reproduce a physical copy of the non-physical real ticket. Therefore, the ontology of the physical and digital has been reversed, leading to a temporal reversal in the way products and services are produced. The digital version is produced first, and the physical version is produced when and where it is deemed necessary.[78]

6.3.2.2 Digital-first strategy in judicial sale

6.39. At present, the process for the online judicial sale in China is virtually paperless. The bids are placed over the internet and they are assessed through an automated process designed by *Taobao*.[79] The courts decided to automate the process in 2016[80] when an unprecedented number of judicial sales proceedings were initiated due to *en masse* bankruptcy in the shipbuilding sector.[81] The decision to digitalise the sale

---

[73] S Nambisan, K Lyytinen, A Majchrzak and M Song, 'Digital Innovation Management: Reinventing Innovation Management Research in a Digital World' (2017) 41(1) MIS Quart 223, 224.

[74] See A Hund, H Wagner, D Beimborn and T Weitzel, 'Digital innovation: Review and novel perspective' (2021) 30(4) J Strateg Inf Syst 5, fig 2.

[75] RL Baskerville, MD Myers and Y Yoo, 'Digital First: The Ontological Reversal and New Challenges for Information Systems Research' (2020) 44(2) MIS Quart 509.

[76] S Nambisan, K Lyytinen and Y Yoo, Digital innovation: towards a Transdisciplinary Perspective, in S Nambisan, K Lyytinen and Y Yoo (eds), *Handbook of Digital Innovation*, 1st edn. (2020, Edward Elgar) 7.

[77] IATA, *Annual Report 2008* <www.iata.org/contentassets/c81222d96c9a4e0bb4ff6ced0126f0bb/iata-annual-report-2008.pdf>.

[78] S Nambisan, Lyytinen and Yoo, supra (n 76) 7.

[79] Cheng, supra (n 3) 81–82.

[80] The decision of the Chinese courts to automate the judicial sale process coincided with the government's decision to remove subsidies from the shipbuilding sector: see Wang, Wei Chong and Hong, supra (n 2).

[81] Wang, Wei Chong and Hong, supra (n 2).

process[82] allowed each ship to be treated as a digital object or resource.[83] *Taobao* could then combine the ship as a resource with its pre-existing resources (e.g., search, registration, documentation, forum, live chat, support, etc.)[84] to facilitate their exchange in innovative ways[85] and create value.[86]

6.40. Furthermore, in online judicial sales, digital innovation is intertwined with the digital platform (i.e., *Taobao*) and the actors (i.e., *Taobao* as the platform owner, the maritime courts in China and the bidders). The digital innovation leads to blurring of boundaries as *Taobao* fulfils certain duties which are ordinarily performed by the Admiralty Marshal, such as arranging the sale of a ship, filing an account of sale and paying the proceeds of the sale of a ship into the court.[87] In addition, *Taobao* undertakes the task of advertising the sale to the world at large based on its network effect to fetch the best possible price for the ship.[88] The actors form an ecosystem for online judicial sale.[89] Eventually, they adopt new strategic approaches and develop new organisational forms and capabilities to align with the auction rules, requirements and payment. The new organisational forms and capabilities further enable digital innovation making it a sequential process.[90] Figure 6.1 diagrammatically represents the aforementioned conceptualisation of the digital transformation process in online judicial sales and elucidates how *Taobao* instigated the digital-first strategy in judicial sales in China.

---

[82] Selling ships online includes strategies for "digitisation", "digitalisation" and "digital transformation" which range from "translating analogue signals to digital ones", "leveraging digitized products to establish new proceedings or offerings" and "adapting the courts to a new organizational form and skill sets needed in a digital landscape", respectively. For a general discussion on digitisation, digitalisation and digital transformation see T Saarikko, UH Westergren and T Blomquist, 'Digital transformation: Five recommendations for the digitally conscious firm' (2020) 63(6) Bus Horiz 825, 828–829.

[83] For a conceptual discussion on a physical object being transformed into a digital object through bit strings: see P Faulkner and J Runde, 'Technological Objects, Social Positions, and the Transformational Model of Social Activity' (2013) 37(3) MIS Quart 803–818.

[84] For a conceptual understanding of how resources are categorised and utilised in the platform economy see A Ghazawneh and O Henfridsson, 'Balancing platform control and external contribution in third-party development: the boundary resources model' (2013) 23 Inf Syst J 173–192.

[85] Y Yoo, O Henfridsson and K Lyytinen, 'Research Commentary: The New Organizing Logic of Digital Innovation: An Agenda for Information Systems Research' (2010) 21(4) Inf Syst Res 724.

[86] *Taobao*, by virtue of the platform design, acts as the central agent in the nexus of a network of value creators and can monitor, control, and use the resources without owning them. For a discussion on platforms as a dominant organisational form of the digital age, see A Gawer, 'Digital Platforms and Ecosystems: Remarks on the Dominant Organizational Forms of the Digital Age' [2021] Innov Organ Manag 5.

[87] The duties of the Admiralty Marshal in the United Kingdom can be gleaned from the CPR rule 61.10, PD 61 s. 9 and Form ADM14: see *The Commercial Court Guide* (11th end 2023) N.12.1.

[88] Traditionally, the advertisement for judicial sales are made through popular maritime trade and transport news channels. However, with *Taobao*, network effect represents the economic phenomenon of demand economies of scale, driven by technological innovation. Demand economies of scale are driven by efficiencies in networks, demand aggregation, application development, etc., that make bigger networks more valuable to users such as the maritime courts. *Taobao* with its hundreds of millions of users gallops on this network effect advantage that is extremely difficult for competitors to overcome. For a detailed discussion on network effect: see Parker, Van Alstyne and Paul Choudary, supra (n 70) Chpt 2.

[89] Ecosystem is defined as community of cooperating actors that collectively produce goods, services, or solutions, that co-evolve their products under an aligned vision and "that must deal with either unique, or supermodular complementarities that are non-generic, requiring the creation of a specific structure of relationships and alignment to create value": see MG Jacobides, C Cennamo and A Gawer, Towards a Theory of Ecosystems (2018) 39(8) Strateg Manag J 2255, 2263. Essentially, ecosystem is about interorganisational relations: see MG Jacobides and I Lianos, 'Ecosystems and competition law in theory and practice' (2021) 30 Ind Corp Change 1199, 1201.

[90] Hund and others, supra (n 74).

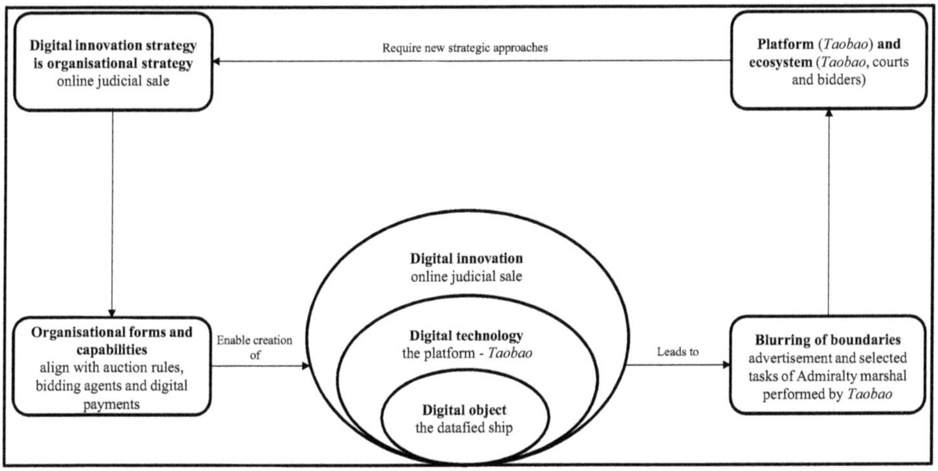

Figure 6.1 The Digital Transformation Process in Online Judicial Sale[91]

6.3.3 Taobao orchestrates the ecosystem through private rules

6.41. The ecosystem for the judicial sale in China emerged in response to a crisis in the shipbuilding sector rather than through purposeful design and implementation activities of *Taobao*. The ecosystem allowed the maritime courts to have quick access to digital capabilities, which would otherwise have been expensive and time-consuming to build on their own.[92] By providing a ready-to-use digital platform, *Taobao* seized the chance to promulgate the rules of engagement to exercise occasional, opportunity-oriented, non-hierarchical control over the actors through persuasion. The maritime courts authorised the rules promulgated by *Taobao*.

6.3.3.1 Ecosystem orchestration in online judicial sales

6.42. *Taobao's* control on the ecosystem would qualify as ecosystem orchestration, which is a "set of deliberate and purposeful actions undertaken by the ecosystem orchestrator [i.e., *Taobao*] to encourage voluntary, value co-creating inputs and effect coordination among hierarchically independent [actors] of the ecosystem".[93] Such control differs significantly from the usual "command and control" coordination found in hierarchical supply chain structure that is usual in public procurement contracts.

6.43. Ecosystem orchestration is a governance challenge. In its role as orchestrator, *Taobao* strives to provide a well-structured governance mechanism that can generate significant value for all actors. Governance, in this context, is perceived as a balancing act between value creation and value capture for multiple sides of the platform where the actors may have divergent incentives.[94] Good governance sends credible

[91] Figure 2 is adapted by the author from Hund and others, supra (n 74).
[92] Jacobides, Cennamo and Gawer, supra (n 89).
[93] E Autio, 'Orchestrating ecosystems: a multi-layered framework' (2022) 24(1) Innov Organ Manag 96, 107.
[94] Ibid.

commitment to actors so that they continue to remain affiliated with the platform. This signalling is especially important for *Taobao* because, theoretically, it is open to competition from other platforms and the courts may switch to those platforms or multi-home.[95]

6.44. Ecosystem orchestration subsists in four layers, namely, technological, economic, institutional and behavioural. The orchestration also varies based on the stage at which the ecosystem is situated, namely, initiation, scaling and growth.[96] For the purpose of this chapter, the institutional layer is of particular interest as it accommodates the rule-setting process during the three stages of ecosystem progression.

6.45. The ecosystem initiation stage requires shaping the roles in which different actors can participate in the ecosystem. At this stage, the institutional layer is of considerable significance because the rules and licencing conditions that regulate actor connectivity to and the use of the platform are negotiated. In addition, practical matters such as the user and supplier rights to data, contributed content and applications are also agreed upon.[97] From a governance viewpoint, the initiation stage is less problematic because the ecosystem orchestrator keeps the rules and licencing conditions reasonably open and negotiable to encourage the participation of actors.

6.46. The next stage of ecosystem development is scaling,[98] where ecosystem actors adjust their roles and redefine their interactions. Various standpoints for ecosystem evolution may emerge as different actors seek to push their own agendas and establish their priorities. An effective conflict resolution mechanism addressing internal discord is important to minimise interference with the scaling process. In practice, this stage allows the actors to further validate and reinforce their ecosystem roles, which acts as a coordination and governance mechanism to mitigate conflicts.[99]

6.47. Progressing then to the final stage, ie growth, the orchestrator has to consider wider societal effects as the ecosystem may give rise to external conflicts. As ecosystems operate in various industry contexts, the orchestrator has to be mindful that the rules of internal governance adapt to the scaling ecosystem and the ecosystem itself proactively adjusts to evolving external regulations.[100]

6.3.3.2 Concern about ecosystem orchestration in online judicial sales

6.48. In the context of online judicial sales, the practical effectiveness of the sale ordered by a court using a third-party digital platform would depend on whether foreign courts recognise and enforce the order. The main concern that could be raised against recognition of the order is that the ecosystem orchestration rules are not

---

[95] For a comprehensive legal discussion on multi-homing: see HJ Hovenkamp, 'Antitrust and Platform Monopoly' (2021) 130 Yale Law J 1952, 1972–1977.

[96] The ecosystem orchestration framework described previously is developed by Autio, supra (n 93) 104, fig 1.

[97] Ibid 106.

[98] Scaling is "'a process by which the operational efficiency of the enterprise increases as it is growing". In case of digital enterprises, the source of the operational efficiency is largely from network effects: see O Henfridsson, Scaling Digital Enterprises, in S Nambisan, K Lyytinen and Y Yoo (eds), *Handbook of Digital Innovation*, 1st edn. (2020, Edward Elgar) 152.

[99] Autio, supra (n 93) 106.

[100] Ibid.

subjected to the rigorous democratic processes of a state legislature.[101] Thus, a way must be devised to demonstrate internationally that "the [c]ourt has acted within its jurisdiction"[102] by delegating some of the tasks to a third-party digital platform as to disposition of the ship. The next sub-section investigates ways in which the Beijing Convention may be able to address the aforementioned concern.

6.3.4 Beijing Convention may facilitate online judicial sales through platforms

6.49. The Beijing Convention is the first international instrument addressing the recognition of foreign judicial sales of ships and their consequences.[103] It is not designed to harmonise the procedure for judicial sales.[104] The initial draft of the Convention text was prepared by the Comité Maritime International (CMI)[105] and was handed over to the United Nations Commission on International Trade Law (UNCITRAL), based on a proposal made in 2017.[106] The finalised text emerged on the basis of deliberations that took place at UNCITRAL Working Group VI, spread over six sessions, from May 2019 to February 2022.[107] What follows in this sub-section is a brief discussion of whether the Convention addresses the issue of online judicial sales of ships and their recognition.

6.3.4.1 Definition may include online judicial sale

6.50. The term "judicial sale of a ship" is used throughout the Convention. Article 2(b) defines "judicial sale" as –

> any sale of a ship: (i) [w]hich is ordered, approved or confirmed by a court or other public authority either by way of public auction or by private treaty carried out under the supervision and with the approval of a court; and (ii) [f]or which the proceeds of sale are made available to the creditors.

6.51. As clarified in the explanatory notes prepared by the UNCITRAL Secretariat, the definition clearly includes private treaty sales, and the sale may be conducted by a court or a public authority that does not exclusively exercise adjudicative functions.[108] The definition allows judicial sale to be "ordered, approved or confirmed" by a "court or other public authority", which leaves room to accommodate a variety of procedures for conducting judicial sale among legal systems.[109]

---

[101] Gawer, supra (n 86) 5.

[102] *Castrique v Imrie* (1869–70) LR 4 HL 414, 429.

[103] See Beijing Convention, supra (n 5).

[104] See Art 4(1) of the Convention, which leaves matters related to the conduct of the judicial sale to the law of the State of judicial sale.

[105] UNCITRAL Doc A/CN.9/WG.VI/WP.82 <documents-dds-ny.un.org/doc/UNDOC/LTD/V19/009/60/PDF/V1900960.pdf?OpenElement>.

[106] UNCITRAL Doc A/CN.9/923 <documents-dds-ny.un.org/doc/UNDOC/GEN/V17/023/36/PDF/V1702336.pdf?OpenElement>.

[107] The session reports and the documents that were used during the deliberations at Working Group VI (Judicial Sale of Ships) are available at UNCITRAL's website <uncitral.un.org/en/working_groups/6/sale_ships>.

[108] UNCITRAL Doc A/CN.9/1110 <documents-dds-ny.un.org/doc/UNDOC/GEN/V22/029/14/PDF/V2202914.pdf?OpenElement> paras 32 and 34.

[109] Note, the term "other public authority" is not defined in the Convention.

6.52. While the definition states that the judicial sale must be carried out either by "public auction" or by "private treaty", the Convention does not prescribe how either type of sale is carried out and leaves that to the law of the state of judicial sale. However, the elements of each type of sale may be gleaned from the minimum information to be included in the notice.[110] Overall, given the broad nature of the definition of "judicial sale", one can argue that it encompasses the online judicial sale of a ship. This argument is strengthened further based on the explanatory notes where it is stated that:[111]

> The Convention is designed to accommodate the use of an online platform or other online service to receive and publish instruments using automated systems, and for instruments to be transmitted and accessed via an online account or other interactive application.

6.3.4.2 Clean title tied to certificate

6.53. Article 3 of the Convention subsumes the approach in *Castrique v Imrie* to the effect that a foreign judicial sale will be recognised if two preconditions are met, namely, "the judicial sale is conducted in a state party; and the ship is physically within the territory of the state of judicial sale at the time of that sale".

6.54. Article 3 does not address clean title as a matter of substantive scope. The Convention leaves it to its substantive provisions, notably Article 6, to limit its regime to judicial sales that confer clean title.[112] "Clean title" is defined in Article 2(c) to mean "title free and clear of any mortgage or hypothèque and of any charge". The clean title is operationalised by Article 6, pursuant to which only a judicial sale for which a certificate of judicial sale that has already been issued has international effect; and Article 5(1), pursuant to which only a judicial sale that confers clean title is issued with a certificate.[113] Article 8, which forbids the arrest of the ship, is triggered by the production of the Certificate of Judicial Sale.

6.3.4.3 Certificate tied to notice

6.55. The issuance of the certificate is tied to giving notice of the sale. Article 4 lays down the notice requirements so that creditors are made aware of the judicial sale, who can then join the proceedings and claim from the sale proceeds.[114] According to paragraphs 4 and 5 of Article 4, the notification is governed by the law of the state of sale, but certain minimum standards regarding the persons to be notified of the judicial sale must be followed.

---

[110] See Beijing Convention, supra (n 5) Annex I, items 11 and 12, which provides that if a judicial sale is conducted by public auction, then anticipated date, time and place of public auction must be provided; and if a judicial sale is conducted by private treaty, then any relevant details, including time period, should be provided for the judicial sale as ordered by the court or other public authority.

[111] UNCITRAL Doc A/CN.9/1110/Add.2 <documents-dds-ny.un.org/doc/UNDOC/GEN/V22/030/61/PDF/V2203061.pdf?OpenElement>, para 43.

[112] UNCITRAL Doc A/CN.9/1110 <documents-dds-ny.un.org/doc/UNDOC/GEN/V22/029/14/PDF/V2202914.pdf?OpenElement>, para 24.

[113] Ibid, para 45.

[114] This scheme follows the common law position of notifying the sale to the wider maritime community to ensure the best possible price and notice to all interested parties: see *The Turtle Bay* [2013] 4 SLR 615, [2013] SGHC 165 [20] (J Ang).

6.56. The notice requirements do not serve as a stand-alone obligation but rather as a condition for the issuance of the certificate of judicial sale under Article 5.[115] Pursuant to Article 9, a claim challenging the validity of a certificate due to non-compliance with the notice requirements is heard in the state of judicial sale.

6.57. However, it is possible that a flagrant failure to comply with the notice requirements could give rise to an application invoking the "public policy" ground in a foreign court under Article 10.

6.3.4.4 Notice through repository

6.58. The public policy ground is generally invoked by a foreign court that is approached to enforce a judicial sale when it perceives that natural justice has been breached, due process has not been followed, or that one party's interests have been elevated above the rest. Generally, it is difficult for a party to argue that natural justice has been breached based on lack of notice in an admiralty context.[116] However, as stated by Myburgh, "an unreasonable refusal by the court to allow an interested party to intervene in admiralty proceedings, or clear evidence of court collusion or bias", is more likely to provide a sound basis for a foreign court to disregard a judicial sale on public policy grounds.[117]

6.59. To address public policy concerns, Article 4(5)(b) of the Convention states that the notice shall be "[t]ransmitted to the repository referred to in Article 11 for publication". Under Article 11, the Repository is the Secretary-General of the IMO or an institution named by UNCITRAL. Upon receipt of a notice of judicial sale, the Repository is required to make it available to the public.

6.60. The notion of a repository was not present in the CMI draft.[118] It was first included during the deliberations at UNCITRAL in 2019, and the technical aspects were developed later in 2021.[119] Under the Convention, the Repository is designed to provide public access to the notice of judicial sale and certificate of judicial sale, as well as any decisions avoiding a judicial sale or suspending its effects.

6.61. The IMO has agreed to be the Repository via an additional module on its GISIS platform.[120] Article 11(2) requires the repository to make the documents received from the state of judicial sale "available to the public in a timely manner,

---

[115] UNCITRAL Doc A/CN.9/1110/Add.1 <documents-dds-ny.un.org/doc/UNDOC/GEN/V22/029/76/PDF/V2202976.pdf?OpenElement>, para 4.

[116] For example, in *The Phoenix* [2014] 1 Lloyd's Rep 449 [28]–[32], the English court rejected arguments of a breach of natural justice in a North Korean judicial sale, because the mortgagee had itself chosen not to participate in the sale.

[117] Myburgh, supra (n 20) 365.

[118] See (n 105).

[119] For references to the preparatory work on the Repository in various UNCITRAL WG VI session reports see UNCITRAL Doc A/CN.9/1110/Add.2 <documents-dds-ny.un.org/doc/UNDOC/GEN/V22/030/61/PDF/V2203061.pdf?OpenElement>, para 44.

[120] GISIS <gisis.imo.org/Public/Default.aspx> is developed, maintained and headed by the IMO. The platform allows online access to information and data supplied to the IMO Secretariat by Maritime Administrations, its Member States and port authorities, in compliance with IMO's instruments, regulations and guidelines. Currently, GISIS consists of several subsystems which include 28 modules, which are further divided into sub-modules dedicated to various themes and topics. In summary, GISIS is an information hub, which could be considered as the proper channel in a contemporary digital context for notifying the global shipping community about a judicial sale.

in the form and language in which it is received". Professor Thomas views this as a "passive duty" as there is no obligation on the Repository to "publish, transmit, circulate or disseminate".[121] Also, the Repository is neither required to review or to ensure the accuracy or completeness of the documents, nor is it under any obligation to translate them. This is because the obligation is to make the information available "as received" and therefore "the repository has no oversight responsibilities".[122]

6.62. In other words, the role of the Repository is purely informational, and the publication of the documents has no particular legal effect under the Convention.[123] Professor Thomas asserts that

> [g]reat reliance is based on [the GISIS] platform by the framers of this Convention to function as an effective system for the international dissemination of notices of judicial sale, certificates of sale and related information, and it is hoped that this confidence is justified.[124]

6.3.4.5 The repository as intermediary fiduciary

6.63. The threshold for entry into force of the Beijing Convention is set at three ratifications. While this number may be criticised for not being large enough to generate any significant effect internationally on judicial sales after the Convention's entry into force, but that number may serve the purpose of making the IMO repository operational relatively soon. An operational repository may be of particular significance in the context of online judicial sales because third-party digital platforms can scale exponentially within a short period of time, leading to the situation of "winner-take-all".[125] Thus, the Beijing Convention has the possibility to lead to a situation where a select number of platforms would disrupt traditional judicial sales and establish the digital-first strategy internationally.

6.64. The challenge of establishing the digital-first strategy internationally by a select few third-party digital platforms is that they may generate different societal effects, both positive and negative. As seen in the recent past, platforms have used the internal governance rules to their advantage to capture a significant part of the value generated inside the ecosystems.[126] Therefore, the ongoing debate in various parts of

---

[121] DR Thomas, 'The United Nations Convention on the International Effects of Judicial Sales of Ships: The Beijing Convention – A Textual Analysis' (2022) 28 J Int Mar Law 378, 367–379.

[122] Ibid.

[123] The publication of the notice of judicial sale does not substitute the requirement to give the notice under Article 4(3) nor does it substitute the requirement to produce the certificate of judicial sale to prompt action on registration of the ship under Article 7 or action to prohibit arrest of the ship under article 8: see UNCITRAL Doc A/CN.9/1110/Add.2 <documents-dds-ny.un.org/doc/UNDOC/GEN/V22/030/61/PDF/V2203061.pdf?OpenElement>, para 41.

[124] Ibid.

[125] Winner-take-all is a market in which specific forces conspire to encourage users to gravitate toward one platform and to abandon others. The four forces that most often characterise winner-take-all markets are supply economies of scale, strong network effects, high multihoming or switching costs, and lack of niche specialization. See Parker, Van Alstyne and Paul Choudary, supra (n 70) 300.

[126] For a general discussion on the opportunistic behaviour of the digital platforms: see Gawer, supra (n 86) 110–124; J Rietveld and MA Schilling 'Platform Competition: A Systematic and Interdisciplinary Review of the Literature' (2021) 47 J Manag 1528–1563; LM Khan, 'Sources of tech platform power' (2018) 325 Geo Law Technol Rev 325–334. For a concise discussion on opportunistic behaviour of digital

the world is how platforms should be regulated, and what form and content such regulation might take.

6.65. The aforementioned debate in relation to judicial sales of ships may be framed in relation to public good. Notably, public good is "non-rivalrous", that is, an individual's consumption of the good does not influence what is available for others; and "non-excludable", that is, no one can be excluded from the consumption of the good. A typical example of a public good is a lighthouse where one ship's use of the beacon does not prevent other ships from using the same.

6.66. In judicial sales, the creditors entrust the state with the power of adjudicative function as a public good.[127] The creditors as individuals rely on the state because they do not have the ability and resources to enjoy and share the benefits of public good in a constant and non-exclusionary manner. Thus, the creditors enter into a fiduciary relationship with the state, where the latter does not act in self-interest, takes a holistic view of public good and does not abuse its power when satisfying the needs of the former.[128] In the absence of a global state, it is submitted that the IMO represents states individually and collectively, and becomes an "intermediary fiduciary" of – adjudication as public good.

6.67. The notion of IMO as intermediary fiduciary is connected to the role of the GISIS platform. To ensure that the adjudication in judicial sales is conclusive, the GISIS platform must be utilised for the benefit of states and the creditors from each state. Therefore, the delivery of information must be precise, especially for the international dissemination of notices of judicial sale, certificates of sale and related information. Any information disorder has the potential to undermine the fiduciary relationship of the IMO. Information disorder is a matter of cybersecurity, and in the shipping context, constitutes part of maritime security.[129]

6.68. Therefore, it is submitted that the IMO must adopt measures to address information disorder as an intermediary fiduciary. The Beijing Convention makes the IMO an intermediary fiduciary in its role as repository because the GISIS platform is interposed between two sides –

(i) The states as fiduciaries of adjudication through national courts, and all states collectively as fiduciaries of global adjudication. Notably, the collective of all states is represented through the IMO.

(ii) The IMO itself, as an actor in digital platforms and ecosystems, who must actively participate therein for the benefit of the global maritime community.

platforms in the context of transport ecosystems: see A Basu Bal, 'The generative carriage of goods' (2023) 29(2) J Int Mar Law 92, 104–109.

[127] For a general discussion on adjudication as a public good: see Joshua Paine, 'International Adjudication as a Global Public Good?' (2018) 29(4) Eur J IntLaw 1223, 1223–1249.

[128] For a general discussion on fiduciary, see A Hudson, *Understanding Equity & Trusts* (2012, Routledge) 72.

[129] Notably, information disorder is misinformation, disinformation or malinformation (often referred to as MDM in cybersecurity literature) that can hinder or thwart the delivery of the public good of adjudication by creating confusion, doubt, division, insularity or exclusion, as well as by preventing action or undermining the state and the courts whose mandate is to serve this public good.

6.69. Thus, the GISIS platform claim for the IMO assuming a distinct and indeed important fiduciary role in the pursuit of the international public good of adjudication, a role that cannot otherwise be justified or legitimised in the digital first world.

6.3.4.6 Addressing the concern of ecosystem orchestration in online judicial sales

6.70. Policymakers at the IMO must exercise due care when laying down the procedures of the Repository to facilitate online judicial sales of ships and find ways to engage with ecosystem orchestration.

6.71. UNCITRAL has clarified that the IMO repository mechanism has been implanted in the Convention to promote use of digital platforms in judicial sales of ships.[130] The Convention does not prescribe rules on functioning of the Repository. The IMO is free to decide by itself the procedures for the receipt and publication of documents required to be transmitted under the Convention.[131]

6.72. Thus, it could be argued that the IMO is free to set certain minimum standards of good governance that could eventually be transplanted into the internal rules of platforms involved in online judicial sales. Such minimum standards could be helpful, because the rules of ecosystem orchestration, as highlighted above, are not subjected to the rigorous democratic processes of a state legislature.

6.73. It is important to appreciate that third-party digital platforms operate in various industry contexts and therefore any regulatory intervention must consider prevailing legislation, which may differ markedly across sectors.[132] The challenge is aggravated in the maritime sector, especially because of its inherent international characteristics and varied levels of digital maturity.[133] An international and sectoral approach seems useful to address the public interests at stake as well as the policy options to safeguard such interests.

6.74. The IMO could learn from the Chinese experience, as their ecosystem for online judicial sale emerged through an organic process and involved multi-actor negotiations between the maritime courts and *Taobao*. When the ecosystem was initiated, the actors did not have a clear idea of what the final ecosystem would look like, and what their position might be in it. The unfolding of the three stages of ecosystem orchestration over a period may have allowed *Taobao* and the maritime courts to participate in the orchestration process organically, based on a bottom-up approach. A bottom-up approach seems plausible because *Taobao* as the ecosystem orchestrator could not rely on an exogenous market to inform on the resource value of online judicial sales, particularly when the offering was so new that a market did not yet exist. As it was not possible to determine the "value" exogenously, it had to

[130] See (n 111).

[131] Ibid.

[132] For a general understanding on how sectoral peculiarities are relevant considerations for legislating in the platform economy see K Frenken, T Vaskelainen, L Fünfschilling and L Piscicelli, An Institutional Logics Perspective on the Gig Economy, in I Maurer, J Mair and A Oberg (eds), *Theorizing the Sharing Economy: Variety and Trajectories of New Forms of Organizing, Research in the Sociology of Organizations Book Series*, vol 66 (2020, Emerald Publishing) 85–105.

[133] Digital maturity is defined as the degree to which organisations have adapted themselves to a digital business environment. For a discussion on digital maturity in the maritime transport and logistics sector: see Z Raza, J Woxenius, C Altuntas Vural and M Lind, 'Digital transformation of maritime logistics: Exploring trends in the liner shipping segment' (2023) 145 Comput Ind 103811.

be negotiated and co-discovered endogenously, in a multi-sided negotiation involving *Taobao* and the maritime courts.

6.75. It is submitted that there is no need to reinvent the wheel every time a court has to approach a digital platform to digitalise the judicial sale process. The IMO in its capacity as the Repository and as a fiduciary intermediary has the possibility of taking a balanced and international approach on behalf of the maritime community at large to develop a set of minimum standards for ecosystem orchestration for online judicial sales.

6.76. An internationally accepted standard could assist a court or public authority in delegating the digitalisation of the judicial sale process to a third-party digital platform with greater ease of negotiation. The standard could then be used as a benchmark, and further negotiations for ecosystem orchestration between the court and the platform owner would mostly be necessary to address local particularities. Such an approach would allow the court or public authority ordering the online sale to justify easily to the rest of the world that it has acted within its jurisdiction.

6.77. Needless to say, any regulatory intervention from the IMO in relation to ecosystem orchestration has to be carefully weighed against stubborn issues such as the balance between digital innovation versus domestic priorities for economic efficiency, political manoeuvring, community building and digital sovereignty.[134] In addition, the governance model for ecosystem orchestration is a critical design choice for digital platforms because that replaces the hierarchical forms of control with indirect forms of control. Platforms would therefore like to protect themselves from too much external scrutiny. However, based on the discussion above, the control stage requires the digital platform as an orchestrator to remain in constant dialogue with regulators and policymakers to minimise and remove any negative effects on society.

6.78. In summary, an international set of minimum standards for ecosystem orchestration set by the IMO could be helpful to thwart possible "public policy" attacks by foreign courts on online judicial sales.[135] In addition, such standards may assist in furthering the digitalisation and digital transformation efforts in both legal and maritime fields.[136]

---

[134] For a discussion on safeguarding societal values through digital sovereignty see H Roberts, J Cowls, E Hine, J Morley, and others, 'Safeguarding European values with digital sovereignty: an analysis of statements and policies' (2021) 10(3) Internet Policy Rev 1–25.

[135] While it is generally accepted that an international instrument cannot compete with a sovereign state's interpretation of the public policy concept, the Beijing Convention sets a high threshold for public policy exception, which reflects recent treaty practice. As elucidated in the explanatory notes to the Convention,

> the threshold is designed to avoid an abusive or overly expansive application of the public policy exception and requires a compelling reason as to why giving effect to the foreign judicial sale is contrary to an identified matter of public policy. It emphasises that the public policy is expected to apply only in exceptional cases.

See UNCITRAL Doc A/CN.9/1110/Add.2 <documents-dds-ny.un.org/doc/UNDOC/GEN/V22/030/61/PDF/V2203061.pdf?OpenElement> paras 35–37.

[136] See (n 82).

6.4 Concluding remarks

6.79. Despite the digital first strategy in judicial sales of ships in China, the uncertainty stemming from the silence of other leading maritime law jurisdictions regarding online sales continues to keep many maritime creditors and debtors from reaping the benefits of platformisation.

6.80. While this chapter asserts that online sales possess inherent advantages over traditional judicial sales, it does not advocate for giving preference to the former over the latter. A level playing field, however, seems necessary for maritime creditors' and debtors' reticence. Ultimately, the goal of judicial sales is to implement guidance and procedures to achieve the highest possible prices in a fair, impartial and independent manner.

6.81. As discussed above, the most compelling argument to restrict online judicial sale is the concern that such sale may undermine the Admiralty Court's impartiality and integrity. This is particularly attributable to the Court's inability to exercise complete control and administration over the online sale process, which may be exacerbated by internally set rules of ecosystem orchestration by the digital platform.

6.82. However, this chapter has argued that ecosystem orchestration can be set up in a bottom-up manner, which may address the concern. In addition, it is submitted that the IMO, in its capacity as the Repository, may proactively develop a set of minimum standards for ecosystem orchestration in online judicial sales, thereby promoting digital transformation in both legal and maritime fields.

6.83. Overall, the Beijing Convention allows online sales to be placed on an equal footing with traditional sales by adopting a wider definition of judicial sale, by linking clean title, certificate and notice, and finally, through the establishment of the Repository under the auspices of the IMO for notifying the global shipping community about a judicial sale.

APPENDIX 1

UN Convention on the International Effects of Judicial Sales of Ships (the Beijing Convention on the Judicial Sales of Ships)[1]

[1] Reprinted with permission of the UNCITRAL Secretariat.

UNITED NATIONS CONVENTION ON THE INTERNATIONAL EFFECTS OF JUDICIAL SALES OF SHIPS

The States Parties to this Convention,

Reaffirming their belief that international trade on the basis of equality and mutual benefit is an important element in promoting friendly relations among States,

Mindful of the crucial role of shipping in international trade and transportation, of the high economic value of ships used in both seagoing and inland navigation, and of the function of judicial sales as a means to enforce claims,

Considering that adequate legal protection for purchasers may positively impact the price realized at judicial sales of ships, to the benefit of both shipowners and creditors, including lienholders and ship financiers,

Wishing, for that purpose, to establish uniform rules that promote the dissemination of information on prospective judicial sales to interested parties and give international effects to judicial sales of ships sold free and clear of any mortgage or *hypothèque* and of any charge, including for ship registration purposes,

Have agreed as follows:

Article 1
Purpose

This Convention governs the international effects of a judicial sale of a ship that confers clean title on the purchaser.

Article 2
Definitions

For the purposes of this Convention:

(a) "Judicial sale" of a ship means any sale of a ship:

(i) Which is ordered, approved or confirmed by a court or other public authority either by way of public auction or by private treaty carried out under the supervision and with the approval of a court; and

(ii) For which the proceeds of sale are made available to the creditors;

(b) "Ship" means any ship or other vessel registered in a register that is open to public inspection that may be the subject of an arrest or other similar measure capable of leading to a judicial sale under the law of the State of judicial sale;

(c) "Clean title" means title free and clear of any mortgage or *hypothèque* and of any charge;

(d) "Mortgage or *hypothèque*" means any mortgage or *hypothèque* that is effected on a ship and registered in the State in whose register of ships or equivalent register the ship is registered;

(e) "Charge" means any right whatsoever and howsoever arising which may be asserted against a ship, whether by means of arrest, attachment or otherwise, and includes a maritime lien, lien, encumbrance, right of use or right of retention but does not include a mortgage or *hypothèque*;

(f) "Registered charge" means any charge that is registered in the register of ships or equivalent register in which the ship is registered or in any different register in which mortgages or *hypothèques* are registered;

(g) "Maritime lien" means any charge that is recognized as a maritime lien or *privilège maritime* on a ship under applicable law;

(h) "Owner" of a ship means any person registered as the owner of the ship in the register of ships or equivalent register in which the ship is registered;

(i) "Purchaser" means any person to whom the ship is sold in the judicial sale;

(j) "Subsequent purchaser" means the person who purchases the ship from the purchaser named in the certificate of judicial sale referred to in article 5;

(k) "State of judicial sale" means the State in which the judicial sale of a ship is conducted.

Article 3
Scope of application

1. This Convention applies only to a judicial sale of a ship if:

(a) The judicial sale is conducted in a State Party; and

(b) The ship is physically within the territory of the State of judicial sale at the time of that sale.

2. This Convention shall not apply to warships or naval auxiliaries, or other vessels owned or operated by a State and used, immediately prior to the time of judicial sale, only on government non-commercial service.

Article 4
Notice of judicial sale

1. The judicial sale shall be conducted in accordance with the law of the State of judicial sale, which shall also provide procedures for challenging the judicial sale prior to its completion and determine the time of the sale for the purposes of this Convention.

2. Notwithstanding paragraph 1, a certificate of judicial sale under article 5 shall only be issued if a notice of judicial sale is given prior to the judicial sale of the ship in accordance with the requirements of paragraphs 3 to 7.

3. The notice of judicial sale shall be given to:

(a) The registry of ships or equivalent registry with which the ship is registered;

(b) All holders of any mortgage or *hypothèque* and of any registered charge, provided that the register in which it is registered, and any instrument required to be registered under the law of the State of registration, are open to public inspection, and that extracts from the register and copies of such instruments are obtainable from the registry;

(c) All holders of any maritime lien, provided that they have notified the court or other public authority conducting the judicial sale of the claim secured by the maritime lien in accordance with the regulations and procedures of the State of judicial sale;

(d) The owner of the ship for the time being; and

(e) If the ship is granted bareboat charter registration:

(i) The person registered as the bareboat charterer of the ship in the bareboat charter register; and

(ii) The bareboat charter registry.

4. The notice of judicial sale shall be given in accordance with the law of the State of judicial sale, and shall contain, as a minimum, the information mentioned in annex I.

5. The notice of judicial sale shall also be:

(a) Published by announcement in the press or other publication available in the State of judicial sale; and

(b) Transmitted to the repository referred to in article 11 for publication.

6. For the purpose of communicating the notice to the repository, if the notice of judicial sale is not in a working language of the repository, it shall be accompanied by a translation of the information mentioned in annex I into any such working language.

7. In determining the identity or address of any person to whom the notice of judicial sale is to be given, it is sufficient to rely on:

(a) Information set forth in the register of ships or equivalent register in which the ship is registered or in the bareboat charter register;

(b) Information set forth in the register in which the mortgage or *hypothèque* or the registered charge is registered, if different to the register of ships or equivalent register; and

(c) Information notified under paragraph 3, subparagraph (c).

Article 5
Certificate of judicial sale

1. Upon completion of a judicial sale that conferred clean title to the ship under the law of the State of judicial sale and was conducted in accordance with the requirements of that law and the requirements of this Convention, the court or other public authority that conducted the judicial sale or other competent authority of the State of judicial sale shall, in accordance with its regulations and procedures, issue a certificate of judicial sale to the purchaser.

2. The certificate of judicial sale shall be substantially in the form of the model contained in annex II and contain:

(a) A statement that the ship was sold in accordance with the requirements of the law of the State of judicial sale and the requirements of this Convention;

(b) A statement that the judicial sale has conferred clean title to the ship on the purchaser;

(c) The name of the State of judicial sale;

(d) The name, address and the contact details of the authority issuing the certificate;

(e) The name of the court or other public authority that conducted the judicial sale and the date of the sale;

(f) The name of the ship and registry of ships or equivalent registry with which the ship is registered;

(g) The IMO number of the ship or, if not available, other information capable of identifying the ship;

(h) The name and address of residence or principal place of business of the owner of the ship immediately prior to the judicial sale;

(i) The name and address of residence or principal place of business of the purchaser;

(j) The place and date of issuance of the certificate; and

(k) The signature or stamp of the authority issuing the certificate or other confirmation of authenticity of the certificate.

3. The State of judicial sale shall require the certificate of judicial sale to be transmitted promptly to the repository referred to in article 11 for publication.

4. The certificate of judicial sale and any translation thereof shall be exempt from legalization or similar formality.

5. Without prejudice to articles 9 and 10, the certificate of judicial sale shall be sufficient evidence of the matters contained therein.

6. The certificate of judicial sale may be in the form of an electronic record provided that:

(a) The information contained therein is accessible so as to be usable for subsequent reference;

(b) A reliable method is used to identify the authority issuing the certificate; and

(c) A reliable method is used to detect any alteration to the record after the time it was generated, apart from the addition of any endorsement and any change that arises in the normal course of communication, storage and display.

7. A certificate of judicial sale shall not be rejected on the sole ground that it is in electronic form.

Article 6
International effects of a judicial sale

A judicial sale for which a certificate of judicial sale referred to in article 5 has been issued shall have the effect in every other State Party of conferring clean title to the ship on the purchaser.

Article 7
Action by the registry

1. At the request of the purchaser or subsequent purchaser and upon production of the certificate of judicial sale referred to in article 5, the registry or other competent authority

of a State Party shall, as the case may be and in accordance with its regulations and procedures, but without prejudice to article 6:

(a) Delete from the register any mortgage or *hypothèque* and any registered charge attached to the ship that had been registered before completion of the judicial sale;

(b) Delete the ship from the register and issue a certificate of deletion for the purpose of new registration;

(c) Register the ship in the name of the purchaser or subsequent purchaser, provided further that the ship and the person in whose name the ship is to be registered meet the requirements of the law of the State of registration;

(d) Update the register with any other relevant particulars in the certificate of judicial sale.

2. At the request of the purchaser or subsequent purchaser and upon production of the certificate of judicial sale referred to in article 5, the registry or other competent authority of a State Party in which the ship was granted bareboat charter registration shall delete the ship from the bareboat charter register and issue a certificate of deletion.

3. If the certificate of judicial sale is not issued in an official language of the registry or other competent authority, the registry or other competent authority may request the purchaser or subsequent purchaser to produce a certified translation into such an official language.

4. The registry or other competent authority may also request the purchaser or subsequent purchaser to produce a certified copy of the certificate of judicial sale for its records.

5. Paragraphs 1 and 2 do not apply if a court in the State of the registry or of the other competent authority determines under article 10 that the effect of the judicial sale under article 6 would be manifestly contrary to the public policy of that State.

Article 8
No arrest of the ship

1. If an application is brought before a court or other judicial authority in a State Party to arrest a ship or to take any other similar measure against a ship for a claim arising prior to a judicial sale of the ship, the court or other judicial authority shall, upon production of the certificate of judicial sale referred to in article 5, dismiss the application.

2. If a ship is arrested or a similar measure is taken against a ship by order of a court or other judicial authority in a State Party for a claim arising prior to a judicial sale of the ship, the court or other judicial authority shall, upon production of the certificate of judicial sale referred to in article 5, order the release of the ship.

3. If the certificate of judicial sale is not issued in an official language of the court or other judicial authority, the court or other judicial authority may request the person producing the certificate to produce a certified translation into such an official language.

4. Paragraphs 1 and 2 do not apply if the court or other judicial authority determines that dismissing the application or ordering the release of the ship, as the case may be, would be manifestly contrary to the public policy of that State.

Article 9
Jurisdiction to avoid and suspend judicial sale

1. The courts of the State of judicial sale shall have exclusive jurisdiction to hear any claim or application to avoid a judicial sale of a ship conducted in that State that confers clean title to the ship or to suspend its effects, which shall extend to any claim or application to challenge the issuance of the certificate of judicial sale referred to in article 5.

2. The courts of a State Party shall decline jurisdiction in respect of any claim or application to avoid a judicial sale of a ship conducted in another State Party that confers clean title to the ship or to suspend its effects.

3. The State of judicial sale shall require the decision of a court that avoids or suspends the effects of a judicial sale for which a certificate has been issued in accordance with article 5, paragraph 1, to be transmitted promptly to the repository referred to in article 11 for publication.

Article 10
Circumstances in which judicial sale has no international effect

A judicial sale of a ship shall not have the effect provided in article 6 in a State Party other than the State of judicial sale if a court in the other State Party determines that the effect would be manifestly contrary to the public policy of that other State Party.

Article 11
Repository

1. The repository shall be the Secretary-General of the International Maritime Organization or an institution named by the United Nations Commission on International Trade Law.

2. Upon receipt of a notice of judicial sale transmitted under article 4, paragraph 5, certificate of judicial sale transmitted under article 5, paragraph 3, or decision transmitted under article 9, paragraph 3, the repository shall make it available to the public in a timely manner, in the form and in the language in which it is received.

3. The repository may also receive a notice of judicial sale emanating from a State that has ratified, accepted, approved or acceded to this Convention and for which the Convention has not yet entered into force and may make it available to the public.

Article 12
Communication between authorities of States Parties

1. For the purposes of this Convention, the authorities of a State Party shall be authorized to correspond directly with the authorities of any other State Party.

2. Nothing in this article shall affect the application of any international agreement on judicial assistance in respect of civil and commercial matters that may exist between States Parties.

Article 13
Relationship with other international conventions

1. Nothing in this Convention shall affect the application of the Convention on the Registration of Inland Navigation Vessels (1965) and its Protocol No. 2 concerning Attachment and Forced Sale of Inland Navigation Vessels, including any future amendment to that convention or protocol.

2. Without prejudice to article 4, paragraph 4, as between States Parties to this Convention that are also parties to the Convention on the Service Abroad of Judicial and Extrajudicial Documents in Civil or Commercial Matters (1965), the notice of judicial sale may be transmitted abroad using channels other than those provided for in that convention.

Article 14
Other bases for giving international effect

Nothing in this Convention shall preclude a State from giving effect to a judicial sale of a ship conducted in another State under any other international agreement or under applicable law.

Article 15
Matters not governed by this Convention

1. Nothing in this Convention shall affect:

(a) The procedure for or priority in the distribution of proceeds of a judicial sale; or

(b) Any personal claim against a person who owned or had proprietary rights in the ship prior to the judicial sale.

2. Moreover, this Convention shall not govern the effects, under applicable law, of a decision by a court exercising jurisdiction under article 9, paragraph 1.

Article 16
Depositary

The Secretary-General of the United Nations is hereby designated as the depositary of this Convention.

Article 17
Signature, ratification, acceptance, approval, accession

1. This Convention is open for signature by all States.

2. This Convention is subject to ratification, acceptance or approval by the signatory States.

3. This Convention is open for accession by all States that are not signatories as from the date it is open for signature.

4. Instruments of ratification, acceptance, approval or accession are to be deposited with the depositary.

Article 18
Participation by regional economic integration organizations

1. A regional economic integration organization that is constituted by sovereign States and has competence over certain matters governed by this Convention may similarly sign, ratify, accept, approve or accede to this Convention. The regional economic integration organization shall in that case have the rights and obligations of a State Party, to the extent that that organization has competence over matters governed by this Convention. For the purposes of articles 21 and 22, an instrument deposited by a regional economic integration organization shall not be counted in addition to the instruments deposited by its member States.

2. The regional economic integration organization shall make a declaration specifying the matters governed by this Convention in respect of which competence has been transferred to that organization by its member States. The regional economic integration organization shall promptly notify the depositary of any changes to the distribution of competence, including new transfers of competence, specified in the declaration under this paragraph.

3. Any reference to a "State", "States", "State Party" or "States Parties" in this Convention applies equally to a regional economic integration organization where the context so requires.

4. This Convention shall not affect the application of rules of a regional economic integration organization, whether adopted before or after this Convention:

(a) In relation to the transmission of a notice of judicial sale between member States of such an organization; or

(b) In relation to the jurisdictional rules applicable between member States of such an organization.

Article 19
Non-unified legal systems

1. If a State has two or more territorial units in which different systems of law are applicable in relation to the matters dealt with in this Convention, it may declare that this Convention shall extend to all its territorial units or only to one or more of them.

2. Declarations under this article shall state expressly the territorial units to which this Convention extends.

3. If a State makes no declaration under paragraph 1, this Convention shall extend to all territorial units of that State.

4. If a State has two or more territorial units in which different systems of law are applicable in relation to the matters dealt with in this Convention:

(a) Any reference to the law, regulations or procedures of the State shall be construed as referring, where appropriate, to the law, regulations or procedures in force in the relevant territorial unit;

(b) Any reference to the authority of the State shall be construed as referring, where appropriate, to the authority in the relevant territorial unit.

Article 20
Procedure and effects of declarations

1. Declarations under article 18, paragraph 2, and article 19, paragraph 1, shall be made at the time of signature, ratification, acceptance, approval or accession. Declarations made at the time of signature are subject to confirmation upon ratification, acceptance or approval.

2. Declarations and their confirmations shall be in writing and formally notified to the depositary.

3. A declaration takes effect simultaneously with the entry into force of this Convention in respect of the State concerned.

4. Any State that makes a declaration under article 18, paragraph 2, and article 19, paragraph 1, may modify or withdraw it at any time by a formal notification in writing addressed to the depositary. The modification or withdrawal shall take effect 180 days after the date of the receipt of the notification by the depositary. If the depositary receives the notification of the modification or withdrawal before entry into force of this Convention in respect of the State concerned, the modification or withdrawal shall take effect simultaneously with the entry into force of this Convention in respect of that State.

Article 21
Entry into force

1. This Convention shall enter into force 180 days after the date of the deposit of the third instrument of ratification, acceptance, approval or accession.

2. When a State ratifies, accepts, approves or accedes to this Convention after the deposit of the third instrument of ratification, acceptance, approval or accession, this Convention shall enter into force in respect of that State 180 days after the date of the deposit of its instrument of ratification, acceptance, approval or accession.

3. This Convention shall apply only to judicial sales ordered or approved after its entry into force in respect of the State of judicial sale.

Article 22
Amendment

1. Any State Party may propose an amendment to this Convention by submitting it to the Secretary-General of the United Nations. The Secretary-General shall thereupon communicate the proposed amendment to the States Parties with a request that they indicate whether they favour a conference of States Parties for the purpose of considering and voting upon the proposal. In the event that within 120 days from the date of such communication at least one third of the States Parties favour such a conference, the Secretary-General shall convene the conference under the auspices of the United Nations.

2. The conference of States Parties shall make every effort to achieve consensus on each amendment. If all efforts at consensus are exhausted and no consensus is reached, the amendment shall, as a last resort, require for its adoption a two-thirds majority vote of the States Parties present and voting at the conference. For the purposes of this paragraph, the vote of a regional economic integration organization shall not be counted.

3. An adopted amendment shall be submitted by the depositary to all States Parties for ratification, acceptance or approval.

4. An adopted amendment shall enter into force 180 days after the date of deposit of the third instrument of ratification, acceptance or approval. When an amendment enters

into force, it shall be binding on those States Parties that have expressed consent to be bound by it.

5. When a State Party ratifies, accepts or approves an amendment following the deposit of the third instrument of ratification, acceptance or approval, the amendment shall enter into force in respect of that State Party 180 days after the date of the deposit of its instrument of ratification, acceptance or approval.

Article 23
Denunciation

1. A State Party may denounce this Convention by a formal notification in writing addressed to the depositary. The denunciation may be limited to certain territorial units of a non-unified legal system to which this Convention applies.

2. The denunciation shall take effect 365 days after the date of the receipt of the notification by the depositary. Where a longer period for the denunciation to take effect is specified in the notification, the denunciation shall take effect upon the expiration of such longer period after the date of the receipt of the notification by the depositary. This Convention shall continue to apply to a judicial sale for which a certificate of judicial sale referred to in article 5 has been issued before the denunciation takes effect.

DONE in a single original, of which the Arabic, Chinese, English, French, Russian and Spanish texts are equally authentic.

Annex I

Minimum information to be contained in the notice of judicial sale

1. Statement that the notice of judicial sale is given for the purposes of the United Nations Convention on the International Effects of Judicial Sales of Ships

2. Name of State of judicial sale

3. Court or other public authority ordering, approving or confirming the judicial sale

4. Reference number or other identifier for the judicial sale procedure

5. Name of ship

6. Registry

7. IMO number

8. (*If IMO number not available*) Other information capable of identifying the ship

9. Name of the owner

10. Address of residence or principal place of business of the owner

11. (*If judicial sale by public auction*) Anticipated date, time and place of public auction

12. (*If judicial sale by private treaty*) Any relevant details, including time period, for the judicial sale as ordered by the court or other public authority

13. Statement either confirming that the judicial sale will confer clean title to the ship, or, if it is not known whether the judicial sale will confer clean title, a statement of the circumstances under which the judicial sale would not confer clean title

14. Other information required by the law of the State of judicial sale, in particular any information deemed necessary to protect the interests of the person receiving the notice

Annex II

Model certificate of judicial sale

Issued in accordance with the provisions of article 5 of the United Nations Convention on the International Effects of Judicial Sales of Ships

This is to certify that:

(a) The ship described below was sold by way of judicial sale in accordance with the requirements of the law of the State of judicial sale and the requirements of the United Nations Convention on the International Effects of Judicial Sales of Ships; and

(b) The judicial sale has conferred clean title to the ship on the purchaser.

1.	**State of judicial sale**	....
2.	**Authority issuing this certificate**	
2.1	Name	....
2.2	Address	....
2.3	Telephone/fax/email, if available	....
3.	**Judicial sale**	
3.1	Name of court or other public authority that conducted the judicial sale	....
3.2	Date of the judicial sale	....
4.	**Ship**	
4.1	Name	....

4.2 Registry ....

4.3 IMO number ....

4.4 (*If IMO number not available*) Other information capable of identifying the ship (*Please attach any photos to the certificate*)

....

....

5. Owner immediately prior to the judicial sale

5.1 Name ....

5.2 Address of residence or principal place of business ....

6. Purchaser

6.1 Name ....

6.2 Address of residence or principal place of business ....

At .... (place) **On** .... (date)

....
Signature and/or stamp of issuing authority or other confirmation of authenticity of the certificate

APPENDIX 2

Explanatory Note Prepared by the UNCITRAL Secretariat

Explanatory note*

I. Overview of the Convention

A. Objective

1. In many States, courts have the authority to order the sale of a ship to satisfy a legal claim. Such a claim is typically brought against the ship or shipowner to foreclose a ship mortgage (in the event of default in repayment) or to enforce a maritime lien against the ship. The judicial sale procedure is typically preceded by the arrest of the ship.

2. While the international community has achieved significant progress in harmonizing rules on the arrest of ships,[1] much less progress has been achieved in harmonizing rules on the judicial sale of ships.[2] As such, it remains for each State to prescribe the rules governing the procedure and legal effect of judicial sales ordered by its courts, although in many States the judicial sale has the legal effect of conferring "clean title" on the purchaser (i.e. it extinguishes all rights and interests that were previously attached to the ship, including mortgages and maritime liens). It also remains for each State to prescribe the rules governing the legal effect within its jurisdiction of foreign judicial sales.

3. The United Nations Convention on the International Effects of Judicial Sales of Ships (hereinafter "Convention") harmonizes the latter rules. Put in another way,

---

* The present explanatory note was prepared by the secretariat of the United Nations Commission on International Trade Law (UNCITRAL) for information purposes. It is not an official commentary on the Convention. A draft of the explanatory note (A/CN.9/1110, A/CN.9/1110/Add.1 and A/CN.9/1110/Add.2) was presented to the fifty-fifth session of UNCITRAL, which requested the secretariat to publish the text of the explanatory note (with updates to reflect the deliberations during the session) together with the text of the convention: *Official Records of the General Assembly, Seventy-seventh Session, Supplement No. 17* (A/77/17), para. 98.

[1] See, e.g., the International Convention Relating to the Arrest of Seagoing Ships (1952), United Nations, *Treaty Series*, vol. 439, No. 6330, and International Convention on Arrest of Ships (1999), United Nations, *Treaty Series*, vol. 2797, No. 49196 (hereinafter the "Arrests Conventions").

[2] Efforts to harmonize rules on the recognition and enforcement of maritime liens and mortgages have addressed judicial sales. See, e.g., article 9 of the International Convention for the Unification of Certain Rules relating to Maritime Liens and Mortgages (1926), League of Nations, *Treaty Series*, vol. CXX, No. 2765, and articles 11 and 12 of the International Convention on Maritime Liens and Mortgages (1993), United Nations, *Treaty Series*, vol. 2276, No. 40538.

the Convention establishes a harmonized regime for giving international effect to judicial sales, while preserving domestic law governing the procedure of judicial sales and the circumstances in which judicial sales confer clean title. By ensuring legal certainty as to the title that the purchaser acquires in the ship as it navigates internationally, the Convention is designed to maximize the price that the ship is able to attract in the market and the proceeds available for distribution among creditors, and to promote international trade.

B. Outline

4. The basic rule of the Convention is that a judicial sale conducted in one State Party which has the effect of conferring clean title on the purchaser has the same effect in every other State Party (article 6). The basic rule is subject only to a public policy exception (article 10).

5. The Convention regime prescribes additional rules which establish how a judicial sale is given effect after completion. The first is a requirement that the ship registry deregister the ship or transfer registration at the request of the purchaser (article 7). The second is a prohibition on arresting the ship for a claim arising from a pre-existing right or interest (i.e. a right or interest extinguished by the sale) (article 8). The third is the conferral of exclusive jurisdiction on the courts of the State of judicial sale to hear a challenge to the judicial sale (article 9).

6. To support the operation of the regime and to safeguard the rights of parties with an interest in the ship, the Convention provides for the issuance of two instruments: a notice of judicial sale (article 4) and a certificate of judicial sale (article 5). It also establishes an online repository of those instruments which is freely accessible to any interested person or entity (article 11).

7. The Convention regime is "closed", in the sense that it applies only among States Parties (article 3). Yet it is "not exclusive", in the sense that it does not displace other bases for giving effect to judicial sales (article 14).

C. Drafting history

8. The Convention was prepared by the United Nations Commission on International Trade Law (UNCITRAL) between 2019 and 2022.

9. The project originated in a proposal by the Comité Maritime International (CMI) to the fiftieth session of the Commission (Vienna, 3–21 July 2017) for possible future work on cross-border issues related to the judicial sale of ships

(A/CN.9/923). The proposal drew attention to problems arising around the world from the failure to give recognition to foreign judgments ordering the sale of ships. It was stated that a short, self-contained instrument along the lines of the Convention on the Recognition and Enforcement of Foreign Arbitral Awards (1958)[3] could provide a solution to those problems by enabling clean title to vessels to be recognized across borders. While swift resolution of the questions raised by the proposal was encouraged, it was agreed within the Commission that additional information in respect of the breadth of the problem would be useful.[4]

10. The Commission therefore requested the CMI to develop and advance the proposal by holding a colloquium so as to provide additional information to the Commission and allow it to take an informed decision in due course. The Commission further agreed that UNCITRAL, through its secretariat, and States would support and participate in the colloquium and to revisit the matter at a future session.[5] To that end, following a request from the Government of Malta, the UNCITRAL secretariat extended a formal invitation to all member and observer States of UNCITRAL to participate in a high-level technical colloquium in respect of the cross-border judicial sale of ships.

11. The colloquium, which took place in February 2018, resulted in a number of findings. It was agreed that the "lack of legal certainty in relation to the clean title which a judicial sale is intended to confer on a buyer" led to problems in the de-registration process in the country of the former flag.[6] It was also agreed that the lack of legal certainty created obstacles in respect of the clearance of all former encumbrances and liens, which in turn created a risk of costly and lengthy proceedings, thereby interrupting trade and shipping. Finally, there was broad agreement that the gap could be filled from a legal perspective by providing an instrument on the recognition of judicial sales of ships.

12. At its fifty-first session (New York, 25 June–13 July 2018), the Commission considered a proposal from the Government of Switzerland on possible future work on cross-border issues related to the judicial sale of ships (A/CN.9/944/Rev.1). The proposal summarized the outcomes and conclusions of the colloquium and requested that UNCITRAL undertake work to develop an international instrument on foreign judicial sales of ships and their recognition.

13. In support of the proposal, it was noted within the Commission that the lack of recognition of the judicial sale of ships had the potential to affect many areas of international trade and commerce, not simply the shipping industry, with several

[3] United Nations, *Treaty Series*, vol. 330, No. 4739.
[4] *Official Records of the General Assembly, Seventy-second Session, Supplement No. 17* (A/72/17), paras. 456–465.
[5] Ibid., paras. 464–465.
[6] See A/CN.9/944/Rev.1, p. 5.

examples of that impact being provided. In support of work being undertaken by UNCITRAL, various parallels were drawn between the work being undertaken on recognition of insolvency-related judgments and a possible instrument on the judicial sale of ships.[7]

14. The Commission considered the proposal together with other suggestions for future work in the context of its deliberations on its work programme at its fifty-first session. After discussion, it was agreed that the topic of judicial sale of ships should be added to the work programme of the Commission.

15. At its thirty-fifth session (New York, 13–17 May 2019), Working Group VI considered the topic for the first time (A/CN.9/973), and decided that the draft convention on the recognition of foreign judicial sales of ships, prepared by the CMI and approved by the CMI Assembly in 2014 (known as the "Beijing Draft"), would provide a useful basis for discussion (ibid., para. 25). At its fifty-second session (Vienna, 8–19 July 2019), the Commission expressed its satisfaction with the progress made by the Working Group.[8]

16. At its thirty-sixth session (Vienna, 18–22 November 2019), the Working Group continued its work on the basis of a first revision of the Beijing Draft (A/CN.9/WG.VI/WP.84), which had been prepared by the Secretariat to incorporate the deliberations and decisions of the Working Group at its thirty-fifth session (A/CN.9/1007). The Working Group considered several key provisions of the first revision (ibid., paras. 11–98) and expressed a preliminary view that the instrument should take the form of a convention, while agreeing that a final decision on the matter should be made at a future session (ibid., para. 99). At the resumed fifty-third session of the Commission (Vienna, 14–18 September 2020), support was expressed for the instrument taking the form of a convention, with the observation being made that only a convention was capable of ensuring the level of uniformity needed to affirm the international effects of judicial sales of ships.[9] The Commission confirmed that the Working Group should continue its work to prepare an international instrument on the topic.[10]

17. At its thirty-seventh session (Vienna, 14–18 December 2020), the Working Group continued its work on the basis of a second revision of the Beijing Draft (A/CN.9/WG.VI/WP.87), which had been prepared by the Secretariat to incorporate the deliberations and decisions of the Working Group at its thirty-sixth session (A/CN.9/1047/Rev.1). The Working Group proceeded with an article-by-article consideration of the second revision (ibid., paras. 19–109) and agreed to

[7] *Official Records of the General Assembly, Seventy-third Session, Supplement No. 17* (A/73/17), para. 243.

[8] Ibid., *Seventy-fourth Session, Supplement No. 17* (A/74/17), para. 189.

[9] Ibid., *Seventy-fifth Session, Supplement No. 17* (A/75/17), part two, para. 47.

[10] Ibid., para. 51(f).

continue working on the assumption that the instrument would take the form of a convention (ibid., para. 15). At its thirty-eighth session (New York, 19–23 April 2021), the Working Group considered several outstanding issues from its thirty-seventh session on the basis of a third revision of the Beijing Draft (A/CN.9/WG.VI/WP.90), as well as proposals relating to the grounds for avoidance and to defining the time of judicial sale (A/CN.9/1053). At the fifty-fourth session of the Commission (Vienna, 28 June–16 July 2021), satisfaction was expressed with the progress made by the Working Group.[11]

18. At its thirty-ninth session (Vienna, 18–22 October 2021), the Working Group proceeded with a further article-by-article review of the draft convention on the basis of a fourth revision of the Beijing Draft (A/CN.9/WG.VI/WP.92), and made progress in its consideration of several open issues, including *(a)* dealing with clean title sales, *(b)* the content and function of the notice requirements for judicial sales benefiting from the recognition regime under the draft convention, *(c)* the content and issuance of the certificate of judicial sale, and *(d)* the functioning of the proposed repository mechanism (A/CN.9/1089).

19. At its fortieth session (New York 7–11 February 2022), the Working Group completed a further article-by-article review of the substantive provisions of a draft convention and considered the preamble and final clauses of the draft convention on the basis of a fifth revision of the "Beijing Draft" that had been prepared by the Secretariat (A/CN.9/WG.VI/WP.94). The Working Group requested the Secretariat to revise the draft convention to reflect its deliberations and decisions during the session, and to transmit the revised draft to the Commission for consideration and possible approval at its fifty-fifth session (A/CN.9/1095). The Working Group also requested the Secretariat to circulate the revised draft to all Governments and relevant international organizations for comment, and to compile the comments received for the consideration of the Commission.

20. At its fifty-fifth session (New York, 27 June–15 July 2022), the Commission considered the revised draft (A/CN.9/1108) and a compilation of comments submitted by States and international organizations (A/CN.9/1109, A/CN.9/1109/Add.1, A/CN.9/1109/Add.2 and A/CN.9/1109/Add.3). The Commission finalized the text and, on 30 June 2022, approved the draft convention and submitted it to the General Assembly for adoption.[12] The General Assembly adopted the Convention on 7 December 2022 by its resolution 77/100.

[11] Ibid., *Seventy-sixth Session, Supplement No. 17* (A/76/17), para. 211.

[12] Ibid., *Seventy-seventh Session, Supplement No. 17* (A/77/17), paras. 24–99.

II. Article-by-article remarks

Preamble

21. The preamble recites the objective of the Convention and the considerations that led to its conclusion. It also recalls the connection between the Convention and the work of UNCITRAL, under whose auspices the Convention was prepared.

22. The first paragraph is common to many legislative texts prepared by UNCITRAL. Together with the second paragraph, it situates the Convention within the mandate of UNCITRAL to promote the "progressive harmonization and unification of the law of international trade".[13] The third paragraph reflects the belief of the drafters that the Convention will contribute to maximizing the price that a ship attracts in the market, and the proceeds available for distribution among creditors, by ensuring legal certainty as to the title that the purchaser acquires in the ship as it navigates internationally. The fourth paragraph reflects the objective of the Convention to establish a harmonized regime for giving international effect to judicial sales. It also alludes to the safeguards in the Convention that are aimed at protecting the rights of parties with an interest in the ship, including lienholders and ship financiers.

References to preparatory work

Document	*Reference*
Report of the fortieth session of Working Group VI	A/CN.9/1095, para. 92
Report of the fifty-fifth session of UNCITRAL	A/77/17, paras. 94–97

Article 1. Purpose

23. Article 1 declares – in positive terms – the basic operation of the Convention. It contrasts with article 3, which delimits its substantive and geographic scope of application.

24. Article 1 makes it clear that the Convention is concerned only with the "effects" of a judicial sale and thus not with the conduct of the judicial sale itself.

[13] General Assembly resolution 2205 (XXI), section I.

This is confirmed in article 4, paragraph 1, although the provisions of the Convention dealing with the notice of judicial sale may have an "indirect" impact on the procedure of the judicial sale (see remarks below on article 4, paragraph 1).

25. Article 1 makes it clear that the Convention is concerned only with the effects of "judicial sales" and thus not with the effects of judgments in respect of such sales (e.g. decisions of a court ordering, approving or confirming a judicial sale). This is confirmed in article 6 (see remarks below on article 6).

26. Article 1 also makes it clear that the Convention is concerned only with judicial sales that (already) confer "clean title". Unlike the International Convention on Maritime Liens and Mortgages (1993),[14] the Convention does not address the question as to whether a judicial sale confers clean title, which is left to the law of the State of judicial sale. In some legal systems, a judicial sale within the meaning of the Convention will always confer clean title, whereas in other legal systems, it will not (see remarks below on the definition of "clean title" in article 2). Because article 3 does not address clean title as a matter of substantive scope, the Convention leaves it to its substantive provisions – notably article 6 – to limit its regime to judicial sales that confer clean title.

27. Article 1 refers to the "international" effects of a judicial sale to reflect the title and focus of the Convention. The reference does not mean that the Convention cannot apply, on its terms, in "domestic" cases. For instance, a certificate of judicial sale may be issued under article 5 for a ship registered in the State of judicial sale, and the certificate may be produced to the authorities of that State to trigger action on registration under article 7 or the prohibition of arrest under article 8.

References to preparatory work

Document	*Reference*
Report of the thirty-sixth session of Working Group VI	A/CN.9/1007, paras. 34, 48
Report of the thirty-seventh session of Working Group VI	A/CN.9/1047/Rev.1, paras. 19–20
Report of the thirty-ninth session of Working Group VI	A/CN.9/1089, paras. 11, 40–42, 46–47
Report of the fortieth session of Working Group VI	A/CN.9/1095, paras. 45, 94
Report of the fifty-fifth session of UNCITRAL	A/77/17, paras. 28–29
Note by the Secretariat on the interaction between a future instrument on the judicial sale of ships and selected HCCH Conventions	A/CN.9/WG.VI/WP.85, paras. 3–7

[14] See note 2 above.

Article 2. Definitions

General

28. Article 2 defines key terms that are used in the Convention. The definitions are not presented in alphabetical order, but rather in order of the prominence of the defined term to the operation of the Convention and its relationship with other defined terms. Accordingly, article 2 starts by defining the meaning of a "judicial sale" of a "ship" that confers "clean title", before defining the component elements of clean title (i.e. "mortgage or *hypothèque*" and "charge", as well as "registered charge" and "maritime lien" that are particular types of charges), followed by selected parties involved in the judicial sale (i.e. "owner", "purchaser" and "subsequent purchaser").

29. Consistent with other legislative texts prepared by UNCITRAL, the use of a term in the singular includes the plural. This rule is particularly applicable for provisions that refer to the parties involved in the judicial sale.

References to preparatory work

Document	*Reference*
Report of the fortieth session of Working Group VI	A/CN.9/1095, paras. 45, 94
Cover note by the Secretariat to the fifth revision of the Beijing Draft	A/CN.9/WG.VI/WP.94, para. 6

Definition of "judicial sale"

30. The term "judicial sale of a ship" is used throughout the Convention. The term defines the scope of application of the Convention and is the focus of its substantive provisions. The Convention defines separately the terms "judicial sale" and "ship".

31. A judicial sale is a device used in many legal systems to allow a creditor to seek the assistance of a court or other public authority to force the disposal of an encumbered asset in order to liquidate the asset and satisfy the creditor's right to payment of a monetary sum through access to the proceeds of sale. In effect, the judicial sale converts a claim against the asset into a claim against the proceeds, according to applicable priority rules.

32. The definition of "judicial sale" recognizes two key features of judicial sales:

(*a*) The first feature is that, despite differences in procedure among legal systems, a judicial sale is conducted with the involvement of a court. This feature is reflected in subparagraph (i) of the definition;

(b) The second feature is that a judicial sale is essentially a device that supports the enforcement of private rights. This feature is reflected in subparagraph (ii) of the definition.

Subparagraph (i)

33. Subparagraph (i) recognizes that a judicial sale may be conducted under the authority of either a court or other public authority. The Convention does not itself confer that authority, which is commonly sourced from the laws of civil or admiralty procedure of the State of judicial sale. Jurisdiction with respect to judicial sales may be conferred on a single court or on multiple courts; the Convention does not interfere with a State's internal allocation of jurisdiction.

34. The term "other public authority" is not defined in the Convention. It is not limited to a judicial authority (cf. article 8, in which the term "court" is used in apposition to "judicial authority"), even if international practice indicates that judicial sales are usually conducted under the authority of a court.[15] Accordingly, a sale does not fail to satisfy subparagraph (i) merely because it is conducted under the authority of a public authority that does not exercise exclusively adjudicative functions. In particular, subparagraph (i) is not intended to narrow the meaning of "judicial sale" beyond the "forced sales" that are addressed in articles 11 and 12 of the International Convention on Maritime Liens and Mortgages (1993).[16] However, the nature of the authority and the functions that it exercises may be indicative of a sale that does not satisfy subparagraph (ii).

35. Subparagraph (i) recognizes that a judicial sale is "ordered, approved or confirmed" by the relevant authority. Those words are designed to accommodate the different procedures for judicial sales among legal systems, according to which the relevant authority may be required to intervene at different stages of the proceedings (e.g. in some legal systems, a judicial sale is not subject to confirmation).

36. Nevertheless, the judicial sale must be carried out either by "public auction" or by "private treaty".[17] The Convention does not prescribe how either type of sale is carried out, which is left to the law of the State of judicial sale.[18] International practice indicates that public auction is the more common – and in some legal systems

[15] A 2010 survey carried out by the CMI on the judicial sale of ships indicated that judicial sales in the jurisdictions surveyed were always conducted either by a court or under the control or supervision of a court: see synopsis of replies to question 1.4 in the CMI Yearbook 2010 (Antwerp, 2011), pp. 267–271.

[16] See note 2 above.

[17] In earlier drafts of the convention, "judicial sale" was defined to include a sale carried out by "any other way provided for by the law of the State of judicial sale".

[18] Some elements of each type of sale can be gleaned from items 11 and 12 of annex I to the Convention.

the only – means by which a judicial sale is carried out.[19] In some legal systems, the judicial sale may involve a call for sealed bids as part of a public tender. The term "public auction" in subparagraph (i) is intended to cover those types of sales (in which case, the reference to the "anticipated date, time and place of public auction" in item 11 of annex I to the Convention is understood to refer to the anticipated date, time and place of "submission of bids").

37. A judicial sale by "private treaty" is not the same as a private sale negotiated between the owner (or mortgagee) and prospective purchaser, but rather a sale that is carried out "under the supervision and with the approval of a court". For that reason, it is sometimes referred to as a "hybrid sale", although terminology differs among those legal systems in which private treaty sales are carried out. In some cases, a private treaty sale may result from a public tender process that is ordered by the court, while in other legal systems, the sale may result from direct arrangements between the mortgagee and prospective purchaser.

38. A public auction is typically held by a judicial officer or other person appointed by the court. In legal systems that recognize private treaty sales, that officer or appointed person may also intermediate in the sale process (e.g. by holding the public tender). The term "other public authority" in subparagraph (i) (and in item 3 of annex I and item 3.1 of annex II to the Convention) does not refer to the officer or appointed person that holds the public auction or public tender. Moreover, if the judicial sale proceedings are commenced on the basis of an enforceable title issued by another authority (e.g. a judgment or arbitral award), the term "other public authority" does not refer that other authority. Accordingly, a sale does not fail to satisfy subparagraph (i) merely because the enforceable title is not issued by a "public authority".

39. In some legal systems, a judicial sale may be ordered and conducted prior to final determination of the claim on the basis of which the judicial sale proceedings were commenced. The definition of judicial sale is intended to accommodate such sales.

References to preparatory work

Document	*Reference*
Report of the thirty-fifth session of Working Group VI	A/CN.9/973, paras. 20, 90–91
Report of the thirty-sixth session of Working Group VI	A/CN.9/1007, paras. 16, 18
Report of the thirty-seventh session of Working Group VI	A/CN.9/1047/Rev.1, paras. 31–33

[19] See synopsis of replies to question 1.5 in the CMI Yearbook 2010 (Antwerp, 2011), pp. 271–276.

Document	*Reference*
Report of the thirty-ninth session of Working Group VI	A/CN.9/1089, paras. 18–23
Report of the fifty-fifth session of UNCITRAL	A/77/17, paras. 30–33

Subparagraph (ii)

40. Subparagraph (ii) is designed to distinguish forced sales for which the proceeds form part of government revenue, as may be the case in sales of ships that are seized in the enforcement of public law, such as tax, customs or criminal law.

41. The Convention does not define the term "creditor". Typically, the term includes a person with a right to payment of a monetary sum that is secured by mortgage, maritime lien or other charge that is attached to the ship (i.e. the mortgagee or holder of the maritime lien or charge). Although a judicial sale is essentially a device that supports the enforcement of private rights, a sale does not fail to satisfy subparagraph (ii) merely because a public authority has a claim against the proceeds. For example, a maritime lien within the meaning of the Convention may secure a claim by a port authority for unpaid port dues. Moreover, a sale does not fail to satisfy subparagraph (ii) merely because it follows seizure of the ship by a public authority (e.g. seizure by tax or customs authorities).

References to preparatory work

Document	*Reference*
Report of the thirty-fifth session of Working Group VI	A/CN.9/973, paras. 19, 89–90
Report of the thirty-sixth session of Working Group VI	A/CN.9/1007, paras. 35–39
Report of the thirty-seventh session of Working Group VI	A/CN.9/1047/Rev.1, paras. 30, 34–35
Report of the thirty-ninth session of Working Group VI	A/CN.9/1089, paras. 49–50

Definition of "ship"

42. As noted above (para. 30), the term "judicial sale of a ship" defines the scope of application of the Convention and is the focus of its substantive provisions. If the definition of "judicial sale" delimits that term by reference to the rights and procedures involved in the forced disposal of an asset, the definition of "ship" further delimits the term by reference to the type of asset involved.

43. The concept of a "ship" at law differs between legal systems and depends on the context in which it is used. The term "ship" has evaded international attempts to

define its intrinsic features,[20] and the Convention does not attempt to formulate such a definition. The definition of "ship" is designed to be broad and does not seek to delimit the types of vessels to which the Convention applies.

44. The definition does not defer to the meaning of "ship" under the law of a particular State. Accordingly, the term should be given an autonomous meaning in accordance with the rules of treaty interpretation. Nevertheless, the requirement for a vessel to be "registered" and the requirement for the vessel to be "subject of an arrest or other similar measure capable of leading to a judicial sale under the law of the State of judicial sale" suggests that, in practice, only a vessel that falls within the meaning of the law of both the State of judicial sale and the State of registration will be a "ship" for the purposes of the Convention.

45. Unlike other maritime law conventions, the Convention does not draw a distinction between "seagoing vessels" and "inland navigation vessels", and the term "ship" is intended to cover both types of vessels. Nevertheless, the requirement for the vessel to be "registered" and for the register to be "open to public inspection" means that, in practice, some inland navigation vessels will fall outside the definition of "ship". Moreover, an inland navigation vessel may fall outside the Convention regime altogether by virtue of article 13, paragraph 1.

46. The term "ship" is not limited to vessels used for commercial navigation and therefore would typically cover pleasure craft (e.g. yachts and recreational boats), provided that the other requirements of the definition are satisfied. Note, however, that paragraph 2 of article 3 excludes from scope warships and certain other State-owned or operated vessels that may be used for non-commercial navigation.

47. The Convention acknowledges that different types of vessels within the meaning of "ship" may be entered in different registers (e.g. registers for pleasure craft, registers for inland navigation vessels, registers for seagoing vessels) and therefore does not assume the existence of a single register of ships in each State. This is confirmed by the definition of "owner" and other provisions of the Convention which recognize that the ship may be registered in the "register of ships" or "equivalent register". Accordingly, a vessel does not fall outside the meaning of the term "ship" merely because of the identity of the register of ships.

[20] For instance, neither the International Convention Relating to the Arrest of Seagoing Ships (1952), International Convention on Maritime Liens and Mortgages (1993) or International Convention on Arrest of Ships (1999) defines the term "ship".

References to preparatory work

Document	*Reference*
Report of the thirty-sixth session of Working Group VI	A/CN.9/1007, paras. 22, 28–32
Report of the thirty-seventh session of Working Group VI	A/CN.9/1047/Rev.1, paras. 26–28
Report of the thirty-ninth session of Working Group VI	A/CN.9/1089, paras. 30–31
Note by the Secretariat accompanying the second revision of the Beijing Draft	A/CN.9/WG.VI/WP.87/Add.1, paras. 4–9

Definition of "clean title"

48. The concept of "clean title" is key to the basic rule of the Convention (i.e. that a judicial sale conducted in one State Party which has the effect of conferring clean title on the purchaser has the same effect in every other State Party). This is operationalized by article 6 (pursuant to which only a judicial sale for which a certificate of judicial sale issued has international effect) and article 5, paragraph 1 (pursuant to which only a judicial sale that confers clean title is issued with a certificate).

49. The concept of "title" refers to property rights in the ship that are vested in the purchaser. That title is "clean" if all other property rights in the ship that were vested in another person immediately prior to the judicial sale (i.e. encumbrances, rights "in re aliena") are extinguished, and if all pre-existing mortgages, *hypothèques* or charges cease to attach to the ship. A sale does not fail to confer "clean title" merely because it does not extinguish a pre-existing right that is not a "charge" (e.g. a right of use that cannot be asserted against the ship).

50. As noted above (para. 26), whether a judicial sale confers clean title is a matter for the law of the State of judicial sale. In some legal systems, a judicial sale will only extinguish pre-existing property rights in the ship that are vested in lower-ranking creditors according to applicable priority rules (i.e. it will not extinguish property rights that have priority over the right of the creditor who commenced judicial sale proceedings). A sale that preserves pre-existing property rights does not confer "clean title" within the meaning of the Convention.

51. In some legal systems, title only becomes effective (in the sense of being opposable against others) once additional formalities are taken (e.g. registering the ship in the name of the purchaser). As the Convention does not address the transfer of ownership, whether a judicial sale confers "clean title" within the meaning of the Convention does not depend on whether those additional formalities are taken.

52. The Convention is concerned with clean title "to the ship", and not with property rights in assets which are not comprised in the "ship". As noted above (para. 44),

the term "ship" should be given an autonomous meaning in accordance with the rules of treaty interpretation.

53. Unlike the International Convention on Maritime Liens and Mortgages (1993),[21] the Convention does not provide for the preservation of pre-existing mortgages or *hypothèques* or of charges that are "assumed by the purchaser". If, under the law of the State of judicial sale, a pre-existing mortgage, *hypothèque* or charge remains attached to the ship, there is no conferral of "clean title" within the meaning of the Convention, and therefore the basic rule of the Convention does not apply. Conversely, whether or not the judicial sale extinguishes rights other than property rights in the ship (e.g. personal rights that may be enforced by a claim brought against the former shipowner) has no bearing on whether clean title has been conferred. This is reinforced by article 15, paragraph 1 (b).

References to preparatory work

Document	*Reference*
Report of the thirty-fifth session of Working Group VI	A/CN.9/973, paras. 33, 81
Report of the thirty-sixth session of Working Group VI	A/CN.9/1007, paras. 15, 49
Report of the thirty-seventh session of Working Group VI	A/CN.9/1047/Rev.1, paras. 37–38

Definition of "mortgage or hypothèque"

54. The term "mortgage or *hypothèque*" is one component of the definition of "clean title". It is also used *(a)* to designate the persons to whom the notice of judicial sale is to be given under article 4 (i.e. "all holders of any mortgage or *hypothèque*" referred to article 4, paragraph 3 (b)), and *(b)* to designate the actions to be taken under article 7 (i.e. action to delete "any mortgage or *hypothèque* . . . attached to the ship" referred to in article 7, paragraph 1 (a)).

55. Mortgages and *hypothèques* are essentially two different devices that create property rights in a ship to secure payment of a monetary sum. The security rights that each device creates differ between legal systems, and international efforts to harmonize rules on the recognition and enforcement of mortgages and *hypothèques* have not sought to define those rights. Moreover, either device may be unknown to the law in some legal systems (e.g. mortgages are more commonly associated with common law legal systems, while *hypothèques* are more commonly associated with civil law legal systems). Despite those differences, both a mortgage and a *hypothèque* attach to the ship and may be enforced by judicial sale regardless of change in shipowner.

[21] See note 2 above.

56. The Convention does not attempt to define "mortgage or *hypothèque*" by reference to their intrinsic features nor does the definition defer to devices recognized as such under the law of a particular State (cf. definition of "maritime lien"). Instead, it is sufficient for the purposes of the Convention for the term "mortgage or *hypothèque*" to be defined by reference to the fact of registration in the State of registration (e.g. entry in the register of ships or separate register of security interests), which will produce the same result regardless of the State in which the issue of the existence of a "mortgage or *hypothèque*" arises. In practice, that issue will arise in the State of judicial sale (i.e. in determining the persons to whom the notice of judicial sale is to be given) and in the State of registration (i.e. in identifying the registry to take action to delete the mortgage or *hypothèque*). In both cases, the fact of registration delimits the scope of the term in a manner that is both suitable and workable.

57. The Convention acknowledges that a mortgage or *hypothèque* may be registered in a different register to the register in which the ship is registered. For example, a State may maintain a separate register of security interests in which ship mortgages are registered. This is confirmed by the definition of "registered charge" and other provisions of the Convention (e.g. article 4, paragraph 7 (b)), and accommodated by the reference in article 7 to action taken by a registry or "other competent authority".

58. The Convention refers to "mortgage or *hypothèque*" as a single defined term, rather than defining "mortgage" to include a *hypothèque* or applying the same definition to either "mortgage" and "*hypothèque*" as two defined (yet synonymous) terms. Referring to "mortgage or *hypothèque*" as a single defined term acknowledges that, in some languages, it may be sufficient to refer to a single device.

References to preparatory work

Document	*Reference*
Report of the thirty-sixth session of Working Group VI	A/CN.9/1007, paras. 21, 97
Report of the thirty-eighth session of Working Group VI	A/CN.9/1053, paras. 45–48
Report of the thirty-ninth session of Working Group VI	A/CN.9/1089, paras. 16–17

Definition of "charge"

59. The term "charge" is the other component of the definition of "clean title". It is also the basis for designating two types of charges – maritime liens and registered charges – whose holders are entitled to notification of the judicial sale under article 4. Singling out maritime liens and registered charges reflects their special treatment in other maritime law conventions.

60. The definition of charge is broad and is designed to cover any property right in the ship. The concept of charge is not limited by how it is denominated (as indicated by the non-exclusive list set out in the definition) or by how it may be asserted against the ship (e.g. by arrest or attachment). While a mortgage or *hypothèque* (and the rights it creates) would typically fall within the definition of "charge", the definition expressly excludes those devices to reflect their separate treatment in other maritime law conventions.

61. Unlike the definition of "maritime lien" (a particular type of charge), the definition of "charge" does not defer to charges recognized as such under the law of a particular State. As the basic rule of the Convention is for a judicial sale that confers clean title in one State Party to confer clean title in every other State Party, and as clean title involves extinguishing all "charges", it is neither necessary nor appropriate for the definition to involve a conflict of law analysis. Accordingly, a pre-existing charge recognized under the law of a State Party other than the State of judicial sale will not continue to attach to the ship merely because the particular type of charge is unknown to the law of the State of judicial sale.

References to preparatory work

Document	*Reference*
Report of the thirty-fifth session of Working Group VI	A/CN.9/973, paras. 78–80
Report of the thirty-sixth session of Working Group VI	A/CN.9/1007, paras. 12–14
Report of the thirty-eighth session of Working Group VI	A/CN.9/1053, paras. 39–42
Report of the thirty-ninth session of Working Group VI	A/CN.9/1089, para. 13

Definition of "registered charge"

62. As noted above (para. 59), a "registered charge" is a special type of "charge" within the meaning of the Convention. The term is used (*a*) to designate the persons to whom the notice of judicial sale is to be given under article 4 (i.e. "all holders of . . . any registered charge" referred to in article 4, paragraph 3(b)), and (*b*) to designate the actions to be taken under article 7 (i.e. action to delete "any registered charge attached to the ship" referred to in article 7, paragraph 1 (a)). As such, a registered charge is treated like a mortgage or *hypothèque* for the purposes of the Convention.

63. The definition of "registered charge" is formulated differently to the definition of "mortgage or *hypothèque*" so that it does not cover charges that are registered in any register, but only *(a)* the register in which the ship is registered, or *(b)* any other register in which mortgages or *hypothèques* are registered. Delimiting the scope of the term by reference to those registers is designed to ensure a greater

connection between the registered charge and the ship registry or court of judicial sale (or other public authority conducting the judicial sale), and thus make the requirements of the Convention regarding notification and deletion more workable (see remarks below on article 4, paragraph 3 (b)).

References to preparatory work

Document	*Reference*
Report of the thirty-eighth session of Working Group VI	A/CN.9/1053, para. 43
Report of the thirty-ninth session of Working Group VI	A/CN.9/1089, paras. 28–29

Definition of "maritime lien"

64. As noted above (para. 59), a "maritime lien" is a special type of "charge" within the meaning of the Convention. The term is used to designate the persons to whom the notice of judicial sale is to be given under article 4 (i.e. "all holders of any maritime lien" referred to in article 4, paragraph 3 (c)).

65. A maritime lien is a device that is peculiar to maritime law. In essence, it is a right to payment of a monetary sum that is secured against a ship in connection with which the right arises, whether by services provided to it, or by loss caused by it, regardless of change in ownership or operation of the ship. Unlike a "registered charge", a maritime lien is not subject to registration. Unlike a "mortgage or *hypothèque*", it is not subject to any formality or expression of consent on the part of the owner or operator of the ship at the time of its creation.

66. Despite international efforts to harmonize the circumstances in which a maritime lien arises (e.g. the types of services provided to, and types of losses caused by, the ship), maritime liens differ between legal systems. Accordingly, the law of one State may create a maritime lien in circumstances that do not give rise to a maritime lien under the law of another State. This is particularly relevant in international shipping, where maritime liens could potentially attach to a ship under the law of the various States through which the ship navigates, giving rise to conflict of law issues.

67. The definition of "maritime lien" accepts the status quo, and thus defers to the law applicable in the State in which the issue of the existence of a maritime lien arises, including its conflict of law rules. In practice, that issue will arise in the State of judicial sale (i.e. in identifying the persons to whom the notice of judicial sale is to be given (i.e. "all holders of any maritime lien")). By deferring to applicable law, the Convention makes it clear that the term "maritime lien" should not be given an autonomous meaning.

References to preparatory work

Document	*Reference*
Report of the thirty-sixth session of Working Group VI	A/CN.9/1007, paras. 19–20
Report of the thirty-eighth session of Working Group VI	A/CN.9/1053, para. 44
Report of the thirty-ninth session of Working Group VI	A/CN.9/1089, para. 14

Definition of "owner"

68. The term "owner" is used to designate the persons to whom the notice of judicial sale is to be given under article 4 (i.e. "the owner of the ship for the time being" referred to in article 4, paragraph 3 (d)). Certain particulars of the owner are also part of the minimum information to be contained in the notice of judicial sale (article 4, paragraph 4) and the certificate of judicial sale (article 5, paragraph 2 (h)). In all cases, the term "owner" refers to the owner prior to judicial sale, in contrast to the "purchaser".

69. Determining ownership of a ship at law differs between legal systems. For the purposes of the Convention, it is not necessary to resort to a conflict of law analysis to identify the "owner". Instead, it is sufficient for the term "owner" to be defined by reference to the fact of registration (or recordation) as the owner in the register in which the ship is registered (or entered). This may be more than one person.

References to preparatory work

Document	*Reference*
Report of the thirty-sixth session of Working Group VI	A/CN.9/1007, para. 22
Report of the thirty-ninth session of Working Group VI	A/CN.9/1089, para. 24
Report of the fifty-fifth session of UNCITRAL	A/77/17, para. 40

Definition of "purchaser"

70. The term "purchaser" is used to designate the person to whom the judicial sale confers clean title to the ship, as well as the person entitled to request action on registration under article 7. Certain particulars of the purchaser are also part of the minimum information to be contained in the certificate of judicial sale (article 5, paragraph 2 (i)). As with the term "owner" (see para. 69 above), more than one person may be a "purchaser".

71. As noted above (para. 69), determining ownership of a ship at law, including passage and opposability of title, differs between legal systems. As the Convention

does not address the transfer of ownership, it is not necessary for the definition of "purchaser" to involve a conflict of law analysis or to refer to ownership. Instead, it is sufficient for the purposes of the Convention for the term "purchaser" to be defined by reference to the fact that the ship was disposed to the purchaser.

References to preparatory work

Document	*Reference*
Report of the thirty-sixth session of Working Group VI	A/CN.9/1007, paras. 25–27
Report of the thirty-ninth session of Working Group VI	A/CN.9/1089, para. 27

Definition of "subsequent purchaser"

72. The term "subsequent purchaser" is used only to designate the persons entitled to request action on registration under article 7. For a discussion on accommodating subsequent purchasers, see remarks below on article 7.

73. While the ship may be disposed to another person in a variety of ways, the definition of "subsequent purchaser" covers only persons who have "purchased" the ship.

References to preparatory work

Document	*Reference*
Report of the thirty-ninth session of Working Group VI	A/CN.9/1089, paras. 34–38
Report of the fortieth session of Working Group VI	A/CN.9/1095, paras. 18–21

Definition of "State of judicial sale"

74. The term "State of judicial sale" is used throughout the Convention. The definition is not limited to States Parties; however, by virtue of paragraph 1 (a) of article 3, the term is effectively used in the Convention to refer only to States Parties.

References to preparatory work

Document	*Reference*
Report of the thirty-sixth session of Working Group VI	A/CN.9/1007, para. 33
Report of the thirty-ninth session of Working Group VI	A/CN.9/1089, para. 33

Other terms not defined

"Bareboat charter registration"

75. Several provisions of the Convention refer to the "bareboat charterer", "bareboat charter registration" and the "bareboat charter registry". None of those terms is defined in the Convention. The United Nations Convention on Conditions for Registration of Ships (1986)[22] defines a "bareboat charter" as a "contract for the lease of a ship, for a stipulated period of time, by virtue of which the lessee has complete possession and control of the ship, including the right to appoint the master and crew of the ship, for the duration of the lease". The lessee is referred to as the "bareboat charterer".

76. The practice of bareboat charter registration is recognized under the law of many States. There are two aspects of bareboat charter registration. The first aspect is the practice whereby a State permits its registered ship to fly a foreign flag. This practice is commonly referred to as "flagging out" or "bareboat charter-out" registration. The second aspect is the practice whereby a State permits a foreign-registered ship to fly its flag temporarily (i.e. for the period of the charter). This practice is commonly referred to as "flagging in", or "bareboat charter-in" registration. In some States, the law provides only for bareboat charter-in registration. The law in other States does not provide for either aspect of bareboat charter registration.

77. The procedures to give effect to bareboat charter registration differ between States. The United Nations Convention on Conditions for Registration of Ships (1986) seeks to harmonize some of the procedures and terminology relating to bareboat charter-in registration among States that recognize the practice. The Convention does not seek to contribute to those harmonization efforts. It does, however, seek to refer to procedures and use terminology consistent with other maritime law conventions. The Convention does not require a State Party to recognize the practice of bareboat charter registration under its law.

Reference to preparatory work

Document	*Reference*
Report of the thirty-sixth session of Working Group VI	A/CN.9/1007, para. 63

"Person"

78. The term "person" is used in the Convention primarily to define the "owner" and "purchaser" of a ship. Consistent with other legislative texts prepared by UNCITRAL, the Convention does not define the term, which should be

[22] The text of the convention is contained in TD/RS/CONF/23.

understood broadly to encompass both legal and natural persons, as well as States and State entities.

References to preparatory work

Document	*Reference*
Report of the thirty-sixth session of Working Group VI	A/CN.9/1007, paras. 23–24
Report of the thirty-ninth session of Working Group VI	A/CN.9/1089, paras. 25–26

"Register" and "registry"

79. In provisions concerning registration, the Convention seeks to use terminology that is consistent with other maritime law conventions. Accordingly, the Convention uses the terms "register" and "registry" as follows:

(*a*) The term "register" refers to the record in which particulars of a ship, mortgage, *hypothèque* or (registered) charge are recorded; and

(*b*) The term "registry" refers to the entity which maintains the register.

80. The Convention uses the term "register of ships" but does not define the term. It does, however, distinguish the "register of ships" from an "equivalent register" in which a ship is registered. The reference to "register of ships" and "equivalent register" acknowledges the broad definition of the term "ship", which, further to the remarks on that definition above (para. 47), covers vessels that are entered in registers other than what might be named or commonly regarded as the "register of ships".

References to preparatory work

Document	*Reference*
Report of the thirty-sixth session of Working Group VI	A/CN.9/1007, para. 22
Report of the fortieth session of Working Group VI	A/CN.9/1095, paras. 95, 104
Report of the fifty-fifth session of UNCITRAL	A/77/17, para. 52

"State of registration"

81. Several provisions of the Convention refer to the "State of registration". Paragraph 3 (b) of article 4 uses the term to refer to the State in which the mortgage, *hypothèque* or registered charge is registered, while paragraph 1 (c) of article 7 uses the term to refer to the State in which the ship is registered. By virtue of the definitions of "mortgage or *hypothèque*" and of "registered charge", these are one and the same State.

"Time of judicial sale"

82. Several provisions of the Convention refer to the time of judicial sale. The Convention purposefully does not define the time of judicial sale but instead defers to the law of the State of judicial sale on that issue (see further remarks on article 4, paragraph 1).

Article 3. Scope of application

83. Article 3 delimits the scope of the Convention. Paragraph 1 prescribes certain judicial sales to which the Convention does not apply by reference to (*a*) whether the State of judicial sale is party to the Convention (the "geographic scope"), and (*b*) whether the ship is physically present within the territory of the State of judicial sale at the time of the sale (the "physical presence requirement"). Paragraph 2 deals with State-owned or operated vessels.

Geographic scope (article 3, paragraph 1 (a))

84. By virtue of paragraph 1 (a) of article 3, the Convention establishes a "closed" regime that applies only among States Parties. Nothing in the Convention prevents a State from giving effect – under its domestic law – to judicial sales conducted in a non-State party on terms similar to those provided for under the Convention.

85. A judicial sale of a ship does not fall outside the scope of application merely because the ship is registered in a State that is not party to the Convention. Of course, that State would not be bound by the Convention, as a matter of international law, to give effect to the judicial sale or to take action on the registration of the ship upon presentation of the certificate of judicial sale issued under article 5 of the Convention, which would limit the protections that the Convention could provide to the sale.

References to preparatory work

Document	*Reference*
Report of the thirty-fifth session of Working Group VI	A/CN.9/973, paras. 47, 52–53
Report of the thirty-seventh session of Working Group VI	A/CN.9/1047/Rev.1, paras. 16–18
Report of the thirty-eighth session of Working Group VI	A/CN.9/1053, para. 49
Report of the thirty-ninth session of Working Group VI	A/CN.9/1089, paras. 32, 39–42
Report of the fifty-fifth session of UNCITRAL	A/77/17, para. 34

Physical presence requirement (article 3, paragraph 1 (b))

86. The physical presence requirement in paragraph 1 (b) of article 3 recognizes that, in practice, the judicial sale of a ship is typically preceded by the arrest of the ship which, under the harmonized rules established in the Arrests Conventions,[23] can only occur in the territory of the State in which the arrest is judicially authorized. The requirement does not apply at the time of arrest but "at the time of the sale".

87. The purpose of the physical presence requirement is to ensure a jurisdictional link between the court (or other public authority) under whose authority the judicial sale was conducted and the ship. The Convention purposefully does not define the time of judicial sale but instead defers to the law of the State of judicial sale on that issue (see article 4, paragraph 1). Nonetheless, the words "at the time of the sale" in paragraph 1 (b) of article 3 need to be understood in the context of the Convention, in particular the definition of "judicial sale" (article 2) and article 4, paragraph 2, which acknowledges that notification of a judicial sale occurs "prior to the judicial sale". Just as the procedure for a judicial sale differs between legal systems, so does the time at which the court of judicial sale (or other public authority) exercises jurisdiction over the ship. Some legal systems may consider jurisdiction to be exercised over a period (e.g. from the commencement to the conclusion of the judicial sale proceedings), while other legal systems may consider jurisdiction to be exercised at a particular time (e.g. when the court orders, approves or confirms the disposal of the ship to the purchaser, or upon completion of the judicial sale). In all cases, paragraph 1 (b) of article 3 requires the physical presence of the ship at the final stage of the judicial sale procedure, when the ship is awarded to the successful purchaser.

88. The physical presence requirement is not intended to prevent existing practices by which *(a)* proceedings for the arrest of a ship or other proceedings leading to a judicial sale can be commenced before the ship enters territorial waters, or *(b)* the ship is released from arrest pending its judicial sale.

References to preparatory work

Document	*Reference*
Report of the thirty-fifth session of Working Group VI	A/CN.9/973, para. 28
Report of the thirty-sixth session of Working Group VI	A/CN.9/1007, paras. 50, 83
Report of the thirty-seventh session of Working Group VI	A/CN.9/1047/Rev.1, paras. 22–25, 82
Report of the thirty-eighth session of Working Group VI	A/CN.9/1053, paras. 50–56
Report of the fifty-fifth session of UNCITRAL	A/77/17, paras. 34–35

[23] See note 1 above.

Exclusion of State-owned or operated vessels (article 3, paragraph 2)

89. Like the International Convention on Maritime Liens and Mortgages (1993),[24] the Convention excludes State-owned or operated vessels from scope. The wording of paragraph 2 of article 3 is based on article 16, paragraph 2, of the United Nations Convention on Jurisdictional Immunities of States and Their Property (2004).[25]

90. In addition to warships and naval auxiliaries, the exclusion in paragraph 2 of article 3 applies to State-owned or operated vessels that are used, "immediately prior to" the time of judicial sale, only on government non-commercial service. Referring to a time immediately prior to the time of sale is designed to ensure that the exclusion is given full effect in practice. Specifically, it acknowledges that, by the time of the sale itself, the ship would be within the jurisdiction of the court of judicial sale (or other public authority conducting the sale) and thus not capable of being used "only on government non-commercial service".

91. The exclusion in paragraph 2 may find little application in practice given that *(a)* such vessels are already immune from arrest under the harmonized rules established in the Arrests Conventions,[26] and *(b)* the definition of "ship" requires the relevant vessel to be capable of being "the subject of an arrest or other similar measure capable of leading to a judicial sale under the law of the State of judicial sale".

References to preparatory work

Document	*Reference*
Report of the thirty-fifth session of Working Group VI	A/CN.9/973, para. 40
Report of the thirty-sixth session of Working Group VI	A/CN.9/1007, paras. 40–42
Report of the thirty-seventh session of Working Group VI	A/CN.9/1047/Rev.1, para. 46
Report of the thirty-ninth session of Working Group VI	A/CN.9/1089, para. 48

Matters of substantive scope not addressed in article 3

Clean title sales

92. As noted above (para. 26), the Convention leaves it to the substantive provisions to limit its scope to judicial sales that confer clean title. This approach

[24] See note 2 above.

[25] The text of the convention is contained in the annex to A/RES/59/38.

[26] See note 1 above.

acknowledges that, for some jurisdictions, the notice requirements in article 4 are applicable at a time in the judicial sale proceedings at which it is not yet known whether the sale will result in the conferral of clean title. It also avoids potential difficulties of introducing a requirement to ascertain the content of foreign law (i.e. whether a judicial sale confers clean title) in order to determine the substantive scope of the Convention.

References to preparatory work

Document	*Reference*
Report of the thirty-fifth session of Working Group VI	A/CN.9/973, paras. 35–38, 92–93
Report of the thirty-sixth session of Working Group VI	A/CN.9/1007, para. 43
Report of the thirty-seventh session of Working Group VI	A/CN.9/1047/Rev.1, paras. 36, 39–45
Report of the thirty-eighth session of Working Group VI	A/CN.9/1053, paras. 13–15
Report of the thirty-ninth session of Working Group VI	A/CN.9/1089, paras. 43–47

Forced sales in the enforcement of tax, customs or criminal law

93. Concerns were expressed during the preparation of the Convention about applying its regime to the sale of ships that are seized in the enforcement of public law, such as tax, customs or criminal law. However, it was felt that it would not be appropriate to address those concerns by excluding such sales from scope, particularly given that, in some jurisdictions, a ship so seized could still be sold by judicial sale with proceeds made available to creditors. Instead, those concerns are addressed in the definition of "judicial sale", particularly the requirement in subparagraph (ii) for the proceeds of sale to be made available to creditors (see remarks above on article 2, paragraph (a)).

References to preparatory work

Document	*Reference*
Report of the thirty-fifth session of Working Group VI	A/CN.9/973, paras. 18–19, 79, 90
Report of the thirty-sixth session of Working Group VI	A/CN.9/1007, paras. 35–39
Report of the thirty-seventh session of Working Group VI	A/CN.9/1047/Rev.1, paras. 30, 34–35
Report of the thirty-ninth session of Working Group VI	A/CN.9/1089, paras. 49–50

Article 4. Notice of judicial sale

Purpose and function of the notice requirements (article 4, paragraphs 1 and 2)

94. Notification of a judicial sale is only one aspect of the judicial sale procedure, but one that is particularly important in safeguarding the interests of creditors, who might otherwise not be party to the proceedings giving rise to the judicial sale. Judicial sale procedures differ significantly between jurisdictions, not only in terms of competent authorities and notification requirements, but also in terms of the circumstances in which a judicial sale procedure starts and ends, and the various stages of the procedure in between (see remarks above on subparagraph (i) of the definition of "judicial sale" in article 2). The Convention is not designed to harmonize the procedure for judicial sales. This is confirmed by paragraph 1 of article 4, which leaves matters related to the conduct of the judicial sale to the law of the State of judicial sale.

95. The notice requirements in the remaining paragraphs of article 4 prescribe minimum standards regarding the persons to be notified of the judicial sale (paragraph 3), the content of the notice (paragraph 4), and the public advertisement of the judicial sale (paragraph 5). The notice requirements in the Convention are adapted to the judicial sale itself and not to related proceedings (e.g. proceedings giving rise to the judicial sale or proceedings related to the distribution of proceeds). In that context, while notification attracts potential bidders and can help maximize the eventual proceeds available to creditors, the primary purpose of the notice requirements in the Convention is to alert creditors to the impending sale and eventual distribution of proceeds. The requirements are designed to strike a fair balance between due process towards creditors and the expediency required in judicial sale proceedings. They acknowledge that creditors and other persons to be notified may have other means at their disposal, including the use of online tools, to track the ship and be informed of its arrest or impending sale.

Relationship with domestic law

96. The notice requirements do not substitute or displace notification requirements under domestic law, including those relating to the service of judicial documents. The distinction between the notice requirements under the Convention and the notification requirements under domestic law, as well as the coexistence of those requirements, is acknowledged in paragraph 4 of article 4 and in paragraph 1 of article 5 of the Convention.

Condition for issuing certificate of judicial sale

97. The notice requirements do not serve as a stand-alone obligation but rather as a condition for the issuance of the certificate of judicial sale under article 5. This is confirmed by paragraph 2 of article 4. Nevertheless, given the central role of the certificate of judicial sale in the Convention regime, compliance with the notice requirements is essential to securing the international effects of a judicial sale. The notice requirements may also have an "indirect" impact on the procedure of the judicial sale, insofar as States might align their procedural law to the notice requirements to ensure that their judicial sales benefit from the Convention regime. This is particularly relevant for States in which the judicial sale is not notified to prescribed classes of persons but rather advertised publicly (e.g. by publishing a notice in the press or maritime periodicals).

98. It follows that a failure to comply with the notice requirements does not constitute a breach of the Convention, but it would prevent the issuance of a certificate of judicial sale. Under the Convention, any claim challenging the validity of a certificate due to a failure to comply with the notice requirements is heard in the State of judicial sale in exercise of the exclusive jurisdiction conferred under article 9. However, it is conceivable that a particularly egregious failure to comply with the notice requirements could give rise to an application invoking the public policy ground under article 10 in another State in which the effect of the judicial sale is sought to be produced.

Procedures for challenging the judicial sale

99. Paragraph 1 of article 4 declares that the law of the State of judicial sale shall "provide procedures for challenging the judicial sale prior to its completion". That provision is designed to strike a balance between due process towards creditors, by ensuring that they have an opportunity to assert their rights, and the objective of the Convention to leave matters of procedure to domestic law. It does not require a State party to take steps to legislate procedures for challenging a judicial sale if such procedures already exist. Paragraph 1 was drafted on an assumption that the law in most States would already have procedures in place for challenging a judicial sale. Such procedures are sourced in legislation (e.g. rules of civil procedure) or in case law, and may be invoked at different stages of the judicial sale procedure.

100. Paragraph 1 of article 4 is concerned with challenging a judicial sale prior to its completion, and thus with the availability of remedies that typically have the effect of delaying or calling off the sale before the procedure has reached its final stage. It is not concerned with challenges after completion, and can thus be contrasted with article 9, which is concerned with avoiding the judicial sale or suspending its effect after completion. Moreover, it is not intended to suggest that challenges

to a judicial sale should be encouraged as a matter of course. As with article 9, paragraph 1 of article 4 does not deal with standing to bring a challenge, nor does it deal with limitation periods, which remain a matter for the law of the State of judicial sale.

Determining the time of the judicial sale

101. Paragraph 1 of article 4 adds that the law of the State of judicial sale "determine[s] the time of the sale for the purposes of this Convention". Several provisions of the Convention refer to the time of judicial sale:

(a) The time of the judicial sale is relevant in determining the scope of the Convention, given that *(a)* the physical presence requirement in paragraph 1 (b) of article 3 applies "at the time of the sale", and *(b)* the exclusion of State-owned or operated vessels in paragraph 2 of article 3 applies by reference to use "immediately prior to the time of judicial sale";

(b) Reference to action taken prior to the time of judicial sale is relevant to the application of the notice requirements, given that paragraph 2 of article 4 provides for the notice of judicial sale to be given "prior to the judicial sale";

(c) The time of the judicial sale is relevant in determining whether the judicial sale has reached completion, and thus in determining *(a)* whether the conditions for issuance of the certificate of judicial sale under paragraph 1 of article 5 have been met, and *(b)* the range of mortgages, *hypothèques* and other registered charges to be deleted from the register under paragraph 1 (a) of article 7.

102. The Convention does not assume that the law of the State of judicial sale makes specific provision for determining the time of a judicial sale. Concepts and principles of broader application under domestic law could guide such a determination.

References to preparatory work

Document	*Reference*
Report of the thirty-fifth session of Working Group VI	A/CN.9/973, paras. 22, 30, 67–70
Report of the thirty-sixth session of Working Group VI	A/CN.9/1007, paras. 55–61
Report of the thirty-seventh session of Working Group VI	A/CN.9/1047/Rev.1, paras. 49–50
Report of the thirty-eighth session of Working Group VI	A/CN.9/1053, paras. 16–17
Report of the thirty-ninth session of Working Group VI	A/CN.9/1089, paras. 52, 57–59, 73
Report of the fortieth session of Working Group VI	A/CN.9/1095, para. 99
Report of the fifty-fifth session of UNCITRAL	A/77/17, paras. 38–39, 60–63

Persons to be notified (article 4, paragraph 3)

103. Paragraph 3 of article 4 prescribes classes of persons to be notified. The application of paragraph 3 is complemented by paragraph 7 of article 4. The law of the State of judicial sale might prescribe additional classes of persons to be notified, for example the holder of any unregistered charge, diplomatic or consular agents of the State of registration in the State of judicial sale, or the insolvency representative (e.g. in the event of that the owner is insolvent). Nothing in the Convention displaces those requirements.

References to preparatory work

Document	*Reference*
Report of the thirty-seventh session of Working Group VI	A/CN.9/1047/Rev.1, paras. 52–53
Report of the thirty-ninth session of Working Group VI	A/CN.9/1089, para. 67
Report of the fifty-fifth session of UNCITRAL	A/77/17, para. 40

Ship registries (article 4, paragraph 3 (a))

104. Paragraph 3 (a) of article 4 requires notification of the ship registry. As noted above (para. 79), the "registry" is the entity which maintains the register. Paragraph 3 (a) refers not only to the registry maintaining the "register of ships" but also to the registry maintaining an "equivalent register in which the ship is registered". Reference to "equivalent register" is a consequence of the broad definition of "ship", which covers different types of vessels that may be registered in different registers under the law of the State of registration (see remarks above on the definition of "ship" in article 2).

105. In some States, the law may not require the ship registry to be notified and the ship registry may not have procedures in place to receive and respond to notices. Moreover, the ship registry may not have an interest in the judicial sale proceedings or in the distribution of proceeds. Nevertheless, the requirement in the Convention to notify the ship registry acknowledges the utility of alerting the ship registry to possible future action on the registration of the ship under article 7.

106. In some States, the law may make special provision for the notification of the registry so that it can *(a)* provide information that is needed for the court of judicial sale to identify other persons to be notified under that law, or *(b)* take action required to notify or otherwise advertise the sale. The Convention does not mandate either role for the registry.

107. The requirement to notify the ship registry applies regardless of the location of the registry. Accordingly, paragraph 3 (a) of article 4 requires the notice of judicial

sale to be given to the registry even if the State of registration is not party to the Convention (see remarks above on paragraph 1 (a) of article 3) or is the State of judicial sale.

References to preparatory work

Document	*Reference*
Report of the thirty-fifth session of Working Group VI	A/CN.9/973, paras. 73–74
Report of the thirty-sixth session of Working Group VI	A/CN.9/1007, para. 63
Report of the thirty-seventh session of Working Group VI	A/CN.9/1047/Rev.1, paras. 57–58

Holders of any mortgage, hypothèque or registered charge (article 4, paragraph 3(b))

108. Paragraph 3 (b) of article 4 requires notification of each holder of a mortgage, *hypothèque* or registered charge attached to the ship, but only if the relevant register (whether it be the register of ships or separate register of security interests) is "open to public inspection". The wording of this precondition is drawn directly from article 1 of the International Convention on Maritime Liens and Mortgages (1993),[27] which defines the conditions for a mortgage, *hypothèque* or registered charges to be recognized and enforceable under that convention (and thus whose holders are to be notified according to the forced sale regime under article 12 thereof). Although the wording is the same, the present Convention is not concerned with the recognition of foreign mortgages, hypothèques or charges; the precondition in paragraph 3 (b) of article 4 should be understood in the context of the Convention and in view of the primary purpose of the notice requirements to alert creditors to the impending sale and eventual distribution of proceeds (as noted in para. 95 above).

109. Public access to the register is a common feature of registry practice both in relation to registers of ships and separate registers of security interests. The practice is reflected in article 6, paragraph 3, of the United Nations Convention on Conditions for Registration of Ships (1986)[28] as well as the Model Registry Provisions of the UNCITRAL Model Law on Secured Transactions.[29] The Convention does not elaborate on the depth and breadth of the enquiry required to determine whether a register is "open to public inspection". As elaborated in the International Convention on Maritime Liens and Mortgages (1993), registers "open to public inspection" include those that issue extracts from the register (e.g., a record of the particulars of any mortgage, *hypothèque* or registered charge effected on a ship) and those that provide

[27] See note 2 above.

[28] See note 22 above.

[29] *UNCITRAL Model Law on Secured Transactions* (2016), United Nations publication, Sales No. E.17.V.1.

copies of those instruments. Paragraph 3 (b) of article 4 does not presuppose that such extracts and copies have in fact been obtained, nor does it prescribe the persons by whom such extracts and copies are obtainable. It should thus not be understood as waiving the requirement to notify a holder of a mortgage, *hypothèque* or registered charge for a particular judicial sale merely because the relevant registry only issues extracts and not copies (or vice versa). Moreover, a register should not fail to satisfy the precondition merely because the regulations and procedures of the State of registration prescribe a fee or form requirements for requesting an extract from the register or copy of a registrable instrument, or require the person making the request to demonstrate a legitimate interest in accessing the register.

Reference to preparatory work

Document	*Reference*
Report of the thirty-seventh session of Working Group VI	A/CN.9/1047/Rev.1, para. 55
Report of the thirty-eighth session of Working Group VI	A/CN.9/1053, para. 48

Holders of any maritime lien (article 4, paragraph 3 (c))

110. Paragraph 3 (c) of article 4 requires notification of each holder of a maritime lien attached to the ship, but only if *(a)* the holder has notified the court of judicial sale (or other public authority conducting the judicial sale) of the claim secured by the maritime lien, and *(b)* the holder has done so "in accordance with the regulations and procedures of the State of judicial sale".

111. The first precondition is inspired by article 11, paragraph 1 (c), of the International Convention on Maritime Liens and Mortgages (1993)[30] but differs insofar as it identifies the person that is required to notify the court of judicial sale of the claim secured by the maritime lien. Various procedures exist under domestic law by which a claim may be notified to the court of judicial sale, but not all provide for the claim to be notified by the holder of the maritime lien. In some jurisdictions, the party requesting the judicial sale is required to inform the court of any maritime lien that is known to the party. In several jurisdictions, the procedure for filing a caveat (or caution) with the court against release of the ship after its arrest allows a holder of a maritime lien to notify the court of particulars of its claim. In other jurisdictions, a special procedure exists for a holder (among other holders of unregistered charges) to intervene in the judicial sale proceedings. Nothing in paragraph 3 (c) of article 4 requires the notice to the court to be in any particular form.

112. The second precondition acknowledges that not all jurisdictions have procedures in place for the court to receive notices from the holders of maritime liens, particularly where the holder is not the party requesting the judicial sale. In some jurisdictions, the holder of a maritime lien will only address the court of judicial

[30] See note 2 above.

sale in proceedings related to the distribution of proceeds once the judicial sale is completed. Nothing in paragraph 3 (c) of article 4 requires the State of judicial sale to amend its regulations and procedures for conducting judicial sales to accommodate the notification of claims. Moreover, the paragraph does not require the holder of a maritime lien to be notified merely because it has given the court an ad hoc or informal notice that is not provided for under the applicable regulations and procedures.

References to preparatory work

Document	*Reference*
Report of the thirty-fifth session of Working Group VI	A/CN.9/973, para. 70
Report of the thirty-seventh session of Working Group VI	A/CN.9/1047/Rev.1, paras. 51–54
Report of the thirty-ninth session of Working Group VI	A/CN.9/1089, paras. 64–66

Shipowners (article 4, paragraph 3 (d))

113. Paragraph 3 (d) of article 4 requires notification of the owner of the ship "for the time being". By virtue of article 4, paragraph 2, that time is the time at which the judicial sale is notified. As noted above (para. 69), more than one person may be the owner.

Reference to preparatory work

Document	*Reference*
Report of the fifty-fifth session of UNCITRAL	A/77/17, para. 40

Bareboat charterers and bareboat charter registries (article 4, paragraph 3 (e))

114. Paragraph 3 (e) of article 4 applies only if the ship has been granted bareboat charter-in registration (i.e. a State other than the State of registration has granted the ship the right to fly its flag). If it applies, subparagraph (i) requires notification of the person registered as the bareboat charterer of the ship in the bareboat charter register, while subparagraph (ii) requires notification of the bareboat charter registry.

115. Paragraph 3 (e) of article 4 acknowledges that the practice of bareboat charter registration differs between States. References to the person "registered", the "register", "registration" and the "registry" therefore cover situations in which particulars of the bareboat charter arrangement are recorded in a record other than a "register". Moreover, that record may not be the same as the register of ships and may be maintained by an entity other than the ship registry of the State of bareboat charter-in registration.

116. Paragraph 3 (e) of article 4 applies regardless of whether the law of the State of judicial sale recognizes the practice of bareboat charter registration.

References to preparatory work

Document	*Reference*
Report of the thirty-sixth session of Working Group VI	A/CN.9/1007, para. 63
Report of the thirty-ninth session of Working Group VI	A/CN.9/1089, para. 68

Content of the notice and methods of notification (article 4, paragraph 4)

117. If paragraph 3 of article 4 requires the notice of judicial sale to be given to prescribed classes of persons, paragraph 4 of article 4 addresses the content of the notice and how it is to be given.

Content of the notice

118. The notice of judicial sale is to contain the minimum information itemized in annex I to the Convention. Recalling that the primary purpose of the notice requirements in the Convention is to alert creditors to the impending sale and eventual distribution of proceeds, the items in annex I are designed to ensure that the notice of judicial sale contains the essential information that a creditor would need to assert its rights. Annex I does not contain a model form, and nothing in the Convention prevents the use of an existing form that is prescribed under the law of the State of judicial sale. Moreover, nothing in the Convention prevents the inclusion of other information in the notice of judicial sale, such as information required by the law of the State of judicial sale.

119. As noted above (para. 38), item 3 of annex I refers to the court (or other public authority) rather than the judicial officer appointed to carry out the public auction (if any). Item 7 refers to the identifier issued under the IMO ship identification number scheme. Item 8 is relevant if no IMO number is issued. Other identifying information referred to in that item could include the name of the shipbuilder, the time and place of shipbuilding, and recent photographs of the ship.

120. Item 11 of annex I is relevant only for a judicial sale carried out by public auction, in which case item 12 is not relevant. Item 11 refers to the anticipated date, time and place of the auction. It thus acknowledges that the date, time or place might not be set at the time of notification or might be subject to change. Unlike the International Convention on Maritime Liens and Mortgages (1993),[31] the Convention does not

[31] See note 2 above.

require a follow-up notice to be given once the date, time and place of the auction are set. Moreover, item 11 is compatible with judicial sales which are carried out using an online platform and open for remote bidding over a period of time. As noted above (para. 36), if the judicial sale is carried out by public tender, the notice is instead to contain the anticipated date, time and place of the submission of bids.

121. Item 12 of annex I is relevant only for a judicial sale carried out by private treaty. It acknowledges that, owing to the nature of private treaty sales, only limited information might be available about the sale at the time of notification, as ordered by the supervising court.

122. Item 13 of annex I refers to either a statement confirming that the judicial sale will confer clean title or a statement of the circumstances under which the judicial sale would not confer clean title. The item thus acknowledges that, for some jurisdictions, the notice may be given at a time in the judicial sale proceedings at which it is not yet known whether the sale will result in the conferral of clean title (see para. 92). Item 14 of annex I refers to other information required by the law of the State of judicial sale, in particular information to protect the interests of the person receiving the notice. The item is inspired by article 11, paragraph 2, of the International Convention on Maritime Liens and Mortgages (1993).[32] Depending on the law of the State of judicial sale, such information might include information about challenging the judicial sale or about participating in subsequent proceedings for the distribution of proceeds.

Methods of notification

123. Paragraph 4 of article 4 defers to the law of the State of judicial sale on other matters related to the manner and form of notification. Accordingly, the law of the State of judicial sale determines the notice period, method of notification, form of the notice, and the persons responsible for giving the notice. That law also determines the language of the notice, although paragraph 6 of article 4 prescribes language requirements for the minimum information when transmitting the notice to the repository.

124. With regard to the method of notification, the law of the State of judicial sale might apply standard procedures for the service of judicial documents to the notice of judicial sale. The default method of service under those procedures typically requires the notice of judicial sale to be given personally (e.g. by hand to the person being notified or their representative). If the default method is not possible or feasible (e.g. due to an evasive addressee or in view of the state of the ship and its crew), the procedures might allow the person giving notice to resort to an alternative method of service, by which the notice is given by post or by email or some other form of electronic

[32] See note 2 above.

communication addressed to the person with confirmation of receipt. To that end, the notification requirements in the Convention are formulated in medium-neutral terms and thus accommodate the issuance and transmission of a notice of judicial sale in electronic form. Failing that, the procedures might allow the notice to be given by public announcement. In those circumstances, a judicial sale should not be regarded as failing to comply with the notice requirements under the Convention merely because the notice of judicial sale was not given "to" the person concerned.

125. The Convention is thus less prescriptive than article 11, paragraph 3, of the International Convention on Maritime Liens and Mortgages (1993),[33] which requires a notice of forced sale to be "either given by registered mail or given by any electronic or other appropriate means which provide confirmation of receipt". Nothing in the Convention requires confirmation of receipt; as noted above (para. 124), any such requirement is a matter for the law of the State of judicial sale, and that law may require the notice to be given personally without the involvement of a postal or email service.

126. With regard to responsibility for giving the notice, the Convention accommodates circumstances in which the law of the State of judicial sale requires the notice to be given by the court of judicial sale (or other public authority conducting the judicial sale), by a judicial officer, or by a party to the proceedings or their representative. Accordingly, a judicial sale does not fail to comply with the notice requirements under the Convention merely because of the identity of the person giving the notice.

127. Consistent with the international nature of shipping, it is anticipated that there may be occasion for the notice of judicial sale to be transmitted outside the State of judicial sale for service in the territory of another State (e.g. the State of registration). Paragraph 4 of article 4 manifests the consent of a State Party to the notice of judicial sale being served in its territory. Accordingly, a judicial sale does not fail to comply with the notice requirements under the Convention merely because the notice of judicial sale is given to a person located in the territory of a State other than the State of judicial sale, and the notice is given in a manner that is not provided for under the law of that place.

128. The transmission of the notice of judicial sale for service abroad may engage the application of a treaty between the State of judicial sale and the other State on judicial assistance in matters relating to the service of judicial documents (see further remarks below on article 13, paragraph 2).

---

[33] See note 2 above.

References to preparatory work

Document	*Reference*
Report of the thirty-fifth session of Working Group VI	A/CN.9/973, paras. 18, 22, 71, 75
Report of the thirty-sixth session of Working Group VI	A/CN.9/1007, paras. 64–66
Report of the thirty-seventh session of Working Group VI	A/CN.9/1047/Rev.1, paras. 59, 61–62
Report of the thirty-ninth session of Working Group VI	A/CN.9/1089, paras. 73–80
Report of the fortieth session of Working Group VI	A/CN.9/1095, paras. 102–106
Report of the fifty-fifth session of UNCITRAL	A/77/17, paras. 38, 44–45

Public advertisement (article 4, paragraph 5)

129. The notice of judicial sale is published by announcement in the press or other publication available in the State of judicial sale. It is also transmitted to the repository. Paragraph 5 of article 4 applies in addition to – and not as an alternative to – the requirement in paragraph 3 to notify the prescribed classes of persons. By virtue of paragraph 4 of article 4, the notice that is published and the notice that is transmitted are to contain the information itemized in annex I to the Convention.

Announcement in the press or other publication (article 4, paragraph 5 (a))

130. Paragraph 5 (a) of article 4 is concerned with the fact of publication and not with the modalities for publication, such as the selection of newspaper or periodical by which the notice of judicial sale is to be published. In accordance with paragraph 4 of article 4, those modalities are left to the law of the State of judicial sale.

131. As noted above (see remarks above on article 4, paragraph 1), the notification requirements acknowledge the use of online tools to track ships and provide information on their arrest and impending sale. Like the other notification requirements, paragraph 5 of article 4 is formulated in medium-neutral terms and thus accommodates the publication of the notice in newspapers and other periodicals that are circulated in electronic form. Accordingly, a judicial sale does not fail to comply with the notice requirements under the Convention merely because the notice is published in electronic form.

132. Paragraph 5 (a) of article 4 offers a choice between two options, namely *(a)* publication by "announcement in the press" and *(b)* publication by "other publication available in the State of judicial sale". The first option typically entails placing an advertisement in a newspaper containing the notice of judicial sale, as opposed to posting an announcement to a noticeboard or website of the court of judicial sale or

other person responsible for notification. Paragraph 5 (a) does not prescribe any requirements regarding circulation if the first option is chosen. The second option typically entails an advertisement placed in a periodical, including an online journal or newsletter published for the shipping industry. Paragraph 5 (a) requires the publication to be "available in the State of judicial sale" if the second option is chosen. For the purposes of that requirement, it does not matter whether the publication is published in the State of judicial sale or abroad. What matters is whether the publication is "available" in the State of judicial sale, which typically entails the circulation of a paper-based publication or accessibility of an online publication in that State.

133. In keeping with the purpose of the notice requirements to alert creditors to the impending sale and eventual distribution of proceeds, and given the international nature of shipping, it is advisable that, whichever option is chosen, the selected newspaper or periodical should be widely available outside the State of judicial sale.

Transmission of notice to repository (article 4, paragraph 5 (b))

134. Paragraph 5 (b) of article 4 is concerned with the fact of transmission and not with the modalities of transmission, such as the method used and person responsible for transmitting the notice to the repository. Those modalities are left to the law of the State of judicial sale, in accordance with paragraph 4 of article 4, and the procedures put in place by the repository in performing its functions under article 11. In keeping with the purpose of the notice requirements to alert creditors to the impending sale and eventual distribution of proceeds, what matters is that the content of the notice is received in a format that can be published by the repository (see remarks below on article 11).

References to preparatory work

Document	*Reference*
Report of the thirty-sixth session of Working Group VI	A/CN.9/1007, para. 66
Report of the thirty-seventh session of Working Group VI	A/CN.9/1047/Rev.1, para. 63
Report of the thirty-ninth session of Working Group VI	A/CN.9/1089, paras. 82–84, 87–88

Language requirements when transmitting notice to repository (article 4, paragraph 6)

135. When transmitted to the repository under paragraph 5 (b) of article 4, the notice of judicial sale is to be accompanied by a translation of the information itemized in annex I to the Convention (i.e. the minimum information to be contained in the notice by virtue of article 4, paragraph 4). The requirement in paragraph 6 of article 4 does not apply when the notice is given under paragraph 3; the words "for

the purpose of communicating the notice to the repository" are intended to clarify that it only applies when the notice is transmitted under paragraph 5 (b). Accordingly, a judicial sale does not fail to comply with the notice requirements under the Convention merely because the notice of judicial sale that is given under paragraph 3 is only in the language of the court of judicial sale and without an accompanying translation. Nevertheless, the person giving the notice under paragraph 3 is encouraged to accompany the notice with a translation of the information itemized in annex I to the Convention, particularly because the translation will eventually need to be transmitted to the repository under paragraph 6.

136. Paragraph 6 of article 4 reflects the balance between due process towards creditors and the expediency required in judicial sale proceedings (see remarks above on article 4, paragraph 1). On the one hand, due process demands that information should be communicated in a manner that can be readily understood by the addressee, including in a language that the addressee knows. This is particularly relevant in international shipping, where creditors can be dispersed around the globe and might not know the language of the court of judicial sale. On the other hand, expediency demands that the judicial sale procedure should not be overburdened by the time and cost of translating documents into multiple languages, let alone identifying the language that is known to each person that is to be notified. It recognizes that most creditors in the international shipping industry are likely to know at least one of the working languages of the repository, which, at the time that the Convention was being prepared, were English, French and Spanish. It also recognizes that the burden of translation will be significantly reduced by focusing on the minimum information itemized in annex I to the Convention. That information is likely to be concise and the translation will already benefit from the text of each item heading being available in English, French and Spanish, among the other official languages of the United Nations in which the text of the Convention is adopted. Indeed, some of the information, such as the "reference number or other identifier for the sale procedure" may require little or no translation.

137. As with transmitting the notice of judicial sale under paragraph 5 (b), the modalities for transmitting the accompanying translation are left to the law of the State of judicial sale and the procedures of the repository. Paragraph 6 does not require the translation to be certified.

References to preparatory work

Document	*Reference*
Report of the thirty-seventh session of Working Group VI	A/CN.9/1047/Rev.1, para. 64
Report of the thirty-ninth session of Working Group VI	A/CN.9/1089, paras. 69–72
Report of the fortieth session of Working Group VI	A/CN.9/1095, paras. 100–101
Report of the fifty-fifth session of UNCITRAL	A/77/17, para. 42

Reliance on registry information (article 4, paragraph 7)

138. While the Convention does not prescribe the method for notification, compliance with paragraph 3 of article 4 typically involves identifying the persons within each prescribed class and determining their name and address. The identity, name and address of holders of any mortgage, *hypothèque* or registered charge, the shipowner and the bareboat charterer are recorded in the register of ships of the State of registration or in any separate register of security interests or bareboat charter-in register. By virtue of the requirement for many of those registers to be open to public inspection, which stems from the definition of "ship" in article 2 and the precondition in paragraph 3 (b) of article 4, the person giving the notice should be in a position to obtain this information from the relevant registry. The identity, name and address of holders of any maritime lien are recorded in the notice given to the court under paragraph 3 (c) of article 4.

139. In that context, the effect of paragraph 7 of article 4 is that the person responsible for notification is not required to consult any other source of information to identify or to determine the accuracy or currency of the name and address of each person to be notified. In so doing, the Convention provides certainty for the person giving the notice of judicial sale, while avoiding needless challenges to the international effect of a judicial sale based on non-compliance with the notification requirements. Paragraph 7 reflects the principle that the person to be notified should bear the risk of inaccurate information in the register, or in the notice given to the court, as that person has greater control over the accuracy and currency of the information.

140. Nothing in paragraph 7 of article 4 precludes the person giving the notice from using other sources of information, including to comply with domestic law requirements. Moreover, paragraph 7 does not oblige the person to search or inspect the register, nor oblige the relevant registry to provide access to the register (as noted in para. 138 above, the requirement for the register to be open to public inspection stems from other provisions of the Convention). Paragraph 7 also does not oblige the court of judicial sale to provide access to notices received from any holder of a maritime lien, although such a procedure might need to be legally enabled to implement the Convention, particularly in those jurisdictions in which the person giving the notice is not the court of judicial sale. In jurisdictions in which the court of judicial sale or a judicial officer gives the notice, cross-border communication between authorities that is provided for under article 12 may assist the operation of paragraph 7.

141. As noted above (para. 78), the term "person" in the chapeau of paragraph 7 of article 4 should be understood broadly to encompass the ship registry and bareboat charter registry.

References to preparatory work

Document	*Reference*
Report of the thirty-eighth session of Working Group VI	A/CN.9/1053, para. 18
Report of the thirty-ninth session of Working Group VI	A/CN.9/1089, para. 63
Report of the fortieth session of Working Group VI	A/CN.9/1095, paras. 96–98
Report of the fifty-fifth session of UNCITRAL	A/77/17, para. 43

Article 5. Certificate of judicial sale

Purpose of the certificate

142. The certificate of judicial sale plays a central role in the overall operation of the Convention regime. It serves two crucial purposes: first, it secures the international effects of the judicial sale in that *(a)* its issuance triggers the basic rule in article 6, and *(b)* its production triggers action on registration under article 7 and the prohibition of arrest under article 8; second, it operationalizes the safeguards under the Convention, which are translated into conditions for the issuance of the certificate under article 5. Nonetheless, the role of the certificate is limited to the purpose of the Convention which, as noted in article 1, is to govern the effects of a judicial sale that confers clean title. In particular, the Convention does not establish the certificate of judicial sale as a document of title.

143. Article 5 addresses a range of matters relating to the issuance, form, content and legal value of the certificate. It is complemented by article 9, which addresses jurisdiction to review the issuance of the certificate.

References to preparatory work

Document	*Reference*
Report of the thirty-fifth session of Working Group VI	A/CN.9/973, para. 41
Report of the thirty-seventh session of Working Group VI	A/CN.9/1047/Rev.1, para. 70
Report of the fortieth session of Working Group VI	A/CN.9/1095, para. 46

Issuing authority (article 5, paragraph 1)

144. The certificate of judicial sale is issued either *(a)* by the court or other public authority that conducted the judicial sale, or *(b)* by another competent authority of the State of judicial sale. Such other authority could be the judicial officer or other person appointed by the court of judicial sale to carry out the public auction, or

another authority not involved in conducting the judicial sale. The designation of the issuing authority is a matter for the law of the State of judicial sale. Competence to issue the certificate may be conferred on a single authority or on multiple authorities.

References to preparatory work

Document	*Reference*
Report of the thirty-fifth session of Working Group VI	A/CN.9/973, para. 84
Report of the thirty-sixth session of Working Group VI	A/CN.9/1007, para. 91
Report of the thirty-ninth session of Working Group VI	A/CN.9/1089, paras. 98–99
Report of the fifty-fifth session of UNCITRAL	A/77/17, para. 47

Procedure for issuance (article 5, paragraph 1)

145. The competent authority issues the certificate of judicial sale to the purchaser "in accordance with its regulations and procedures". Those regulations and procedures are a matter for the law of the State of judicial sale. In the context of paragraph 1 of article 5, they typically provide for a range of matters relating to procedure, including the time frame for issuance, whether the issuing authority acts on application (e.g. the certificate is issued at the request of the purchaser) or on its own motion (e.g. the certificate is issued automatically), whether a fee can be charged for issuing the certificate, whether the certificate can be issued to the purchaser's representative or nominee, and the standard of review required to determine whether the conditions for issuance have been met. The regulations and procedures might also provide for the issuance of multiple certificates for the same judicial sale, as well as the issuance of certificates in paper or electronic form (see remarks below on article 5, paragraph 6).

References to preparatory work

Document	*Reference*
Report of the thirty-sixth session of Working Group VI	A/CN.9/1007, paras. 90–91
Report of the thirty-eighth session of Working Group VI	A/CN.9/1053, paras. 24–25
Report of the thirty-ninth session of Working Group VI	A/CN.9/1089, para. 100

Conditions for issuance (article 5, paragraph 1)

146. A certificate of judicial sale is issued if the following conditions are met:

(*a*) The judicial sale has reached completion;

(*b*) The judicial sale has conferred clean title to the ship under the law of the State of judicial sale;

(*c*) The judicial sale was conducted in accordance with the requirements of the law of the State of judicial sale;

(*d*) The judicial sale was conducted in accordance with the requirements of the Convention.

Condition 1 – completion of the judicial sale

147. The term "completion" gives effect to the principle of finality, according to which the Convention regime should only apply to judicial sales for which the procedure has been concluded and is no longer subject to ordinary review, whether by appeal against an order of the court of judicial sale or otherwise, even if additional formalities remain to be taken (e.g. action under article 7). The Convention purposefully does not define "completion" since terms commonly used to describe finality in the context of judgments, such as "final and conclusive", "effective and enforceable" and "no longer subject to appeal", might not find uniform meaning. Instead, consistent with the rule in paragraph 1 of article 4, the Convention defers to the law of the State of judicial sale for determining when a judicial sale has reached completion (e.g. the date of judicial sale, such as the date of the public auction or the date on which the sale is approved or confirmed by the court of judicial sale).

Condition 2 – conferral of clean title

148. Whether or not a judicial sale confers clean title is a matter for the law of the State of judicial sale (see remarks above on the definition of "clean title" in article 2). The conferral of clean title could coincide with the completion of the judicial sale.

Condition 3 – compliance with requirements of the law of the State of judicial sale

149. As noted above (para. 145), the regulations and procedures of the issuing authority determine the standard of review required to determine whether the conditions for issuance have been met. In determining whether condition 3 is met, the Convention does not require the issuing authority to carry out a full review of the judicial sale. Such a requirement would be inconsistent with the principle of finality reflected in condition 1, as well as with the objective of the Convention to leave the procedure of judicial sales to domestic law.

Condition 4 – compliance with requirements of the Convention

150. The final condition for issuance is concerned with compliance with the notice requirements in paragraph 3 and following of article 4.

151. It is conceivable that the condition could encompass a review of whether the judicial sale and the ship correspond with the definitions of those terms in article 2. However, it does not encompass a review of whether the judicial sale falls within the scope of application of the Convention under article 3, as its application necessarily assumes that the Convention applies.

References to preparatory work

Document	*Reference*
Report of the thirty-sixth session of Working Group VI	A/CN.9/1007, para. 90
Report of the thirty-seventh session of Working Group VI	A/CN.9/1047/Rev.1, paras. 65–69
Report of the thirty-eighth session of Working Group VI	A/CN.9/1053, paras. 22–23, 26
Report of the thirty-ninth session of Working Group VI	A/CN.9/1089, paras. 92–97
Report of the fifty-fifth session of UNCITRAL	A/77/17, para. 32

Form and content of the certificate (article 5, paragraph 2)

152. The certificate of judicial sale is issued substantially in the form of the model contained in annex II to the Convention. A requirement to use a model form for certificates is not unusual in international conventions and promotes standardization and thus greater acceptance of the certificate when produced abroad. The model contained in annex II sets out the basic layout for the content of the certificate. The requirement for the certificate to the "substantially" in the form of the model emphasizes that the Convention does not mandate a particular design for the certificate nor the use of a particular language for the item headings or for filling in the corresponding blanks. The certificate of judicial sale will typically be issued in the language of the issuing authority and may be issued in multiple languages.

153. The certificate of judicial sale contains the information prescribed in paragraph 2 of article 5, which corresponds to the information itemized in the model. The certification in the headnote of the model corresponds to the information prescribed in paragraphs 2 (a) and 2 (b), which in turn is designed to match the conditions for issuance in article 5, paragraph 1. As noted above (para. 144), the authority referred to in item 2 of the model and paragraph 2 (d) of article 5 (i.e. the issuing authority) may be the same as the authority referred to in item 3.1 of the model and paragraph 2 (e) of article 5 (i.e. the court or other public authority that conducted the judicial sale).

154. Both the model and paragraph 2 (k) of article 5 refer to the inclusion of the signature or stamp of the issuing authority or "other confirmation of authenticity of the certificate". Confirmation of authenticity provides assurance as to the origin of the certificate (i.e. that it was issued by the issuing authority). The most common device used to confirm authenticity besides a signature or stamp is a seal, but in the case of electronic certificates, other devices are also possible. The Convention does not mandate the use of any device other than a signature or stamp. Moreover, the reference to "other confirmation of authenticity of the certificate" is not intended to suggest any additional formality to authenticate the certificate, such as legalization (see further remarks below on article 5, paragraph 4).

References to preparatory work

Document	*Reference*
Report of the thirty-fifth session of Working Group VI	A/CN.9/973, paras. 44–45, 47, 57
Report of the thirty-sixth session of Working Group VI	A/CN.9/1007, para. 93
Report of the thirty-seventh session of Working Group VI	A/CN.9/1047/Rev.1, paras. 71–72
Report of the thirty-ninth session of Working Group VI	A/CN.9/1089, paras. 103–105
Report of the fortieth session of Working Group VI	A/CN.9/1095, para. 109
Report of the fifty-fifth session of UNCITRAL	A/77/17, paras. 46, 48

Transmission of certificate to repository (article 5, paragraph 3)

155. The certificate is issued to the purchaser, who will use it, as need be, to prompt action on registration of the ship under article 7 and to prohibit arrest of the ship under article 8. In addition, the certificate is transmitted to the repository. As with paragraph 5 (b) of article 4, paragraph 3 of article 5 is concerned with the fact of transmission and not with the modalities of transmission, such as the method used and person responsible for transmitting the certificate to the repository. Those modalities are left to the law of the State of judicial sale and the procedures put in place by the repository in performing its functions under article 11 (see remarks below on article 11).

156. In practice, it may be more convenient for a copy of the certificate to be transmitted to the repository. While paragraph 3 of article 5 refers to "the" certificate, it should not be understood as preventing a copy (including an electronic copy) of the certificate from being transmitted to the repository.

References to preparatory work

Document	*Reference*
Report of the thirty-ninth session of Working Group VI	A/CN.9/1089, paras. 106–107
Report of the fortieth session of Working Group VI	A/CN.9/1095, para. 108

No legalization (article 5, paragraph 4)

157. Consistent with the international nature of shipping, it is anticipated that the certificate of judicial sale will be produced in a State other than the State in which it is issued. That other State may have a practice of requiring foreign public documents to be legalized. "Legalization" is a term often used for the formality by which a diplomatic or consular agent of the State in which the document is to be produced certifies the authenticity of the signature, the capacity in which the person signing the document has acted and, where appropriate, the identity of the seal or stamp on the document. Legalization procedures can be cumbersome and time-consuming owing to the involvement of various authorities at different levels in both the State in which the document is issued and the State in which it is to be produced.

158. In the interests of expediency, paragraph 4 of article 5 exempts the certificate of judicial sale from legalization. It also exempts the certificate from any "similar formality" to legalization. The most notable example of such a formality is the addition of a certificate – known as an "Apostille" – issued under the Hague Convention Abolishing the Requirement of Legalisation for Foreign Public Documents (1961)[34] by the State in which the document is issued.

159. The effect of paragraph 4 of article 5 is that the registry or other competent authority may not require a foreign certificate of judicial sale to be legalized or produced with an Apostille as a condition for taking action under article 7, nor may the court or other judicial authority do so as a condition for taking action under article 8. If the authority has doubts about the authenticity of the document produced, it can verify the issuance of the certificate by communicating with the issuing authority using the contact details included for that purpose in the certificate, as provided for in article 12, or compare the certificate with the certificate published by the repository. Nothing in the Convention prevents the authority from rejecting a document purporting to be a certificate issued under the Convention because it is not authentic. However, by virtue of article 9, it is not the role of the authority to ascertain whether the conditions for issuance of a certificate under the Convention have been met or whether the certificate is otherwise valid.

[34] United Nations, *Treaty Series*, vol. 527, No. 7625.

160. The exemption in paragraph 4 of article 5 is extended to "any translation" of the certificate of judicial sale. Under paragraph 3 of article 7 and paragraph 3 of article 8, the authority to which the certificate is submitted may request production of a certified translation. It is conceivable that, if the authority accepts a certified translation done in another State (e.g. in the State of judicial sale), the certified translation itself would be treated as a foreign public document that is subject to legalization. In those circumstances, exempting only the certificate of judicial sale from legalization would not achieve the expediency that paragraph 4 of article 5 pursues. For more on certified translations, see remarks below on article 7, paragraph 3.

References to preparatory work

Document	*Reference*
Report of the thirty-fifth session of Working Group VI	A/CN.9/973, para. 45
Report of the thirty-eighth session of Working Group VI	A/CN.9/1053, paras. 33–34
Report of the thirty-ninth session of Working Group VI	A/CN.9/1089, para. 108
Report of the fortieth session of Working Group VI	A/CN.9/1095, paras. 90–91
Report of the fifty-fifth session of UNCITRAL	A/77/17, paras. 80–82

Evidentiary value (article 5, paragraph 5)

161. The production of the certificate of judicial sale triggers action on registration under article 7 and the prohibition of arrest under article 8. For those provisions to be effective, the content of the certificate needs to be accepted by the authorities to which the certificate is produced. In other words, the content of the certificate needs to have evidentiary value.

162. By virtue of paragraph 5 of article 5, the information contained in the certificate of judicial sale is "sufficient evidence" of the matters certified. An authority to which the certificate is produced may not request additional information to identify the ship or to establish that the ship was sold by judicial sale, that the sale was conducted in accordance with the requirements of the law of the State of judicial sale and the requirements of the Convention, or that the judicial sale conferred clean title to the ship on the purchaser.

163. Paragraph 5 of article 5 does not require the information contained in the certificate of judicial sale to be treated as conclusive or irrefutable evidence. For example, it does not prevent an authority from considering other information as to the matters certified. In particular, it would not prevent a court in the State of judicial sale exercising jurisdiction under article 9 from considering information outside the certificate in hearing an application to avoid the judicial sale or to challenge the

issuance of judicial sale certificate, nor would it prevent a court in another State Party from considering information outside the certificate in hearing an application invoking the public policy ground under article 10. This is confirmed by the inclusion of the words "without prejudice to articles 9 and 10" in paragraph 5 of article 5.

Reference to preparatory work

Document	*Reference*
Report of the thirty-ninth session of Working Group VI	A/CN.9/1089, paras. 109–112

Electronic form (article 5, paragraphs 6 and 7)

164. The certificate of judicial sale may be issued electronically and cannot be rejected merely because it is in electronic form. While paragraph 2 of article 5 is formulated in medium-neutral terms, the Convention makes special provision in paragraphs 6 and 7 of article 5 for the issuance and acceptance of electronic certificates. Those provisions are modelled on rules contained in the United Nations Convention on the Use of Electronic Communications in International Contracts (2005) (hereinafter "Electronic Communications Convention").[35]

165. Nothing in the Convention prevents a certificate from being issued in both electronic and paper form for the same judicial sale (i.e. multiple certificates). Nor does it oblige or authorize the competent authority to issue certificates in electronic form. Those matters are left to the regulations and procedures of the issuing authority under the law of the State of judicial sale.

Requirements for electronic certificates (article 5, paragraph 6)

166. Paragraph 6 of article 5 is modelled on the rules in article 9 of the Electronic Communications Convention, which establish functional equivalence between paper-based and electronic communications with respect to legal requirements of recordation, authenticity and integrity. Those requirements are translated into the conditions set out in paragraph 6 (a) to (c), respectively. The term "electronic record" is not defined in the Convention and should be given the same meaning as an "electronic communication" under the Electronic Communications Convention or an "electronic record" under the UNCITRAL Model Law on Electronic Transferable Records.[36] Article 2 of the Model Law defines "electronic record" to

[35] United Nations, *Treaty Series*, vol. 2898, No. 50525.

[36] *UNCITRAL Model Law on Electronic Transferable Records* (2017), United Nations publication, Sales No. E.17.V.5.

mean “information generated, communicated, received or stored by electronic means, including, where appropriate, all information logically associated with or otherwise linked together so as to become part of the record, whether generated contemporaneously or not”.

167. Paragraph 6 (a) requires information contained in an electronic certificate of judicial sale to be “accessible so as to be usable for subsequent reference”. This condition, which is modelled on article 9, paragraph 2, of the Electronic Communications Convention, establishes equivalence for the function of a paper document in recording information in writing (i.e. in a format that can be read and can thus allow the information to be recalled). As stated in the explanatory note on the Electronic Communications Convention, the word “accessible” is intended to imply that information in the form of computer data should be readable and interpretable, and that the software that might be necessary to render such information readable should be retained, while the word “usable” is intended to cover both human use and computer processing.[37]

168. Paragraph 6 (b) requires the use of a reliable method to identify the issuing authority. While the content of the certificate itself identifies the issuing authority by name, this condition, which is modelled on article 9, paragraph 3, of the Electronic Communications Convention, establishes equivalence for the function of a signature or stamp in confirming the authenticity of a paper document (i.e. that it was issued by the issuing authority). Unlike the Electronic Communications Convention, paragraph 6 (b) does not require the electronic certificate to indicate the authority’s intention in respect of the content of the certificate. In the context of the Convention, identifying the authority issuing the certificate is sufficient both to identify the authority and to associate it with the content of the certificate.

169. Paragraph 6 (c) requires the use of a reliable method to detect any alteration to the electronic record after the time it was generated. This condition establishes equivalence for the function of the original of a paper document in allowing the integrity of the certificate to be confirmed (i.e. whether its content has remained unchanged since being issued). It is modelled on article 9, paragraph 4 (a), read with article 9, paragraph 5, of the Electronic Communications Convention, but has been reformulated to maintain consistency with paragraph 6 (b).

170. Paragraph 6 (b) and (c) require the use of a “reliable method” to fulfil the functions described therein. Whether a method is reliable depends on the circumstances and not on the use of a particular technology. Relevant considerations include international standards and practices. In some jurisdictions, the issuing authority will be required by law to use an approved method to issue electronic

[37] *United Nations Convention on the Use of Electronic Communications in International Contracts* (2007), United Nations publication, Sales No. E.07.V.2, para. 146.

certificates, whereas in others, the issuing authority can decide the method to use. In both cases, paragraph 6 provides for the reliability of the method to be determined on a case-by-case basis, which necessarily implies an enquiry after the certificate is issued and only if the issue arises.

Acceptance of electronic certificates (article 5, paragraph 7)

171. If the requirements of paragraph 6 of article 5 are satisfied, the electronic certificate is a certificate of judicial sale for the purposes of the Convention and must be accepted as such. For additional certainty, paragraph 7 of article 5 reinforces that principle by providing that an electronic certificate cannot be rejected merely because it is in electronic form. It is modelled on article 8, paragraph 1, of the Electronic Communications Convention, which embodies the principle of non-discrimination against the use of electronic means. Nothing in paragraph 7 of article 5 obliges a court or other authority of a State Party to give effect to an electronic record purporting to be a certificate of judicial sale issued under the Convention if the court finds that the record does not comply with the requirements of paragraph 6.

References to preparatory work

Document	*Reference*
Report of the thirty-sixth session of Working Group VI	A/CN.9/1007, para. 92
Report of the thirty-seventh session of Working Group VI	A/CN.9/1047/Rev.1, para. 75
Report of the thirty-eighth session of Working Group VI	A/CN.9/1053, paras. 35–38
Report of the fortieth session of Working Group VI	A/CN.9/1095, paras. 12–14

Article 6. International effects of a judicial sale

172. Article 6 contains the basic rule of the Convention: a judicial sale conducted in one State Party which has the effect of conferring clean title on the purchaser has the same effect in every other State Party. Article 6 is triggered by the issuance of a certificate for the judicial sale under article 5. It requires no special procedure to give effect to the foreign judicial sale, such as confirmation by a competent court in the State in which the effects are sought to be produced. The judicial sale produces its effects automatically, i.e. by operation of law.

173. Article 6 is concerned with the effect of the foreign judicial sale in "conferring clean title". Giving effect to the conferral of clean title will most commonly be manifested in action taken on the registration of the ship under article 7 and action on the prohibition of arrest of the ship under article 8. However, the operation of

article 6 may be manifested in other ways (e.g. in the event of a dispute concerning ownership in the ship).

174. Article 6 and other provisions of the Convention purposefully refer to "giving effect" to a foreign judicial sale and not to the "recognition" of that sale. As noted in the remarks on article 1, the Convention is concerned with the effects of judicial sales and not with the recognition of judgments. The Convention is only concerned with the sale as a legal fact produced under the aegis of a foreign legal system. It is a device that enforces private rights; where those private rights are adjudged by a court on the merits of a claim (e.g. against the shipowner), the judicial sale becomes the measure by which the judgment is enforced. To emphasize that it is not concerned with the recognition and enforcement of foreign judgments, the Convention avoids the term "recognition". Similarly, the Convention contains no provision addressing its interaction with treaties on the recognition and enforcement of foreign judgments (cf. article 13), nor does it contain a provision preserving bases for recognizing foreign judgments under domestic law (cf. article 14).

175. If article 6 is triggered by the issuance of a certificate of judicial sale, it does not deal with the situation in which the certificate is subsequently invalidated by a court exercising jurisdiction under article 9. This is confirmed in paragraph 2 of article 15, which provides that, at most, the question of the international effect of invalidating a certificate of judicial sale is governed by the law applicable in the State in which the issue arises.

References to preparatory work

Document	*Reference*
Report of the thirty-fifth session of Working Group VI	A/CN.9/973, paras. 27, 49
Report of the thirty-sixth session of Working Group VI	A/CN.9/1007, paras. 46–47
Report of the thirty-seventh session of Working Group VI	A/CN.9/1047/Rev.1, paras. 82–83, 89
Report of the thirty-eighth session of Working Group VI	A/CN.9/1053, paras. 19–21

Article 7. Action by the registry

Actions to be taken (article 7, paragraphs 1 and 2)

176. Despite international efforts to harmonize conditions for the registration of ships, including the conclusion of the United Nations Convention on Conditions

for Registration of Ships (1986),[38] practice varies between jurisdictions. The Convention does not seek to contribute to those efforts. Rather, it identifies actions to be taken by the competent authorities in the State of registration to realize the effects of a judicial sale, as required by article 6. Those actions are prescribed in paragraph 1 of article 7. Paragraph 2 of article 7 prescribes additional action to be taken if the ship is subject to a bareboat charter arrangement.

177. Paragraphs 1 and 2 of article 7 are triggered by the production of the certificate of judicial sale and therefore only apply after completion of a judicial sale that confers clean title. They also require a request by the purchaser or subsequent purchaser (see remarks in paras. 188–192 below on procedure for taking action). The prescribed actions are required to be taken if the judicial sale is conducted in the State of registration (in the case of article 7, paragraph 1) or the State of bareboat charter-in registration (in the case of article 7, paragraph 2), or in another State Party.

178. With regard to paragraph 1 of article 7, not every sale will require all prescribed actions to be taken. For instance, if action is taken to register the ship in the name of the purchaser under paragraph 1 (c), no action would be required to delete the ship from the register under paragraph 1 (b). The non-cumulative nature of the actions prescribed follows from the requirement for the competent authority to act "at the request of the purchaser or subsequent purchaser" and is reinforced by the addition of the words "as the case may be" in the chapeau of paragraph 1. In other words, the prescribed actions are to be taken if applicable and to the extent applicable.

References to preparatory work

Document	*Reference*
Report of the thirty-fifth session of Working Group VI	A/CN.9/973, para. 48
Report of the thirty-seventh session of Working Group VI	A/CN.9/1047/Rev.1, para. 89
Report of the fifty-fifth session of UNCITRAL	A/77/17, para. 55

Deleting pre-existing mortgages, ***hypothèques*** *and registered charges (article 7, paragraph 1 (a))*

179. As noted above (para. 49), the conferral of clean title means that all pre-existing mortgages, *hypothèques* and charges cease to attach to the ship. By definition, mortgages, *hypothèques* and registered charges are registered in the State of registration. By requiring action to delete registration, paragraph 1 (a) of article 7

[38] See note 22 above.

implements the effect of the judicial sale with respect to mortgages, *hypothèques* and registered charges.

References to preparatory work

Document	*Reference*
Report of the fortieth session of Working Group VI	A/CN.9/1095, paras. 30–31
Report of the fifty-fifth session of UNCITRAL	A/77/17, para. 55

Deleting the ship from the register (article 7, paragraph 1 (b))

180. As noted above (para. 49), the conferral of clean title means that all pre-existing property rights in the ship are extinguished, including the title vested in the previous shipowner. A ship is typically registered in a State in the name of the shipowner and will not be able to be registered in another State unless the previous registration is deleted. By requiring action to delete the ship from the register and issue a certificate of deletion, paragraph 1 (b) of article 7 implements the effect of the judicial sale with respect to title and facilitates the "new" registration of the ship in another State in the event that the purchaser wishes to "reflag" the ship. However, it does not require action to register the ship in that other State, which remains a matter for the law of that State.

181. Recalling the differences in registration practice between States, the procedure for deregistering a ship might be known in the State of registration by a term other than "deletion".

References to preparatory work

Document	*Reference*
Report of the thirty-sixth session of Working Group VI	A/CN.9/1007, paras. 96–97
Report of the fortieth session of Working Group VI	A/CN.9/1095, paras. 32–34

Registering the ship in the name of the purchaser (article 7, paragraph 1(c))

182. Alternatively, the purchaser may wish the ship to remain registered in the State of registration, and wish therefore to be registered as the new owner. By requiring action to register the ship in the name of the purchaser, paragraph 1 (c) of article 7 implements the effect of the judicial sale with respect to title. This is subject, however, to a proviso that "the ship and the person in whose name the ship is to be registered meet the requirements of the law of the State of registration". This proviso acknowledges that States have different requirements for registering ships, including

requirements stemming from article 5 of the Convention on the High Seas (1958),[39] article 91 of the United Nations Convention on the Law of the Sea (1982),[40] and other domestic laws.

183. Paragraph 1 (c) extends to action taken to register the ship in the name of the "subsequent purchaser" which, by virtue of the definition of that term in article 2, is limited to the first subsequent purchaser. This limited extension reflects a balance between acknowledging the practice whereby a purchaser transfers ownership in the ship to a separate legal entity in order to meet the requirements of the law of the State of registration, on the one hand, and the burden on the registry of verifying the regularity of dealings concerning ships entered in the register, on the other hand.

References to preparatory work

Document	*Reference*
Report of the thirty-sixth session of Working Group VI	A/CN.9/1007, paras. 96–97
Report of the fortieth session of Working Group VI	A/CN.9/1095, paras. 32–34

Updating the register (article 7, paragraph 1 (d))

184. Paragraph 1 (d) of article 7 requires additional information on the judicial sale to be recorded in the register of ships or equivalent register in which the ship is registered. It is concerned with updating the register with particulars in the certificate that may not have been recorded in the register pursuant to action taken under paragraph 1 (a) to (c), such as the name of the court of judicial sale and the date of the sale. It is not concerned with updating the register to enter the ship in the register or to record the purchaser as the new owner.

References to preparatory work

Document	*Reference*
Report of the thirty-seventh session of Working Group VI	A/CN.9/1047/Rev.1, para. 96
Report of the fortieth session of Working Group VI	A/CN.9/1095, para. 35

Deleting bareboat charter registration (article 7, paragraph 2)

185. A bareboat charter grants the charterer a right of use over the ship. While the obligation under article 6 requires the State to recognize the extinguishment of any right of use so far as it can be asserted against the ship, paragraph 1 (b) of article 15 makes it clear that the Convention does not affect the ability of the bareboat

[39] United Nations, *Treaty Series*, vol. 450, No. 6465.
[40] United Nations, *Treaty Series*, vol. 1833, No. 31363.

charterer (as lessee) to assert that right in a personal claim against the former shipowner (as lessor) for breach of contract. However, the purchaser is not bound to honour the right of use of the bareboat charter (unless of course the purchaser assumes the obligations of the former owner). Paragraph 2 of article 7 implements the effective termination of the bareboat charter arrangement, by which the State of bareboat charter-in registration revokes its permission for the ship to fly its flag.

186. Recalling the differences in practice between States (see para. 77), the procedure for terminating the bareboat charter registration might be known in the State of bareboat charter-in registration by a term other than "deletion".

Reference to preparatory work

Document	*Reference*
Report of the thirty-sixth session of Working Group VI	A/CN.9/1007, para. 96

Competent authority

187. The actions prescribed in paragraphs 1 and 2 of article 7 are taken either by the registry or by another competent authority of the State of registration (in the case of article 7, paragraph 1) or the State of bareboat charter-in registration (in the case of article 7, paragraph 2). Competence to take any of the prescribed actions is a matter for the law of that State, which may confer competence on a single authority or multiple authorities, including by function of geographic location (e.g. port of registration) or type of register (e.g. register of ships, register of security interests, bareboat charter register). Nevertheless, the Convention assumes an alignment between the authorities taking action under article 7 and the registers and registries referred to in article 4, paragraph 3. Specifically:

(a) The authority competent to take action under paragraph 1 (a) of article 7 will typically be the registry that maintains the register referred to in paragraph 3 (b) of article 4;

(b) The authority competent to take action under paragraph 1 (b) and (c) of article 7 will typically be the registry referred to in paragraph 3 (a) of article 4; and

(c) The authority competent to take action under paragraph 2 of article 7 will typically be the bareboat charter registry referred to in paragraph 3 (e), subparagraph (ii), of article 4.

References to preparatory work

Document	*Reference*
Report of the thirty-sixth session of Working Group VI	A/CN.9/1007, para. 97
Report of the thirty-seventh session of Working Group VI	A/CN.9/1047/Rev.1, para. 90
Report of the fortieth session of Working Group VI	A/CN.9/1095, para. 22

Procedure for taking action

188. The competent authority takes action "in accordance with its regulations and procedures". Those regulations and procedures are a matter for the law of the State of registration. In the context of paragraph 1 of article 7, they typically provide for a range of matters relating to procedure, including how documents are to be produced and whether a fee can be charged for the action taken. However, as noted in the remarks above on paragraph 5 of article 5, those regulations and procedures cannot be applied to require additional information to establish the matters certified in the certificate of judicial sale.

189. The regulations and procedures of the competent authority should not be invoked in a manner that is inconsistent with the obligation of the State of registration under article 6 to give effect to the clean title conferred by the judicial sale. A risk of inconsistency can arise, for example, if regulations make action conditional on the purchaser paying outstanding taxes levied against the former shipowner or paying out unsatisfied creditors. The chapeau of paragraph 1 of article 7 therefore provides that the allowance for the competent authority to take action "in accordance with its regulations and procedures" is "without prejudice to article 6".

190. The regulations and procedures of the competent authority will typically determine whether the authority acts on application (e.g. action is taken at the request of the purchaser) or on its own motion (e.g. action is taken automatically). However, as paragraph 1 of article 7 requires action to be taken "at the request of the purchaser or subsequent purchaser", the regulations and procedures of the competent authority should not be invoked to deny the purchaser or subsequent purchaser the right to seize the competent authority. Paragraph 1 does not prevent the competent authority from taking action on its own motion, for example a registry in the State of judicial sale taking action on the basis of an order of the court of judicial sale. Nevertheless, action to delete the ship from the register under paragraph 1 (b) implies motivation on the part of the purchaser or subsequent purchaser for that action to be taken. And in any case, it is worth recalling that, in the event of action taken in a State other than the State of judicial sale, article 6 requires no special procedure to give effect to the foreign judicial sale, such as confirmation by a competent court in that State.

191. In practice, it is only the actions prescribed in paragraph 1 (c) and (d) that the competent authority will take at the request of the subsequent purchaser. The regulations and procedures of the competent authority may provide for a person acting as subsequent purchaser to produce documentation (e.g. a bill of sale) establishing that they have purchased the ship from the person named as the purchaser in the certificate of judicial sale, and thus qualifying as "subsequent purchaser" within the meaning of the Convention. For the purposes of paragraph 1 (c), the regulations and procedures may provide for the production of other documentation establishing that the "requirements of the law of the State of registration" are met.

192. Nothing in the Convention prevents the competent authority from taking subsequent action on registration at the request of a purchaser further down the chain of transfers.

References to preparatory work

Document	*Reference*
Report of the thirty-sixth session of Working Group VI	A/CN.9/1007, para. 97
Report of the thirty-seventh session of Working Group VI	A/CN.9/1047/Rev.1, paras. 91–95
Report of the fortieth session of Working Group VI	A/CN.9/1095, paras. 17, 23–26
Report of the fifty-fifth session of UNCITRAL	A/77/17, paras. 53–54

Translation and copy of the certificate of judicial sale (article 7, paragraphs 3 and 4)

193. As noted above (para. 152), the certificate of judicial sale will typically be issued in the language of the issuing authority in the State of judicial sale. Paragraph 3 of article 7 allows the competent authority to request production of a certified translation of the certificate. While the term "certified translation" is not defined, in the context of the actions prescribed in paragraphs 1 and 2 of article 7, the requirements for certification should be left to the regulations and procedures of the competent authority, which typically provide for a document bearing an endorsement by a recognized person or entity (e.g. a sworn translator) that the document is an accurate translation. Nothing in the Convention prevents the competent authority from dispensing with the requirement to produce a certified translation (e.g. if the competent authority accepts uncertified translations or no translation at all). It is worth recalling that nothing in the Convention requires the issuing authority to issue a certificate of judicial sale in a particular language.

194. Paragraph 4 of article 7 allows the competent authority to request production of a certified copy of the certificate for its records. This provision acknowledges that a single certificate of judicial sale may need to be produced to multiple

authorities to trigger all of the actions prescribed in paragraphs 1 and 2. If requested, the production of the certified copy supplements, but does not substitute, the production of the certificate of judicial sale itself. While the term "certified copy" is not defined, as with certified translations under paragraph 3, the requirements for certification should be left to the regulations and procedures of the competent authority, which typically provide for a document bearing an endorsement by a recognized person or entity that the document is a true copy. Nothing in the Convention prevents the competent authority from dispensing with the requirement to produce a certified copy (e.g. if the competent authority accepts an uncertified copy or makes a copy itself).

195. By virtue of paragraph 4 of article 5, the competent authority may not request evidence of legalization or the production of an "Apostille" for the certificate or for any translation.

References to preparatory work

Document	*Reference*
Report of the thirty-fifth session of Working Group VI	A/CN.9/973, para. 48
Report of the thirty-sixth session of Working Group VI	A/CN.9/1007, para. 98
Report of the thirty-seventh session of Working Group VI	A/CN.9/1047/Rev.1, para. 101
Report of the fortieth session of Working Group VI	A/CN.9/1095, para. 36
Report of the fifty-fifth session of UNCITRAL	A/77/17, para. 57

Refusal to take action (article 7, paragraph 5)

196. The competent authority is not required to take any actions prescribed in paragraphs 1 or 2 of article 7 if a court in the State of registration (in the case of article 7, paragraph 1) or the State of bareboat charter-in registration (in the case of article 7, paragraph 2) determines under article 10 that giving effect to the judicial sale would be manifestly contrary to the public policy of that State. As the preclusive effect of such a determination already flows from article 10 itself, paragraph 5 of article 7 is designed to provide an additional signpost to the competent authority. It acknowledges that a request for the competent authority to take action under article 7 may trigger a challenge invoking the public policy exception. The competent authority might not be well-placed to make a public policy determination and should not have the burden of dealing with a public policy challenge, but neither should it be expected to take any actions prescribed in paragraphs 1 or 2 where that would contravene a decision by a competent court. See further remarks on article 10 (including regarding the meaning of "determination" and "manifestly contrary").

References to preparatory work

Document	*Reference*
Report of the thirty-seventh session of Working Group VI	A/CN.9/1047/Rev.1, paras. 97–100
Report of the fortieth session of Working Group VI	A/CN.9/1095, paras. 37–40
Report of the fifty-fifth session of UNCITRAL	A/77/17, para. 58

Article 8. No arrest of the ship

General rule (article 8, paragraphs 1 and 2)

197. The international community has achieved significant progress in harmonizing rules on the arrest of ships. In broad terms, those rules permit a ship to be arrested in respect of a maritime claim only if the person who owns the ship at the time of arrest is the person who owned the ship at the time the claim arose, unless the maritime claim is secured by a maritime lien or is based on a mortgage, *hypothèque* or charge of similar nature. Where the judicial sale not only vests title of the ship in the purchaser, but does so free and clear of any mortgage, *hypothèque* or charge (including maritime lien and registered charge), it follows that the ship should not be subject to arrest for any maritime claim or maritime lien arising prior to the judicial sale. Paragraphs 1 and 2 of article give effect to that principle.

198. Paragraph 1 of article 8 deals with the case in which an arrest is applied for, while paragraph 2 deals with the case in which an arrest has been effected. Like article 7, article 8 is triggered by the production of the certificate of judicial sale and therefore only applies after completion of a judicial sale in a State Party that confers clean title. Moreover, it applies if the judicial sale is conducted in the State in which the arrest is applied for or effected, or in another State Party.

199. Both paragraphs refer to the "arrest" of the ship or any other "similar measure" against the ship. The reference to "similar measure" against the ship is designed to align article 8 with the terminology used in the definition of "ship" in article 2 (which refers to a vessel that "may be the subject of an arrest of other similar measure capable of leading to a judicial sale") and in the definition of "charge" (which refers to rights being asserted against a ship "whether by means of arrest, attachment or otherwise"). It is not designed to modify the understanding of "arrest" under the Arrests Conventions.[41]

[41] See note 1 above.

200. Both paragraphs refer to arrest for a "claim". The term is not designed to affect the range of claims in respect of which a ship may be arrested under the Arrests Conventions. Nor is it intended to affect any rights or powers of seizure in the enforcement of public law, such as tax, customs or criminal law.

201. Both paragraphs refer to action by a court or "other judicial authority". This terminology is designed to further align article 8 with the Arrests Conventions. Consistent with the Arrests Conventions and the objective of the Convention, matters of procedure relating to actions taken under article 8 are left to the law of the State in which the arrest has been applied for or effected, as the case may be.

References to preparatory work

Document	*Reference*
Report of the thirty-seventh session of Working Group VI	A/CN.9/1047/Rev.1, paras. 102–103
Report of the fortieth session of Working Group VI	A/CN.9/1095, para. 42
Report of the fifty-fifth session of UNCITRAL	A/77/17, para. 59

Translation of the certificate of judicial sale (article 8, paragraph 3)

202. In similar terms to paragraph 3 of article 7, paragraph 3 of article 8 allows the court or other judicial authority to request production of a certified translation of the certificate (see further remarks above on article 7, paragraph 3).

Refusal to take action (article 8, paragraph 4)

203. The court or other judicial authority is not required to take action to prohibit the arrest of the ship under paragraphs 1 or 2 of article 8 if it determines that that action would be manifestly contrary to the public policy of the State. Paragraph 4 of article 8 differs from paragraph 5 of article 7 in two respects. First, it refers to the court itself making the public policy determination. Second, it links and adapts the public policy exception to cases in which an arrest is applied for or effected. Paragraph 4 of article 8 does not itself confer jurisdiction on the court or other judicial authority to hear an application invoking the public policy ground, which is left to the law of the State in which the arrest is applied for or effected. Moreover, it does not limit the generality of article 10 (see further remarks below on article 10, including regarding the meaning of "determination" and "manifestly contrary").

References to preparatory work

Document	*Reference*
Report of the thirty-seventh session of Working Group VI	A/CN.9/1047/Rev.1, paras. 104–106
Report of the fortieth session of Working Group VI	A/CN.9/1095, para. 42

Article 9. Jurisdiction to avoid and suspend judicial sale

Exclusive jurisdiction (article 9, paragraphs 1 and 2)

204. Article 9 is concerned solely with jurisdiction to review a judicial sale. Paragraph 1 declares that the courts of the State of judicial sale have exclusive jurisdiction. Paragraph 2 reinforces the exclusivity of that jurisdiction by requiring the courts in every other State Party to decline jurisdiction.

205. Article 9 is concerned specifically with jurisdiction to avoid a judicial sale and jurisdiction to suspend the effects of a judicial sale. The Convention does not define "avoidance" of a judicial sale, which is understood to refer to a judicial remedy that renders the sale null and void and restores the parties to their respective positions prior to the sale. In some jurisdictions, such a remedy might be referred to by a different name. The term "avoidance" is consistent with usage in other treaties dealing with sales, including the United Nations Convention on Contracts for the International Sale of Goods (1980),[42] and emphasizes that the Convention is concerned with judicial sales and not with judgments in respect of such sales. In yet other jurisdictions, the remedy of avoidance might not exist at all. Paragraph 1 does not require a State Party to make the remedy available, nor does it affect the availability of other remedies available under the law of the State of judicial sale (e.g. remedies in tort). In that regard, remedies may be available at different stages of the judicial sale procedure, including after the sale is ordered but before the auction takes place, after the auction takes place but before it is confirmed, and after the sale has reached completion. Paragraph 1 applies only to a judicial sale that confers clean title and the remedy of avoidance itself assumes that the sale has reached completion. Avoidance can thus be contrasted to other remedies that have the effect of delaying or calling off the sale before the procedure has reached its final stage (i.e. prior to completion), which are addressed in paragraph 1 of article 4. In some jurisdictions, such other remedies may be referred to as "suspending" the sale, which in turn can be contrasted to suspending the effects of a sale once it has reached completion, which is the other remedy referred to in paragraph 1 of article 9.

[42] United Nations, *Treaty Series*, vol. 1489, No. 25567.

206. While differences exist between jurisdictions, grounds for avoidance may include *(a)* non-compliance with requirements under domestic law relating to notification and the procedures for holding public auctions or public tenders (including as specified in the decision ordering the sale), *(b)* approving or confirming a sale at a price below market price, and *(c)* fraud or other wrongdoing on the part of bidders. Consistent with the objective of the Convention to leave matters of procedure to domestic law, paragraph 1 of article 9 does not deal with grounds for avoidance or with standing to bring a claim or application. In particular, while compliance with the requirements of the Convention is a condition for issuance of the certificate of judicial sale, and the exclusive jurisdiction under paragraph 1 extends to any claim or application to challenge the issuance of the certificate of judicial sale, the Convention does not require the State of judicial sale to make non-compliance a ground for avoidance.

207. In practice, avoidance of a judicial sale is exceedingly rare. It is a remedy of limited availability given the difficulty of unwinding the effects of a judicial sale and restoring the parties to their previous positions once action has been taken on registration under article 7 and the proceeds of sale have been distributed. For many creditors, it is also unlikely to be an adequate remedy, with the possible exception of creditors who put in an unsuccessful bid or who allege that the sale was conducted in a manner that failed to maximize the proceeds. The inclusion of article 9 in the Convention is not intended to suggest that challenges to a judicial sale should be encouraged as a matter of course; rather it is designed to ensure that the validity of a certificate of judicial sale and the conditions for issuance are scrutinized exclusively by the State of judicial sale.

References to preparatory work

Document	*Reference*
Report of the thirty-fifth session of Working Group VI	A/CN.9/973, paras. 51–52, 54–57
Report of the thirty-sixth session of Working Group VI	A/CN.9/1007, paras. 59, 68–78
Report of the thirty-seventh session of Working Group VI	A/CN.9/1047/Rev.1, paras. 82, 107, 109
Report of the thirty-eighth session of Working Group VI	A/CN.9/1053, paras. 29, 57–60
Report of the thirty-ninth session of Working Group VI	A/CN.9/1089, para. 45
Report of the fortieth session of Working Group VI	A/CN.9/1095, paras. 43–47
Report of the fifty-fifth session of UNCITRAL	A/77/17, paras. 60–63

Effects of avoidance and suspension (article 9, paragraph 3; article 15, paragraph 2)

208. The effects of a judgment avoiding a judicial sale in exercise of jurisdiction conferred under paragraph 1 of article 9 are limited to the State of judicial sale under its domestic law. Nevertheless, the Convention acknowledges that, while exceptional, the avoidance of a judicial sale may have an impact on the Convention regime. For instance, a judicial sale may be avoided, or a certificate of judicial sale invalidated, for reasons that are apt to trigger a challenge on public policy grounds in another State under article 10. The Convention does not seek to find an answer to the international effect of avoidance or suspension, which is left to the law applicable in the State in which the issue arises, as provided for in paragraph 2 of article 15.

209. What the Convention does instead is to require any decision that avoids a judicial sale or suspends the effects thereof to be transmitted to the repository. This only applies to judicial sales for which a certificate has been issued. As with paragraph 3 of article 5, paragraph 3 of article 9 is concerned with the fact of transmission and not with the modalities of transmission, such as the method used and person responsible for transmitting the certificate to the repository. Those modalities are left to the law of the State of judicial sale and the procedures put in place by the repository in performing its functions under article 11 (see remarks below on article 11).

References to preparatory work

Document	*Reference*
Report of the thirty-seventh session of Working Group VI	A/CN.9/1047/Rev.1, paras. 74, 108
Report of the thirty-eighth session of Working Group VI	A/CN.9/1053, paras. 27–31
Report of the thirty-ninth session of Working Group VI	A/CN.9/1089, para. 113
Report of the fortieth session of Working Group VI	A/CN.9/1095, paras. 52–54
Report of the fifty-fifth session of UNCITRAL	A/77/17, para. 64

Article 10. Circumstances in which judicial sale has no international effect

Function of article 10

210. Article 10 provides the sole exception to the basic rule contained in article 6. While article 9 deals with jurisdiction to hear a challenge to a judicial sale in the State of judicial sale, article 10 deals with the right of any other State Party to refuse the international effects of a judicial sale. The ground for refusal is limited to the

public policy exception and requires a determination of a court. That determination has effect only in that State and does not affect the international effects of the judicial sale in any other State Party. The Convention acknowledges that the public policy exception will be most likely invoked in the States in which action under articles 7 or 8 is sought.

References to preparatory work

Document	*Reference*
Report of the thirty-fifth session of Working Group VI	A/CN.9/973, paras. 59–66
Report of the thirty-sixth session of Working Group VI	A/CN.9/1007, paras. 58, 79–89
Report of the thirty-seventh session of Working Group VI	A/CN.9/1047/Rev.1, paras. 84–85, 87–88

Public policy exception

211. Public policy is widely admitted among legal systems as a ground for refusing to recognize or enforce a foreign judgment. While the public policy exception in article 10 has been inspired by recent treaty practice, including article 7, paragraph 1 (c), of the Convention on the Recognition and Enforcement of Foreign Judgments in Civil or Commercial Matters (2019),[43] it is adapted to the international effects of judicial sales (recalling that the Convention is not concerned with the recognition and enforcement of foreign judgments; see remarks above on article 6). Matters of public policy can differ between judicial sales and foreign judgments. But as with foreign judgments, the concept of public policy under article 10 differs between States, which is recognized by the reference to the public policy "of that other State Party".

212. Article 10 requires the effect of the judicial sale in the State concerned to be "manifestly contrary" to public policy. This sets a high threshold, which reflects recent treaty practice. The threshold is designed to avoid an abusive or overly expansive application of the public policy exception and requires a compelling reason as to why giving effect to the foreign judicial sale is contrary to an identified matter of public policy. It emphasizes that the public policy is expected to apply only in exceptional cases.

213. In the context of judicial sales, matters of public policy may include the extinguishment of rights that are considered a mandatory rule of the State concerned, the avoidance of the sale in the State of judicial sale, infringement of sovereignty or security occasioned by the sale, the procurement of the sale by fraud committed by the purchaser, and conducting the judicial sale in a manner that violates

[43] Kingdom of the Netherlands, *Treaty Series*, 2019, No. 13672.

fundamental principles of due process. As noted above (para. 98), a particularly egregious failure to comply with the notice requirements under the Convention could give rise to an application invoking the public policy ground. However, consistent with recent treaty practice, a simple breach of a mandatory rule would typically not amount to a matter of public policy. Public policy requires the fundamental values of the State concerned to be engaged.

References to preparatory work

Document	*Reference*
Report of the thirty-fifth session of Working Group VI	A/CN.9/973, paras. 38, 62
Report of the thirty-sixth session of Working Group VI	A/CN.9/1007, paras. 84–86
Report of the thirty-seventh session of Working Group VI	A/CN.9/1047/Rev.1, paras. 85–86, 107
Report of the thirty-eighth session of Working Group VI	A/CN.9/1053, para. 28
Report of the thirty-ninth session of Working Group VI	A/CN.9/1089, paras. 37, 55
Report of the fifty-fifth session of UNCITRAL	A/77/17, para. 65

Determination

214. The public policy exception requires the determination of a court. The Convention does not specify the form of that determination or the procedure for invoking the public policy exception. Consistent with the objective of the Convention, those matters are left to the law of the State concerned. Article 10 refers to the court determining that the effect of the foreign judicial sale would be manifestly contrary to public policy. The word "determines" implies a decision based on a consideration of information relevant to matters of public policy. The use of the words "would be" reflects the formulation of the public policy exception in recent treaty practice. It is not intended to suggest that a provisional or conditional assessment by the court, let alone a mere allegation, would be sufficient.

References to preparatory work

Document	*Reference*
Report of the thirty-seventh session of Working Group VI	A/CN.9/1047/Rev.1, para. 100
Report of the fortieth session of Working Group VI	A/CN.9/1095, paras. 39–40

Article 11. Repository

Purpose of the repository mechanism

215. The Convention establishes a repository mechanism to enhance the operation of the Convention regime by providing public access to instruments that are required to circulate under the Convention. The repository also has the potential to promote the dissemination of information on the judicial sale of ships, thereby raising awareness of the function of judicial sales and supporting research and analysis for the benefit of the global maritime community.

Identity of the repository (article 11, paragraph 1)

216. Paragraph 1 of article 11 designates the Secretary-General of the International Maritime Organization (hereinafter "IMO") as the repository. As an alternative, it designates an institution named by UNCITRAL. This provision, which is based on the UNCITRAL Rules on Transparency in Treaty-based Investor-State Arbitration, recognizes that the Convention does not bind IMO and that the assumption of the repository function by the IMO Secretary-General is subject to approval by IMO's governing bodies.

Function of the repository (article 11, paragraph 2)

217. The function of the repository is to receive and publish the notice of judicial sale and certificate of judicial sale, as well as any decisions avoiding a judicial sale or suspending its effects. To that end, paragraph 2 of article 11 requires the repository to publish the instruments in a timely manner upon receipt. All of these instruments emanate from the State of judicial sale and are required to be transmitted to the repository under the Convention. The function of the repository is purely informational, and the publication of instruments has no particular legal effect under the Convention. In particular, the publication of the notice of judicial sale does not substitute the requirement to give the notice under paragraph 3 of article 4, nor does it substitute the requirement to produce the certificate of judicial sale to prompt action on registration of the ship under article 7 or action to prohibit arrest of the ship under article 8.

218. The Convention imposes no requirement on the repository to review or to ensure the accuracy or completeness of instruments transmitted for publication nor any requirement to translate them for publication. This is confirmed by the requirement in paragraph 2 of article 11 that the repository publish each instrument "in the form and in the language in which it is received".

219. The Convention purposefully does not prescribe how the repository performs its function but rather leaves it to the repository to put in place procedures for the receipt and publication of instruments required to be transmitted under the Convention. The Convention is designed to accommodate the use of an online platform or other online service to receive and publish instruments using automated systems, and for instruments to be transmitted and accessed via an online account or other interactive application.

Transitional application (article 11, paragraph 3)

220. Paragraph 3 of article 11 makes provision for the repository to receive and publish notices of judicial sale emanating from a contracting State (within the meaning of article 2 (f) of the Vienna Convention on the Law of Treaties (1969)[44]) for which the Convention has not yet entered into force. This provision supports the transitional application of the Convention (see further remarks below on article 21, paragraph 3).

References to preparatory work

Document	*Reference*
Report of the thirty-fifth session of Working Group VI	A/CN.9/973, paras. 46, 73
Report of the thirty-sixth session of Working Group VI	A/CN.9/1007, paras. 67, 94
Report of the thirty-seventh session of Working Group VI	A/CN.9/1047/Rev.1, paras. 50, 74, 76–81
Report of the thirty-eighth session of Working Group VI	A/CN.9/1053, para. 32
Report of the thirty-ninth session of Working Group VI	A/CN.9/1089, paras. 85–91
Report of the fortieth session of Working Group VI	A/CN.9/1095, paras. 49–51, 56–62
Report of the fifty-fifth session of UNCITRAL	A/77/17, para. 66

Article 12. Communication between authorities of States Parties

221. Paragraph 1 of article 12 provides for the communication between authorities in different States Parties. It is based on article 14 of the International Convention on Maritime Liens and Mortgages (1993)[45] and provides for communication for the purposes of the Convention as a whole rather than for specific provisions. In

[44] United Nations, *Treaty Series*, vol. 1155, No. 18232.
[45] See note 2 above.

particular, it facilitates direct communication between the court of judicial sale (or other public authority conducting the judicial sale) and registries for the purposes of the notice requirements in article 4, and communication between the issuing authority and the competent authority under article 7 with respect to the issuance of the certificate of judicial sale. Paragraph 1 of article 12 is premised on an assumption that, without authorization, the authorities in a particular State might only be able to communicate with foreign authorities via diplomatic channels, which would not be suited to the expediency required in judicial sale proceedings.

222. Paragraph 1 of article 12 authorizes, but does not require, communication. Moreover, it does not limit the use of other channels of communication, including those established under judicial assistance treaties between the States concerned. This is confirmed by paragraph 2 of article 12. Paragraph 2 is not concerned with other mechanisms for giving effect to foreign judicial sales that might exist under such treaties; the application of those other mechanisms is addressed in article 14.

References to preparatory work

Document	*Reference*
Report of the thirty-fifth session of Working Group VI	A/CN.9/973, para. 74
Report of the fortieth session of Working Group VI	A/CN.9/1095, para. 64–65
Report of the fifty-fifth session of UNCITRAL	A/77/17, paras. 67–68

Article 13. Relationship with other international conventions

223. According to the general principle stated in article 30, paragraph 3, of the Vienna Convention on the Law of Treaties (1969), a later treaty prevails over an earlier treaty to the extent of any incompatibility between the two. Article 13 addresses cases in which the application of the Convention is incompatible with two treaties identified during the preparation of the Convention. Ultimately, the existence and extent of any incompatibility is a matter of the interpretation of both instruments in a particular case.

224. Paragraph 1 of article 13 addresses the Convention on the Registration of Inland Navigation Vessels (1965) and its Protocol No. 2 Concerning Attachment and Forced Sale of Inland Navigation Vessels (hereinafter "Protocol No. 2").[46] That convention is open to members of the United Nations Economic Commission for Europe (UNECE), as well as States admitted to UNECE with a consultative status.

[46] United Nations, *Treaty Series*, vol. 1281, No. 21114.

Protocol No. 2 governs the attachment (including arrest) and forced sale (including judicial sale) of "any vessel used in inland navigation" (article 2) and makes provision regarding various matters related to judicial sales that are addressed in the Convention, namely notice requirements (article 21), the international effects of a judicial sale (article 19), and action on registration following a judicial sale (article 22). As noted in the remarks on the definition of "ship" above (para. 45), the Convention is applicable to the judicial sale of inland navigation vessels, and thus its provisions are potentially incompatible with the provisions of Protocol No. 2 in a particular case. In the event of such incompatibility, paragraph 1 of article 13 provides for the provisions of the Convention to "give way" to the protocol so that, in accordance with the general principle stated in article 30, paragraph 2, of the Vienna Convention on the Law of Treaties (1969), Protocol No. 2 prevails.

225. Paragraph 2 of article 13 addresses the Convention on the Service Abroad of Judicial and Extrajudicial Documents in Civil or Commercial Matters (hereinafter "Service Convention").[47] The Service Convention makes provision for the transmission of judicial documents emanating from one State for service in another State. If it applies, the Service Convention provides several channels of transmission, although for documents to be served in some States Parties, only transmission through a central authority or through diplomatic and consular channels is provided. Insofar as the Service Convention provides exclusively for the channels of transmission of judicial documents for service abroad, its provisions are potentially incompatible with the provisions of the Convention that allow for the notice of judicial sale to be given under the law of the State of judicial sale (article 4, paragraph 4). Specifically, the notification times involved in using the channels of transmission available under the Service Convention for giving notice to a person located in a particular State may not be suited to the expediency required in judicial sale proceedings, and the law of the State of judicial sale may provide for the notice to be given using channels other than those provided in the Service Convention. In that case, paragraph 2 of article 13 is designed not to displace the application of the Service Convention entirely but rather to avoid the exclusivity of the channels of transmission provided thereunder. In other words, those channels can be used, but they do not have to be used. States that have enacted legislation to give effect to the Service Convention may need to amend that legislation if they wish for the notice of judicial sale to be given using channels other than those provided in the Service Convention.

226. As noted above (para. 174), the Convention is not concerned with the recognition of foreign judgments and therefore does not address its relationship with treaties such as the Convention on the Recognition and Enforcement of Foreign Judgments in Civil or Commercial Matters (2019).

---

[47] United Nations, *Treaty Series*, vol. 658, No. 9432.

References to preparatory work

Document	*Reference*
Report of the thirty-fifth session of Working Group VI	A/CN.9/973, para. 72
Report of the thirty-sixth session of Working Group VI	A/CN.9/1007, paras. 31, 65
Report of the thirty-seventh session of Working Group VI	A/CN.9/1047/Rev.1, paras. 29, 60
Report of the thirty-ninth session of Working Group VI	A/CN.9/1089, para. 81
Report of the fortieth session of Working Group VI	A/CN.9/1095, para. 71
Report of the fifty-fifth session of UNCITRAL	A/77/17, para. 69
Note by the Secretariat on the interaction between a future instrument on the judicial sale of ships and selected HCCH Conventions	A/CN.9/WG.VI/WP.85, paras. 12–30

Article 14. Other bases for giving international effect

227. The purpose of article 14 is to clarify that the Convention does not displace other treaties or domestic law that provide a more favourable basis for giving effect to foreign judicial sales. In the preparation of the Convention, it was acknowledged that foreign judicial sales could be recognized under the International Convention on Maritime Liens and Mortgages (1993),[48] as well as under domestic law in circumstances not covered by the Convention, including on the basis of comity.

228. Article 14 is not strictly a "give way" clause like paragraph 1 of article 13 because *(a)* it applies to avoid incompatibility in the first place, *(b)* it applies to judicial sales conducted in States that are not party to the Convention, as well as judicial sales that fall outside the scope of the Convention, and *(c)* it addresses the interaction of the Convention with domestic law (in addition to that with other treaties). If, however, the provisions of the Convention are incompatible with the bases under another treaty for giving effect to a foreign judicial in a particular case, article 14 provides for the provisions of the Convention to "give way" to the application of those bases.

229. Article 14 is not concerned with other treaties and domestic law that, in a particular case, would deny giving effect to foreign judicial sales. As such, article 14 would not give way to the application of grounds for refusal under another treaty. In that case, the provisions of the Convention, notably article 6, would apply to their fullest extent, in accordance with the general principle stated in article 30, paragraph 3, of the Vienna Convention on the Law of Treaties (1969). In the case of the

[48] See note 2 above.

incompatibility with domestic law, the general principle stated in articles 26 and 27 of the Vienna Convention on the Law of Treaties (1969) would be engaged.

References to preparatory work

Document	*Reference*
Report of the thirty-seventh session of Working Group VI	A/CN.9/1047/Rev.1, para. 17
Report of the fortieth session of Working Group VI	A/CN.9/1095, paras. 68–70
Report of the fifty-fifth session of UNCITRAL	A/77/17, paras. 68, 70

Article 15. Matters not governed by this Convention

Purpose

230. The purpose of article 15 is to clarify that the application of the Convention does not extend to matters (hereinafter "extraneous matters") that the Convention is not intended to govern, namely *(a)* the distribution of the proceeds of the judicial sale, *(b)* personal claims against the former shipowner, and *(c)* the international effect of a judgment avoiding or suspending a judicial sale or invalidating a certificate of judicial sale. As such, article 15 is designed to provide a clear signpost to creditors that those extraneous matters are governed by other applicable law, namely domestic law. Strictly speaking, article 15 does not deal with exclusions from scope since the substantive provisions of the Convention are not intended to apply to the extraneous matters in the first place. For that reason, the paragraphs of article 15 are not located in article 3. Nevertheless, given the close connection of the extraneous matters prescribed in article 15 with matters that are governed by the Convention, and the fact that they were raised during the preparation of the Convention, it was felt that, to avoid doubt, an express provision clarifying the application of the Convention to those extraneous matters would be useful.

References to preparatory work

Document	*Reference*
Report of the thirty-seventh session of Working Group VI	A/CN.9/1047/Rev.1, paras. 47–48
Report of the fortieth session of Working Group VI	A/CN.9/1095, paras. 72, 75
Report of the fifty-fifth session of UNCITRAL	A/77/17, para. 71

Distribution of proceeds

231. The availability of proceeds to creditors is a defining feature of a judicial sale within the meaning of the Convention (see remarks above on subparagraph (ii) of the definition of "judicial sale" in article 2). However, unlike the International Convention on Maritime Liens and Mortgages (1993),[49] the Convention does not regulate how those proceeds are distributed or how claims against the proceeds are prioritized. These matters are governed by the law of the State of judicial sale.

References to preparatory work

Document	*Reference*
Report of the thirty-fifth session of Working Group VI	A/CN.9/973, paras. 22, 29
Report of the thirty-sixth session of Working Group VI	A/CN.9/1007, paras. 53, 54

Personal claims against the former shipowner

232. As article 1 makes it clear, the Convention is concerned only with judicial sales that (already) confer clean title. The Convention is not concerned with the effects of a judicial sale on the survival of personal claims against the former shipowner that arise prior to the judicial sale. This includes claims arising under contract or in tort, as well as other personal claims which, but for the judicial sale, could have been enforced by attachment against the ship following a court judgment, or which, by virtue of the judicial sale, could have been enforceable against the proceeds but were not fully satisfied. Paragraph 1 (b) of article 15 clarifies this position. It does not create any claim or revive any claim that was extinguished by the judicial sale.

233. The reference to "person who owned or had proprietary rights in the ship" as opposed to "owner" is designed to further distinguish matters governed by the Convention, which makes limited provision with respect to the notification of the "owner", and the preservation of personal claims.

References to preparatory work

Document	*Reference*
Report of the thirty-fifth session of Working Group VI	A/CN.9/973, para. 34
Report of the thirty-sixth session of Working Group VI	A/CN.9/1007, paras. 51–54
Report of the thirty-seventh session of Working Group VI	A/CN.9/1047/Rev.1, paras. 47–48
Report of the fortieth session of Working Group VI	A/CN.9/1095, para. 73

[49] See note 2 above.

Effects of avoidance and suspension

234. Paragraph 2 of article 15 clarifies that the Convention does not offer an answer to the question, which is expected only ever to arise in exceedingly rare circumstances, as to the international effects of avoidance and suspension of a judicial sale under article 9 (see remarks above on article 9).

Other matters not governed by the Convention

235. As already noted in the remarks above on article 1, the Convention does not address the conduct of judicial sales, the recognition of judgments in respect of judicial sales, or whether a judicial sale confers clean title. This is consistent with the objective of the Convention to establish a harmonized regime for giving international effect to judicial sales, while preserving domestic law governing the procedure of judicial sales and the circumstances in which judicial sales confer clean title. A number of other matters connected with judicial sales were raised during the preparation of the Convention, but not included in article 15. Those other matters include the coordination of insolvency proceedings and parallel judicial sale proceedings, as well as remedies for wrongful arrest.

References to preparatory work

Document	*Reference*
Report of the thirty-fifth session of Working Group VI	A/CN.9/973, paras. 22, 29–30
Report of the thirty-sixth session of Working Group VI	A/CN.9/1007, paras. 44, 46, 70–71
Report of the thirty-seventh session of Working Group VI	A/CN.9/1047/Rev.1, para. 100
Report of the thirty-ninth session of Working Group VI	A/CN.9/1089, paras. 52–61

Final clauses

General

236. The final clauses of the Convention (articles 16–23) are modelled on other multilateral treaties prepared by UNCITRAL. Time periods specified in the final clauses are measured in days rather than years for greater certainty.

References to preparatory work

Document	*Reference*
Report of the fortieth session of Working Group VI	A/CN.9/1095, para. 76
Report of the fifty-fifth session of UNCITRAL	A/77/17, para. 86

Depositary (article 16)

237. Article 16 designates the Secretary-General of the United Nations as depositary of the Convention. The depositary is entrusted with the custody of the authentic texts of the Convention and of any full powers delivered to the depositary. The depositary also performs a number of administrative services in connection with the Convention, including *(a)* preparing certified copies of the original text, *(b)* receiving signatures to the Convention, *(c)* receiving and keeping custody of any instruments, notifications and communications relating to the Convention, and *(d)* informing States of instruments, notifications and communications relating to the Convention.

238. The depositary is a different institution and has a different function to the repository established under article 11.

Reference to preparatory work

Document	*Reference*
Report of the fifty-fifth session of UNCITRAL	A/77/17, para. 72

Consenting to be bound (article 17)

239. Establishing a harmonized regime for giving international effect to judicial sales is best served by securing broad appeal for the Convention among States. Paragraph 1 of article 17 declares that the Convention is open for signature by "all States", which is a formula frequently used in multilateral treaties to promote the widest possible participation.

240. The Secretary-General, as depositary, has stated on a number of occasions that it would fall outside his or her competence to determine whether a territory or other such entity would fall within the "all States" formula. Pursuant to a general understanding adopted by the General Assembly on 14 December 1973, in discharging depositary functions relating to a treaty with the "all States" clause, the Secretary-General will follow the practice of the General Assembly and, whenever advisable, will request the opinion of the General Assembly before receiving a signature or an instrument of ratification or accession.[50]

[50] See *United Nations Juridical Yearbook* (1973), United Nations publication, Sales No. E.75.V.1, part two, chap. IV, sect. A.3 (p. 79, note 9), and *United Nations Juridical Yearbook* (1974), United Nations publication, Sales No. E.76.V.1, part two, chap. VI, sect. A.9 (pp. 157–159).

241. While some treaties provide that a State may express its consent to be bound by signature alone, the Convention, like most modern multilateral treaties, provides that it is subject to ratification, acceptance or approval by the signatory State. Providing for signature subject to ratification, acceptance or approval allows the State time to seek approval for the Convention at the domestic level and to enact any legislation necessary to implement the Convention internally, prior to undertaking the legal obligations from the Convention at the international level. Upon ratification, the Convention legally binds the State.

242. Acceptance or approval of a treaty following signature has the same legal effect as ratification, and the same rules apply. Accession has the same legal effect as ratification, acceptance or approval. However, unlike ratification, acceptance or approval, which must be preceded by signature, accession requires only the deposit of an instrument of accession. Unlike some multilateral treaties, accession to the Convention is not subject to any special conditions. Accession is a means by which a State may become party to a treaty without signing the treaty.

243. The Convention uses the term "State Party" to refer to a State which has consented to be bound by the Convention and for which the Convention is in force (see remarks below on article 21). This is extended to regional economic integration organizations under article 18.

References to preparatory work[51]

Document	*Reference*
Report of the fortieth session of Working Group VI	A/CN.9/1095, para. 76
Report of the fifty-fifth session of UNCITRAL	A/77/17, paras. 73–75

REIO clause (article 18)

Meaning of "regional economic integration organization"

244. In addition to "States", the Convention allows participation by international organizations of a particular type, namely "regional economic integration organizations" (hereinafter "REIOs"). Article 18 acknowledges the growing importance of REIOs, which already participate in a range of trade-related treaties.

245. The Convention does not define "regional economic integration organization". Nevertheless, article 18 encompasses two key elements: the grouping of States

[51] As the date of the signing ceremony was not set at the time of adoption by the General Assembly, article 17 makes no reference to the time and place for opening the convention for signature.

in a certain region for the realization of common purposes, and the transfer of competencies relating to those common purposes from those States to the REIO. Although the notion of an REIO is a flexible one, participation in the Convention is not open to international organizations at large. Most international organizations do not have the power to enact legally binding rules, since that function typically requires the exercise of certain attributes of State sovereignty that only few organizations have received from their member States.

Extent of competence of the REIO

246. Article 18 is not concerned with the internal procedures leading to signature, ratification, acceptance, approval or accession by an REIO. The Convention itself does not require a separate act of authorization by the member States of the REIO and does not answer, in one way or the other, the question as to whether the REIO has the right to consent to be bound by the Convention if none of its member States decides to do so. For the Convention, the extent of treaty powers given to an REIO – and whether it expresses its consent to be bound by ratification, acceptance, approval or accession – is an internal matter concerning the relations between the organization and its own member States. Article 18 does not prescribe the manner in which REIOs and their member States divide competences and powers among themselves.

247. Nonetheless, paragraph 1 of article 18 provides that an REIO may only express its consent to be bound if it "has competence over certain matters governed by this Convention". Moreover, this competence needs to be demonstrated by a declaration made to the depositary pursuant to paragraph 2 of article 18 specifying the matters governed by the Convention in respect of which competence has been transferred to the REIO by its member States. Article 18 does not provide a basis for consenting to be bound by the Convention if the REIO has no competence on the subject matter covered by the Convention.

248. The REIO does not need to have competence over all the matters governed by the Convention; such competence may be partial or concurrent with its member States. Accordingly, both an REIO and any or all of its member States may become party to the Convention. In recognition of this, paragraph 1 of article 18 provides that an instrument deposited by the REIO is not counted (in addition to those deposited by its member States) for the purposes of the entry into force of the Convention (article 21) or of any adopted amendment (article 22).

249. By expressing its consent to be bound by the Convention, an REIO becomes a party to the Convention in its own right. This is confirmed by paragraph 3 of article 18, which provides that any reference to a "State" or "State Party" in the Convention applies equally, where the context so requires, to an REIO.

Relationship between the Convention and REIO rules

250. Like other recent multilateral treaties prepared by UNCITRAL, paragraph 4 of article 18 contains a "disconnection clause" to regulate the relationship between the Convention and the rules enacted by an REIO. It is intended to cover the member States of the REIO in their mutual relations and not in their relations with other States. On its terms, it applies regardless of whether the REIO participates in the Convention following the procedures established in paragraphs 1 and 2 of article 18.

251. Paragraph 4 of article 18 acknowledges that the rules of an REIO may apply to the transmission of the notice of judicial sale from one member State to another, as well as the allocation of jurisdiction among member States in matters governed by the Convention, and provides that the Convention does not displace the operation of those rules.

References to preparatory work

Document	*Reference*
Report of the fortieth session of Working Group VI	A/CN.9/1095, para. 78
Report of the fifty-fifth session of UNCITRAL	A/77/17, paras. 76–78

Non-unified legal systems (article 19)

Mechanism for applying the Convention to territorial units

252. According to the general principle stated in article 29 of the Vienna Convention on the Law of Treaties (1969), a treaty is binding upon each party in respect of its entire territory, unless a different intention appears from the treaty or is otherwise established. Paragraph 1 of article 19 permits a State to declare that the Convention is to extend to all its territorial units or only to one or more of them. Article 20 deals with the timing of that declaration. If no declaration is made, the Convention extends to all territorial units of the State (article 19, paragraph 3).

253. This provision, which is often called the "federal clause", is particularly relevant to States with a federal system of government under which the constituent states, provinces or other "territorial units" of the State have legislative power over matters governed by the Convention. For some federal States, while the central government retains treaty powers, it does not have the power to enact legislation necessary to implement the Convention in all or some of those territorial units. Paragraph 1 of article 19 addresses this situation by allowing the State to declare that the Convention applies only to those territorial units that have enacted legislation to implement the Convention. Article 20 allows the declaration to be amended at any

time, which acknowledges that the State may apply the Convention progressively to its constituent territorial units.

254. Article 19 is not limited to federal States, and may be used by other States with separate territorial units, including autonomous territories and overseas territories. However, as with federal States, a declaration can only be made under paragraph 1 of article 19 if "different systems of law are applicable" in those territorial units "in relation to matters dealt with in [the] Convention". Article 19 is not designed to be used by REIOs.

Interpretation of the Convention in its application to territorial units

255. Paragraph 4 of article 19 establishes rules for interpreting certain terms in the Convention in its application to territorial units of a State Party. It applies regardless of whether the State Party has made a declaration under paragraph 1.

References to preparatory work

Document	*Reference*
Report of the fortieth session of Working Group VI	A/CN.9/1095, paras. 79–80
Report of the fifty-fifth session of UNCITRAL	A/77/17, paras. 68, 79

Procedure and effects of declarations (article 20)

256. Article 20, which is modelled on article 21 of the Electronic Communications Convention,[52] establishes common rules on how declarations under the Convention are made and take effect. The Convention contemplates two types of declaration, which are provided for in paragraph 2 of article 18 (declaration by REIO on transferred competence) and paragraph 1 of article 19 (declaration by State on territorial units), respectively.

257. The second sentence of paragraph 4 of article 20 deals with the situation in which a State makes a declaration on territorial units under paragraph 2 of article 18 and modifies or withdraws the declaration less than 180 days before the Convention enters into force. For ease of administration, the Convention provides that the modification or withdrawal take effect simultaneously with the entry into force of the Convention for that State.

[52] See note 34 above.

Reference to preparatory work

Document	*Reference*
Report of the fifty-fifth session of UNCITRAL	A/77/17, paras. 83–87

Entry into force (article 21)

Entry into force generally

258. Multilateral treaties prepared by UNCITRAL have required as few as three and as many as 10 States to express their consent to be bound in order for the treaty to enter into force. Paragraph 1 of article 21 requires three States to express their consent to be bound, which follows the modern trend in commercial law conventions and promotes the application of the Convention as early as possible in those States that seek to apply its provisions to their commerce. By virtue of paragraph 1 of article 18, the instrument of ratification, acceptance, approval or accession of an REIO is not counted. A 180-day period from the date of deposit of the third instrument of ratification, acceptance, approval or accession is provided so as to give States that become parties to the Convention sufficient time to notify all relevant authorities and other interested parties of its impending entry into force.

Entry into force for States consenting after the Convention has entered into force

259. Paragraph 2 of article 21 deals with the entry into force of the Convention for States that express their consent to be bound once the Convention has entered into force. For those States, the Convention provides for a similar 180-day period as is provided under paragraph 1 of article 21 for the third instrument of ratification, acceptance, approval or accession.

Transitional application

260. While judicial sale procedures are typically expedient, it is conceivable – albeit unlikely – that the Convention will enter into force for a State after the procedure has commenced but before completion of the sale. To avoid doubt as to the application of the Convention, paragraph 3 of article 21 provides that the Convention only applies to judicial sales that are "ordered or approved" after entry into force for the State of judicial sale. This reflects paragraph 1 (a) of article 3, which already limits the scope of application of the Convention to judicial sales that are "conducted in a State Party", and thus in a State for which the Convention is in force (cf. article 2 (g) of the Vienna Convention on the Law of Treaties (1969)). The words "ordered or approved" refer to identifiable actions that are taken with respect to a judicial sale, as

reflected in the definition of "judicial sale", for which the timing can be readily determined. While several provisions of the Convention refer to "conducting" a judicial sale, the operation of those provisions does not depend on pinpointing the time at which, or period during which, a judicial sale is "conducted".

261. To address the case in which the Convention enters into force for a State after notification of a judicial sale (but before the sale is ordered or approved) – and to avoid needless challenges to the international effect of the judicial sale based on non-compliance with the notice requirements, in particular the requirement for the notice of judicial sale to be transmitted to the repository – paragraph 3 of article 11 makes provision for the repository to receive and publish notices of judicial sale emanating from a State that has consented to be bound by the Convention but before its entry into force for that State.

References to preparatory work

Document	*Reference*
Report of the fortieth session of Working Group VI	A/CN.9/1095, paras. 76, 81–85
Report of the fifty-fifth session of UNCITRAL	A/77/17, paras. 88–90

Amendment (article 22)

262. Article 22 establishes a mechanism for amending the Convention. Amendment provisions are common in multilateral treaties, even if they are not commonly invoked. By virtue of paragraph 1 of article 18, the instrument of ratification, acceptance, approval or accession of an REIO is not counted (in addition to those of its member States) for the purpose of entry into force of any adopted amendment. The application of adopted amendments to territorial units to which the Convention has been extended by declaration is covered by article 19.

References to preparatory work

Document	*Reference*
Report of the fortieth session of Working Group VI	A/CN.9/1095, paras. 86–88
Report of the fifty-fifth session of UNCITRAL	A/77/17, paras. 91–92

Denunciation (article 23)

263. Paragraph 1 of article 23 allows a State Party to denounce the Convention. Denunciation releases the State from its obligation further to perform the Convention,

and thus the Convention ceases to be in force for that State. Just as paragraph 1 of article 19 allows a State to apply the Convention to a particular territorial unit, paragraph 1 of article 23 allows the State to denounce the Convention for a territorial unit.

264. Under paragraph 2 of article 23, denunciation takes effect 365 days after the notification is received by the depositary, unless a longer period is specified. The default period, which is approximately twice the period for entry into force of the Convention under article 21, is intended to give sufficient time to notify authorities and other interested parties in the denouncing State and in other States Parties of the change in the legal regime with respect to the international effect of judicial sales involving that State.

Reference to preparatory work

Document	*Reference*
Report of the fifty-fifth session of UNCITRAL	A/77/17, para. 93

Annex

Table of concordance between the Convention and earlier drafts

Final text	*Draft submitted to Commission*[a]	*Fifth revision of the Beijing Draft*[b]
Art. 1. Purpose	Art. 1	Art. 1
Art. 2 (a) (definition of "judicial sale")	Art. 2 (a)	Art. 2 (a)
Art. 2 (b) (definition of "ship")	Art. 2 (b)	Art. 2 (b)
Art. 2 (c) (definition of "clean title")	Art. 2 (c)	Art. 2 (c)
Art. 2 (d) (definition of "mortgage or *hypothèque*")	Art. 2 (d)	Art. 2 (d)
Art. 2 (e) (definition of "charge")	Art. 2 (e)	Art. 2 (e)
Art. 2 (f) (definition of "registered charge")	Art. 2 (f)	Art. 2 (f)
Art. 2 (g) (definition of "maritime lien")	Art. 2 (g)	Art. 2 (g)
Art. 2 (h) (definition of "owner")	Art. 2 (h)	Art. 2 (h)

[a] A/CN.9/1108, considered by the Commission at its fifty-fifth session (A/77/17, paras. 24–99).
[b] A/CN.9/WG.VI/WP.94, considered by Working Group VI at its fortieth session (A/CN.9/1095).
[c] A/CN.9/WG.VI/WP.92, considered by Working Group VI at its thirty-ninth session (A/CN.9/1089).
[d] A/CN.9/WG.VI/WP.90, considered by Working Group VI at its thirty-eighth session (A/CN.9/1053).
[e] A/CN.9/WG.VI/WP.87, considered by Working Group VI at its thirty-seventh session (A/CN.9/1047/Rev.1).
[f] A/CN.9/WG.VI/WP.84, considered by Working Group VI at its thirty-sixth session (A/CN.9/1007).
[g] A/CN.9/WG.VI/WP.82, considered by Working Group VI at its thirty-fifth session (A/CN.9/973).

Final text	*Draft submitted to Commission*[a]	*Fifth revision of the Beijing Draft*[b]	*Fourth revision of the Beijing Draft*[c]
Art. 2 (i) (definition of "purchaser")	Art. 2 (i)	Art. 2 (i)	Art. 2 (h)
Art. 2 (j) (definition of "subsequent purchaser")	Art. 2 (j)	Art. 2 (j)	Art. 2 (l)
Art. 2 (k) (definition of "State of judicial sale")	Art. 2 (k)	Art. 2 (k)	Art. 2 (k)
Art. 3, para. 1 (a) (geographic scope)	Art. 3, para. 1 (a)	Art. 3, para. 1 (a)	Art. 1
Art. 3, para. 1 (b) (physical presence requirement)	Art. 3, para. 1 (b)	Art. 3, para. 1 (b)	Art. 3, para. 1 (a)

Fourth revision of the Beijing Draft[c]	*Third revision of the Beijing Draft*[d]	*Second revision of the Beijing Draft*[e]	*First revision of the Beijing Draft*[f]	*Beijing Draft*[g]
Art. 1	Art. 1	Art. 1	—	Art. 2
Art. 2 (c)	Art. 2 (c)	Art. 2 (c); see also art. 3, para. 2(a)	Art. 1 (c); see also art. 2, para. 1(a)	Art. 1 (h)
Art. 2 (j)	Art. 2 (i)	Art. 2 (i)	Art. 1 (i)	Art. 1 (q)
Art. 2 (b)	Art. 2 (b)	Art. 2 (b)	Art. 1 (b)	Art. 1 (c)
Art. 2 (e)	Art. 2 (e)	Art. 2 (e)	Art. 1 (e)	Art. 1 (j)
Art. 2 (a)	Art. 2 (a)	Art. 2 (a)	Art. 1 (a)	Art. 1 (b)
Art. 2 (i)	—	—	—	Art. 1 (o)
Art. 2 (d)	Art. 2 (d)	Art. 2 (d)	Art. 1 (d)	Art. 1 (i)
Art. 2 (f)	Art. 2 (f)	Art. 2 (f)	Art. 1 (f)	Art. 1 (k)

Third revision of the Beijing Draft[d]	*Second revision of the Beijing Draft*[e]	*First revision of the Beijing Draft*[f]	*Beijing Draft*[g]
Art. 2 (h)	Art. 2 (h)	Art. 1 (h)	Art. 1 (l)
Art. 2 (k)	Art. 2 (k)	Art. 1 (k)	Art. 1 (u)
Art. 2 (j)	Art. 2 (j)	Art. 1 (j)	Art. 1 (s)
Art. 1; see also art. 6	Art. 1 (see also art. 6, para. 1 (chapeau))	Art. 4, para. 1 (chapeau)	— (c.f. art. 9)
Art. 3, para. 1 (a)	Art. 3, para. 1 (a) (see also art. 6, para. 1 (a))	Art. 4, para. 1 (a)	Art. 4, para. 1 (a)

Final text	*Draft submitted to Commission*[a]	*Fifth revision of the Beijing Draft*[b]	*Fourth revision of the Beijing Draft*[c]
Art. 3, para. 2 (exclusion of State-owned or operated vessels)	Art. 3, para. 2	Art. 3, para. 2	Art. 3, para. 2
Art. 4, para. 1 (relationship with domestic law; procedures; procedures for challenging the judicial sale)	Art. 4, para. 1	Art. 4, para. 1	Art. 4, para. 1bis
Art. 4, para. 2 (condition for issuing certificate of judicial sale)	Art. 4, para. 2	Art. 4, para. 2	Art. 4, para. 1 (chapeau)
Art. 4, para. 3 (a) (notification of ship registry)	Art. 4, para. 3 (a)	Art. 4, para. 3 (a)	Art. 4, para. 1 (a)
Art. 4, para. 3 (b) (notification of holders of any mortgage, *hypothèque* or registered charge)	Art. 4, para. 3 (b)	Art. 4, para. 3 (b)	Art. 4, para. 1 (b)
Art. 4, para. 3 (c) (notification of holders of any maritime lien)	Art. 4, para. 3 (c)	Art. 4, para. 3 (c)	Art. 4, para. 1 (c)
Art. 4, para. 3 (d) (notification of shipowner)	Art. 4, para. 3 (d)	Art. 4, para. 3 (d)	Art. 4, para. 1 (d)
Art. 4, para. 3 (e) (notification of bareboat charterers and bareboat charter registries)	Art. 4, para. 3 (e)	Art. 4, para. 3 (e)	Art. 4, para. 1 (e)
Art. 4, para. 4; annex I (content of notice and methods of notification)	Art. 4, para. 4; appendix I	Art. 4, para. 4; appendix I	Art. 4, para. 2; appendix I
Art. 4, para. 5 (a) (publication of announce-ment in the press or other publication)	Art. 4, para. 5 (a)	Art. 4, para. 5 (a)	Art. 4, para. 3 (a)
Art. 4, para. 5 (b) (transmission of notice to repository)	Art. 4, para. 5 (b)	Art. 4, para. 5 (b)	Art. 4, para. 3 (b)
Art. 4, para. 6 (language requirements when transmitting notice to repository)	Art. 4, para. 6	Art. 4, para. 6	—
Art. 4, para. 7 (reliance on registry information)	Art. 4, para. 7	Art. 4, para. 7	Art. 4, para. 4
Art. 5, para. 1 (issuance of certificate of judicial sale)	Art. 5, para. 1	Art. 5, para. 1 (chapeau)	Art. 5, para. 1 (chapeau)
Art. 5, para. 2; annex II (form and content ofcertificate)	Art. 5, para. 2; appendix II	Art. 5, para. 1; appendix II	Art. 5, paras. 1 and 2; appendix II

Third revision of the Beijing Draft[d]	*Second revision of the Beijing Draft*[e]	*First revision of the Beijing Draft*[f]	*Beijing Draft*[g]
Art. 3, para. 2	Art. 3, para. 2 (b)	Art. 2, para. 1 (b)	—
—	—	—	—
— (c.f. art. 6)	— (c.f. art. 6, para. 1 (b))	— (c.f. art. 4, para. 1 (b))	— (c.f. art. 4, para. 1 (b))
Art. 4, para. 1 (a)	Art. 4, para. 1 (a)	Art. 3, para. 1 (a)	Art. 3, para. 1 (a)
Art. 4, para. 1 (b)	Art. 4, para. 1 (b)	Art. 3, para. 1 (b)	Art. 3, para. 1 (b)
Art. 4, para. 1 (c)	Art. 4, para. 1 (c)	Art. 3, para. 1 (c)	Art. 3, para. 1 (c)
Art. 4, para. 1 (d)	Art. 4, para. 1 (d)	Art. 3, para. 1 (d)	Art. 3, para. 1 (d)
Art. 4, para. 1 (e) and (f)	Art. 4, para. 1 (e) and (f)	Art. 3, para. 1 (e)	Art. 3, para. 2
Art. 4, para. 2; appendix I	Art. 4, para. 2; appendix I	Art. 3, paras. 2 and 3	Art. 3, paras. 3, 4 (a) and 7; see also art. 3, para. 1 (chapeau)
Art. 4, para. 3 (a)	Art. 4, para. 3 (a)	Art. 3, para. 4 (a)	Art. 3, para. 4 (b)
Art. 4, para. 3 (b)	Art. 4, para. 3 (b)	Art. 3, para. 4 (b)	—
—	—	—	—
Art. 4, para. 4	Art. 4, para. 4	Art. 3, para. 5	Art. 3, para. 6
Art. 5, para. 1 (chapeau)	Art. 5, para. 1 (chapeau)	Art. 5, para. 1 (chapeau)	Art. 5, para. 1 (chapeau)
Art. 5, paras. 1 and 2; appendix II	Art. 5, paras. 1 and 2; appendix II	Art. 5, paras. 1 and 2; annex	Art. 5, paras. 1 and 2; annex

Final text	*Draft submitted to Commission*[a]	*Fifth revision of the Beijing Draft*[b]	*Fourth revision of the Beijing Draft*[c]
Art. 5, para. 3 (transmission of certificate to repository)	Art. 5, para. 3	Art. 5, para. 2	Art. 5, para. 3
Art. 5, para. 4 (no legalization)	Art. 5, para. 4 (see also art. 20)	Art. 5, para. 3	Art. 5, para. 4
Art. 5, para. 5 (evidentiary value)	Art. 5, para. 5	Art. 5, para. 4	Art. 5, para. 5
Art. 5, paras. 6 and 7 (electronic form)	Art. 5, paras. 6 and 7	Art. 5bis	Art. 5bis
Art. 6 (international effects of a judicial sale)	Art. 6	Art. 6	Art. 6
Art. 7, paras. 1 and 2 (actions to be taken by the registry)	Art. 7, paras. 1 and 2	Art. 7, paras. 1 and 2	Art. 7, paras. 1 and 2
Art. 7, paras. 3 and 4 (translation and copy of the certificate of judicial sale)	Art. 7, paras. 3 and 4	Art. 7, paras. 3 and 4	Art. 7, paras. 3 and 4
Art. 7, para. 5 (refusal to take action)	Art. 7, para. 5	Art. 7, para. 5	Art. 7, para. 5
Art. 8, paras. 1 and 2 (general rule)	Art. 8, paras. 1 and 2	Art. 8, paras. 1 and 2	Art. 8, paras. 1 and 2
Art. 8, para. 3 (translation of the certificate of judicial sale)	Art. 8, para. 3	Art. 8, para. 3	Art. 8, para. 3
Art. 8, para. 4 (refusal to take action)	Art. 8, para. 4	Art. 8, para. 4	Art. 8, para. 4
Art. 9, paras. 1 and 2 (exclusive jurisdiction to avoid and suspend judicial sale)	Art. 9, paras. 1 and 2	Art. 9, paras. 1 and 2	Art. 9, paras. 1 and 2
Art. 9, para. 3 (transmission of avoidance/ suspension decision to repository)	Art. 9, para. 3	—	Art. 5, para. 7
Art. 10 (circumstances in which judicial sale has no international effect)	Art. 10	Art. 10	Art. 10
Art. 11 (repository)	Art. 11	Art. 11	Art. 11
Art. 12 (communication between authorities of States Parties)	Art. 12	Art. 12	Art. 12
Art. 13 (relationship with other international conventions)	Art. 13	Art. 13, paras. 2 and 4	Art. 13, para. 2
Art. 14 (other bases for giving international effect)	Art. 14	Art. 13, paras. 1 and 3	Art. 13, para. 1
Art. 15, para. 1 (matters not governed by the Convention)	Art. 15, para. 1	Art. 14	Art. 14

Third revision of the Beijing Draft[d]	*Second revision of the Beijing Draft*[e]	*First revision of the Beijing Draft*[f]	*Beijing Draft*[g]
Art. 5, para. 3	Art. 5, para. 3	Art. 5, para. 3	—
Art. 11, para. 1	Art. 11, para. 1	Art. 11	—
Art. 5, para. 5	Art. 5, para. 5	Art. 5, para. 5	Art. 7, para. 5
Art. 11, paras. 2 and 3	Art. 11, paras. 2 and 3	—	—
Art. 6	Art. 6, para. 1	Art. 6	Art. 7, para. 1
Art. 7, paras. 1 and 2	Art. 7, paras. 1 and 2	Art. 7, para. 1	Art. 6, paras. 1 and 2
Art. 7, paras. 3 and 4	Art. 7, paras. 3 and 4	Art. 7, paras. 3 and 4	Art. 6, paras. 3 and 4
Art. 7, para. 5	Art. 7, para. 5	—	—
Art. 8, paras. 1 and 2	Art. 8, paras. 1 and 2	Art. 8, paras. 1 and 2	Art. 7, para. 2
Art. 8, para. 3	Art. 8, para. 3	Art. 8, para. 4	—
Art. 8, para. 4	Art. 8, para. 4	—	—
Art. 9, paras. 1 and 2	Art. 9, paras. 1 and 2	Art. 9, paras. 1 and 2	Art. 7, para. 3
Art. 5, para. 7	—	—	—
Art. 10	Art. 10	Art. 10, para. 1	Art. 8, paras. (a) and (c)
Art. 12	Art. 12	Art. 12	—
Art. 13	Art. 13	Art. 13	—
Art. 14, para. 2	Art. 14, para. 2	—	Art. 3, para. 5
Art. 14, para. 1	Art. 14, para. 1	Art. 14	Art. 10
Art. 14bis	Art. 6, para. 2	Art. 4, para. 3	Art. 4, para. 2

Final text	*Draft submitted to Commission*[a]	*Fifth revision of the Beijing Draft*[b]	*Fourth revision of the Beijing Draft*[c]
Art. 15, para. 2 (effects of avoidance/ suspension)	Art. 15, para. 2	Art. 9, para. 5 (c.f. art. 9, paras. 3 and 4)	Art. 9, para. 5 (c.f. art. 5, para. 6 and art. 9, paras. 3 and 4)
Art. 16 (depositary)	Art. 16	Art. 15	Art. 15
Art. 17 (consenting to be bound)	Art. 17	Art. 16	Art. 16
Art. 18 (REIO clause)	Art. 18	Art. 17	Art. 17
Art. 19 (non-unified legal systems)	Art. 19	Art. 18	Art. 18
Art. 20 (procedure and effects of declarations)	Art. 21	—	—
Art. 21 (entry into force)	Art. 22	Art. 19	Art. 19
Art. 22 (amendment)	Art. 23	Art. 20	Art. 20
Art. 23 (denunciation)	Art. 24	Art. 21	Art. 21

Third revision of the Beijing Draft[d]	*Second revision of the Beijing Draft*[e]	*First revision of the Beijing Draft*[f]	*Beijing Draft*[g]
— (c.f. art. 5, para. 6 and art. 9, paras. 3 and 4)	— (c.f. art. 5, para. 6 and art. 9, paras. 3 and 4)	— (c.f. art. 10, paras. 2 and 3)	— (c.f. art. 8, para. (b))
Art. 15	—	—	—
Art. 16	—	—	—
Art. 17	—	—	—
Art. 18	—	—	—
—	—	—	—
Art. 19	—	—	—
Art. 20	—	—	—
Art. 21	—	—	—

APPENDIX 3

International Convention Relating to the Arrest of Seagoing Ships 1952*

* A United Nations publication.

INTERNATIONAL CONVENTION[1] RELATING TO THE ARREST OF SEAGOING SHIPS. SIGNED AT BRUSSELS, ON 10 MAY 1952

The High Contracting Parties,

Having recognised the desirability of determining by agreement certain uniform rules of law relating to the arrest of seagoing ships, have decided to conclude a convention, for this purpose and thereto have agreed as follows:

Article 1

In this Convention the following words shall have the meanings hereby assigned to them:

(1) "Maritime Claim" means a claim arising out of one or more of the following:

(a) damage caused by any ship either in collision or otherwise;

(b) loss of life or personal injury caused by any ship or occurring in connexion with the operation of any ship;

(c) salvage;

(d) agreement relating to the use or hire of any ship whether by charter-party or otherwise;

(e) agreement relating to the carriage of goods in any ship whether by charter-party or otherwise;

---

[1] In accordance with article 14 (a), the Convention came into force on 24 February 1956, six months after the date of deposit of the second instrument of ratification. Here follows a list of States which have deposited their instruments of ratification or accession *(a)* with the Ministry of Foreign Affairs of Belgium, indicating the date of deposit and the date of entry into force of the Convention for each State:

State	*Date of deposit*	*Date of entry into force*
Spain	8 December 1953	24 February 1956
Switzerland.	28 May 1954 (*a*)	24 February 1956
Haiti.	4 November 1954 (*a*)	24 February 1956
Costa Rica (with reservations)*	13 July 1955 (*a*)	24 February 1956
Egypt (Confirming the reservation made at the time of signature; see p. 210 of this volume)	24 August 1955	24 February 1956
Holy See.	10 August 1956	10 February 1957
Cambodia (with reservation)	12 November 1956 (*a*)	12 May 1957
Portugal	4 May 1957	4 November 1957
France**	25 May 1957	25 November 1957
United Kingdom of Great Britain and Northern Ireland (with reservations)*	18 March 1959	18 September 1959
Belgium	10 April 1961	10 October 1961

* For the text of these reservations, see p. 214 of this volume.

** A notification of application to the French Overseas Territories, the Trust Territories of Togoland and Cameroon under French administration was received by the Government of Belgium on 23 April 1958 and took effect on 23. October 1958.

(f) loss of or damage to goods including baggage carried in any ship;

(g) general average;

(h) bottomry;

(i) towage;

(J) pilotage;

(k) goods or materials wherever supplied to a ship for her operation or maintenance;

(l) construction, repair or equipment of any ship or dock charges and dues;

(m) wages of Masters, Officers, or crew;

(n) Master's disbursements, including disbursements made by shippers, charterers or agents on behalf of a ship or her owner;

(o) disputes as to the title to or ownership of any ship;

(p) disputes between co-owners of any ship as to the ownership, possession employment or earnings of that ship;

(q) the mortgage or hypothecation of any ship.

(2) "Arrest" means the detention of a ship by judicial process to secure a maritime claim, but does not include the seizure of a ship in execution or satisfaction of a judgment.

(3) "Person" includes individuals, partnerships and bodies corporate, Governments, their Departments, and Public Authorities.

(4) "Claimant" means a person who alleges that a maritime claim exists in his favour.

Article 2

A ship flying the flag of one of the Contracting States may be arrested in the jurisdiction of any of the Contracting States in respect of any maritime claim, but in respect of no other claim; but nothing in this Convention shall be deemed to extend or restrict any right or powers vested in any Governments or their Departments, Public Authorities, or Dock or Harbour Authorities under their existing domestic laws or regulations to arrest, detain or otherwise prevent the sailing of vessels within their jurisdiction.

Article 3

(1) Subject to the provisions of para 4) of this Article and of Article 10, a claimant may arrest either the particular ship in respect of which the maritime claim arose, or any other ship which is owned by the person who was, at the time when the maritime claim arose, the owner of the particular ship, even though the ship arrested be ready to sail; but no ship, other than the particular ship in respect of which the claim arose, may be arrested in respect of any of the maritime claims enumerated in Article 1, 1) o), *p)* or *q)*.

(2) Ships shall be deemed to be in the same ownership when all the shares therein are owned by the same person or persons.

(3) A ship shall not be arrested, nor shall bail or other security be given more than once in any one or more of the jurisdictions of any of the Contracting States in respect of the same maritime claim by the same claimant : and, if a ship has been arrested in any one of such jurisdictions, or bail or other security has been given in such jurisdiction either to release the ship or to avoid a threatened arrest, any subsequent arrest of the ship or of any ship in the same ownership by the same claimant for the same maritime claim shall be set aside, and the ship released by the Court or other appropriate judicial authority of that State, unless the claimant can satisfy the Court or other appropriate judicial authority that the bail or other security had been finally released before the subsequent arrest or that there is other good cause for maintaining that arrest.

(4) When in the case of a charter by demise of a ship the charterer and not the registered owner is liable in respect of a maritime claim relating to that ship, the claimant may arrest such ship or any other ship in the ownership of the charterer by demise, subject to the provisions of this Convention, but no other ship in the ownership of the registered owner shall be liable to arrest in respect of such maritime claims.

The provisions of this paragraph shall apply to any case in which a person other than the registered owner of a ship is liable in respect of a maritime claim relating to that ship.

Article 4

A ship may only be arrested under the authority of a Court or of the appropriate judicial authority of the Contracting State in which the arrest is made.

Article 5

The Court or other appropriate judicial authority within whose jurisdiction the ship has been arrested shall permit the release of the ship upon sufficient bail or other security being furnished, save in cases in which a ship has been arrested in respect of any of the maritime claims enumerated in Article 1 1), *o)* and *p)*. In such cases the Court or other appropriate judicial authority may permit the person in possession of the ship to continue trading the ship, upon such person furnishing sufficient bail or other security, or may otherwise deal with the operation of the ship during the period of the arrest.

In default of agreement between the parties as to the sufficiency of the bail or other security, the Court or other appropriate judicial authority shall determine the nature and amount thereof.

The request to release the ship against such security shall not be construed as an acknowledgment of liability or as a waiver of the benefit of the legal limitation of liability of the owner of the ship.

Article 6

All questions whether in any case the claimant is liable in damages for the arrest of a ship or for the costs of the bail or other security furnished to release or prevent the arrest of a ship, shall be determined by the law of the Contracting State in whose jurisdiction the arrest was made or applied for.

The rules of procedure relating to the arrest of a ship, to the application for obtaining the authority referred to in Article 4, and to all matters of procedure which the arrest may entail, shall be governed by the law of the Contracting State in which the arrest was made or applied for.

Article 7

(1) The Courts of the country in which the arrest was made shall have jurisdiction to determine the case upon its merits if the domestic law of the country in which the arrest is made gives jurisdiction to such Courts, or in any of the following cases namely:

(a) if the claimant has his habitual residence or principal place of business in the country in which the arrest was made;
(b) if the claim arose in the country in which the arrest was made;
(c) if the claim concerns the voyage of the ship during which the arrest was made;
(d) if the claim arose out of a collision or in circumstances covered by Article 13 of the International Convention for the unification of certain rules of law with respect to collisions between vessels, signed at Brussels on 23rd September 1910;[2]
(e) if the claim is for salvage;
(f) if the claim is upon a mortgage or hypothecation of the ship arrested.

(2) If the Court within whose jurisdiction the ship was arrested has not jurisdiction to decide upon the merits, the bail or other security given in accordance with Article 5 to procure the release of the ship shall specifically provide that it is given as security for the satisfaction of any judgment which may eventually be pronounced by a Court having jurisdiction so to decide; and the Court

[2] *British and Foreign State Papers,* Vol. CIII, p. 434, and League of Nations, *Treaty Series,* Vol. CCV, p. 220.

or other appropriate judicial authority of the country in which the arrest is made shall fix the time within which the claimant shall bring an action before a Court having such jurisdiction.

(3) If the parties have agreed to submit the dispute to the jurisdiction of a particular Court other than that within whose jurisdiction the arrest was made or to arbitration, the Court or other appropriate judicial authority within whose jurisdiction the arrest was made may fix the time within which the claimant shall bring proceedings.

(4) If, in any of the cases mentioned in the two preceding paragraphs, the action or proceedings are not brought within the time so fixed, the defendant may apply for the release of the ship or of the bail or other security.

(5) This article shall not apply in cases covered by the provisions of the revised Rhine Navigation Convention of 17. October 1868.[3]

Article 8

(1) The provisions of this Convention shall apply to any vessel flying the flag of a Contracting State in the jurisdiction of any Contracting State.

(2) A ship flying the flag of a non-Contracting State may be arrested in the jurisdiction of any Contracting State in respect of any of the maritime claims enumerated in Article 1 or of any other claim for which the law of the Contracting State permits arrest.

(3) Nevertheless any Contracting State shall be entitled wholly or partly to exclude from the benefits of this Convention any Government of a non-Contracting State or any person who has not, at the time of the arrest, his habitual residence or principal place of business in one of the Contracting States.

(4) Nothing in this Convention shall modify or affect the rules of law in force in the respective Contracting States relating to the arrest of any ship within the jurisdiction of the State of her flag by a person who has his habitual residence or principal place of business in that State.

(5) When a maritime claim is asserted by a third party other than the original claimant, whether by subrogation, assignment or otherwise, such third party shall, for the purpose of this Convention, be deemed to have the same habitual residence or principal place of business as the original claimant.

Article 9

Nothing in this Convention shall be construed as creating a right of action, which, apart from the provisions of this Convention, would not arise under the law applied by the Court which had seisin of the case, nor as creating any maritime liens which do not exist under such law or under the Convention on Maritime Mortgages and Liens, if the latter is applicable.

[3] De Martens, *Nouveau Recueil général de Traités,* tome XX, p. 355.

Article 10

The High Contracting Parties may at the time of signature, deposit or ratification or accession, reserve

(a) the right not to apply this Convention to the arrest of a ship for any of the claims enumerated in paragraphs *o)* and *p)* of Article 1, but to apply their domestic laws to such claims;

(b) the right not to apply the first paragraph of Article 3 to the arrest of a ship, within their jurisdiction, for claims set out in Article 1, paragraph *q)*.

Article 11

The High Contracting Parties undertake to submit to arbitration any disputes between States arising out of the interpretation or application of this Convention, but this shall be without prejudice to the obligations of those High Contracting Parties who have agreed to submit their disputes to the International Court of Justice.

Article 12

This Convention shall be open for signature by the States represented at the Ninth Diplomatic Conference on Maritime Law. The protocol of signature shall be drawn up through the good offices of the Belgian Ministry of Foreign Affairs.

Article 13

This Convention shall be ratified and the instruments of ratification shall be deposited with the Belgian Ministry of Foreign Affairs which shall notify all signatory and acceding States of the deposit of any such instruments.

Article 14

(a) This Convention shall come into force between the two States which first ratify it, six months after the date of the deposit of the second instrument of ratification.

(b) This Convention shall come into force in respect of each signatory State which ratifies it after the deposit of the second instrument of ratification six months after the date of the deposit of the instrument of ratification of that State.

Article 15

Any State not represented at the Ninth Diplomatic Conference on Maritime Law may accede to this Convention.

The accession of any State shall be notified to the Belgian Ministry of Foreign Affairs which shall inform through diplomatic channels all signatory and acceding States of such notification.

The Convention shall come into force in respect of the acceding State six months after the date of the receipt of such notification but not before the Convention has come into force in accordance with the provisions of Article 14 *a)*.

Article 16

Any High Contracting Party may three years after coming into force of this Convention in respect of such High Contracting Party or at any time thereafter request that a conference be convened in order to consider amendments to the Convention.

Any High Contracting Party proposing to avail itself of this right shall notify the Belgian Government which shall convene the conference within six months thereafter.

Article 17

Any High Contracting Party shall have the right to denounce this Convention at any time after the coming into force thereof in respect of such High Contracting Party. This denunciation shall take effect one year after the date on which notification thereof has been received by the Belgian Government which shall inform through diplomatic channels all the other High Contracting Parties of such notification.

Article 18

(a) Any High Contracting Party may at the time of its ratification of or accession to this Convention or at any time thereafter declare by written notification to the Belgian Ministry of Foreign Affairs that the Convention shall extend to any of the territories for whose international relations it is responsible. The Convention shall six months after the date of the receipt of such notification by the Belgian Ministry of Foreign Affairs extend to the territories named therein, but not before the date of the coming into force of the Convention in respect of such High Contracting Party.

(b) A High Contracting Party which has made a declaration under para graph *a)* of this Article extending the Convention to any territory for whose international relations it is responsible may at any time thereafter declare by notification given to the Belgian Ministry of Foreign Affairs that the Convention shall cease to extend to such territory and the Convention shall one year after the receipt of the notification by the Belgian Ministry of Foreign Affairs cease to extend thereto.

(c) The Belgian Ministry of Foreign Affairs shall inform through diplomatic channels all signatory and acceding States of any notification received by it under this Article.

DONE in Brussels, on May 10, 1952, in the French and English languages, the two texts being equally authentic.

APPENDIX 4

International Convention on Arrest of Ships 1999[1]

[1] **A United Nations publication.**

INTERNATIONAL CONVENTION ON ARREST OF SHIPS, 1999

The States *Parties* to *this Convention,*

Recognizing the desirability of facilitating the harmonious and orderly development of world seaborne trade,

Convinced of the necessity for a legal instrument establishing international uniformity in the field of arrest of ships which takes account of recent developments in related fields,

Have agreed as follows:

Article 1
Definitions

For the purposes of this Convention:

1. "Maritime Claim" means a claim arising out of one or more of the following:

(a) loss or damage caused by the operation of the ship;

(b) loss of life or personal injury occurring, whether on land or on water, in direct connection with the operation of the ship;

(c) salvage operations or any salvage agreement, including, if applicable, special compensation relating to salvage operations in respect of a ship which by itself or its cargo threatened damage to the environment;

(d) damage or threat of damage caused by the ship to the environment, coastline or related interests; measures taken to prevent, minimize, or remove such damage; compensation for such damage; costs of reasonable measures of reinstatement of the environment actually undertaken or to be undertaken; loss incurred or likely to be incurred by third parties in connection with such damage; and damage, costs, or loss of a similar nature to those identified in this subparagraph (d);

(e) costs or expenses relating to the raising, removal, recovery, destruction or the rendering harmless of a ship which is sunk, wrecked, stranded or abandoned, including anything that is or has been on board such ship, and costs or expenses relating to the preservation of an abandoned ship and maintenance of its crew;

(f) any agreement relating to the use or hire of the ship, whether contained in a charter party or otherwise;

(g) any agreement relating to the carriage of goods or passengers on board the ship, whether contained in a charter party or otherwise;

(h) loss of or damage to or in connection with goods (including luggage) carried on board the ship;

(i) general average;

(j) towage;

(k) pilotage;

(l) goods, materials, provisions, bunkers, equipment (including containers) supplied or services rendered to the ship for its operation, management, preservation or maintenance;

(m) construction, reconstruction, repair, converting or equipping of the ship;

(n) port, canal, dock, harbour and other waterway dues and charges;

(o) wages and other sums due to the master, officers and other members of the ship's complement in respect of their employment on the ship, including costs of repatriation and social insurance contributions payable on their behalf;

(p) disbursements incurred on behalf of the ship or its owners;

(q) insurance premiums (including mutual insurance calls) in respect of the ship, payable by or on behalf of the shipowner or demise charterer;

(r) any commissions, brokerages or agency fees payable in respect of the ship by or on behalf of the shipowner or demise charterer;

(s) any dispute as to ownership or possession of the ship;

(t) any dispute between co-owners of the ship as to the employment or earnings of the ship;

(u) a mortgage or a "hypothèque" or a charge of the same nature on the ship;

(v) any dispute arising out of a contract for the sale of the ship.

2. "Arrest" means any detention or restriction on removal of a ship by order of a Court to secure a maritime claim, but does not include the seizure of a ship in execution or satisfaction of a judgment or other enforceable instrument.

3. "Person" means any individual or partnership or any public or private body, whether corporate or not, including a State or any of its constituent subdivisions.

4. "Claimant" means any person asserting a maritime claim.

5. "Court" means any competent judicial authority of **a** State.

Article 2
Powers of arrest

1. A ship may be arrested or released from arrest only under the authority of a Court of the State Party in which the arrest is effected.

2. A ship may only be arrested in respect of a maritime claim but in respect of no other claim.

3. A ship may be arrested for the purpose of obtaining security notwithstanding that, by virtue of a jurisdiction clause or arbitration clauoe in any relevant contract, or otherwise, the maritime claim in respect of which the arrest is effected is to be adjudicated in a State other than the State where the arrest is effected, or is to be arbitrated, or is to be adjudicated subject to the law of another State.

4. Subject to the provisions of this Convention, the procedure relating to the arrest of a ship or its release shall be governed by the law of the State in which the arrest was effected or applied for.

Article 3
Exercise of right of arrest

1. Arrest is permissible of any ship in respect of which a maritime claim is asserted if:

(a) the person who owned the ship at the time when the maritime claim arose is liable for the claim and is owner of the ship when the arrest is effected; or

(b) the demise charterer of the ship at the time when the maritime claim arose is liable for the claim and is demise charterer or owner of the ship when the arrest is effected; or

(c) the claim is based upon a mortgage or a "hypothèque" or a charge of the same nature on the ship; or

(d) the claim relates to the ownership or possession of the ship; or

(e) the claim is against the owner, demise charterer, manager or operator of the ship and is secured by a maritime lien which is granted or arises under the law of the State where the arrest is applied for.

2. Arrest is also permissible of any other ship or ships which, when the arrest is effected, is or are owned by the person who is liable for the maritime claim and who was, when the claim arose:

(a) owner of the ship in respect of which the maritime claim arose; or

(b) demise charterer, time charterer or voyage charterer of that ship.

This provision does not apply to claims in respect of ownership or possession of a ship.

3. Notwithstanding the provisions of paragraphs 1 and 2 of this article, the arrest of a ship which is not owned by the person liable for the claim shall be permissible only if, under the law of the State where the arrest is applied for, a judgment in respect of that claim can be enforced against that ship by judicial or forced sale of that ship.

Article 4
Release from arrest

1. A ship which has been arrested shall be released when sufficient security has been provided in a satisfactory form, save in cases in which a ship has been arrested in respect of any of the maritime claims enumerated in article 1, paragraphs 1 (s) and (t). In such cases, the Court may permit the person in possession of the ship to continue trading the ship, upon such person providing sufficient security, or may otherwise deal with the operation of the ship during the period of the arrest.

2. In the absence of agreement between the parties as to the sufficiency and form of the security, the Court shall determine its nature and the amount thereof, not exceeding the value of the arrested ship.

3. Any request for the ship to be released upon security being provided shall not be construed as an acknowledgement of liability nor as a waiver of any defence or any right to limit liability.

4. If a ship has been arrested in a non-party State and is not released although security in respect of that ship has been provided in a State Party in respect of the same claim, that security shall be ordered to be released on application to the Court in the State Party.

5. If in a non-party State the ship is released upon satisfactory security in respect of that ship being provided, any security provided in a State Party in respect of the same claim shall be ordered to be released to the extent that the total amount of security provided in the two States exceeds:

(a) the claim for which the ship has been arrested, or

(b) the value of the ship,

whichever is the lower. Such release shall, however, not be ordered unless the security provided in the non-party State will actually be available to the claimant and will be freely transferable.

6. Where, pursuant to paragraph 1 of this article, security has been provided, the person providing such security may at any time apply to the Court to have that security reduced, modified, or cancelled.

Article 5
Right of rearrest and multiple arrest

1. Where in any State a ship has already been arrested and released or security in respect of that ship has already been provided to secure a maritime claim, that ship shall not thereafter be rearrested or arrested in respect of the same maritime claim unless:

(a) the nature or amount of the security in respect of that ship already provided in respect of the same claim is inadequate, on condition that the aggregate amount of security may not exceed the value of the ship; or

(b) the person who has already provided the security is not, or is unlikely to be, able to fulfil some or all of that person's obligations; or

(c) the ship arrested or the security previously provided was released either:

(i) upon the application or with the consent of the claimant acting on reasonable grounds, or

(ii) because the claimant could not by taking reasonable steps prevent the release.

2. Any other ship which would otherwise be subject to arrest in respect of the same maritime claim shall not be arrested unless:

(a) the nature or amount of the security already provided in respect of the same claim is inadequate; or

(b) the provisions of paragraph 1 (b) or (c) of this article are applicable.

3. "Release" for the purpose of this article shall not include any unlawful release or escape from arrest.

Article 6
Protection of owners and demise charterers of arrested ships

1. The Court may as a condition of the arrest of a ship, or of permitting an arrest already effected to be maintained, impose upon the claimant who seeks to arrest or who has procured the arrest of the ship the obligation to provide security of a kind and for an amount, and upon such terms, as may be determined by that Court for any loss which may be incurred by the defendant as a result of the arrest, and for which the claimant may be found liable, including but not restricted to such loss or damage as may be incurred by that defendant in consequence of:

(a) the arrest having been wrongful or unjustified; or

(b) excessive security having been demanded and provided.

2. The Courts of the State in which an arrest has been effected shall have jurisdiction to determine the extent of the liability, if any, of the claimant for loss or damage caused by the arrest of a ship, including but not restricted to such loss or damage as may be caused in consequence of:

(a) the arrest having been wrongful or unjustified, or

(b) excessive security having been demanded and provided.

3. The liability, if any, of the claimant in accordance with paragraph 2 of this article shall be determined by application of the law of the State where the arrest was effected.

4. If a Court in another State or an arbitral tribunal is to determine the merits of the case in accordance with the provisions of article 7, then proceedings relating to the liability of the claimant in accordance with paragraph 2 of this article may be stayed pending that decision.

5. Where pursuant to paragraph 1 of this article security has been provided, the person providing such security may at any time apply to the Court to have that security reduced, modified or cancelled.

Article 7
Jurisdiction on the merits of the case

1. The Courts of the State in which an arrest has been effected or security provided to obtain the release of the ship shall have jurisdiction to determine the case upon its merits, unless the parties validly agree or have validly agreed to submit the dispute to a Court of another State which accepts jurisdiction, or to arbitration.

2. Notwithscanding the provisions of paragraph 1 of this article, the Courts of the State in which an arrest has been effected, or security provided to obtain the release of the ship, may refuse to exercise that jurisdiction where that refusal is permitted by the law of that State and a Court of another State accepts jurisdiction.

3. In cases where a Court of the State where an arrest has been effected or security provided to obtain the release of the ship:

(a) does not have jurisdiction to determine the case upon its merits; or

(b) has refused to exercise jurisdiction in accordance with the provisions of paragraph 2 of this article,

such Court may, and upon request shall, order a period of time within which the claimant shall bring proceedings before a competent Court or arbitral tribunal.

4. If proceedings are not brought within the period of time ordered in accordance with paragraph 3 of this article then the ship arrested or the security provided shall, upon request, be ordered to be released.

5. If proceedings are brought within the period of time ordered in accordance with paragraph 3 of this article, or if proceedings before a competent Court or arbitral tribunal in another State are brought in the absence of such order, any final decision resulting therefrom shall be recognized and given effect with respect to the arrested ship or to the security provided in order to obtain its release, on condition that:

(a) the defendant has been given reasonable notice of such proceedings and a reasonable opportunity to present the case for the defence; and

(b) such recognition is not against public policy (ordre *public)*.

6. Nothing contained in the provisions of paragraph 5 of this article shall restrict any further effect given to a foreign judgment or arbitral award under the law of the State where the arrest of the ship was effected or security provided to obtain its release.

Article 8
Application

1. This Convention shall apply to any ship within the jurisdiction of any State Party, whether or not that ship is flying the flag of a State Party.

2. This Convention shall not apply to any warship, naval auxiliary or other ships owned or operated by a State and used, for the time being, only on government non-commercial service.

3. This Convention does not affect any rights or powers vested in any Government or its departments, or in any public authority, or in any dock or harbour authority, under any international convention or under any domestic law or regulation, to detain or otherwise prevent from sailing any ship within their jurisdiction.

4. This Convention shall not affect the power of any State or Court to make orders affecting the totality of a debtor's assets.

5. Nothing in this Convention shall affect the application of international conventions providing for limitation of liability, or domestic law giving effect thereto, in the State where an arrest is effected.

6. Nothing in this Convention shall modify or affect the rules of law in force in the States Parties relating to the arrest of any ship physically within the jurisdiction of the State of its flag procured by a person whose habitual residence or principal place of business is in that State, or by any other person who has acquired a claim from such person by subrogation, assignment or otherwise.

Article 9
Non-creation of maritime liens

Nothing in this Convention shall be construed as creating a maritime lien.

Article 10
Reservations

1. Any State may, at the time of signature, ratification, acceptance, approval, or accession, or at any time thereafter, reserve the right to exclude the application of this Convention to any or all of the following:

(a) ships which are not seagoing;

(b) ships not flying the flag of a State Party;

(c) claims under article 1, paragraph 1 (s).

2. A State may, when it is also a State Party to a specified treaty on navigation on inland waterways, declare when signing, ratifying, accepting, approving or acceding to this Convention, that rules on jurisdiction, recognition and execution of court decisions provided for in such treaties shall prevail over the rules contained in article 7 of this Convention.

Article 11
Depositary

This Convention shall be deposited with the Secretary-General of the United Nations.

Article 12
Signature, ratification, acceptance, approval and accession

1. This Convention shall be open for signature by any State at the Headquarters of the United Nations, New York, from 1 September 1999 to 31 August 2000 and shall thereafter remain open for accession.

2. States may express their consent to be bound by this Convention by:

(a) signature without reservation as to ratification, acceptance or approval; or

(b) signature subject to ratification, acceptance or approval, followed by ratification, acceptance or approval; or

(c) accession.

3. Ratification, acceptance, approval or accession shall be effected by the deposit of an instrument to that effect with the depositary.

Article 13
States with more than one system of law

1. If a State has two or more territorial units in which different systems of law are applicable in relation to matters dealt with in this Convention, it may at the time of signature, ratification, acceptance, approval or accession declare that this Convention shall extend to all its territorial units or only to one or more of them and may modify this declaration by submitting another declaration at any time.

2. Any such declaration shall be notified to the depositary and shall state expressly the territorial units to which the Convention applies.

3 In relation to a State Party which has two or more systems of law with regard to arrest of ships applicable in different territorial units, references in this Convention to the Court of a State and the law of a State shall be respectively

construed as referring to the Court of the relevant territorial unit within that State and the law of the relevant territorial unit of that State.

Article 14
Entry into force

1. This Convention shall enter into force six months following the date on which 10 States have expressed their consent to be bound by it.

2. For a State which expresses its consent to be bound by this Convention after the conditions for entry into force thereof have been met, such consent shall take effect three months after the date of expression of such consent.

Article 15
Revision and amendment

1. A conference of States Parties for the purpose of revising or amending this Convention shall be convened by the Secretary-General of the United Nations at the request of one third of the States Parties.

2. Any consent to be bound by this Convention, expressed after the date of entry into force of an amendment to this Convention, shall be deemed to apply to the Convention, as amended.

Article 16
Denunciation

1. This Convention may be denounced by any State Party at any time after the date on which this Convention enters into force for that State.

2. Denunciation shall be effected by deposit of an instrument of denunciation with the depositary.

3. A denunciation shall take effect one year, or such longer period as may be specified in the instrument of denunciation, after the receipt of the instrument of denunciation by the depositary.

Article 17
Languages

This Convention is established in a single original in the Arabic, Chinese, English, French, Russian and Spanish languages, each text being equally authentic.

DONE AT Geneva this twelfth day of March, one thousand nine hundred and ninety-nine.

IN WITNESS WHEREOF the undersigned being duly authorized by their respective Governments for that purpose have signed this Convention.

APPENDIX 5

International Convention for the Unification of Certain Rules Relating to Maritime Liens and Mortgages (with Protocol of Signature) 1926

Article 1

Mortgages, hypothecations and other similar charges upon vessels, duly effected in accordance with the law of the Contracting State to which the vessel belongs, and registered in a public register either at the port of the vessel's registry or at a central office, shall be regarded as valid and respected in all the other Contracting countries.

Article 2

The following give rise to maritime liens on a vessel, on the freight for the voyage during which the claim giving rise to the lien arises, and on the accessories of the vessel and freight accrued since the commencement of the voyage;

(1) Law costs due to the State, and expenses incurred in the common interest of the creditors in order to preserve the vessel or to procure its sale and the distribution of the proceeds of sale; tonnage dues, light or harbour dues, and other public taxes and charges of the same character; pilotage dues; the cost of watching and preservation from the time of the entry of the vessel into the last port;
(2) Claims arising out of the contract of engagement of the master, crew and other persons hired on board.
(3) Remuneration for assistance and salvage, and the contribution of the vessel in general average;
(4) Indemnities for collision or other accident of navigation, as also for damage caused to works forming part of harbours, docks, and navigable ways; indemnities for personal injury to passengers or crew; indemnities for loss of or damage to cargo or baggage;
(5) Claims resulting from contracts entered into or acts done by the master, acting within the scope of his authority away from the vessel's home port, where such contracts or acts are necessary for the preservation of the vessel or the continuation of its voyage, whether the master is or is not at the same time owner of the vessel, and whether the claim is his own or that of ship-chandlers, repairers, lenders, or other contractual creditors.

Article 3

The mortgages, hypothecations, and other charges on vessels referred to in Article 1 rank immediately after the secured claims referred to in the preceding Article.

National laws may grant a lien in respect of claims other than those referred to in the said last-mentioned Article, so, however, as not to modify the ranking of claims secured by mortgages, hypothecations, and other similar charges, or by the liens taking precedence thereof.

Article 4

The accessories of the vessel and the freight mentioned in Article 2 mean:

(1) Compensation due to the owner for material damage sustained by the vessel and not repaired, or for loss of freight;
(2) General average contributions due to the owner, in respect of material damage sustained by the vessel and not repaired, or in respect of loss of freight;
(3) Remuneration due to the owner for assistance and salvage services rendered at any time before the end of the voyage, any sums allotted to the master or other persons in the service of the vessel being deducted.

The provision as to freight apply also to passage money, and, in the last resort, to the sums due under Article 4 of the Convention on the limitation of shipowners' liability.

Payments made or due to the owner on policies of insurance, as well as bounties, subventions, and other national subsidies are not deemed to be accessories of the vessel or of the freight.

Notwithstanding anything in the opening words of Article 2.(2), the lien in favour of persons in the service of the vessel extends, to the total amount of freight due for all voyages made during the subsistence of the same contract of engagement.

Article 5

Claims secured by a lien and relating to the same voyage rank in the order in which they are set out in Article 2. Claims included under any one heading share concurrently and rateably in the event of the fund available being insufficient to pay the claims in full.

The claims mentioned under Nos. 3 and 5 in that Article rank, in each of the two categories, in the inverse order of the dates on which they came into existence.

Claims arising from one and the same occurrence are deemed to have come into existence at the same time.

Article 6

Claims secured by a lien and attaching to the last voyage have priority over those attaching to previous voyage.

Provided that claims, arising on one and the same contract of engagement extending over several voyages, all rank with claims attaching to the last voyage.

Article 7

As regards the distribution of the sum resulting from the sale of the property subject to a lien, the creditors whose claims are secured by a lien have the right to put forward their claims in full, without any deduction on account of the rules relating to limitation of liability provided, however, that the sum apportioned to them may not exceed the sum due having regard to the said rules.

Article 8

Claims secured by a lien follow the vessel into whatever hands it may pass.

Article 9

The liens cease to exist, apart from other cases provided for by national laws, at the expiration of one year, and, in the case of liens for supplies mentioned in No.5 of Article 2, shall continue in force for not more than six months.

The periods for which the lien remains in force in the case of liens securing claims in respect of assistance and salvage run from the day when the services terminated, in the case of liens securing claims in respect of collision and other accidents and in respect of bodily injuries from the day when the damage was caused; in the case of liens for the loss of or damage or cargo or baggage from the day of the delivery of the cargo or baggage or from the day when they should have been delivered; for repairs and supplies and other cases mentioned in No.5 of Article 2 from the day the claim originated. In all the other cases the period runs from the enforceability of the claim.

The fact that any of the persons employed on board, mentioned in No. 2 of Article 2 has a right to any payment in advance or on account does not render his claim enforceable.

As respects the cases provided for in the national laws in which a lien is extinguished, a sale shall extinguish a lien only if accompanied by formalities of publicity which shall be laid down by the national laws.

These formalities shall include a notice given in such form and within such time as the national laws may prescribe to the authority charged with keeping the registers referred to in Article 1 of this Convention.

The grounds upon which the aforementioned periods may be interrupted are determined by the law of the court where the case is tried.

The High Contracting Parties reserve to themselves the right to provide by legislation in their respective countries, that the said periods shall be extended in cases where it has not been possible to arrest the vessel to which a lien attaches in the territorial waters of the state in which the claimant has his domicile or his principal place of business, provided that the extended period shall not exceed three years from the time when the claim originated.

Article 10

A lien on freight may be enforced so long as the freight is still due or the amount of the freight is still in the hands of the master or the agent of the owner. The same principle applies to a lien on accessories.

Article 11

Subject to the provisions of this Convention, liens established by the preceding provisions are subject to no formality and to no special condition of proof. This provision does not affect the right of any State to maintain in the legislation provisions requiring the master of a vessel to fulfil special formalities in the case of certain loans raised on the security of the vessel, or in the case of the sale of its cargo.

Article 12

National laws must prescribe the nature and the form of documents to be carried on board the vessel in which entry must be made of the mortgages. hypothecations, and other charges referred to in Article 1; so, however, that the mortgagees requiring such entry in the said form be not held responsible for any omission, mistake, or delay in inscribing the same on the said documents.

Article 13

The foregoing provisions apply to vessels under the management of a person who operates them without owning them or to the principal charterer, except in cases where the owner has been dispossessed by an illegal act or where the claimant is not a bona fide claimant.

Article 14

The provisions of this Convention shall be applied in each Contracting State in cases in which the vessel to which the claim relates belongs to a Contracting State as well as in any other cases provided for by the national laws.

Nevertheless the principle formulated in the preceding paragraph does not affect the right of the Contracting States not to apply the provisions of this Convention in favour of the nationals of a non-contracting State.

Article 15

This Convention does not apply to vessels of war, nor to government vessels appropriated exclusively to the public service.

Article 16

Nothing in the foregoing provisions shall be deemed to affect in any way the competence of tribunals, modes of procedure or methods of execution authorised by the national law.

Article 17

After an interval of not more than two years from the day on which the Convention is signed, the Belgian Government shall place itself in communication with the Governments of the High Contracting Parties which have declared themselves prepared to ratify the Convention, with a view to deciding whether it shall be put into force. The ratifications shall be deposited at Brussels at a date to be fixed by agreement among the said Governments. The first deposit of ratifications shall be recorded in a process-verbal signed by the representatives of the powers which take part therein and by the Belgian Minister for Foreign Affairs.

The subsequent deposits of ratifications shall be made by means of a written notification, addressed to the Belgian Government, and accompanied by the instrument of ratification.

A duly certified copy of the process-verbal relating to the first deposit of ratifications, of the notification referred to in the previous paragraph, and also of the instruments of ratification accompanying them, shall be immediately sent by the Belgian Government through the diplomatic channel to the powers who have signed this Convention or who have acceded to it. In the cases contemplated in the preceding paragraph the said Government shall inform them at the same time of the date on which it received the notification.

Article 18

Non-signatory States may acceded to the present Convention whether or not they have been represented at the international Conference at Brussels.

A State which desires to accede shall notify its intention in writing to the Belgian Government, forwarding to it the document of accession which shall be deposited in the archives of the said Government.

The Belgian Government shall immediately forward to all the states which have signed or acceded to the Convention a duly certified copy of the notification and of the act of accession, mentioning the date on which it received the notification.

Article 19

The High Contracting Parties may at the time of signature, ratification, or accession declare that their acceptance of the present Convention does not include any or all of the self-governing dominions, or of the colonies, overseas possession, protectorates, or territories under their sovereignty or authority, and they may subsequently accede separately on behalf of any self-governing dominion, colony, overseas possession, protectorate or territory excluded in their declaration, They may also denounce the Convention separately in accordance with its provision in respect of any self-governing dominion, or any colony, overseas possession, protectorate, or territory under their sovereignty or authority.

Article 20

The present Convention shall take effect, in the case of the states which have taken part in the first deposit of ratifications, one year after the date of the process-verbal recording such deposit. As respects the states which ratify subsequently or which accede and also in cases in which the convention is subsequently put into effect in accordance with Article 19, it shall take effect six months after the notifications specified in Article 17, §2, and Article 18, §2, have been received by the Belgian Government.

Article 21

In the event of one of the Contracting States wishing to denounce the present Convention, the denunciation shall be notified in writing to the Belgian Government, which shall immediately communicate a duly certified copy of the notification to all the other states informing them of the date on which it was received.

The denunciation shall only operate in respect of the state which made the notification and on the expiration of one year after the notification has reached the Belgian Government.

Article 22

Any one of the Contracting States shall have the right to call for a new conference with a view to considering possible amendments.

A state which would exercise this right should give one year advance notice of its intention to the other states through the Belgian Government which would make arrangements for convening the conference.

Protocol of Signature

In proceeding to the signature of the International Convention for the unification of Certain rules relating to maritime liens and mortgages, the undersigned plenipotentiaries have adopted the present Protocol, which will have the same force and the same value as if the provisions were inserted in the text of the Convention to which it relates:

I. It is understood that the legislation of each state remains free
   (1) to establish among the claims mentioned in No.1 of Article 2, a definite order of priority with a view to safeguarding the interests of the Treasury;
   (2) to confer on the authorities administering harbours, docks, lighthouses, and navigable ways, who have caused a wreck or other obstruction to navigation to be removed, or who are creditors in respect of harbour dues, or for damage caused by the fault of a vessel, the right, in case of non-payment, to detain the vessel, wreck, or other property, to sell the same, and to indemnify themselves out of the proceed in priority to other claimants, and
   (3) to determine the rank of the claimants for damages done to works otherwise than as stated in Article 5 and in Article 6.

II. There is no impairment of the provisions in the national laws of the Contracting States conferring a lien upon public insurance associations in respect of claims arising out of the insurance of the personnel of vessels.

Done at Brussels, in a single copy, 10 April 10 1926 of a non-contracting State.

APPENDIX 6

International Convention for the Unification of Certain Rules Relating to Maritime Liens and Mortgages 1967[1]

[1] **A United Nations publication.**

International Convention for the Unification of Certain Rules relating to Maritime Liens and Mortgages

(Brussels, 27 May 1967)

THE CONTRACTING PARTIES,

HAVING RECOGNIZED the desirability of determining by agreement certain rules relating to maritime liens and mortgages,

HAVE RESOLVED to conclude a convention for this purpose, and thereto agreed as follows:

Article 1

Mortgages and "hypothèques" on sea-going vessels shall be enforceable in Contracting States provided that:

(a) such mortgages and "hypothèques" have been effected and registered in accordance with the law of the State where the vessel is registered;

(b) the register and any instruments required to be deposited with the registrar in accordance with the law of the State where the vessel is registered are open to public inspection, and that extracts of the register and copies of such instruments are obtainable from the registrar, and

(c) either the register or any instruments referred to in paragraph (b) above specifies the name and address of the person in whose favour the mortgage or "hypothèque" has been effected or that it has been issued to bearer, the amount secured and the date and other particulars which, according to the law of the State of registration, determine the rank as respects other registered mortgages and "hypothèques".

Article 2

The ranking of registered mortgages and "hypothèques" as between themselves and, without prejudice to the provisions of this Convention, their effect in regard to third parties shall be determined by the law of the State of registration; however, without prejudice to the provisions of this Convention, all matters relating to the procedure of enforcement shall be regulated by the law of the State where enforcement takes place.

Article 3

1. Subject to the provisions of Article 11, no Contracting State shall permit the deregistration of a vessel without the written consent of all holders of registered mortgages and "hypothèques".

2. A vessel which is or has been registered in a Contracting State shall not be eligible for registration in another Contracting State, unless:

(a) a certificate has been issued by the former State to the effect that the vessel has been deregistered, or

(b) a certificate has been issued by the former State to the effect that the vessel will be deregistered on the day when such new registration is effected.

Article 4

1. The following claims shall be secured by maritime liens on the vessel:

(i) wages and other sums due to the master, officers and other members of the vessel's complement in respect of their employment on the vessel;

(ii) port, canal and other waterway dues and pilotage dues;

(iii) claims against the owner in respect of loss of life or personal injury occurring, whether on land or on water, in direct connection with the operation of the vessel;

(iv) claims against the owner, based on tort and not capable of being based on contract, in respect of loss of or damage to property occurring, whether on land or on water, in direct connection with the operation of the vessel;

(v) claims for salvage, wreck removal and contribution in general average.

The word "owner" mentioned in this paragraph shall be deemed to include the demise or other charterer, manager or operator of the vessel.

2. No maritime lien shall attach to the vessel securing claims as set out in paragraph 1 (iii) and (iv) of this Article which arise out of or result from the radioactive properties or a combination of radioactive properties with toxic, explosive or other hazardous properties of nuclear fuel or of radioactive product or waste.

Article 5

1. The maritime liens set out in Article 4 shall take priority over registered mortgages and "hypothèques", and no other claim shall take priority over such maritime liens or over mortgages and "hypothèques" which comply with the requirements of Article 1, except as provided in Article 6(2).

2. The maritime liens set out in Article 4 shall rank in the order listed, provided however that maritime liens securing claims for salvage, wreck removal and contribution in general average shall take priority over all other maritime liens which have attached to the vessel prior to the time when the operations giving rise to the said liens were performed.

3. The maritime liens set out in each of sub-paragraphs (i), (ii), (iii) and (iv) of paragraph (1) of Article 4 shall rank pari passu as between themselves.

4. The maritime liens set out in sub-paragraph (v) of paragraph (1) of Article 4 shall rank in the inverse order of the time when the claims secured thereby accrued. Claims for contribution in general average shall be deemed to have accrued on the date on which the general average act was performed; claims for salvage shall be deemed to have accrued on the date on which the salvage operation was terminated.

Article 6

1. Each Contracting State may grant liens or rights of retention to secure claims other than those referred to in Article 4. Such liens shall rank after all maritime liens set out in Article 4 and after all registered mortgages and "hypothèques" which comply with the provisions of Article 1; and such rights of retention shall not prejudice the enforcement of maritime liens set out in Article 4 or registered mortgages or "hypothèques" which comply with the provisions of Article 1, nor the delivery of the vessel to the purchaser in connection with such enforcement.

2. In the event that a lien or right of retention is granted in respect of a vessel in possession of:

(a) a shipbuilder, to secure claims for the building of the vessel, or

(b) a ship repairer, to secure claims for repair of the vessel effected during such possession,

such lien or right of retention shall be postponed to all maritime liens set out in Article 4, but may be preferred to registered mortgages or "hypothèques". Such lien or right of retention may be exercisable against the vessel notwithstanding any registered mortgage or "hypothèque" on the vessel, but shall be extinguished when the vessel ceases to be in the possession of the shipbuilder or ship repairer, as the case may be.

Article 7

1. The maritime liens set out in Article 4 arise whether the claims secured by such liens are against the owner or against the demise or other charterer, manager or operator of the vessel.

2. Subject to the provisions of Article 11, the maritime liens securing the claims set out in Article 4 follow the vessel notwithstanding any change of ownership or of registration.

Article 8

1. The maritime liens set out in Article 4 shall be extinguished after a period of one year from the time when the claims secured thereby arose unless, prior to the expiry of such period, the vessel has been arrested, such arrest leading to a forced sale.

2. The one year period referred to in the preceding paragraph shall not be subject to suspension or interruption, provided, however, that time shall not run during the period that the lienor is legally prevented from arresting the vessel.

Article 9

The assignment of or subrogation to a claim secured by a maritime lien set out in Article 4 entails the simultaneous assignment of or subrogation to such maritime lien.

Article 10

Prior to the forced sale of a vessel in a Contracting State, the competent authority of such State shall give, or cause to be given at least thirty days written notice of the time and place of such sale to:

(a) all holders of registered mortgages and "hypothèques" which have not been issued to bearer;

(b) such holders of registered mortgages and "hypothèques" issued to bearer and to such holders of maritime liens set out in Article 4 whose claims have been notified to the said authority;

(c) the registrar of the register in which the vessel is registered.

Article 11

1. In the event of the forced sale of the vessel in a Contracting State all mortgages and "hypothèques", except those assumed by the purchaser with the consent of the holders, and all liens and other encumbrances of whatsoever nature shall cease to attach to the vessel, provided however that:

(a) at the time of the sale, the vessel is in the jurisdiction of such Contracting State, and

(b) the sale has been effected in accordance with the law of the said State and the provisions of this Convention.

No charter party or contract for the use of the vessel shall be deemed a lien or encumbrance for the purpose of this Article.

2. The cost awarded by the Court and arising out of the arrest and subsequent sale of the vessel and the distribution of the proceeds shall first be paid out of the proceeds of such sale. The balance shall be distributed among the holders of maritime liens, liens and rights of retention mentioned in paragraph 2 of Article 6 and registered mortgages and "hypothèques" in accordance with the provisions of this Convention to the extent necessary to satisfy their claims.

3. When a vessel registered in a Contracting State has been the object of a forced sale in a Contracting State, the Court or other competent authority having jurisdiction shall, at the request of the purchaser, issue a certificate to the effect that the vessel is sold free of all mortgages and "hypothèques", except those assumed by the purchaser, and all liens and other encumbrances, provided that the requirements set out in paragraph 1, sub-paragraphs (a) and (b) have been complied with, and that the proceeds of such forced sale have been distributed in compliance with paragraph 2 of this Article or have been deposited with the authority that is competent under the law of the place of the sale. Upon production of such certificate the registrar shall

be bound to delete all registered mortgages and "hypothèques", except those assumed by the purchaser, and to register the vessel in the name of the purchaser or to issue a certificate of deregistration for the purpose of re-registration, as the case may be.

Article 12

1. Unless otherwise provided in this Convention, its provisions shall apply to all sea-going vessels registered in a Contracting State or in a non-Contracting State.

2. Nothing in this Convention shall require any rights to be conferred in or against, or enable any rights to be enforced against any vessel owned, operated or chartered by a State and appropriated to public non-commercial services.

Article 13

For the purposes of Articles 3, 10 and 11 of this Convention, the competent authorities of the Contracting States shall be authorized to correspond directly between themselves.

Article 14

Any Contracting Party may at the time of signing, ratifying or acceding to this Convention make the following reservations:

1. to give effect to this Convention either by giving it the force of law or by including the provisions of this Convention in its national legislation in a form appropriate to that legislation;

2. to apply the International Convention relating to the limitation of the liability of owners of sea-going ships, signed at Brussels on 10 October 1957.

Article 15

Any dispute between two or more Contracting Parties concerning the interpretation or application of this Convention which cannot be settled through negotiation shall, at the request of one of them, be submitted to arbitration. If within six months from the date of the request for arbitration the Parties are unable to agree on the organization of the arbitration, any one of those Parties may refer the dispute to the International Court of Justice by request in conformity with the Statute of the Court.

Article 16

1. Each Contracting Party may at the time of signature or ratification of this Convention or accession thereto, declare that it does not consider itself bound by Article 15 of the Convention. The other Contracting Parties shall not be bound by this Article with respect to any Contracting Party having made such a reservation.

2. Any Contracting Party having made a reservation in accordance with paragraph 1 may at any time withdraw this reservation by notification to the Belgian Government.

Article 17

This Convention shall be open for signature by the States represented at the twelfth session of the Diplomatic Conference on Maritime Law

Article 18

This Convention shall be ratified and the instruments of ratification shall be deposited with the Belgian Government.

Article 19

1. This Convention shall come into force three months after the date of the deposit of the fifth instrument of ratification.

2. This Convention shall come into force in respect of each signatory State which ratifies it after the deposit of the fifth instrument of ratification, three months after the date of the deposit of the instrument of ratification.

Article 20

1. States, Members of the United Nations or Members of the specialized agencies, not represented at the twelfth session of the Diplomatic Conference on Maritime Law, may accede to this Convention.

2. The instruments of accession shall be deposited with the Belgian Government.

3. The Convention shall come into force in respect of the acceding State three months after the date of deposit of the instrument of accession of that State, but not before the date of entry into force of the Convention as established by Article 19(1).

Article 21

Each Contracting Party shall have the right to denounce this Convention at any time after the coming into force thereof in respect of such Contracting Party. Nevertheless, this denunciation shall only take effect one year after the date on which notification thereof have been received by the Belgian Government.

Article 22

1. Any Contracting Party may at the time of signature, ratification or accession to this Convention or at any time thereafter declare by written notification to the Belgian Government which, among the territories under its sovereignty or for whose international relations it is responsible, are those to which the present Convention applies.

The Convention shall three months after the date of the receipt of such notification by the Belgian Government, extend to the territories named therein.

2. Any Contracting Party which has made a declaration under paragraph (1) of this Article may at any time thereafter declare by notification given to the Belgian Government that the Convention shall cease to extend to such territories.

This denunciation shall take effect one year after the date on which notification thereof has been received by the Belgian Government.

Article 23

The Belgium Government shall notify the States represented at the twelfth session of the Diplomatic Conference on Maritime Law, and the acceding States to this Convention, of the following:

1. The signatures, ratifications and accessions received in accordance with Articles 17, 18 and 20.

2. The date on which the present Convention will come into force in accordance with Article 19.

3. The notifications with regard to Articles 14, 16 and 22.

4. The denunciations received in accordance with Article 21.

Article 24

Any Contracting Party may three years after the coming into force of this Convention, in respect of such Contracting Party, or at any time thereafter request that a Conference be convened in order to consider amendments to this Convention.

Any Contracting Party proposing to avail itself of this right shall notify the Belgian Government which, provided that one-third of the Contracting Parties are in agreement, shall convene the Conference within six months thereafter

Article 25

In respect of the relations between States which ratify this Convention or accede to it, this Convention shall replace and abrogate the International Convention for the unification of certain rules relating to Maritime Liens and Mortgages and Protocol of signature, signed at Brussels on 10 April 1926.

IN WITNESS WHEREOF the undersigned plenipotentiaries, duly authorized, have signed this Convention.

DONE at Brussels, this 27th day of May 1967, in the French and English languages, both texts being equally authentic, in a single copy, which shall remain deposited in the archives of the Belgian Government, which shall issue certified copies.

APPENDIX 7

International Convention on Maritime Liens and Mortgages 1993[1]

[1] A United Nations publication.

The States Parties to this Convention,

Conscious of the need to improve conditions for ship financing and the development of national merchant fleets,

Recognizing the desirability of international uniformity in the field of maritime liens and mortgages, and therefore

Convinced of the necessity for an international legal instrument governing maritime liens and mortgages,

Have decided to conclude a Convention for this purpose and have therefore agreed as follows:

Article 1

Recognition and enforcement of mortgages, "hypothèques" and charges

Mortgages, "hypothèques" and registrable charges of the same nature, which registrable charges of the same nature will be referred to hereinafter as "charges", effected on seagoing vessels shall be recognized and enforceable in States Parties provided that:

(a) such mortgages, "hypothèques" and charges have been effected and registered in accordance with the law of the State in which the vessel is registered;

(b) the register and any instruments required to be deposited with the registrar in accordance with the law of the State in which the vessel is registered are open to public inspection, and that extracts from the register and copies of such instruments are obtainable from the registrar; and

(c) either the register or any instruments referred to in subparagraph (b) specifies at least the name and address of the person in whose favour the mortgage, "hypothèque" or charge has been effected or that it has been issued to bearer, the maximum amount secured, if that is a requirement of the law of the State of registration or if that amount is specified in the instrument creating the mortgage, "hypothèque" or charge, and the date and other particulars which, according to the law of the State of registration, determine the ranking in relation to other registered mortgages, "hypothèques" and charges.

Article 2

Ranking and effects of mortgages, "hypothèques" and charges

The ranking of registered mortgages, "hypothèques" or charges as between themselves and, without prejudice to the provisions of this Convention, their effect in regard to third parties shall be determined by the law of the State of registration; however, without prejudice to the provisions of this Convention, all matters relating to the procedure of enforcement shall be regulated by the law of the State where enforcement takes place.

Article 3

Change of ownership or registration

1. With the exception of the cases provided for in articles 11 and 12, in all other cases that entail the deregistration of the vessel from the register of a State Party, such State Party shall not permit the owner to deregister the vessel unless all registered mortgages, "hypothèques" or charges are previously deleted or the written consent of all holders of such mortgages, "hypothèques" or charges is obtained. However, where the deregistration of the vessel is obligatory in accordance with the law of a State Party, otherwise than as a result of a voluntary sale, the holders of registered mortgages, "hypotheques" or charges shall be notified of the pending deregistration in order to enable such holders to take appropriate action to protect their interests; unless the holders consent, the deregistration shall not be implemented earlier than after a lapse of a reasonable period of time which shall be not less than three months after the relevant notification to such holders.

2. Without prejudice to article 12, paragraph 5, a vessel which is or has been registered in a State Party shall not be eligible for registration in another State Party unless either:

(a) a certificate has been issued by the former State to the effect that the vessel has been deregistered; or

(b) a certificate has been issued by the former State to the effect that the vessel will be deregistered with immediate effect, at such time as the new registration is effected. The date of deregistration shall be the date of the new registration of the vessel.

Article 4

Maritime liens

1. Each of the following claims against the owner, demise charterer, manager or operator of the vessel shall be secured by a maritime lien on the vessel:

(a) claims for wages and other sums due to the master, officers and other members of the vessel's complement in respect of their employment on the vessel, including costs of repatriation and social insurance contributions payable on their behalf;

(b) claims in respect of loss of life or personal injury occurring, whether on land or on water, in direct connection with the operation of the vessel;

(c) claims for reward for the salvage of the vessel;

(d) claims for port, canal, and other waterway dues and pilotage dues;

(e) claims based on tort arising out of physical loss or damage caused by the operation of the vessel other than loss of or damage to cargo, containers and passengers' effects carried on the vessel.

2. No maritime lien shall attach to a vessel to secure claims as set out in subparagraphs (b) and (e) of paragraph 1 which arise out of or result from:

(a) damage in connection with the carriage of oil or other hazardous or noxious substances by sea for which compensation is payable to the claimants pursuant to international conventions or national law providing for strict liability and compulsory insurance or other means of securing the claims; or

(b) the radioactive properties or a combination of radioactive properties with toxic, explosive or other hazardous properties of nuclear fuel or of radioactive products or waste.

Article 5

Priority of maritime liens

1. The maritime liens set out in article 4 shall take priority over registered mortgages, "hypothèques" and charges, and no other claim shall take priority over such maritime liens or over such mortgages, "hypothèques" or charges which comply with the requirements of article 1, except as provided in paragraphs 3 and 4 of article 12.

2. The maritime liens set out in article 4 shall rank in the order listed, provided however that maritime liens securing claims for reward for the salvage of the vessel shall take priority over all other maritime liens which have attached to the vessel prior to the time when the operations giving rise to the said liens were performed.

3. The maritime liens set out in each of subparagraphs (a), (b), (d) and (e) of paragraph 1 of article 4 shall rank pari passu as between themselves.

4. The maritime liens securing claims for reward for the salvage of the vessel shall rank in the inverse order of the time when the claims secured thereby accrued. Such claims shall be deemed to have accrued on the date on which each salvage operation was terminated.

Article 6

Other maritime liens

Each State Party may, under its law, grant other maritime liens on a vessel to secure claims, other than those referred to in article 4, against the owner, demise charterer, manager or operator of the vessel, provided that such liens:

(a) shall be subject to the provisions of articles 8, 10 and 12;

(b) shall be extinguished

(i) after a period of 6 months, from the time when the claims secured thereby arose unless, prior to the expiry of such period, the vessel has been arrested or seized, such arrest or seizure leading to a forced sale; or

(ii) at the end of a period of 60 days following a sale to a bona fide purchaser of the vessel, such period to commence on the date on which the sale is registered in accordance with the law of the State in which the vessel is registered following the sale;

whichever period expires first; and

(c) shall rank after the maritime liens set out in article 4 and also after registered mortgages, "hypothèques" or charges which comply with the provisions of article 1.

Article 7

Rights of retention

1. Each State Party may grant under its law a right of retention in respect of a vessel in the possession of either:

(a) a shipbuilder, to secure claims for the building of the vessel; or

(b) a shiprepairer, to secure claims for repair, including reconstruction of the vessel, effected during such possession.

2. Such right of retention shall be extinguished when the vessel ceases to be in the possession of the shipbuilder or shiprepairer, otherwise than in consequence of an arrest or seizure.

Article 8

Characteristics of maritime liens

Subject to the provisions of article 12, the maritime liens follow the vessel, notwithstanding any change of ownership or of registration or of flag.

Article 9

Extinction of maritime liens by lapse of time

1. The maritime liens set out in article 4 shall be extinguished after a period of one year unless, prior to the expiry of such period, the vessel has been arrested or seized, such arrest or seizure leading to a forced sale.

2. The one-year period referred to in paragraph 1 shall commence:

(a) with respect to the maritime lien set out in article 4, paragraph 1(a), upon the claimant's discharge from the vessel;

(b) with respect to the maritime liens set out in article 4, paragraph 1 (b) to (e), when the claims secured thereby arise;

and shall not be subject to suspension or interruption, provided, however, that time shall not run during the period that the arrest or seizure of the vessel is not permitted by law.

Article 10

Assignment and subrogation

1. The assignment of or subrogation to a claim secured by a maritime lien entails the simultaneous assignment of or subrogation to such a maritime lien.

2. Claimants holding maritime liens may not be subrogated to the compensation payable to the owner of the vessel under an insurance contract.

Article 11

Notice of forced sale

1. Prior to the forced sale of a vessel in a State Party, the competent authority in such State Party shall ensure that notice in accordance with this article is provided to:

(a) the authority in charge of the register in the State of registration;

(b) all holders of registered mortgages, "hypotheques" or charges which have not been issued to bearer;

(c) all holders of registered mortgages, "hypothèques" or charges issued to bearer and all holders of the maritime liens set out in article 4, provided that the competent authority conducting the forced sale receives notice of their respective claims; and

(d) the registered owner of the vessel.

2. Such notice shall be provided at least 30 days prior to the forced sale and shall contain either:

(a) the time and place of the forced sale and such particulars concerning the forced sale or the proceedings leading to the forced sale as the authority in a State Party conducting the proceedings shall determine is sufficient to protect the interests of persons entitled to notice; or,

(b) if the time and place of the forced sale cannot be determined with certainty, the approximate time and anticipated place of the forced sale and such particulars concerning the forced sale as the authority in a State Party conducting the proceedings shall determine is sufficient to protect the interests of persons entitled to notice.

If notice is provided in accordance with subparagraph (b), additional notice of the actual time and place of the forced sale shall be provided when known but, in any event, not less than seven days prior to the forced sale.

3. The notice specified in paragraph 2 of this article shall be in writing and either given by registered mail, or given by any electronic or other appropriate means which provide confirmation of receipt, to the persons interested as specified in paragraph 1, if known. In addition, the notice shall be given by press announcement in the State where the forced sale is conducted and, if deemed appropriate by the authority conducting the forced sale, in other publications.

Article 12

Effects of forced sale

1. In the event of the forced sale of the vessel in a State Party, all registered mortgages, "hypothèques" or charges, except those assumed by the purchaser with the consent of the holders, and all liens and other encumbrances of whatsoever nature, shall cease to attach to the vessel, provided that:

(a) at the time of the sale, the vessel is in the area of the jurisdiction of such State; and

(b) the sale has been effected in accordance with the law of the said State and the provisions of article 11 and this article.

2. The costs and expenses arising out of the arrest or seizure and subsequent sale of the vessel shall be paid first out of the proceeds of sale. Such costs and expenses include, inter alia, the costs for the upkeep of the vessel and the crew as well as wages, other sums and costs referred to in article 4, paragraph 1 (a), incurred from the time of arrest or seizure. The balance of the proceeds shall be distributed in accordance with the provisions of this Convention, to the extent necessary to satisfy the respective claims. Upon satisfaction of all claimants, the residue of the proceeds, if any, shall be paid to the owner and it shall be freely transferable.

3. A State Party may provide in its law that, in the event of the forced sale of a stranded or sunken vessel following its removal by a public authority in the interest of safe navigation or the protection of the marine environment, the costs of such removal shall be paid out of the proceeds of the sale, before all other claims secured by a maritime lien on the vessel.

4. If at the time of the forced sale the vessel is in the possession of a shipbuilder or of a shiprepairer who under the law of the State Party in which the sale takes place enjoys a right of retention, such shipbuilder or shiprepairer must surrender possession of the vessel to the purchaser but is entitled to obtain satisfaction of his claim out of the proceeds of sale after the satisfaction of the claims of holders of maritime liens mentioned in article 4.

5. When a vessel registered in a State Party has been the object of a forced sale in any State Party, the competent authority shall, at the request of the purchaser, issue a certificate to the effect that the vessel is sold free of all registered mortgages, "hypothèques" or charges, except those assumed by the purchaser, and of all liens and other encumbrances, provided that the requirements set out in paragraph 1 (a) and (b) have been complied with. Upon production of such certificate, the registrar shall be bound to delete all registered mortgages, "hypothèques" or charges except those assumed by the purchaser, and to register the vessel in the name of the purchaser or to issue a certificate of deregistration for the purpose of new registration, as the case may be.

6. States Parties shall ensure that any proceeds of a forced sale are actually available and freely transferable.

Article 13

Scope of application

1. Unless otherwise provided in this Convention, its provisions shall apply to all seagoing vessels registered in a State Party or in a State which is not a State Party, provided that the latter's vessels are subject to the jurisdiction of the State Party.

2. Nothing in this Convention shall create any rights in, or enable any rights to be enforced against, any vessel owned or operated by a State and used only on Government non-commercial service.

Article 14

Communication between States Parties

For the purpose of articles 3, **11** and 12, the competent authorities of the States Parties shall be authorized to correspond directly between themselves.

Article 15

Conflict of conventions

Nothing in this Convention shall affect the application of any international convention providing for limitation of liability or of national legislation giving effect thereto.

Article 16

Temporary change of flag

If a seagoing vessel registered in one State is permitted to fly temporarily the flag of another State, the following shall apply:

(a) For the purposes of this article, references in this Convention to the "State in which the vessel is registered" or to the "State of registration" shall be deemed to be references to the State in which the vessel was registered immediately prior to the change of flag, and references to "the authority in charge of the register" shall be deemed to be references to the authority in charge of the register in that State.

(b) The law of the State of registration shall be determinative for the purpose of recognition of registered mortgages, "hypothèques" and charges.

(c) The State of registration shall require a cross-reference entry in its register specifying the State whose flag the vessel is permitted to fly temporarily; likewise, the State whose flag the vessel is permitted to fly temporarily shall require that the authority in charge of the vessel's record specifies by a cross-reference in the record the State of registration.

(d) No State Party shall permit a vessel registered in that State to fly temporarily the flag of another State unless all registered mortgages, "hypotheques" or charges on that vessel have been previously satisfied or the written consent of the holders of all such mortgages, "hypotheques" or charges has been obtained.

(e) The notice referred to in article 11 shall be given also to the competent authority in charge of the vessel's record in the State whose flag the vessel is permitted to fly temporarily.

(f) Upon production of the certificate of deregistration referred to in article 12 paragraph 5, the competent authority in charge of the vessel's record in the State whose flag the vessel is permitted to fly temporarily shall, at the request of the purchaser, issue a certificate to the effect that the right to fly the flag of that State is revoked.

(g) Nothing in this Convention is to be understood to impose any obligation on States Parties to permit foreign vessels to fly temporarily their flag or national vessels to fly temporarily a foreign flag.

Article 17

Depositary

This Convention shall be deposited with the Secretary-General of the United Nations.

Article 18

Signature, ratification, acceptance, approval and accession

1. This Convention shall be open for signature by any State at the Headquarters of the United Nations, New York, from 1 September 1993 to 31 August 1994 and shall thereafter remain open for accession.

2. States may express their consent to be bound by this Convention by:

(a) signature without reservation as to ratification, acceptance or approval; or

(b) signature subject to ratification, acceptance or approval, followed by ratification, acceptance or approval; or

(c) accession.

3. Ratification, acceptance, approval or accession shall be effected by the deposit of an instrument to that effect with the depositary.

Article 19

Entry into force

1. This Convention shall enter into force 6 months following the date on which 10 States have expressed their consent to be bound by it.

2. For a State which expresses its consent to be bound by this Convention after the conditions for entry into force thereof have been met, such consent shall take effect 3 months after the date of expression of such consent.

Article 20

Revision and amendment

1. A conference of States Parties for the purpose of revising or amending this Convention shall be convened by the Secretary-General of the United Nations at the request of one-third of the States Parties.

2. Any consent to be bound by this Convention, expressed after the date of entry into force of an amendment to this Convention, shall be deemed to apply to the Convention, as amended.

Article 21

Denunciation

1. This Convention may be denounced by any State Party at any time after the date on which this Convention enters into force for that State.

2. Denunciation shall be effected by the deposit of an instrument of denunciation with the depositary.

3. A denunciation shall take effect one year, or such longer period as may be specified in the instrument of denunciation, after the receipt of the instrument of denunciation by the depositary.

Article 22

Languages

This Convention is established in a single original in the Arabic, Chinese, English, French, Russian and Spanish languages, each text being equally authentic.

DONE AT Geneva this sixth day of May, one thousand nine hundred and ninety-three.

IN WITNESS WHEREOF the undersigned being duly authorized by their respective Governments for that purpose have signed this Convention.

INDEX

For Product Safety Concerns and Information please contact our EU representative GPSR@taylorandfrancis.com
Taylor & Francis Verlag GmbH, Kaufingerstraße 24, 80331 München, Germany

www.ingramcontent.com/pod-product-compliance
Ingram Content Group UK Ltd.
Pitfield, Milton Keynes, MK11 3LW, UK
UKHW050315071126
477531UK00012B/631
* 9 7 8 1 0 3 2 8 1 4 5 7 5 *